THE ORIGIN OF AMHARIC

The Origin of Amharic

GIRMA A. DEMEKE

THE RED SEA PRESS
Trenton | London | New Delhi | Cape Town | Nairobi | Addis Ababa | Asmara | Ibadan

THE RED SEA PRESS
541 West Ingham Avenue | Suite B
Trenton, New Jersey 08638

Copyright © 2009 Girma A. Demeke
First Edition, 2009
Second Edition, 2014

All rights reserved. No part of this publication may be reproduced, stored in a retrieval system or transmitted in any form or by any means electronic, mechanical, photocopying, recording or otherwise without the prior written permission of the publisher.

Book design: Lemlem Taddese
Cover design modified by: Saverance Publishing Services

Library of Congress Cataloging-in-Publication Data

Demeke, Girma A.

The origin of Amharic / Girma A. Demeke. -- [2nd ed.]

   p. cm.

"The first edition of this book was published first in 2009 in Addis Ababa by the French Center for Ethiopian Studies and later in the same year (with minor editing) in Germany by LINCOM Europa Academic publishers."--Preface.

Includes bibliographical references and index.

ISBN 978-1-56902-378-5 (hard cover) -- ISBN 978-1-56902-379-2 (pbk.) 1. Amharic language--History. 2. Language and languages--Origin. 3. Language and culture. I. Title.

PJ9209.D46 2013

492.87--dc23

                                    2013001620

In memory of my father Awgichew Demeke Wolde-Amanuel (1928-2000 EC) and Prof. Marvin Lionel Bender (1934-2008)

Table of Contents

List of Illustrations xi
    Figures xi
    Tables xi
    Maps xii
Preface (to the second edition) xiii
Preface (to the first edition) xvii
Chapter One: Introduction 1
Chapter Two: An Overview of the Pidgin Origin Hypothesis 9
    2.1 Introduction 9
    2.2 The Major Points of the Pidgin Origin Hypothesis 10
    2.3 The Spread and Development of Amharic 12
    2.4 Historical Facts Presented in Support of the Pidgin Hypothesis 14
    2.5 Social Genesis and Identity of the Amhara 16
    2.6 Linguistic Issues: The Grammar and Lexicon of Amharic 22
Chapter Three: The Place of Amharic in Genetic Classification 23
    3.1 Introduction 23
    3.2 Classification of Ethio-Semitic 24
    3.3 Amharic as a Semitic Language 26
    3.4 The Non-Semitic Elements in Amharic 27
        3.4.1 Phonology 27
        3.4.2 Morphology 27
        3.4.3 Syntax 28
        3.4.4 Lexicon 28
    3.5 Summary 29
Chapter Four: An Examination of the Pidgin Origin Hypothesis 31
    4.1 Introduction 31

4.2 Date of Origin: Examination of the Contradiction 31
4.3 Historical, Chronological and Logical Questions 33
    4.3.1 The Issue of Argobba 34
    4.3.2 The Relation of Amharic with the other South
           Ethio-Semitic 40
    4.3.3 Chronological Issues 41
4.4 The Issue of Place of origin 43
4.5 Linguistic Issues: Grammar and Lexicon 45
    4.5.1 Loanwords in Amharic 45
    4.5.2 Syntax 48
    4.5.3 Phonology 50
    4.5.4 On Morphology 52
4.6 The Issue of Identity 52
4.7 Summary 52
Chapter Five: The Origin of Ethio-Semitic 55
5.1 Introduction 55
5.2 The Terms "Semitic" and "Cushitic" 56
    5.2.1 The Term "Semitic" 56
    5.2.2 The Term "Cushitic" 57
5.3 The Hypotheses on the Origin of Ethio-Semitic 58
    5.3.1 The Migration Hypothesis 58
    5.3.2 The Non-migration Hypothesis 66
5.4 Classification of Semitic 70
    5.4.1 Introduction 70
    5.4.2 An Overview of Semitic Classification 71
        5.4.2.1 West vs. East Semitic 73
        5.4.2.2 South vs. Central 73
        5.4.2.3 Ethio-Semitic vs. Old South-Arabian 74
    5.4.3 Examination of the Classification 74
        5.4.3.1 On the Grouping of Ethio-Semitic and Old South
               Arabian: On Western South Semitic Innovations 74
        5.4.3.2 On Proto-Ethio-Semitic: The Grouping of NES
               and SES 76
        5.4.3.3 On the Grouping of Ethio-Semitic and South Arabian:
               On South Semitic Innovations 78
        5.4.3.4 On the Grouping of Ethio-Semitic under West Semitic 82
        5.4.3.5 Further Examination/Examining the Alternatives 83
    5.4.4 Proposed Position of ES 86
    5.4.5 Conclusion 87
5.5 Examination and Discussion of the Hypotheses 88
    5.5.1 The Position of ES in the General Classification of Semitic 88

5.5.2 Date of Origin	89
5.5.2 On "Pidginization"	90
5.5.3 Diversity, Least-move and other Issues	92
5.5.3.1 Diversity and Least-move	92
5.5.3.2 Other Issues	96
5.5.4 On the "Immigrant" Civilization	100
5.5.4.1 Agriculture	101
5.5.4.2 The Art of Building	103
5.5.4.3 Literacy	105
5.5.4.4 Summary	114
5.6 An Outline of the Origin and Diffusion of Ethio-Semitic	117
5.7 Summary	124
Chapter Six: An Outline of the Origin of Amharic	129
6.1 Introduction	129
6.2 Place of Origin of Amharic/Proto-Amharic-Argobba	129
6.3 The Spread of Amharic	133
6.3.1 The Expansion of Amharic before the 13th Century	134
6.3.2 The Spread of Amharic after the 13th Century	138
6.5 A Few Points on Amhara	139
6.6 Summary	142
Chapter Seven: The Development of Amharic as a Written Language	145
7.1 Introduction	145
7.2 An Overview of the Development of Amharic Writing	146
7.3 The Amharic Script	159
7.3.1 Date of Origin of the Amharic Script	163
7.3.2 Development/Changes in the Amharic Script	169
7.3.3 The Study of Amharic Script	174
7.4 Summary	177
Chapter Eight: A Grammatical Sketch of Old Amharic	179
8.1 Introduction	179
8.2 Phonology	181
8.2.1 Phonemic features	183
8.2.2 Phonological process	187
8.3 Morphology and Syntax	193
8.3.1 Agreement	193
8.3.2 Tense	196
8.3.3 Sentential Negation	198
8.3.4 Relative clause constructions	200
8.3.5 Word Order	202
8.3.6 Impersonal constructions	206

8.3.7 Copular constructions 208
8.4 Summary 211
Chapter Nine: Concluding Remarks 213
References 215
Appendices 227
  Appendix I. Abbreviations and Transcriptions 227
    1.1 Abbreviations 227
    1.2 Notes on Transcriptions 228
  Appendix II: Bruce on the Origin of Ethiopic Script 229
  Appendix III: Sample Amharic Texts 232
    3.1 Imperial Songs 232
      3.1.1 Amdä Seyon (1314-1344) 232
      3.1.2 Emperor Yishaq (1413-1428) (from Bruce 88) 233
      3.1.3 Zär'a Ya'qob (1433-1467) 237
      3.1.4 Gälawdewos (1540-1559) (from Bruce 88) 240
    3.2 Timhirte Haymanot 265
    3.3 Fragmentum Piquesii 273
    3.3 Texts from the 19th century 286
      3.3.1 Däbtära Zeneb's Mäshafä č'äwata Sïgawi Wämänfäsawi 286
      3.3.2 Letters 293
    3.4 Sample Amharic Texts of the Early 20th Century 296
    3.5 Remarks 304
Index 305

List of Illustrations

Figures
Figure 1: An early Amharic advertisement 19
Figure 2: Ethio-Semitic classification 25
Figure 3: Semitic classification according to Faber (1997)......... 65
Figure 4: Hetzron's classification of Semitic 71
Figure 5: Tentative classification of Semitic 83
Figure 6: The ancient Egyptian representation of their voyage
    to Ethiopia.. 98
Figure 7: Bender classification of Afroasiatic 117
Figure 8: The Amharic additional symbols 170
Figure 9: The Amharic Alphabet from Ludolph (1682)............ 172

Tables
Table 1: The ethnic composition of Addis Ababa in 1910.................... 18
Table 2: Summary of the TAM-system in Semitic 72
Table 3: The distribution of -k in the so-called South Semitic
    languages.. 80
Table 4: South Semitic innovations 82
Table 5: Perfective, suffix conjugations and Jussive 84
Table 6: Akkadian and ES... 85
Table 7: South Arabian and Ge'ez scripts... 112
Table 8: Basic Amharic characters... 160
Table 9: Labiovelars.. 162
Table 10: Phonological process with pharyngeal and glottal sounds.. 189
Table 11: Varieties in Argobba 190
Table 12: Semantic and phonological changes of ከብት käbt............... 191

Maps

Map 1: The Amhara and its neighboring regions in the early 16th century 17
Map 2: Semitic migration as proposed by Sergew 60
Map 3: The diffusion of Afroasiatic according to Bernal 68
Map 4: The diffusion of Semitic according to Bernal 69
Map 5: The diffusion of Afroasiatic languages according to Bender .. 118
Map 6: The diffusion of Afroasiatic languages according to Blench (2006) 119
Map 7: The birthplace of ES and its two branches 123
Map 8: The diffusion of ES 124
Map 9: The diffusion of TSES 132
Map 10: The spread of Proto-Amharic-Argobba before the 13th century 136
Map 11: The land occupied by Amharic-Argobba speakers around the 13th century 137

Preface (to the second edition)

The first edition of this book was published first in 2009 in Addis Ababa by the French Center for Ethiopian Studies and later in the same year (with minor editing) in Germany by LINCOM Europa Academic publishers.

In this edition, I have added a new chapter on the diachronic grammar of Amharic in addition to a thorough editing of each chapter. Though this book might be beginning to look more like a history of Amharic as opposed to a mere origin, its lack of thorough engagement with diachronic aspects of the language does not merit it to be considered so. For instance, the diachronic grammar part covers only a certain period. The chapter on the development of Amharic as a written language is also still far from comprehensive. I have not made major changes to the literature chapter except the addition of sample texts. Moreover, the major thrust and central point of the book are still origin. All the chapters in fact rotate on this central point rather than on the historical aspect of Amharic. I feel that a fair history of Amharic should have a balanced discussion including a comprehensive analysis of the diachronic grammar covering all the periods and a critical account of its historical development as a written language among other issues.

I confess from the outset that the grammar chapter included here is adopted from a recent publication of mine. It examines the grammar of Old Amharic based on pre-17th century manuscripts. It is my hope that this chapter will fill a gap in the study of the diachronic grammar of Amharic as the earliest of such work only dates back to the 17th century in the work of Ludolf (1698a). This chapter should make research on the diachronic grammar of Amharic smoother and easier as there are grammar works on later periods starting from Ludolf (just mentioned), Isenberg (1842), Praetorius (1879), Armbruster (1908), Mersie Hazen (1935EC) and Leslau (1995).

Cowley (1974, 1983) presents a good discussion of the two important Amharic manuscripts of the 16th century, i.e. Timherte Haymanot and a manuscript about Mary who anointed Jesus' feet. He appended photocopies of these manuscripts. I too have attached photocopies of these manuscripts in the appendix. This will also make access easier for researchers who would not normally have a chance to examine the original manuscripts. Thanks to Brook Abdu, I was able to hold in my hand the Bodleian library manuscript copy referred to as Bruce 88 that contains the pre-17th century Amharic imperial songs. "This manuscript was written between 1592 and 1605" and the oldest of all other known manuscripts that contain copies of the imperial songs (Huntingford 1965:38). In this edition, I also appended photocopies of the imperial songs from this manuscript, i.e. Bruce 88, in addition to the typed version.

I received a lot of encouragement and many comments on the first edition of the book which helped me to go ahead with this second edition. I cannot do justice here and list all who have contributed in one way or another to the publication of this second edition. However, I would like to mention at least some of them. I especially would like to thank Lawrence Youngman, Samey Gebremengist, Ahmed Zekaria, Ayele Meshesha, Tsegay Demoz, Zelealem Leyew, Hailu Habtu, Amanuel Gebreyesus, Eyob Keno, Ronny Meyer, Hiruy Abdu, Henock Yared, Shimels Gizaw, Alemayehu Dogamo, Atsede Wudneh, Tagel Seifu, and James King. I am most grateful to Brook Abdu. He discussed with me lots of points and provided me some valuable materials which I used in this edition. I am highly indebted for the enthusiastic support of my former MA students at Addis Ababa University. I thank especially Leulseged Asefa and Teshome Belay. Thanks also to Prasanna Sree Sathupati from Andhra University, Visakhapatnam, India for the many exchanges of ideas. I am most grateful to Grover Hudson and Muhammed Jemal, for providing me detailed written comments on the first edition, which helped me to do this revised edition.

If there is anyone I should acknowledge the most, it is my colleague and friend, Stephen Woerner. Not only did he thoroughly edit the whole manuscript, he also went out of his way to make comments on the side which were very educational. Thank you, Stephen!

This edition was possible by the kind support of the Institute of International Education-Scholar Rescue Fund and the Institute of Semitic Studies. I am indebted to both institutions. Last but not least, I would like to express my deep gratitude to Kassahun Checole, publisher of Red Sea Press and Africa World Press, and Ephraim Isaac, director of the Institute of Semitic Studies, for their moral support, and friendship.

Girma A. Demeke
February 2013, Princeton, New Jersey.

Preface (to the first edition)

This work investigates the origin of Amharic. The historical investigation focuses more on establishing and identifying Amharic's origin than on illustrating its historical development through time.

Proper linguistic studies on the origin of Amharic are not many. To the best of my knowledge, Bender (1983) is the first and so far the only one who tried to give detailed linguistic explanations from theoretical and historical perspectives. Most of the other works are not substantially different from Bender's (1983).

Bender's hypothesis is that Amharic originated as a pidgin with a Semitic superstratum and a Cushitic substratum. In fact, Bender claims that Omotic and probably Nilo-Saharan languages as well were involved in the pidginization process. This hypothesis, which also has a base in oral traditions, is widely propagated and found in many works and in various fields such as history, anthropology and linguistics. A closer examination of this hypothesis, however, reveals that the evidence presented in support of it is very weak. On the contrary, Amharic exhibits many features of a Semitic ancestry but not of a pidgin origin.

Amharic was and still serves as lingua franca in this extremely multi-lingual nation for about a millennium. However, it is a language that has been highly influenced by Cushitic and to some extent Omotic languages. It can, therefore, be considered as a good example of how language contact may affect the nature and structure of a language. Although Amharic exhibits a number of non-Semitic features mostly those of Cushitic and Omotic languages both in its grammar and lexicon, it cannot be considered as one which is created through pidginization. I have argued that the non-Semitic features that Amharic exhibits are due to contact with different languages.

This work is not a mere re-examination of the pidgin origin hypothesis. Based on critical examination of the linguistic evidence and historical documents, it outlines the origin of Amharic and its early development. As Amharic is considered a Semitic language, the different hypotheses with regard to its origin in one way or another are connected with the origin of Ethio-Semitic. This work critically examines the origin of the latter as well.

I argue that Argobba and Amharic, the two most closely related speech varieties, diverged and developed on their own as independent languages not because of geographical differences but because of religion: The two were once sociolects, not geographical dialects. This, in turn, means that Amharic's place of origin cannot be different from that of Argobba or from that of their common ancestral language, Proto-Central South Ethio-Semitic. It is a linguistic as well as a historical fact that although the dialectal distinction may have already started in the 9th century, Argobba and Amharic became distinct languages only very recently – in the 17th or 18th century.

The spread and development of Amharic is divided in this work into two periods, taking the 13th century as a dividing point. However, I argue that the spread of Amharic before the 13th century cannot be thought of independent from Argobba. Such spread was caused by the expansion of the Central South Ethiopic, i.e. Proto-Amharic-Argobba, speakers from their place of origin in the central part of Ethiopia to various locations in the north, east and south. The spread of Amharic independent of Argobba only took place when Amharic became a language of administration, especially starting from the 13th century.

I examine two competing hypotheses with regard to the origin of Ethio-Semitic and argue that it is an indigenous group still living in its home of origin. I propose a hypothesis about the place and time at which the two major branches of Ethio-Semitic diverged. In connection with this, the various historical, anthropological and linguistic suggestions are examined. Moreover, this work thoroughly discusses the case of Argobba. It is my hope that the present work will also provide some clues about the ancient and medieval period of Ethiopian history.

Although I seriously started to work on this specific topic some five years ago, the question regarding the history of Amharic occupied my mind since a term paper assignment in 1996 during my MA studies at Addis Ababa University. My research encompassing the entire Ethio-

Semitic language group definitely had a big impact on the outcome of this work. During my research, many people shared their ideas and works with me. I acknowledge, therefore, all who directly or indirectly helped me to produce this book.

An earlier version of the core part of this work was presented in a Seminar at Addis Ababa University and later in a workshop at Mainz University, both in 2007. I thank the participants of both institutions for their valuable comments and suggestions.

Dr. Hailu Habtu and Dr. Ronny Meyer have read some parts of the earlier manuscript and made some suggestions. Aboneh Ashagre, Ahmed Zekaria and Emmanuel Gebreyesus have discussed with me their comments. Dr. Yimer Kifle and Dr. Mousumi Roy Chowdhury helped me with proofreading and editing the manuscript. Dr. François-Xavier Fauvelle-Aymar, the director of the French Center for Ethiopian Studies, has made available his unpublished works. He raised some important points and gave me written comments on an earlier draft of this work. Dr. Marie-Laure Derat also commented on an earlier draft. Prof. Grover Hudson gave me important comments on the pre-final manuscript. He also helped me to get Bender's picture. Daniel Wolde provided me some reference materials and encouraged me in every aspect during the preparation of this work. Lemlem Tadesse typed most of the Amharic texts, scanned some of the pictures used here and helped me in the preparation of the final camera-ready copy. Addis Alemu and Addis Getachew prepared the cover design. I thank all of them.

I would like to thank also Girmame Negero, Gashaw Kifle, Eyob Keno, Alemayehu Gurmu, Dr. Garoma Kena, Alemayehu Dogamo, Dr. Fikru Tafese, Hinsene Mukria, Dr. Wondwosen Tesfaye, Jebessa Keno, Shemels Gizaw and Eshetu Taddese for their moral support and encouragement.

Girma A. Demeke
July 2009, Addis Ababa

Chapter One: Introduction

The Semitic group is one of the three language families of the Afroasiatic phylum found in Ethiopia. The Semitic languages spoken in this country (and Eritrea) are generally referred to as Ethio–Semitic or Ethiopian Semitic. In a genealogical classification of languages, the Ethio-Semitic languages (ES) are therefore grouped into the language family called Semitic. The Afroasiatic phylum is also referred to, especially in earlier literature, by the name Hamito-Semitic.[1] Besides Semitic, this phylum contains five other language families; namely, Berber, Chadic, Cushitic, Omotic and Old Egyptian.[2]

Amharic is the second most widely spoken Semitic language next to Arabic. According to the latest reports, Amharic is spoken approximately

---

[1] The term Hamito-Semitic has a racial connotation. Moreover, there is no linguistic proof that lead us to consider the so-called Hamitic language groups to be a single linguistic entity distinct from the Semitic language family (see chapter five).

[2] Most recent works suggest that the relation between these six families is not uniform. It would be better to consider some to form their own distinct group. For instance, Omotic is now widely acknowledged to be the first separated branch of the group. On the other hand, some of the groups, which were considered to belong in a certain family, may better be considered separate Afroasiatic families on their own. For instance, the relation between the various sub-families of Cushitic, i.e. North Cushitic, East Cushitic, Central Cushitic and South Cushitic, is perhaps too distant to consider them within one branch of Afroasiatic. They should rather be considered as separate branches of this phylum, i.e. separate language families by their own comparable to the other families of Afroasiatic (see chapter five for further discussion and relevant references).

by 80 percent of the Ethiopian population as a first and second language (cf. Meyer and Richter 2003: 40). Furthermore, there are various expatriate Amharic-speaking communities. It has about 80,000 native speakers in Israel. Amharic is also spoken by a significant number of immigrants of Ethiopian origin in the USA and Europe.[3] Among the Ethiopian languages, it is by far the most well-described and studied language. However, its origin is not well known.

Although the origin of Amharic is not clear, there is a widely propagated hypothesis that it originated as a pidgin. This is often due to Bender's (1983) influential work. Amharic is a language which exhibits a number of non-Semitic features (cf. Hetzron 1972, Ullendorff 1955). It is mostly due to this that Bender (1983) claims that Amharic has originated through a pidgin-induced process with a Semitic superstratum and a Cushitic substratum. It originated somewhere in the northwestern highlands of Ethiopia out of a necessity for a common means of communication among soldiers who spoke an amalgamation of different languages. For Bender, it then spread through the whole of Ethiopia by ways of military expeditions.[4] Baye (2000 E.C.) took a similar position with Bender and discussed the hypothesis at length in the preface of his book on Amharic Grammar.[5] We find similar proposal in Bender and Fulass (1978). This hypothesis has also a base in oral traditions and is found here and there in some historical and other non-linguistic works.[6]

---

[3] For instance, due to the large number of speakers, Amharic is recognized as an official language in Washington DC, USA, and a number of official activities are carried out in Amharic in Israel.

[4] In fact, it is also claimed that the substratum probably consisted of more than one language or language group (cf. Bender and Fulass 1978, Bender 1983, Baye 2000 E.C.).

[5] Baye (2000 E.C.) is the second revision of the Amharic Grammar (in Amharic) published in 1987 E.C.

[6] For instance, Alamirew Gebre-Hiwot claims that Amharic evolved out of Ge'ez and Agew during the Zague dynasty (in Ayalew n.d.: 206-207) and expanded to the south, east and central parts of Ethiopia with military expeditions. Gamst (1969) suggests that with the Axumite military force expedition to the south, pre-Amharic started to mix with the Agew languages and created the language, which we know today as Amharic. In the Amhara entry of *Encyclopaedia Aethiopica*, Levine states that Amharic was "emerged from a process of pidginization and creolization, combining Ethiopian Semitic with a large component of Cushitic vocabulary and syntax. ... The language began to spread into adjacent areas, includmg Šäwa, Lasta, Bägemdər and Goǧǧam, replacing Central Cushitic languages and other South Semitic

INTRODUCTION

In the oral traditions, one account claims that Amharic was created by a group of church scholars. According to this account the dominant languages at the time (in the Ethiopian Empire in the North), Ge'ez and Tigrinya, were not good for communication. Due to this, the scholars gathered and decided to create a language with a smooth pronunciation that made for easier communication. This group of scholars then created Amharic from Tigrinya and Ge'ez.[7]

As the account goes the term *Amhariñña* comes from a Tigrinya word *Amhiruläy* meaning 'becomes fine, beautiful', etc.[8] The legend claims that this term was used when the scholars finally saw their creation.[9] The suggestion that Amharic is smooth and easy for pronunciation has also a root in historical works such as that of Aleqa Taye (1914 E.C./1964 E.C.). Aleqa Taye, in his short book called የኢትዮጵያ ሕዝብ ታሪh 'The History of the People of Ethiopia' claims that Amharic was advanced as an administrative language during Emperor Yikuno Amlak's (1270-1285) period, because it was considered to be "modern", attractive, beloved, smooth for pronunciation and easy for communication (1914 E.C./1964 E.C.: 51).

Amharic is grouped under South Ethio-Semitic (SES) but not under North Ethio-Semitic (NES) to which Tigrinya and Ge'ez belong (see chapter three). Thus, there is not the slightest genealogical evidence to support the legend that Amharic originated through a pidginization involving Ge'ez and Tigrinya. In fact, the literal translation of the term

---

languages like Gafat and Argobba. Its use as the language of the court and official documents after the 13th cent[ury] aided its diffusion" (Levine 2003:230)

[7] A slightly different version of this story is found in Belay (1995 E.C: 131ff.). Although Belay does not claim that Amharic was created by church scholars, he suggested that it evolved out of the mix of Ge'ez and Tigrinya, used first as a secret language of the Axumite solders and spread with military expedition. According to Belay, Amharic spread easily because it was found smooth for communication. Belay states that his sources are oral traditions and elderly people.

[8] The root word of *amhiruläy* is *amharä* and its meaning is as given above. See, for instance, Ethiopian Languages Academy (1989: 510), a monolingual Tigrinya dictionary.

[9] Indeed, this account varies from person to person, but it is basically the same. See, for instance, Belay (1995 E.C.) for a similar but slightly different story. When we were in the final editing of the first edition, a similar account appeared in the Amharic weekly Newspaper, "Käadmas Bashagär", in the edition of Genbot 22, 2001 EC, Vol. 9, No. 487 (Girum Teffera 2001).

3

Amhiruläy is 'It became beautiful for me' and does not refer to 'we'. If the legend's claim that Amharic was originated by a group of scholars is correct, the "source" word for Amharic language should have been *Amhirulna* with a plural reference 'It became good for us' but not *Amhiruläy* that refers to the singular.

On the other hand, whether we try to correct the aforementioned legend either by changing the term *Amhiruläy* to its plural form *Amhirulna* or whether we correct the story leaving the word *Amhiruläy* as it is and assume that Amharic was created by a single person, the problem still exists with the word *Amhiruläy* itself. This term is native neither to Ge'ez nor to Tigrinya. It is a loanword in Tigrinya borrowed from Amharic (Hailu Habtu p.c.). Indeed, I have not mentioned the legend or the suggestions of Belay and Aleq Taye because of their scientific relevance, but to demonstrate how the origin of Amharic is perceived in the oral traditions and by certain historians.

In addition to the pidgin origin hypothesis, there is also a non-pidgin origin hypothesis. However, to the best of my knowledge, this latter hypothesis is not well developed and lacks convincing evidence to support such a claim. It is, in fact, an opinion reflected in some works such as Amsalu (1976 E.C.) and Appleyard (2003). Accordingly, this present work examine point by point the hypothesis that posits Amharic's origination to be the result of a pidgin-induced process (henceforth referred to as either the "pidgin origin hypothesis" or the shorter "pidgin hypothesis") and then follow to propose a plausible origin and development for Amharic based on its thorough examination.

In the analysis and examination, I have used historical data obtained from various sources. However, since the historical data are scarce, I have also used historical linguistic methods to determine the origin of Amharic and its early development. The work is organized as follows:

In chapter 2, I discuss the pidgin origin hypothesis. In chapter 3, I discuss the place of Amharic in the genetic classification. I show Amharic's place in the overall classification of Ethio-Semitic (ES) and examine how much Semitic Amharic is and how much it is not, i.e. how much it exhibits the non-Semitic features.

Chapter 4 examines the pidgin origin hypothesis, introduced in chapter two, point by point from various angles. Indeed, as Amharic is genetically classified as a Semitic language, in this chapter I try to answer the question whether the non-Semitic features that it exhibits are due to a result of a past pidgin stage or due to later contact-induced linguistic changes.

Although there are various suggestions for the origin of Ethio-Semitic, all of them essentially fall into two basic hypotheses; the migration hypothesis and the non-migration hypothesis. The former hypothesis considers the Ethio-Semitic languages to have developed as the result of South Arabian immigrants into Ethiopia. According to this hypothesis, the people who presently speak the Ethio-Semitic languages were basically of Cushitic stock. These Cushitic people later adopted the language of the immigrants. The latter hypothesis maintains that Ethio-Semitic is not a result of South Arabian migration but instead that Semitic languages themselves are indigenous to Ethiopia.

Of the two hypotheses, the migration hypothesis until recently is the most prominent one upon which the pidgin origin hypothesis for Amharic is premised. With the increase of linguistic studies, the non-migration hypothesis is gaining ground in recent days. In chapter 5, I shall examine these two hypotheses and propose where and when Proto-Ethio-Semitic possibly originated, where and when its various groups diverged, and how they occupy their present locations.

Based on both the examination of the pidgin origin hypothesis and the suggestion made in chapter four and also on the discussion made in chapters three and five, chapter six develops and outlines in some detail the non-pidgin hypothesis for the origin and little known earlier development and expansion of Amharic. It also begins to explore the implication this hypothesis has on the very controversial issue regarding the ethnic identity and origin of the Amhara people.

Chapter seven presents an overview of the development of Amharic as a written language. An attempt has been made to determine when the peculiar Amharic characters, known as Arabi Fidels, developed. The earliest attested Amharic text only dates back to the 14th century, which was created in praise of the deeds of the great Emperor Amdä Seyon (1314-1344). In the 16th century Amharic was employed by European missionaries to preach the locals. They produced some religious texts. The Ethiopian Orthodox church also produced some texts in Amharic in defence of their faith. In 17th and 18th centuries we find also some Amharic manuscripts that include magic scrolls. Amharic promoted as an official written language during the reign of Emperor Theodore II (1855-1868) in the 19th century. Amharic was developed as a standard written language in the 20th century. The introduction of printing press, the establishment of government schools and its subsequent promotion as a language of instruction have played major role for such development.

Chapter eight outlines the grammar of Old Amharic based on the limited pre-17th century Amharic manuscripts. It examines particularly the royal songs written in praise of the deeds of Amdä Seyon (1314-1344), Dawit (1375-1404), Yishaq (1413-1428), Zär'a Ya'qob (1433-1467), Gälawdewos (1540-1559), two manuscripts discussed by Cowley (1974, 1983); and a glossary manuscript discussed by Getatchew Haile (1970) all of which can be dated back to the 16th and pre-16th centuries. The chapter focuses mainly on the peculiar grammatical features of that period which are not observable in modern Amharic.

Pre-17th century Amharic exhibits all the pharyngeal and glottal phonemes typical of Semitic languages. Modern Amharic (MA) has rigid an SOV order. Relative clauses and adjectives must also follow their head noun in MA. However, pre-17th century Amharic was not rigid in this regard. Although structures like those in modern Amharic are also attested, we find a VSO order in pre-17th century Amharic. Relative clauses and adjectives also follow the noun they modify. Pre-17th century Amharic in general shows more Semitic features than present-day Amharic. This is, in fact, to be expected if Amharic is seen as a descendant of a Semitic language; not as one created through a pidgin-induced process. In this chapter I have also examined in brief the copular construction.

The affirmative present tense copular clauses in modern Amharic (MA) are constructed with the verbal copula *n*-. Ancient manuscripts in old Amharic (OA) show a number of constructions - a similar one as in MA, without any visible copula as in Ge'ez, or with the element *-t* as in Silte and Zay. The copula *n*- is developed out of a focus marker and has neither semantic nor structural, i.e. syntactic, similarity with experiential verbs. The usage of the element *-t* in copular constructions in OA was an issue of much debate. Similar to a number of related languages, a closer examination of this element shows that it was a focus marker in OA. The element *-t* however developed as a copula in Harari; like Amharic taking NSA for the identification of subjects. A trace of this element is also found in some copular constructions in MA.

Besides the conclusion chapter and the reference section, the book has a large appendix. The appendix contains abbreviations and transcriptions used in the book, ancient manuscripts and sample Amharic texts from different periods. The ancient manuscripts attached here rare materials which are not widely available for the public and especially for Ethiopian students at home.

Chapter Two: An Overview of the Pidgin Origin Hypothesis

2.1 Introduction

Proper historical linguistic studies on the origin of Amharic are rare. With regard to the pidgin origin hypothesis, the most prominent proponents are Bender (1983), Bender and Fulass (1978) and Baye (2000 E.C.). Bender (1983) is a continuation of Bender and Fulass (1978). However, some linguistic issues, examined in Bender and Fulass (1978), were not considered in Bender (1983). Baye (2000 E.C) has discussed the matter in his Amharic work on Amharic grammar. Although Baye is highly dependent on Bender (1983), he presents some points that differ from those of Bender. Baye's proposal was also taken directly into the 12th grade Amharic textbook and as a result the pidgin origin hypothesis became a nationally learned fact.

In section 2.2, I discuss the major points of the pidgin origin hypothesis. In section 2.3, I discuss how the spread of Amharic is perceived in the pidgin origin hypothesis. In section 2.4, I discuss the historical issues presented in support of the pidgin origin hypothesis. The social genesis and the identity of the so-called Amhara people have been cited to strengthen the pidgin origin hypothesis. I discuss these points in section 2.5. Section 2.6 discusses the supposed core linguistic issues that characterize Amharic as a pidgin language.

2.2 The Major Points of the Pidgin Origin Hypothesis

As pointed out above, for Bender (1983), Amharic probably originated as a pidgin with a Semitic superstratum and a Cushitic substratum. In fact, he claims that Omotic (at that time widely known as West-Cushitic) and probably Nilo-Saharan languages as well took part in the pidginization process. For him, the pidginization process started around the fourth century AD following the expansion of the Semitic speakers' territory to the south. It started particularly around the Bashilo River at a place called Amhara.[10] Bender outlines the general historical processes as follows:

> In the first three centuries A.D., Semitic-speaking people were building a South Arabian type of civilization in Eritrea, later centering about Aksum. As early as the middle of the fourth century, military expeditions may have reached the area later known as Amhara. By the mid-ninth century, four centuries later, a distinctive Amhara region was recognized. The conquering Semitic-speakers spoke a language which was perhaps only four to seven centuries removed from a common origin with Giiz [Ge'ez]. This pre-Amharic may have been as similar to Giiz [Ge'ez] as Icelandic is to Norwegian, or even more so. But meanwhile an interesting process was taking place among the subjugated peoples. The military forces were drawn from a number of diverse ethnic groups: perhaps largely Agew, but with significant numbers of speakers of Omotic and Cushitic languages –

---

[10] "Amharic or pre-Amharic came into being in the Bashilo River basin area known as Amhara during the period beginning in about the 4th century, probably being a distinct variety by the middle of the 9th century, and being first attested in the 14th century. The social setting was one of a forging colony — religious and military — imposing itself on an Agew-speaking population, but in frequent contact with neighboring peoples speaking several other languages, very likely including both Cushitic and Omotic ones (Nilo-Saharan is more doubtful, but possible)" (Bender 1983: 46-47). In this quotation, although Bender suggests that Amharic became a distinct variety by the middle of the 9th century, in the same paper at another point he claims this date to be the 14th century: "By the fourteenth century, the standard would be as far removed in time from its [i.e. Amharic} common origin with Giiz [Ge'ez]" (Bender 1983: 49). Others also suggest different dates of origin as we will see in a moment. We will examine these different suggestions vis-à-vis the general outline of the pidgin origin hypothesis in chapter four.

they may have had Nilo-Sharan speaking servants, slaves, and artisans. A lingua franca based on "Cushomotic" syntax (i.e. Verb-final) and Semitic lexicon was being used for communication in the ranks and among many of the Agew servants of Amhara.

This situation may have persisted for centuries, as have similar situations in the Caribbean and elsewhere. In short, a complicated diglossic situation had been created, with the ruling elite speaking a slowly-changing Semitic tongue out of old Aksum, the military ranks using a creole based on Semitic (plus use of their own native tongues) and the peasantry using the creole and also Agew. As the Agew slowly began to fuse with their conquerors, and military and missionary campaigns extended ever further west, south and east, other linguistic groups were added to the creole brew and it was shifting but ever based on Semitic lexicon and 'Cushomotic' syntax.

The Agew rise to power came after upwards of seven centuries of this diglossic situation. It meant a resurgence of Agew, but also meant an acceleration of the process of the creole impinging on the standard Semitic language (Bender 1983: 49).

Baye (2000 E.C.) elaborates in some detail how the linguistic situation looks like in the pidginization process. According to Baye (2000: xv), the military force that spoke different languages started to speak the language of its commanders but by mixing it with their own language: "Like present day Amharic speakers adopt the word 'type' and making it productive as in ተየበ [täyyäbtä, Verb, perfective], ተያቢ [täyabi, Agentive noun], ትይታባ [tiytäba, Process noun], ትይብ [tiyb, Result noun] etc., the soldiers made the Semitic vocabularies in the same way by modifying and adopting with their own language" (own translation).[11] Baye (ibid: xv-xvi) continues his discussion as follows:

In the syntax, the soldiers made the language to finish

---

[11] This explanation is, indeed, questionable. The scenario that non-Semitic speakers, i.e. solders, took the Semitic vocabulary and modified it in accordance to their own language morphology is linguistically unfounded. One of the strong reasons for considering Amharic as a Semitic language besides its core vocabularies is its morphology (see chapter four).

the sentence with a verb clause-finally like their own language. In time, the syntax and the form of the vocabulary became more un-Semitic and around the fourth century, it became distinct from the earlier Semitic language and needed a new name. Then, taking its name from the place where it was spoken, it started to be known as Amhariñña (own translation).[12]

According to Bender (1983), Bender and Fulass (1978) and Baye (2000 E.C.), Amharic developed out of a pidgin language, which received its Semitic features from the commanders and non-Semitic features from both the soldiers and conquered Agew people. It is a creation resulting from an extreme case of language contact where "multilingualism created a creole which became a post-creole, and by the accidents of history became the dominant language of Ethiopia" (cf. Bender 1983: 50).

2.3 The Spread and Development of Amharic

As we know from history, not only during the Axumite period but also during the Zague and Solomonic dynasties till the 19th century of Emperor Theodore II, the language the government used for its writing purposes was Ge'ez. Baye (2000 E.C.) suggests that during the Zague dynasty the government was using Ge'ez whereas the military forces were using Amharic. According to Baye, Amharic rose from being a language spoken by military forces to being a language spoken by the king as the result of a power struggle within the Agews, probably during the reign of king Lalibela (1140-1180).[13] He suggests that king Lalibela promoted Amharic to be his government's language in order to secure the support of the military (ibid.). On the other hand, some such as Cohen (1958) and Ludolph (1682) suggest that Amharic became the *lisane niguss* lit. 'language of the king' during the reign of Yikuno Amlak (1270-1285), the first emperor of the so-called restored Solomonic line.

> For the Zagean line failing, when they set up a Sewan [Shoan] Prince, where the Amharic Dialect is vulgarly spoken, and that some others who are exiles in the Rock

---

[12] Note that here, there is a huge difference between Baye's and Bender's (1983) suggested dates for Amharic's origin.
[13] For Alamrew Gebre-Hiwot (in Ayalew n.d: 206-207), however, Amharic was first functioning as a secret language of the kings. The military force learned it later.

of Amhara, were called to the Governments, the Amharic Dialect came into request. For the new king not well understanding the language of Tygra, and having advanced about his person his own friends that speak the same language with him, brought his own dialect into the court and camp; which being long fixed there, and in the parts adjoining, was seldom removed into Tygra. In imitation of whom, the rest of the nobility and great personages used the same speech. Thus, the Amharic dialect, otherwise called the King's language, being carried along with the camp and court over the kingdom (t) got the upper hand of all the other dialects, and the ancient and more noble Ethiopic language itself: and at length became so familiar to all the chiefs of Abissines, that you may easily by the use of that one dialect travel the whole empire, though in several parts so extremely differing in dialect from one another (Ludolph 1682: 77-78).

Indeed, it is generally believed that Amharic spread into the surroundings of northwestern and central highlands of Ethiopia after it became *lisane niguss* or *afe niguss* ("lit. mouth/tongue of the king").[14] Amharic spread much further to the southern lowlands during the reign of Emperors Amdä Seyon (1314-1344) and Zär'a Ya'qob (1434-68) who expanded their territory further south than their immediate predecessors. Indeed, during the reign of Zär'a Ya'qob (1434-1468), it is suggested that Amharic spread further to the south because his soldiers started to settle in newly conquered (or more appropriately re-conquered) areas for the first time (Lapiso 1982 E.C.: 109).

After the 14th and 15th centuries, another major expansion that helped the spread of Amharic to south is assumed to have taken place during the reign of Menelik II at the beginning of the 20th century. It is then thought that Amharic continued to spread because of its high status in the subsequent governments.[15]

---

[14] See, for instance, Cohen (1958), Amsalu (1976 E.C.), Appleyard (2003), Bender (1983), Cooper (1976), and Meyer (2006) among others.

[15] "The spread of Amharic over an increasing area of the Ethiopian highlands accompanied the conquests of various Ethiopian rulers, consolidated by the practice adopted first by Amdetsyon I [Amdä Seyon] in the 14th century and more recently by Menelik II and Hayle Sellasse I in the late 19th and first half

When secular education began at the beginning of the 20th century with the establishment of government schools, Amharic was first taught as a subject and then, later in the in the 1950s, a language in which instruction was conducted. According to Baye (2000 E.C.) and many others, it is due to the aforementioned historical coincidences that Amharic became first a lingua franca in many parts of the Ethiopian empire and then the national language of the country.

2.4 Historical Facts Presented in Support of the Pidgin Hypothesis

Sergew points out that "Ethiopian tradition attributes the birth of the Amharic language to the period of Zagwé rule" (1972: 278) that is with the shift of the Ethiopian empire from Axum to the south.[16] Indeed, such shift is an undisputed historical fact (among many others see, for instance Taddese 1972, Lapiso 1982 E.C., Sergew 1972, Ayalew n.d.). In the pidgin hypothesis, particularly as propagated by Bender (1983) and Bender and Fulass (1978), the emergence of Amharic is somewhat connected with the Zague dynasty. Its essence, however, goes back to the fourth century with the Axumite military expeditions to the south.[17] These early military expeditions by the Axumites to the south are reported in some historical works such as Taddese (1972) and Sergew (1972). Moreover, besides the Axumite military expeditions, Christianity also started to spread to the south at least beginning from the 7th century. Corroborating this, Taddese (1972) mentions the establishment of the Orthodox Church in the first quarter of the 7th century in the central parts of the Agew Land. The pidginization process that brought Amharic is specifically thought to have started around the Bashilo River in the place called Amhara not only with the Axumite expedition but also with a permanent settlement of the military. A further point that seems to strengthen the hypothesis of such Axumite expedition and their settlement in the place called Amhara is also found within the oral traditions. According to Levine (2003: 230), "oral traditions of inhabitants of Amhara claim direct descent from ancient Aksum and folk etymologies claim that the term Amhara means 'a free people'".

Recall that according to the pidgin hypothesis, the military campaigns from Axum to the south were made by soldiers speaking different Cushitic, Omotic and Nilo-Saharan languages and with commanders

---

of the 20th century of settling Amhara colonialists in the newly absorbed areas" (Appleyard 2003: 233).
[16] This tradition is also reflected in many works (see for instance Meyer 2006).
[17] That is, long before the administrative shift from north to south took place.

AN OVERVIEW OF THE PIDGIN ORIGIN HYPOTHESIS

speaking a Semitic language slightly different from that of Ge'ez. Recall also that according to the pidgin hypothesis, the Semitic tongue spoken by the commanders was the one that provided the Semitic features to Amharic. Indeed, there is historical support for the existence of such a Semitic tongue in the north before the administrative shift took place from north, Axum, to the South, Zague. Pre-Amharic or an Amharic-like language existed in the northern part in this early times, according to Aleqa Taye (1964 E.C.: 52) as evidenced from the names of some kings such as ጉም (721-725), አስገምጉም (725-730), ለትም (730-746) and ተላተም (746-767) of the Axumite Empire. As Aleqa Taye (Ibid) also points out, such names do not fall to any of the present ES, but to Amharic.[18] In fact, the traditional list of kings provided in Aleqa Taye and other traditional works are questionable (see, for instance, Sergew 1972, Munro-Hay 1991). However, the existence of such names in the north seems an undeniable fact. There are other names as well that do not belong to any of the Northern Ethio-Semitic languages from the same Axumite period. For instance, in a funeral inscription dated to the second half of the eighth century found in Tigray we have the name *Mängäsha* /mängäša/ which was of course written as መንገሃ, as the symbol for 'sh', /š/, in the Ethiopic script was not developed at that time (Sergew 1972: 198). Although this name is now very popular among the Tigrinya speakers, it clearly has an Amharic pattern. It is the infinitive form plus the derivational morpheme *–ya* as in **mängäs-ya → mängäša* with a palatalization of the final radical of the base root caused due to the glide /y/.[19] This pattern is unknown in Tigrinya. Ge'ez has also a completely different pattern for the infinitive.[20]

According to the pidgin hypothesis, Amharic spread further south by way of military expedition especially after it came to be known as *lisane niguss* (that is, the 'language of the king').[21] This too is a historical fact.

---

[18] Argobba is an exception, as it is closer to Amharic.

[19] This is a very productive derivation in Amharic. Almost every infinitive, at the lexical level, takes the derivational morpheme *-ya* and becomes an agentive noun, a petient noun or an adjective.

[20] Tigrinya and Ge'ez have in fact a similar process but the derivational morpheme is *i*, not *-ya*. Moreover the internal pattern of the infinitives is often different from the Amharic one and palatalization is not a feature of the Ge'ez and Tigrinya. See Tsehaye (1979) for Tigrinya and Dillmann (1899) for Ge'ez.

[21] In fact, this suggestion is not only promoted by those who advocate a pidgin origin hypothesis but also by some of those who consider Amharic to be a linear descendant of a Semitic language such as Amsalu (1976 E.C.), Meyer (2006) and Appleyard (2003).

Especially after the restoration of the Solomonic dynasty in the 13th century, there were military campaigns further to the south. Among the most successful military campaigns to the very southern territories were the ones conducted by Amdä Seyon (1314-1344) and Zär'a Ya'qob (1434-68) and later by Menelik II (see Lapiso 1982 E.C. among many others). Another point presented in some works to support the pidgin hypothesis is the identity of the so-called Amhara and the usage of the term Amhara itself among the Amharic speakers to which I turn now.

2.5 Social Genesis and Identity of the Amhara

The term Amhara is used with different meanings. One of its usages is associated with the term Christian since, at least, the 14th century (see Maqrizi).[22] Even now when one is required to specify one's own ethnic identity, an Amharic speaker (who is unfamiliar with any other ethnic identy apart from "Amhara") may use Amhara to mean that he/she is a Christian and "not Amhara" to mean that he/she is a Muslim. Moreover, as a number of historians point out, the term Amhara did not refer to an ethnic group until as early as the 20th century. It was only used as a toponym: "In the Ethiopian chronicles of the 14th-18th centuries the term 'Amhara' occurs to be a toponym, not an ethnonym, and designates a province, not people" (Chernetsov 1993: 97). Chernetsov (Ibid.) further states that this term "remains a toponym up to the 19th century both in Christian also Muslim written traditions".[23] Levine describes the region that this term Amhara referred to in earlier times as follows:

> The term Amhara referred originally to a region of historic Ethiopia bounded on the west by the Abbay and its tributary the Bashilo River; on the north by the regions of Angot and Lasta; on the east by the escarpment leading down to the Dankil Desert (Afar); and by the Wänc'it River to the south (the southwestern part of Wällo province) (Levine 2003: 230).[24]

---

[22] Maqrizi is a 15th century document written in Arabic. The reference I used here and throughout this work is the English translation of it made by Huntingford (1955). For simplicity and ease of reference, I refer to this translation "Maqrizi as translated by Huntingford (1955)".

[23] Levine confirming this suggestion also writes as follows: "Royal chronicles of the 14th-18th century consistently refer to Amhara only as a geographical region in Wällo, never as an ethnic name, and the same is true of Christian and Muslim annals up through the 19th century" (2003: 230).

[24] See also for an earlier account of this region Job Ludolph/Ludolf (1682), *A*

AN OVERVIEW OF THE PIDGIN ORIGIN HYPOTHESIS

The following is a rough estimation of the 16th century political map of Ethiopia. The map, however, only indicates the Amhara province and its immediate neighboring provinces.

Map 1: The Amhara and its neighboring regions in the early 16th century

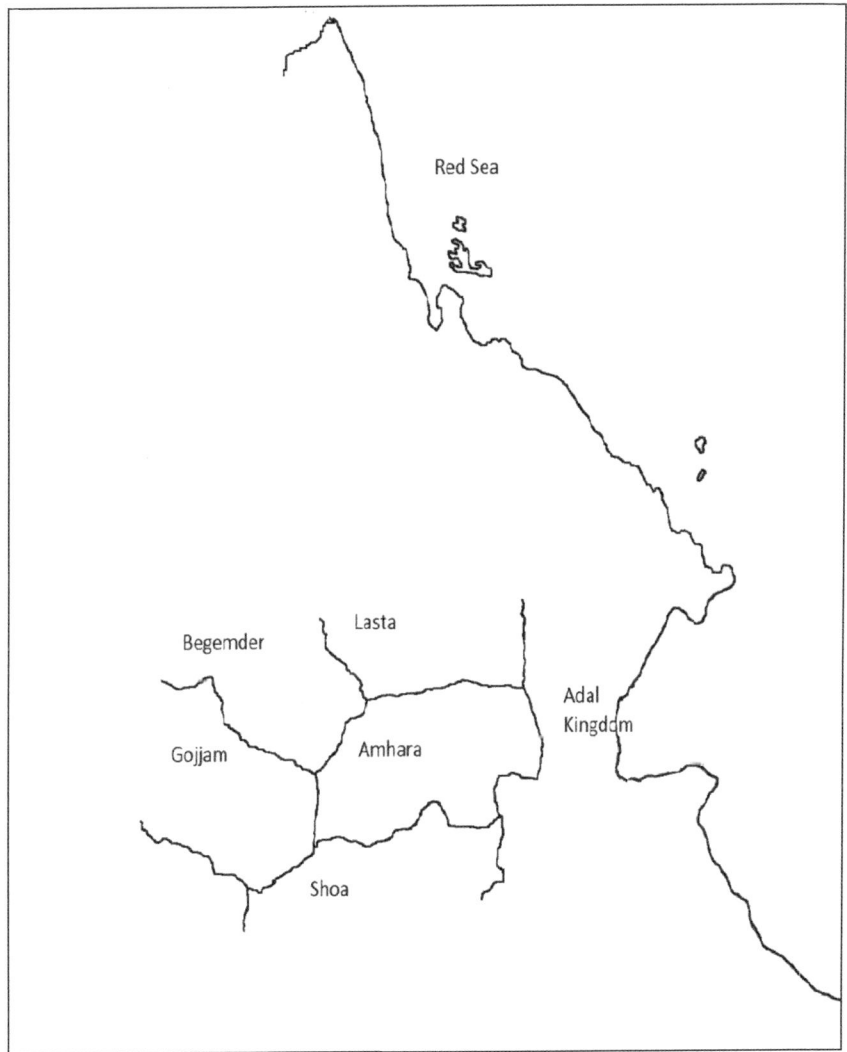

As can be seen above, the indicated region does not include all predominantly Amharic-speaking places of today such as Gonder, Gojjam, and Shoa. The early 20th century account of the "ethnic"

New History of Ethiopia.

composition of Addis Ababa does not refer to the Shoan and the Gojjame as Amhara. Consider the following table:

Table 1: The ethnic composition of Addis Ababa in 1910[25]

Ethnic group	Percentage	Number
[Oromo]	30.8	20,020
Shankalla[26]	23.1	15,015
Shewan	23.1	15,015
[Welayitta]	7.7	5,005
Amhara	4.6	2,990
Gurage	3.1	2,015
Tigre	1.5	975
Gojjami	1.5	975
Other Ethiopian	4.6	2,990
Total	100.0	65,000

Beside the aforementioned meanings, the term Amhara is used to mean "Ethiopian" as opposed to *färänj* meaning "foreigner". This is true until recently. Consider, for instance, the following advertisement of horse races during Empress Zewditu's time taken from Eadie (1924: 134):

---

[25] See Mérab in Cooper and Horvath (1976: 203)
[26] This is a collective term which was used to refer to many different ethnic groups (Ibid.).

Figure 1: An early Amharic advertisement

ያዲስ፡ አበባ፡ የፈረስ፡ እሽቅድምያ፡ በሰኔ፡ በ፪፡ ቀን፡ ለሰኞ፡ በ፪ሰዓት።	The Addis Ababa (Horse) Races. On Monday Sane 2nd, 8 a.m.
መጀመሪ፡ እሽቅድም፡ ኖቢስቴክ። ፩ኛ፡ ፴ብር፡ ፪ተኛ፡ ፲ብር፡ ፫ተኛ፡ ፭ብር።	The First Race. Novice Stake. 1st \$30. 2nd \$10. 3rd \$5.
፪ተኛ፡ እሽቅድም፡ ሰርክል፡ ደሉንዮን፡ ፩ኛ፡ ፶ብር፡ ፪ተኛ፡ ፳ብር፡ ፫ተኛ፡ ፲ብር።	Second Race. Cercle de l'Union. 1st \$50. 2nd \$20. 3rd \$10.
፫ተኛ፡ እሽቅድም፡ የሺ፡ አምበል። ፩ኛ፡ ፶ብር፡ ፪ተኛ፡ ፳ብር፡ ፫ተኛ፡ ፭ብር።	Third Race. Officers' Race. 1st \$50. 2nd \$20. 3rd \$5.
፬ተኛ፡ እሽቅድም፡ የሙሴ፡ ሴይሲገር፡ የወርቅ፡ ዋንጫ። ፩ኛ፡ ዋንጫና፡ ፶ብር፡ ፪ተኛ፡ ፳፭ብር፡ ፫ተኛ፡ ፲፩ብር።	Fourth Race. Monsieur Thesiger's Gold Cup. 1st Cup and \$50. 2nd \$25. 3rd \$11.
፭ተኛ፡ የእንጦጦ፡ ማሽቀዳደም፡ ለአማራ፡ ብቻ።[27] ፩ኛ፡ ፲፭ብር፡ ፪ተኛ፡ ፲ብር፡ ፫ተኛ፡ ፭ብር።	Fifth Race. Entotto Race. For Abyssinians Only 1st \$15. 2nd \$10. 3rd \$5.
፮ተኛ፡ ማሽቀዳደም፡ የፈረንጆች፡ ማሕበር፡ ፩ኛ፡ ፵፭ብር፡ ፪ተኛ፡ ፴፭ብር፡ ፫ተኛ፡ ፳ብር።	Sixth Race. Of the European Club. 1st \$45. 2nd \$35. 3rd \$20.
፯ተኛ፡ ማሽቀዳደም፡ ከቡር፡ ያልጋ፡ ወራሽ። ፩ኛ፡ ፶ብር፡ ፪ተኛ፡ ፳፭ብር፡ ፫ተኛ፡ ፲፭ብር።	Seventh Race. H.H the Heir Apparent's Race. 1st \$50. 2nd \$25. 3rd \$15.

---

[27] Bold is mine.

ጩኸኛ፡ እሽቅድድም፡፡ የማስዘለል፡ የፊሪክ ዋንጫ፡፡ ፩ኛ፡ ፶ብር፡፡ ፪ተኛ፡ ፳ብር፡ ፫ተኛ፡ ፲ብር፡፡	Eighth Race. Steeplechase. The Frick Cup. 1st $50. 2nd $20. 3rd $10.

In the above advertisement, the fifth race was restricted to Ethiopians alone, who were called Amhara in the Amharic text. Indeed, there are ample written works done in the Haile Selassie I period too where the term Amhara was used in the same way to refer to Ethiopians. Chernetsov (1993) points out about the people having a different ethnic background with little knowledge of Amharic who identify themselves as Amhara:

> The people of Marabete are partly of [Oromo] descent and [Oromo] living in the nearby Shoan fief of Fiche, though many speak only a few words of Amharic, tend increasingly to describe themselves as Shewan and Amhara (Chernetsov 1993: 101).

Until recently, although the ruling elites of Amharic speakers have been referred to as "Amhara kings", they identify themselves as Ethiopians or on a regional basis (Tegegne 1998: 119). Moreover, as Chernetsov (1993: 98) points out, the usage of this phrase, i.e. "Amhara kings", does not refer to an ethnic identity. Because "the dynastic ties of Ethiopian kings with their native province were quite strong", it is only meant to refer to kings who descended from the Amhara province, i.e. from Yikuno Amlak (1270-1285), the first king of the restored Solomonic line.

In the social genesis, it has been widely reported that most of the Amhara especially those who live in Gojjam, Gonder and other neighboring areas are essentially semitized Agews (cf. Taddese 1972). "More recently many Amharized former speakers of Oromo, Sidamo, etc. have been added to the 'melting pot'" (cf. Bender 1983: 48). Bender (ibid.) further states that the "present day phenotypes, i.e. the physical appearances, of present day highland plateau Amhara are quite varied, but certainly are in the range of what Amharized Agews would presumably look like". I do not know exactly what Bender meant by this as most Ethiopians especially those of Cushitic and Semitic stocks have similar physical appearance. However, it is generally true that a number of non-Amharic speakers have adopted Amharic as their native language due to their conversion to Christianity and due to Amharic's high status.

This is the case for instance, with a number of groups in Wällo (Aleqa Taye 1914 E.C.) and Qemant (see Gamst 1969, Zelealem 2003). In some cases, a whole ethnic group may adopt Amharic as their native language, as is the case with Gafat (Leslau 1944a, 1945). With the recent spread of Amharic especially to the newly re-conquered regions by Menelik II, other non-Amharic speaking people started to speak Amharic and might have replaced their own native languages by it. This is especially true with peoples who live in towns, as can be inferred, among others, from the studies of Cooper (1976) and Meyer and Richter (2003).

Besides the various usages of the term Amhara and the diverse social genesis on the making of the Amhara, Amharic speakers do not have a rigid ethnic identity. This is exhibited in a number of ways. For instance, a person from Wällo is often referred to as *Wälloye*, a person from Yifat as *Yifate*, Gojjam as *Gojjame*, Tägulät as *Täguläte*, Mänz as *Mänze* etc.[28]

> Only in the last quarter of the 20th century has the term Amhara come to be a common ethnic appellation, comparable to the way in which Oromo has become generalized to cover people who long knew themselves primarily as Boorana (Boräna), Guğği, Mäčč and the like. Even so, Amharic-speaking Šäwans still feel themselves closer to non-Amharic-speaking Šäwans than to Amharic-speakers from distant regions like Gondär and there are few members of the Šäwans nobility who do not have Oromo genealogical links... Indeed, despite the recent ethnicization of political discourse, many if not most people considered "Amhara" continue to identify themselves primarily as "Ethiopians", beyond being residents of some local area (Levine 2003: 231).

Chernetsov (1993: 101) concludes that "Amhara probably never had a close definition and always meant more social than ethnic group".

It is a fact that the so-called Amhara do not have a rigid ethnic identity and that the term is used in a number of different ways. Furthermore, most of the aforementioned discussions are indeed historical facts. The point here is, "are such facts best explained by the pidgin hypothesis?" For this, the crucial point in turn is, whether Amharic exhibits a pidgin past, i.e. whether it has characteristics of a pidgin language. For Bender

---

[28] In fact, Amharic speakers born in the Amhara regional state used also to identify themselves as *Yifate, Gojjame, Täguläte, Mänze* etc. tracing the origin of their ancestors.

(1983) and some others that promote the pidgin hypothesis, it has. I discuss this point below.

2.6 Linguistic Issues: The Grammar and Lexicon of Amharic

Although Amharic is classified as a Semitic language, it exhibits a number of non-Semitic features both in its grammar and lexicon. For instance, Amharic has SOV word order like Cushitic and Omotic languages, 25% of its core vocabulary is non-Semitic and has some other un-Semitic features. Amharic has non-concatenative morphology like Semitic languages. However, it has some morphological pattern similar with Cushitic and Omotic languages. Today's Amharic does not exhibit the common pharyngeal sounds of Semitic and is in the process of losing the glottal sounds but has, except few, some of the typical Cushitic and Omotic sounds. For those who promote the pidgin hypothesis, this is due to its pidgin past.

Although questionable, Baye (2000: xvi) claims that because of Cushitic vocabularies, Amharic received palatal phonemes such as ሽ š, ች č, ጅ ğ, ጭ č', and ኝ ñ, which make it distinct from both Geʻez and a number of Semitic languages outside Ethiopia and got ጵ p' and also received ፕ p from Greek. According to Baye (ibid) due to such process, i.e. pidginization, "Amharic lost the Semitic sounds, such as ሐ, ኽ, ዐ, ቐ, which we find today in languages like Tigrinya" (own translation).

Furthermore, for Baye (ibid), the structure of phrases and many Amharic affixes are closer to Cushitic languages such as Oromo and Omotic languages such as Wolayitta. "For this, we can site ቀበ-ኛ, ጠነ-ኛ of Oromo which Amharic takes -ኛኛ and makes extensive use of it like ኃያለኛ, ጥፋተኛ, ተንኮለኛ, ፈረሰኛ etc. This type of word formation is fundamentally that of Cushitic but not of Semitic" (own translation).

On the other hand, as pointed out above, although neither Meyer (2006) nor Amsalu (1976) present their arguments in detail, they claim that Amharic may not have originated as a pidgin despite the aforementioned facts. Appleyard (2003) also claims that Amharic may not have originated as a pidgin. Before I explore the non-pidgin alternative and examine point by point the plausibility of Bender's hypothesis, i.e. the pidgin hypothesis, I will first discuss the place of Amharic in genetic classification in the following chapter.

Chapter Three: The Place of Amharic in Genetic Classification

3.1 Introduction

Grouping languages in terms of their genetic relation is not always a straightforward matter. There are language isolates, which cannot be grouped genetically. Pidgins and/or creoles are also in most cases excluded from genetic groupings. In the Afroasiatic phylum alone, some consider the Omotic languages to belong to the Cushitic family while others consider them to form their own family as a direct descendent of the Afroasiatic phylum. Beja finds itself in the same controversy. Although most works consider Beja as a branch of Cushitic, some suggest that it should be considered as a direct descendant of Afroasiatic. The classification of Biraile (known also by the name Onogota) is another unsettled issue within this phylum. Much controversy also surrounds the internal classification of Semitic.[29]

On the other hand, although there is much controversy with regard to the internal classification of Semitic, there is no controversy as to which language is Semitic. The Semitic languages have unique grammatical

---

[29] For instance, in a recent paper Girma (2001) considers the Ethio-Semitic group as a direct descendant of Proto-Semitic. Although Girma's classification falls in line with Murtonen's (1967) suggestion, it is unlike most previous works that consider Ethio-Semitic as branching from South Semitic (see chapter five for more).

features that make them distinct from the other language families. Among others, the non-concatenative morphology and the various types of agreement markers found attached to verbs are two of the core unique morphological features of the Semitic languages.

Although pidgins and/or creoles are often outside genetic classification and, as discussed in the preceding chapter, Amharic, in Bender (1983) and some other works, suggested to have a pidgin past, i.e. origin, in almost all other works, it is considered to be a Semitic language and is grouped under the Ethio-Semitic language group. Hence, in the following section, I shall focus only on the internal classification of this group and show to which group Amharic belongs. The general classification of the whole Semitic family is presented in the following chapter. For an elaborate discussion of this family, however, see among others Hetzron (1972), Faber (1997) and the references cited there.

The major concern of this chapter is to examine the placement of Amharic in the genetic grouping of languages. Following the classification of Ethio-Semitic, in section 3.3 I discuss the major features that led to Amharic's being considered a Semitic language. In section 3.4 I discuss the non-Semitic elements found in Amharic.

3.2 Classification of Ethio-Semitic

The Ethio-Semitic language group comprises 80% of all spoken languages within the entire Semitic family (Hudson 2002) and is divided into two groups; North Ethio-Semitic, NES, and South Ethio-Semitic, SES (see Leslau 1969, Hetzron 1972, 1977 among many others).

The North Ethio-Semitic sub-family consists of Tigre, Tigrinya and Ge'ez. These three languages have a higher similarity between each other in their lexicon than any of them has to the South Ethio-Semitic languages. Moreover, they have unique grammatical features that make them distinct from the South. For instance, gemination of the penultimate consonant of "type A" roots in the imperfective is only attested in the North but not in the South. Such gemination is attested in the South in the perfective, which is not the case in the North. Moreover, broken plural is a typical feature of the Northern languages but not of the Southern ones.[30]

The Southern languages are grouped into two sub-families, which are named Transversal and Outer South Ethiopic (Hetzron 1972). These two

---

[30] See for detailed list of such features Hetzron (1972) and for a counter argument of such division Voigt (2007).

sub-families are also divided into other mini-sub-families. The Transversal is divided into Central and Southern, according to Hetzron (1977), and the Outer is divided into *n*-group and *tt*-group (Hetzron 1972, 1977) or GMS-group and Western Gurage (Girma 2001). The general classification of the Ethiopian Semitic languages, as adopted from Girma (2001) with minor modifications, is as follows:[31]

Figure 2: Ethio-Semitic classification
Ethio-Semitic
1. North Ethio-Semitic
    - Ge'ez
    - Tigre
    - Tigrinya
2. South Ethio-Semitic
   A. Transversal South Ethiopic
    i. Southern
      - Silte, Wolane
      - Harari
      - Zay
    ii. Central
      - Amharic
      - Argobba
   B. Outer South Ethiopic
    i. GMS-group
      a. Gafat
      b. North Gurage
        - AMCM-Group
      - Soddo
      - Gogot
        - Mäsqan
    ii. Western Gurage
      a. Central Western Gurage
        - Muher
        - Ezha, Chaha, Gumer, Gura, Ennemor
      b. Peripheral Western Gurage
        - Geyto, Endegeñ, Ener, Mesmes

As we can see from the above chart, Amharic is grouped under South Ethio-Semitic. It is grouped, especially, along with Argobba under the

---

[31] Some of the languages listed below have other alternative names (see Hetzron 1972, ELRC 2005).

Central South ES within the Transversal South ES. This is because Amharic is more closely related to Argobba than to any of the other languages. Some even suggest that these two speech varieties are dialects of the same language.[32] Compared to the major nationalities of Ethiopia, Argobba is spoken by a minority people. Since most of the Argobba do not speak their language any more, it is considered as an endangered language (Leslau 1997, Hussien et al 2006).[33]

3.3 Amharic as a Semitic Language

Amharic is considered a Semitic language because it has the basic Semitic features. Bender (1983) who suggests the idea of pidgin-induced origin to Amharic, contradicts himself when it comes to the Semitic features exhibited in Amharic which make it indisputably Semitic as can be seen from his own statement below.

> Amharic is clearly a Semitic language: its basic word stock is up to 75% recognizably Semitic, containing such universal Semitic items as "bite, blood, die, eat, eye, hand, hear, long, mouth, name, sea, short, spit, what". In morphology, the Semitic verbal prefix system is seen clearly in Amharic i-, ti-, yi-, ni-, ti-, yi- 1,2,3 sg., 1,2,3, pl. respectively, (ignoring gender distinctions); Semitic prepositions are found: la-, 'for, to', ba- 'in, by'; passive intransitive ta- is found, also active transitive verbs with doubled penultimate consonant, etc. (Bender 1983: 41).

Besides the features stated above in Bender, Amharic has a number of other core Semitic features. For instance, like other Semitic languages it has non-concatenative morphology: "Verb" roots, which are abstract and consist of only consonants called radicals, carry the lexical meaning where vowels, inserted in between the radicals to form various types of stems, carry the grammatical information. That is, vowels mark grammatical categories such as aspect (especially perfective and imperfective) and mood (like jussive and imperative) and determine the class to which the stem belongs in the same way as other Semitic languages do. In addition to the basic Semitic subject agreement features

---

[32]This suggestion does not seem to be the case, however. See the following chapter.
[33] According to the latest national census of Ethiopia (2007), the number of ethnic Argobba is 140,134. UNESCO considers Argobba a critically endangered language, estimating the number of Argobba speakers at 8,000.

that Amharic exhibits, in this language the person marker in the imperative verb form is only morphologically visible in the negation. To the best of our knowledge, this is true of all Semitic languages. The negative marker *al-* of Proto-Semitic is also preserved in Amharic, which is in fact lost in Geʻez, for instance.[34] However, it has also non-Semitic elements both in its lexicon and grammar, which I turn to now.

3.4 The Non-Semitic Elements in Amharic

Amharic exhibits a number of un-Semitic grammatical features, although most of these features are not particular to this language. They are also found in most of the other Ethio-Semitic languages. Amharic has also some non-Semitic lexical items in its basic and cultural lexicons. I discuss these issues point by point below.

3.4.1 Phonology

Amharic lacks the pharyngeal and the glottal sounds such as ħ, and ʕ which are assumed to be typical of Semitic languages. Amharic has palatal sounds which are not attested, for instance in Geʻez. Palatalization is also a very common process in Amharic. It has more or less a complete sound system of Cushitic and Omotic languages.

3.4.2 Morphology

Hetzron (1972) and Bender and Fulass (1978) have mentioned some morphological facts in Amharic which are un-Semitic. For instance, according to Hetzron (1972: 85ff.) *-acc-* in bound pronouns such as in *-accihu* '2pl' and *-accäw* '3pl' is a redundant plural marker which is developed in analogy with similar redundant plural markers (having different phonological shapes) in Agew varieties. "A further extension is the use of the original plural pronouns with the extra marker as polite forms" (Bender and Fulass 1978: 9-10). Broken plural, which is typical of Semitic, is not attested in Amharic.

According to Bender (1983: 42) a very un-Semitic pattern in Amharic morphology is the extensive use of post-posed particles such as *wist* 'inside', *lay* 'up', *tac* 'down', *fit* 'face', *hwala*, 'behind', *zuriya* 'around'.[35] Bender (ibid.) also states that, "some of the common Semitic

---

[34] There is one exception to this in Geʻez with the verb *bo* 'there is' where its negation form takes *al-* as in *al-bo* 'there is not'.

[35] Bender, however, states that "most of these are recognizable Semitic roots, e.g. *wist*, inside; *lay* up; *tač* down; fit face *hwala*, behind; *zuriya*, around" (1983: 42). The status of these items is controversial: They can equally be considered as nouns than adpositions. We will come to this point later.

verb markers are lacking: prefix *n-* and prefix *s-* are preserved in traces only, and the function of the doubled penultimate consonant is quite different from the pattern productive in old Semitic". There are also some un-Semitic morphological patterns in Amharic. However, it is believed that Amharic morphology exhibits basic Semitic features. The un-Semitic morphological features in this language are minimal and insignificant.

3.4.3 Syntax

Amharic exhibits a truly un-Semitic appearance in its syntax. For instance, it has SOV word order in most constructions which are un-Semitic; relative clauses precede nouns that they modify; construct state, which is typical of Semitic languages is lacking in Amharic; phrasal verb construction, with dummy "compounding" verb *al-* the "verb-to-say" (in the case of intransitive) and √*drg* 'to do' (in the case of transitive) is common in Amharic which is un-Semitic. As Bender points out, "it is the un-Semitic syntax which has aroused the doubts of scholars, and led to endless speculation about the unorthodoxy of Amharic" (Bender 1983: 42). However, the un-Semitic syntax of Amharic is not greater than any of the other modern Ethio-Semitic languages. For instance, all the aforementioned un-Semitic syntactic features that Amharic exhibits are also found in all modern Ethio-Semitic languages (see also Hetzron 1972, Ullendorff 1955, Girma 2003).

3.4.4 Lexicon

As pointed in the preceding chapter, 25% of Amharic core vocabularies are non-Semitic. Some of such basic vocabularies are the following: the third person pronouns, *wiha* 'water', *joro* 'ear', *siga* 'meat', *wiša* 'dog', *bäga* 'dry season', *asa* 'fish', *kara* 'knife', etc. Amharic has also a number of cultural terms with non-Semitic origins. Most of the non-Semitic basic vocabularies of Amharic are from Cushitic. However, loanwords of cultural terms in Amharic can also be traced from the other Semitic languages such as Ge'ez and Arabic, and from the non-Semitic languages such as Greek (probably via Ge'ez), Portuguese (which can be traced to the 17th century), Italian (this can also be traced to the five year Italian occupation period), and recently from English.

3.5 Summary

In this chapter, I have pointed out that although Amharic morphology is the least affected one, its phonology exhibits more un-Semitic pattern. Amharic has also non-Semitic lexical items in its cultural as well as basic lexicon. The very un-Semitic pattern that Amharic shows is, in fact, in syntax. In spite of this, however, Amharic is considered a Semitic language because it contains the core Semitic features.

Chapter Four: An Examination of the Pidgin Origin Hypothesis

4.1 Introduction

In chapter two, I discussed the core points of the pidgin origin hypothesis. In chapter three, I examined the place of Amharic in the genetic classification of Semitic languages. In that chapter I also discussed the extent to which Amharic does exhibit Semitic features. In this chapter, I examine Bender's hypothesis point by point.

4.2 Date of Origin: Examination of the Contradiction

As we have seen in chapter two, the pidiginization process that yielded the present Amharic language, according to Bender (1983), Baye (2000 EC) and Bender and Fulass (1978), should have started around the middle of the 4th century. However, the date when exactly Amharic became distinct varies from work to work and sometimes even within a single work. While Bender (1983) at one point claims that Amharic became distinct around the 9th century (p. 46), at another point, he claims that it became distinct by the 14th century (p. 49). Baye (2000 EC: xv-xvi), as pointed out earlier, suggests that Amharic became distinct by the 4th century. Bender and Fulass (1978) claim that Amharic became distinct by the 14th century;[36] by the 9th century it was only the place

---

[36] "By the fourteenth century, the standard itself would be as far removed in time from its common origin with Giiz [Ge'ez] as present-day English is from

◈ *THE ORIGIN OF AMHARIC*

known as Amhara that became distinct.[37]

The contradiction regarding the date of origin may indicate that the pidgin origin hypothesis is not a well-thought theory.[38] When we closely examine Bender (1983), we find that his overall discussion favors the 14th century date of origin but not the 9th century. Bender suggests that the pidginization process was accelerated when the Agew rose to power around the middle of the 12th century (1983: 49). If the pidginization process of Amharic was still ongoing in the 12th century, it can only be the case that Amharic became distinct at a date later than the 12th century.[39] Now, let us come to Baye's (2000 E.C.) suggestion that Amharic became distinct around the 4th century.

First, as Baye (2000 E.C.) following Bender (1983) adopted the suggestion that the Axumite military expeditions to the south took place starting from the middle of the 4th century, the idea that Amharic became distinct around the same century, i.e. at the same time while the pidiginization process started, is theoretically impossible. A pidgin can only be promoted to a creole when it becomes a mother tongue, i.e. through a process known as nativization, which often takes centuries. Moreover, for a creole to be developed as a "standard" language, it needs its own time. Hence, a very convincing assumption (that can be compatible with Baye's 2000 E.C. and Bender's 1983 outline of the historical process of the pidgin hypothesis) is rather to consider that Amharic has become distinct at a later period than the 4th century or even the 9th century. This, therefore, means that we are left only with Bender's (1983) and Bender and Fulass' (1978) alternative suggestion that Amharic evolved in the 14th century.[40] This, however, poses other serious

---

that of Alfred the Great" (Bender and Fulass 1978: 8).

[37] "By the mid-ninth century, a distinctive Amhara region was recognized" (Bender and Fulass 1978: 7).

[38] This is true especially as the contradictory suggestion is also found within a single work, surprisingly in Bender (1983). However, let us examine which date of proposed origin is compatible with their explanation.

[39] Bender's (1983) suggestion that Amharic came into existence as a language in the 9th century is probably based on Taddese (1972) who mentions that a distinct Amhara region was recognized by the end of the 9th century on the upper basin of the Bashilo River. Levine also mentioned that "the earliest references to the region appear in connection with the traditions narrating of the reign of a 9th century Axumite king, Degnajan who brought Christian missionaries to teach there" (2003: 230).

[40] Assuming that Amharic was evolved out of Ge'ez, some historians and

problems with regard to historical and linguistic facts, which I turn to now.

4.3 Historical, Chronological and Logical Questions

Amharic is assumed to have spread south during the reign of the famous Emperor Amdä Seyon (1314-1344), who is considered to be the greatest of the early "Solomonic" monarchs.[41] If Amharic were spoken only in the northwestern parts of Ethiopia and spread with the former kings, I should not find it in an area where no former emperors reached. However, the 14th century Arab historian Al 'Umari describes that in the kingdom of Yifat, which Amdä Seyon fought against to establish his rule, the same language as in Amdä Seyon's kingdom was spoken (cf. Pankhurst 1997). The other 15th century Arab historian Maqrizi also mentions the same thing (Maqrizi as translated by Huntingford 1955).

The Kingdom of Yifat was founded by the people known as Argobba (Abebe 1992: 83 ff., Ahmed 1999 E.C.). The Argobba language is genetically the closest relative of Amharic (chapter three, Hetzron 1972, Leslau 1997). Presently Argobba speaking people or people who once used to speak this language are found among other places in the environs of Harar, eastern Shoa, and some parts of Wällo (Wetter 2003, Hussien et al 2006, and Girma 2011). These people are assumed to have been living there at least before the tenth century and some of the Argobba lands are fully incorporated into the Christian kingdom starting from the end of the 19th century with the reign of Emperor Menelik II. What is not questioned in the pidgin hypothesis is the presence of Argobba in non-Christian territory at an earlier date and their relation to the Amharic-speaking population.

I believe that addressing the aforementioned point is crucial not only for the sake of examining the pidgin hypothesis but also for the understanding of the origin of Amharic, in general. In section 4.3.1, we, therefore, discuss the Argobba issue in more detail. The genetic relation of Amharic with other Ethio-Semitic languages especially with the Transversal South Ethio-Semitic that I pointed out in chapter three will

---

philologists also advocate that Amharic became a distinct language by the 14th century. For instance, Getatchew and Huntingford suggest based on the imperial lyrics composed in praise of the deeds of Amdä Seyon (1314-1344) that "these songs are written in a transitional form of Amharic during the period of its emergence from Ge'ez" (Huntingford 1965:14).

[41] Amdä Seyon expands his territory to the south beyond what had been that of his predecessors.

be examined against the pidgin origin hypothesis in section 4.3.2. With the consideration of other factors, the dialectal differences within a language may indicate how old that language is. In a similar way, although not with hundred percent precision, the subgrouping of languages in the genetic classification may also indicate dates of separation of the genetically related languages in question. Hence, in section 4.3.3 I examine dates of origin for the various Ethio-Semitic groups against Bender's (1983) suggestion in the pidgin hypothesis.

4.3.1 The Issue of Argobba

Argobba is closely related to Amharic. It is often considered to be a dialect of Amharic[42], which, actually does not seem to be the case (cf. Hussien et al. 2006, Wetter 2011, Girma 2011).[43] However, there is no doubt that Amharic and Argobba derived from a single Proto-language (Leslau 1997, Hetzron 1972 among others). Abebe quoting other sources states as follows:

> It is during the first Muslim period of Shoa and Yefat — roughly between the tenth and the thirteenth centuries — that the differentiation of a common Proto-Amharic-Argobba language into Amharic and Argobba took place. Although Argobba is not a dialect of Amharic, structurally it is the closest. Separated from the main block of Amharic-speaking highlanders by a different religion and culture, having a different outlook and relations to the outside world, and living in a very different natural habitat, the Argobba preserved a language of an ancient pattern (Abebe 1992: 86).

It is due to their close similarity that Argobba and Amharic are considered to form their own group even within the smaller group of Transversal South Ethio-Semitic (cf. chapter three). If Amharic originated in the surroundings of the Bashilo River or somewhere in the northwest around the 4^h century as a pidgin and became a distinct language around the 14th century as proposed in Bender (1983) and Bender and Fulass (1978) and if, on the other hand, Argobba were separated from Amharic around the 10th or 11th century, then it means

---

[42] For instance, Bender and Fulass state that "Amharic does have one quite divergent dialect: Argobba. This is probably best considered as a 'Muslim dialect'" (1978: 59).

[43] As we will see in a moment, Amharic, besides Argobba, is closely related with the other Transversal South Ethio-Semitic languages.

that Argobba separated from Amharic before Amharic became a fully functional language. This assumption linguistically is, therefore, implausible because the differences exhibited between Amharic and Argobba at present should been higher than what they are. As pointed out above, Amharic and Argobba are very closely related, though not to the extent that they are dialects of the same language. Though Bender's (contradictory) proposal that Amharic became distinct around the 9th century could avoid this problem, as discussed above, this or any other earlier date is not compatible with the general outline of the pidgin hypothesis. Even if this proposed date were seriously considered despite not fitting the outline, a number of other difficult questions are raised. Among these, one is a logical question: How would the Argobba speakers spread eastward around Harar and many other far eastern and southern areas of the country prior to the expansion of the Christian kingdom?

According to a recent survey by a group of scholars from SIL-Ethiopia, the Argobba people are living, among other places, in the east scattered along the way to Harar:

> The Argobba people are somewhat spread out, living in parts of the Amhara, Oromiya and Afar regions of northeastern Ethiopia. They are generally distinguished by being either "northern" Argobba or "southern" Argobba. The precise locations of these "northern" and "southern" Argobba are unclear. Generally, the "southern" live around the road that goes from Addis Ababa to Harar while the "northern" live between and around the two roads that travel north from Addis Ababa on either side of the Rift Valley, as far north as the town of Kemise (Hussein et al 2006: 415).

In the introduction of the recently published Argobba textbook, Muhamed and Jewhar (n.d.: 2) state that the Argobba reside in areas stretching from Bale in the south to Eritrea in the north. Although, it is difficult presently to prove some of the claims, such as their existence far in Eritrea, the 1994 census reports that they live in Tigray. Seid Omur, the head of the Argobba Development Association, (P.C) confirms me that they live in Gondor and far south in Bale. Moreover, there are Argobba people in Arsi, especially in the former Arba Gugu district.

Currently, most of the Argobba people, probably 80 percent of their total population, do not speak their language any more (Hussien et al 2006).[44] However, although the Argobba people reside scattered in different regions and most of them do not speak their language any more, all claim descent from the same ancestor and that they therefore have the same origin (Abebe 1992, Ahmed 1999 E.C.).

The Argobba are Muslims and are one of the first groups that converted to Islam in the horn of Africa (Abebe 1992, Ahmed 1999 E.C.). As pointed out above, it is claimed that they are the ones who founded the Yifat sultanate, which was the successor of the Makzumite sultanate.[45] In fact, the Makzumite sultanate, the first Muslim sultanate founded in Ethiopia around the 9th century, was established in the heartland of Argobba. The "Mahzumi dynasty [...] is said to have reigned on a sultanate of Shoa from ca. H. 283/AD 896-897 to ca. H. 684/AD 1285, at which terminal date it was absorbed by the sultanate of Ifat that flourished somewhere in eastern Ethiopia" (Fauvelle-Aymar and Hirsch 2011: 37, See also Abebe 1992: 84).

On the other hand, in the early medieval period, the highland Christian kingdom had contacts with the people in central Shoa called Gobah, i.e. Argobba (Taddese 1972).[46] Moreover, especially starting from the Solomonic dynasty in the 13th century, military campaigns to the south took place regularly. The Ethiopian Orthodox faith, too, might also have reached further south to the heartland of Gurage, even before the 10th century.[47] Indeed, quoting Al 'Umari , Lapiso (1982: 106) states that

---

[44] The SIL report and our field work show that some areas have totally given up their language recently. For instance, the people around Harar have only preserved their language in some songs. In fact, these people do not understand the meanings of such songs.

[45] "As a result of the connection between the Argobba and Wälashma and the fortunes of the Muslim sultanates which developed in north-eastern Shoa between 1270-1415, there is evidence indicating that the present Argobba of Shoa and Wällo are a remnant population of the sultanate of Ifat" (Abebe 2003: 333).

[46] The Gobah people are assumed to be the Argobba. Indeed, in one of the legends of Argobba, Abebe reports the following: "Argobba elders assert that the term Argobba is in fact a derivative of the compound word "Har" and "Gubba" – meaning "silk" and "mountain top" respectively. That is, the early inhabitants of the Rift Valley System were silk traders inhabiting mountaintops. This alternative folk etymology not only does establish the past and present occupational status of the Argobba but it also rightly describes their settlement pattern" (Abebe 1992: 80).

[47] According to tradition when the Axumite kingdom was attacked by Yodit,

from the beginning of the 14th century, the administrative parts of the Ethiopian empire included Semhar, Saho, Hamasen, Nara, Baria, Tigray, Sehart, Amhara, Shoa, Damot, Gänz, Adal, Mora, Yifat, Däwaro, Arababini, Hadiya, Sharka, Bali and Dära.[48] The 15th century Arab historian Maqrizi also states that Ethiopia had twelve regions during his time. The twelve regions of Ethiopia that Maqrizi mentions are the following:

> Abyssinia begins where the land stretches north from east at that strait of Bab al Mandib. In Abyssinia is the river Sihun, of Sweet water, which is a tributary of the Nile of Egypt. On the west Abyssinia extends to the region of Tekrur where it turns southwards. Here in the desert is the Wadi Baraka. Thence to the former metropolis of the kingdom of Sahart, also called Ahsum [Axum] and Zarafrata, which was the seat of the Najasi. Then comes the district of Amhar, now the main part of the kingdom, also called Marada. Next are the regions (clima) of Shawah [Shewa], Damut, Lamanan, Sanhu, Zeng, Adal al umara, Hamasa, Barya, and Tiraz al islami, which is called Zayla. Each of these twelve regions has its own king, but all are subject to the Hati, who is called Sultan in Arabic (Maqrizi as translated by Huntingford 1955: 1-2).

Zayla, the Muslim region which belongs to the country of Abyssinia had seven kingdoms, namely Yifat (in Maqrizi term Awfat), Dawaro, Arababni, Hadya, Sharha, Bali, and Darah (Maqrizi as translated by Huntingford 1955: 7). However, the military expeditions and the establishment of the Ethiopian-Orthodox church could not have been sufficient to spread Amharic and to make other people adopt it.

Although the Christian kingdoms in the Ethiopian highlands fought with the Muslim sultanates and made them pay taxes, it was only under emperor Zär'a Ya'qob (1434-1468) that the Christian kingdom posted its soldiers in the heartland of Yifat (cf. Lapiso 1982 E.C: 109, Maqrizi as translated by Huntingford 1955: 14). A complete and permanent

---

some priests migrated to the islands of Lake Zway taking with them the *Tabot* of Axum Tsion and lived there for 40 years before taking the *Tabot* back with them.
[48] See also Pankhurst (1997), and Huntingford (1965).

inclusion of Yifat took place after the 19th century (Abebe 2003: 333).[49]

As the two kingdoms had different religions and the contact was mostly power struggle, it is hard to assume that the Muslim sultanate adopted the language of the Christians who made them pay taxes. Furthermore, the contact between these two kingdoms was limited before the reign of Zär'a Ya'qob (1434-1468). In order for a language shift to occur, there must be sufficent social contact.

Moreover, if Argobba diverged from Amharic later in the 15th century, I should not find archaic features in Argobba which are not found any more in Amharic. For example, Argobba has heavy and light object suffixes like some of the Gurage languages, which Amharic lacks (Andreas Wetter 2010: 180ff.). This feature can be considered at least as a feature of South Ethio-Semitic. Some of the core Semitic and Proto-South Ethio-Semitic vocabularies that Amharic lost are preserved in Argobba. Consider, for instance, *käme* (Argobba) vs. *indet* (Amharic) 'how', *gey* (Argobba) vs. *agar* (Amharic) 'country, place, land', *wägär* (Argobba) vs. *dähna* (Amharic) 'good'. Note that also, in Old Amharic some of these lexemes are attested. From the above vocabularies, *wägär and gey* are used in Old Amharic as evidenced, for example, in the poems written to praise emperors Gälawdewos (1540-1559 E.C.) and Zär'a Ya'qob (1434-1468), respectively (see these poems in the appendix). There are also more archaic features in Argobba which Amharic lacks. Moreover, there is a historical fact that disproves the pidgin hypothesis.

As pointed out above, the first Muslim sultanate already existed in the central parts of Shoa in the 9th century. 'There were ten rulers of this state – one a woman – between 896 and 1280, when the neighbouring Moslem state Ifat gained control of it under Omar Walasma'"(Huntingford 1965: 14-15). The Yifat sultanate was the most powerful sultanates among the seven Moslem sultanets which were

---

[49] "The rise of Shoa during the late 17th and 18th centuries became a prelude to the Amhara penetration into the escarpment slopes. Under *negus* Sahleselasse and his successors, the Argobba homelands were incorporated into the expanding Shäwan kingdom in the 19th century. During the same century, the erosion of Wälashma authority and Argobba regional economy was facilitated through state taxation and gradual arrival of Christian Amhara settlers from the highlands" (Abebe 2003: 333).

subject to the Emperor of Ethiopia in the 14th century.⁵⁰ We know from Al 'Umari that both the Christian kingdom and the Muslim sultanate used to speak the same language long before the settlement of Emperor Zär'a Ya'qob's "Chäwa" troops in the heartland of Yifat.⁵¹ Abebe (1992: 99), based on Al 'Umari's description, states that "the inhabitants of the Sultanate [i.e. the Yifat Sultanate] were followers of the *shafi* school of Muslim law. The people spoke their own language and Arabic." The local language was reported in Al 'Umari as Abyssinian, and interpreted in many historical writings as Amharic (see, for instance, Pankhurst 1997). Even the language of the Makzumite Sultanate, i.e. the indigenous language spoken by the local people, is suggested to be a Semitic language, which possibly was Proto-Amharic-Argobba (Lapiso 1982: 153).⁵² If such historical facts are true, and if Amharic was created through a pidginization process, it must have been created not in the 14th century but long before this date, as the language was already spoken before this time by the Argobba people as well. This also puts Bender's hypothesis into question.

Recall that according to the pidgin origin hypothesis, Amharic should have been created by soldiers of the Christian kingdom and then spread along with Christianity: "The ensuing process of 'Amharainzation' entailed not only the adoption of the Amharic language, but also the acceptance of the Ethiopian Orthodox faith such that the two became an inseparable trend" (Appleyard 2003: 233). Although this can be true for many groups, for the reason discussed above, it is very difficult to suggest that the Argobba adopted their language due to the Christian kingdom expansion.

It seems that the first language of the Argobba people is Argobba itself, which separated from Amharic due to religious differences that took place probably around the 10th or 11th century as suggested in Hetzron

---

⁵⁰ See the Glorious Victory of Amde Seyon (Huntingford 1965) among others.

⁵¹ See Crummey (2003) for "Chäwa".

⁵² Although most of the Argobba names that we get from historical records are Arabic, in a few cases we find local names which are exactly the same with Amharic. Even in some cases, the Yifat Sultanate officials use similar nicknames as those of the Christian kingdom. For example, Ahmed who ruled Yifat in the time of Newaye Kirstos, known also Säyf Ar'ed (1344-1372), was known by the name Harb Arad. Note that also the person who killed Ahmed (Harb Arad) was his uncle named Mola Asfah (Maqrizi, translated by Huntingford 1955:13). The names Mola and Asfah are still common among the Amhara communities.

(1972) or even in the 9th century with the establishment of the Muslim sultanate, and later the linguistic differences intensified when the Amhara took control of the Christian kingdom in the 13th century. As the distinctiveness of the Argobba and the Amhara people is attributed to religion (cf. Abebe 1992), and they live either in adjacent territories or intermingled with each other, it is plausabile to assume that the two speech varieties developed as distinct languages due to cultural differences, i.e. religion (see chapter six for further discussion).

4.3.2 The Relation of Amharic with the other South Ethio-Semitic

In genetic classification, Amharic and Argobba are considered as originating from a single Proto-language and grouped as Central South Ethio-Semitic. This group, in turn, is derived from the Proto-Transversal South Ethio-Semitic which encompasses also Southern Transversal Ethio-Semitic languages (cf. chapter three).[53] It is due to the great number of grammatical and lexical similarities that Amharic and Argobba have with the Southern Transversal Ethio-Semitic languages, i.e. Harari, Zay, Silte and Wolane, that they are grouped under one subfamily, (see Hetzron 1972, Hudson 2000, among others). From a pidginization theory point of view, it is difficult to explain the reason why Amharic exhibits such close affiliations with these language.

Bender himself states that the un-Semitic behavior of Amharic also occurs in its related Southern Ethio-Semitic languages stating: "the same or a similar solution must then be proposed for the other Southern Ethio-Semitic languages, since Harari, the various Gurage languages, and the extinct Gafat show the same general characteristics" (1983: 42). For me, the only conceivable solution which would be compatible with the pidgin origin hypothesis is that each of the South Ethio-Semitic languages or its subgroups, too, originated from a pidgin. However, this is doubtful.

First, if Amharic or Proto-Amharic-Argobba, i.e. Central Transversal South Ethio-Semitic, originated from a pidgin, the diversification between the Central and the Southern Transversal languages should be higher than what they are today. Second, not only Amharic but also any of the Transversal South Ethio-Semitic (or South Ethio-Semitic generally) would show unnatural language change that supports separate pidginization. If at all pidginization plays a role in the formation of

---

[53] Note that Transversal South Ethio-Semitic is directly derived from South Ethio-Semitic where the other direct descendant of the latter is Outer South Ethio-Semitic (cf. chapter three).

Amharic, it should have taken place before the formation of Proto-Amharic-Argobba, i.e. with Proto-Transversal South Ethio-Semitic. Moreover, as the relation between this group and the Outer South Ethio-Semitic is crystal clear, no independent pidgin-induced origin would possibly be the case for Proto-Transversal either. As Hetzron (1972: 22) states, "common features characterized all the SE languages suggest that there was a common SE stage in their development". Hence, the pidgin theory for Amharic alone is not plausible in any case.

4.3.3 Chronological Issues

Recall that according to Bender (1983), Amharic originated from a Semitic superstratum and a Cushitic and probably Omotic and Nilo-Saharan substratum. It became a distinct language in the 14th century. The pre-Amharic Semitic language, however, was removed from a common origin with Ge'ez only four to seven centuries before the middle of the 4th century. If this is true, then the SES and NES would have been separated (from Proto-ES) around 2000 years ago, 300 BC to 100 AD.[54] With this suggestion, not only is there a serious chronological problem from the theoretical point of view but also a factual/historical error.

If Ge'ez, a North Ethio-Semitic language, and Amharic, a South Ethio-Semitic language, had been separated from the same parent language around 300 B.C.E to 100 A.C.E. as Bender (1983) and Bender and Fulass (1978) claim, Ge'ez and its sister languages, Tigre and Tigrinya, must have been separated after Proto-North Ethio-Semitic fully developed its distinctive features. In historical linguistics it is assumed that dialects need 500 to 1000 years of separation to become distinctive languages. If I apply this linguistic prediction to Bender's date of separation, it means that Ge'ez, Tigre and Tigrinya were separated from their parent Proto-North Ethio-Semitic in between 200 to 700 A.D. However, it is a historically attested fact that Ge'ez was already a spoken language on its own even before 300 BC (see Drewes 1958 and the following chapter). Tigrinya and Tigre, as well, were assumed to be spoken at the same time (cf. Hetzron 1972).

Recall that Amharic and Argobba are assumed to have been separated around 10th or 11th century (or even as early as the 9th century. As Amharic and Argobba are presently distinct languages, the suggested separation date, i.e. 9th, 10th or 11th century, seems plausible.

---

[54] This is because Ge'ez is a North Ethio-Semitic language and Amharic a South Ethio-Semitic.

In the preceding section, I have argued that no pidginization can be postulated for the creation of Amharic or Central South ES, i.e. Proto-Amharic-Argobba, alone because they show close affinity with the Southern Transversal Ethio-Semitic languages. If we follow the 500-1000 years of separation period for dialects to become distinctive languages, the division of Central and Southern Transversal should have taken place at least some 2000 years ago.

If we try to postulate the separation date of Outer and Transversal from their common parent language Proto-South Ethio-Semitic, it should take place between 3000 to 4000 years ago. The separation of South Ethio-Semitic from the North Ethio-Semitic should not be less than 5000 years, if not more (cf. Murtonen 1967). Recall that for Murtonen such separation might have been occuring since Proto-Semitic time. Bender rejecting his former assumption, in his recent works (Bender 1997, 2003) also suggests a similar hypothesis with Murtonen. According to Bender (1997, 2003), the diversity observed in the various Ethiopian Semitic languages and their known close relation with Akkadian, the ancient attested Semitic language, can only be explained if we give for the origin of ES a longer date than the often claimed 500 BC. For Bender (ibid.) this date most probably is a proto-Semitic time, as he proposed a Semitic homeland to be Ethiopia. Although Hetzron (1972, 1977) does not propose a specific date, he also suggests that the diversity in the various Ethiopian Semitic languages cannot be explained with the assumed South Arabian migration in the first millennium BCE. It needs a much longer period than this. This means, if we take Bender's (1983) proposed date of separation (between Pre-Amharic and Pre-Ge'ez), i.e. 300 B.C.E.-100 A.C.E., there is not enough time for the separation of the various Ethio-Semitic languages. Hence, neither the Amharic's pidginzation date nor pre-Amharic's and pre-Ge'ez's separation date suggested by Bender (1983) can be true. Moreover, the suggestion that Amharic became a distinct language around the 14th century (section 4.1 above) and later spread further south with military expedition cannot also be the case. This is so for the following historical facts:

First, as pointed out in the preceding section, the social contact which could have brought the Amharic expansion into the Muslim lands of the Yifat sultanate can only be assumed starting from the Zär'a Ya'qob (1434-1468) period when the Christian soldiers permanently settled there. However, this Muslim Sultanate was assumed to speak the same language with the Christian kingdom long before this date. Second, Amharic was promoted to be an administrative language during the

Zague period specifically during the reign of king Lalibela (1140-1180) (Sergew 1972: 278, Ayalew n.d.: 155ff.). This indicates that Amharic was a distinct language long before the 14th century.

4.4 The Issue of Place of origin

Based on Hetzron (1972), Bender and Fulass (1978) outline how the South Ethio-Semitic languages came to their present location as follows:

> When Axum was under pressure from the Beja and other invaders, the main retreat route was to the south. The southerners passed through Agew – Speaking territory, and this meant Agew influence on the language also. The picture gets more complicated: a vanguard group went far south and this migration led to the eventual development of most of the "Gurage" languages, with Highland East Cushitic as main "substratum". From an unspecified center further north, at a later date, another group moved southeast and split into two: One section went south and under Sidamo or Somali or other influence, gave rise to Harari and East Gurage languages. The other group remained in touch with the old northern civilization, and inherited it when the northern empire collapsed. These were the people who brought Semitic speech to the Amhara region (Bender and Fulass 1978:4).

Bender remarks, however that the above "outline is quite controversial and that many problems remain to be resolved" (Ibid). This is indeed controversial for a number of reasons.

I have pointed out in the above section that the first language of Argobba people is Argobba itself which separated from Amharic due to religious differences probably around the 9th century (or 10th or 11th century as suggested by Hetzron). The difference intensified later when the Amhara took control of the Christian kingdom in the 13th century. I know that the Argobba people used to live in some of their present locations long before the Amhara took over the Christian Kingdom, and they who reside in such places claim that they are indigenous.[55] If the Argobba

---

[55] "The strip of narrow lowland area separating Rasa from the rest of Adal country in the east is full of ruined buildings, walls of mosques and countless number of tombs, <u>dorih</u>. For the Argobba, this too gives them a sense of [being] 'the first indigenous people to settle in the place" (Abebe 1992: 84).

people did not adopt their language at a later period, and it is in fact their native language, Proto-Amharic-Argobba could not have beencreated in the northwest, i.e. around the Bashilo River. Note that, before the Oromo expansion, the area from Harar to the present Gurage Zone was assumed to be inhabited by the Semitic people of Ethiopia: "While Harari now is a speech island, in the time before the sixteenth-century Oromo invasion, there might have been a coherent Semitic speaking area up to the eastern Gurage languages" (Wagner 1997: 486). The settlements of the Argobba community confirm such a continuum. Currently the Argobba people are found in small pockets scattered around from the surrounding of Nazret all the way to Harar: Methara – Awash – Asebot – Harar. Bender and Fulass (1978: 8) also assert that "Harari is one of the remnants of a probable East Gurage continuum extending from the present East Gurage area south of Addis Ababa to Harer".[56]

There is one further point that renders the pidgin hypothesis questionable with regard to the place of origin. The Ethiopian Semitic languages are spoken in their place of origin and are divided into northern and southern branches (cf. Hudson 1977, 1978, Girma 2001 among many others). The common stage of origin is not attested for these languages either (Murtonen 1967). Although the common origin of North Ethio-Semitic and South Ethio-Semitic is a workable theory, the distinction between the two seems justified (Hetzron 1972: 22) and the diversification of the South Ethio-Semitic languages most probably took place in the south (see chapter six). Amharic is grouped with South Ethio-Semitic languages for a number of its features. If the Amharic superstratum language was spoken in the northern parts of Ethiopia along with the other north Ethio-Semitic languages, why does Amharic not show the innovative features of North Ethio-Semitic languages? The only explanation is that the superstratum language was also a South Ethio-Semitic language. If this is the case, then it becomes difficult to explain *when* the superstratume language migrated to the north within the pidginization theory.[57] The pidgin origin hypothesis has some other

---

[56] In fact, as pointed out above a trace of an earlier Semitic tongue that we have today from the present East Gurage area to Harar is Argobba. Hence, the probable Semitic tongue continuum in the time before the sixteenth-century Oromo expansion could be the Transversal South Ethiopic group at a large, not its Southern sub-group alone.

[57] In fact, the pidgin theory is built on the previous dominant hypothesis that Ethio-Semitic languages are brought by Semitic speaking emigrants from South Arabia sometime in the first millennium BC. They are not an autochthonous group living in their place of origin and that the migration was from north to

serious problems, to which I now turn below.

4.5 Linguistic Issues: Grammar and Lexicon

As we have seen in chapter three, Amharic exhibits a number of non-Semitic features. Recall that for Bender (1983) and for those who promote a pidgin origin hypothesis, this is due to its pidgin past. However, for some it is due to later influence. Consider, for instance, the following statement from Appleyard:

> Like all the modern Ethiopian Semitic languages, Amharic has been heavily influenced by the Cushitic language ..., initially the Agäw languages, especially the central block ... and then, as Amharic spread, Highland East Cushitic and later Oromo. This influence can be seen not only in lexicon, but also in syntax and typology. As the language of the ruling elite and thus the inheritors of Ethiopian Christian culture from Aksum, Amharic was also open to borrowing from Ge'ez which in more recent times has provided a rich source for the expansion of the Amharic lexicon to satisfy the need for technical, political and other vocabulary (Appleyard 2003: 235).

In this section, I examine whether the grammar and lexicon of Amharic exhibit the characteristics of a pidgin language or later influence as Appleyard and many other suggest.

4.5.1 Loanwords in Amharic

It is a well-known fact that Amharic has a lrage loan vocabulary in both its cultural lexicon and in its basic lexicon. According to Appleyard (2003), and also Bender (1983), the main sources of Amharic's loanwords seem to be in earlier time Agew, then High Land East Cushitic and later Oromo. Due to expansions of usage, Amharic has a number of vocabularies from Ge'ez. Amharic has also a number of loanwords from non-Ethiopian languages such as English, Arabic etc. Although I do not have the actual figure, Amharic has probably around 40% of loanwords relating to cultural terms. Important to note that, English has 50% loanwords with no claim to a pidgin past. As Amharic has a relatively well-developed written language, and most of its loanwords in its cultural terms can be traced historically, I focus here only on the loanwords in its basic lexicon, which are claimed to amount to about 25%.

---

south but not vice versa.

Bender and Fulass (1978) have examined whether the loanwords in Amharic are a result of later influence or due to its pidgin past. They then claim that it is difficult "to pin down the degrees of specific language or specific group influences" on Amharic exhaustively (Bender and Fulass 1978: 10). As a result, they claim that the loanword evidence supports the pidgin hypothesis. However, unlike what Bender and Fulass suggest, the loanword evidence can equally be supportive of the assumption that Amharic is a linear descendant of a Semitic language.

The Cushitic loanwords, quoted in Bender and Fulass (1978), are indeed not from a specific language, as can be seen below:[58]

- č'oma 'fat' (noun; Agew, Oromo, Sidama);
- siga 'meat' (Agew);
- wiha 'water' and wisha 'dog' (H.E.C)
- č'ira 'tail' (Agew, H.E.C)

As pointed out above, the various Cushitic sources for the Amharic loanwords are taken as evidence for a pidgin stage in Bender and Fulass (1978). However, according to Appleyard (2003), these loanwords represent later Cushitic influence on a fully functional Amharic language. As the loanwords are not from a single group, Appleyard (2003), among others, suggests that such loanwords entered the language in different periods of contact with different groups. Indeed there is much evidence that supports this assumption.

Contact between Oromo and Amharic started in the 16th century, i.e. long after Amharic became the language of administration of the Christian kingdom. Hence, the Oromo vocabularies in Amharic have nothing to do with the pidgin stage of Amharic. In other words, they cannot provide any information about Amharic's origin.

Excluding Oromo, when I examine other loanwords, some basic lexicons that Amharic is missing today are found in the 15th and 16th centuries texts of Old Amharic. Some are also found in Argobba (see section 4.3.1). Thus, the 25% non-Semitic vocabularies of today's Amharic did not enter the language at once. This means also that the non-Semitic basic vocabularies will be reduced significantly in Old Amharic. The non-Semitic basic vocabulary that can be assumed to have entered into Amharic in contacts with different languages in its earlier days may not be more than 5%.

---

[58] The examples are from Bender and Fulass (1978: 9-10).

If we consider the entire 25% of non-Semitic basic vocabularies in Amharic, more than 70 percent of them are not specific to Amharic. They are also found in the other South Ethio-Semitic languages. Furthermore, some basic vocabularies which are assumed to be that of Cushitic are found not only in Amharic and other South Ethio-Semitic languages but also in Tigrinya, a northern Ethio-Semitic language. In a recent paper Hudson (to appear) has made an interesting observation. He examines ten vocabularies that Ehret (2011) considers Ethio-Semitic has borrowed from Agew and argues that six of them are not Agew loanwords at all. Among the ten words, nine of them are found in Amharic. It is not only that the so-called non-Semitic basic vocabularies of Amharic are shared by the other Ethio-semitic languages but also that some of the words may not be borrowed at all. The loanword evidence in Amharic, therefore, can in no way be taken to support the pidgin origin hypothesis.

Indeed, it is mainly Bender and Fulass (1978) who consider the existence of non-Semitic basic vocabularies in Amharic as evidence of its pidgin past. In Bender (1983), where the pidgin theory is developed in full detail, the loanword evidence is not considered as supportive of a pidgin hypothesis. Bender rather suggests the contrary:

> [The Amharic loanword] is not unusual: consider Swahili, a Bantu language, but with plenty of non-Bantu lexical items even in basic lexicon: *lakini* 'but', *karibu* 'near'. The fact remains that if a language has well over half of its basic lexicon in common with a family, it cannot be borrowing; such massive borrowing of basic vocabulary does not occur (Bender 1983: 41).

Although there are some reservations, in historical linguistics it is assumed that an average of 19.5 percent of core vocabularies of any language is expected to be lost, i.e. replaced by others, in one thousand years. As Amharic has existed for at least 1000 years, the retention of 75% of its Semitic core vocabulary is indeed a natural expectation. Note also that, as Amharic is not a direct descendant of the Proto-Semitic, the 75% of core vocabulary retention does not make it an unnatural language change.

Besides the loanword issue, the most striking non-Semitic characteristics of Amharic are related to syntax, which does not reveal specific language contacts.

4.5.2 Syntax

According to Bender (1983: 42), "the syntax [of Amharic] is much more like Oromo, Somali, [Wolayitta] and other languages of neighboring Cushitic and Omotic groups than it is like Tigrinya, Giiz [Ge'ez], or Classical Arabic". This is the main reason for Bender (1983) to consider Amharic to be a language that has developed out of a pidgin-induced process. It is true that Amharic deviates more from Semitic languages in its syntax than in its phonology and morphology. Amharic, for instance, has in most constructions SOV word order, which is non-Semitic. This is one of the major non-Semitic syntactic features taken as a reason to support pidgin hypothesis. However, if we closely examine the Amharic word order, it shows "underlying" VSO structure (see also Bach 1970). I explain this below.

In generative linguistics, it is assumed that VSO is a result of V movement to a higher functional category where the other constituents remain in the syntactical lower projections. With regard to the VSO order in Ge'ez, Girma (2003) suggests that V moves to one of the C projections found lower than the projection that hosts the complementizer preceding all the other constituents. Amharic also exhibits a similar kind of movement. The difference between Ge'ez and Amharic in this regard is only minute. Amharic, unlike Ge'ez and the other VSO Semitic languages, has further derivation where the remnant movement takes place to the Spec of the higher C projection that hosts the complementizer.[59] According to Girma (2003), it is due to this derivation that complementizers are found preceding verbs but follow the other constituents of the sentence in Amharic. This synchronic analysis may show that the Amharic SOV order is a historical development out of VSO.[60]

Moreover, Amharic does not exhibit the typical SOV languages behavior. In SOV languages, it is typical that complementizers follow the verb and adpositions are realized as postpositions. In Amharic, complementizers precede verbs like in VSO languages and adpositions

---

[59] Note that the usual assumption in the derivation of SOV is that V remains in situ while the object moves preceding the verb.

[60] Indeed, this change may not happen in pre-Amharic but may take place in its parent language, i.e. either Proto-transversal SES or even Proto-SES. Whatever the reason could be, the SOV order of Amharic cannot be an original order created by pidgnization. It is rather a natural language change probably resulting due to contact with Cushitic and Omotic languages. We will come to the issue of influence vs. pidgin in more detail in the following section.

are prepositions, like in Ge'ez and the non-Ethio-Semitic languages. This phenomenon is assumed to be the feature of Proto-Semitic. Moreover, most of these prepositions are assumed to be Semitic (see Hetzron 1972 among many others).

On the other hand, Bender (1983: 42) claims that Amharic has many post-posed particles such as *wist* 'inside'; *lay* 'up'; *tacc* 'down'; *fit* 'in front of, face'; *h^wala* 'behind'; *zurya* 'around'. First, although using post-posed particle is truly an un-Semitic feature, as Bender himself states, most of the aforementioned vocabularies have recognizable Semitic roots.[61] Second, the status of these items as postpositions is controversial: They can equally (or preferably) be considered nouns rather than adpositions. For instance, like any other noun, these items can inflect for grammatical categories such as definiteness, number and case as in *wist-u-n* 'inside-def-Acc', *lay-u-n* 'upward-def-Acc' etc. They can also be bases for the formation of other word classes either by taking a derivational morpheme as in *tacc-iñña-w* down-*iñña*(derivational morpheme)-def 'down (Adjective)', *lay-iñña-w* upward-*iñña*(derivational morpheme)-def 'upward (Adjective)' or by combining with other words as in *wist awäq* 'insider'. Moreover these items can be combined with prepositions to form a prepositional phrase, *kä-lay* lit. 'from upward', *kä-tacc* lit. 'from down', *kä-wist* 'from inside', etc.

Modern Ethio-Semitic languages share a number of syntactic features with Cushitic and Omotic languages.[62] For instance, when we consider the syntactic features set by Ferguson (1976) to be shared by Cushitic, Omotic and Amharic, they are equally shared by modern Ethio–Semitic languages.[63] As such syntactic features are not peculiar to Amharic, it is not convincing to suggest that Amharic inherited those features because of its pidgin past.[64] Those features must be due to a later influence. Bender and Fulass (1978: 7) state that such syntactic "distribution

---

[61] "There is the extensive use of post-posed particles: a very un-Semitic pattern. But most of them are recognizable Semitic roots" (cf. Bender 1983:42).

[62] Ge'ez ceased to be spoken around 8th or 10th century.

[63] For instance, not only Amharic, but also Tigrinya shares all the eight syntactic features set by Ferguson (Bender and Fulass 1978: 6). It is not also the case that every Cushitic and Omotic language equally shares these eight features.

[64] Note that whether the Cushomotic syntactic influence was exerted on individual languages at a later date or on Proto-languages at an earlier date does not matter for the controversies pidgin vs. non-pidgin hypotheses as both alternatives go against the pidgin origin suggestion for Amharic.

certainly suggests that there is a common Cushitic-Omotic ('Cushomotic') syntactic pattern and that it spread to the modern Ethio-Semitic languages after Giiz [Ge'ez] ceased to be a spoken language".[65]

As people question the unorthodoxy of Amharic mostly because of its syntax, the clear indication of the un-Semitic syntactic pattern resulting from an influence (exerted either later on Amharic or earlier before it split from its sister languages) is sufficient to counter argue that Amharic did not originate as a pidgin, at least not alone. I examine below the phonology and morphology of Amharic, particularly focusing on its so-called non-Semitic features.

4.5.3 Phonology

Bender and Fulass (1978) have examined Amharic phonology based on Ferguson's (1976) set of phonological features and found out that the distribution is quite different from the syntactic one.

> Ethio-Semitic languages, including Giiz [Ge'ez], are high; Cushitic (except Awngi) and Arabic are intermediate; Omotic is low; English and Anywa (also Awngi) are clearly outside the pattern. No argument for Cushitic or even simply Cushitic influence can be made here: rather, Ethio-Semitic would appear to have developed its own set of phonological features. In fact, one might argue for diffusion from Ethio-Semitic to Cushitic and more weakly to Omotic (Bender & Fulass 1978:7).

Bender and Fulass (1978: 9) also examine a list of phonological features which Leslau (1945,1959) considers to be the result result of a [Sidama] influence on South-Ethiopic, and they argue that "'Cushomotic' and especially Highland East Cushitic phonological influence on Amharic is probable". The Amharic phonology, in fact, does not provide any evidence for the pidgin hypothesis. However, before I come to this conclusion let me examine some specific phonological features mentioned in Baye (2000 EC) to support the pidgin origin hypothesis.

According to Baye (2000 EC: xv), recall that, due to its pidgin past, Amharic lacks the pharyngeal and the glottal sounds such as ħ, ʔ, and ʕ which are assumed to be typical of Semitic languages. However, it has more or less a complete sound system, similar to that of Cushitic and

---

[65] When it comes to the phonological features, the picture is different as we will see in a moment in the following section.

Omotic languages. The non-Semitic sounds of Amharic mentioned in Baye (ibid.), are as follows: *š*, *č*, *ǧ*, *ñ*, and *č'*. The sounds *p* and *p'* are assumed to have entered into Amharic along with borrowed Greek words.

Indeed, Amharic at present does not have the pharyngeal sounds quoted above although it still uses all the letters representing those sounds without having distinct phonetic/phonemic representation. For instance, the letters ሐ and ዐ have different phonetic representation in Tigrinya. In current Amharic these letters and the letter ኀ represent a single phoneme and are used interchangeably. However, the distinction between these sounds existed in Old Amharic. For instance, in the first known written documents of Amharic that go back to the 14th and 15th centuries we have the pharyngeal sounds (see chapter seven, chapter eight and the Appendix). The existence of such sounds goes also at least to the 17th century. See for instance Ludolf (1698a&b). Getatchew Haile (1979a: 234) also listed the following examples from one of the seventeenth-century texts, ጎርቦኛ, ጎንድ, የአነን, ሰፊሐ, እንጅዕ, ሐንዳይገደፍ, ሲሰእን, ብትጥሀል, and ልአረፍ. As can be seen from these examples, and as discussed in Ludolf (1698a) even as late as the 17th century Amharic retains almost all the basic glottal and pharyngeal sounds of Semitic.

On the other hand, although the usage of *Ɂ* is not frequent, it is found in some words such as *säɁat* 'time', 'watch' and *siɁil* 'picture'. Although the usage of *x* is rare in standard Amharic, it is frequently used in the Mänz dialect as in *yixä* 'this' which in the standard dialect is *yih*. The only sound that we can be sure of to have not existed in Amharic, both in old and present Amharic, is the velar ejective *q*. Indeed, Amharic shows some deviation in its phonology from Semitic, but not greater than any of the other South Ethio-SE languages does (see for more discussion chapter eight in this work and Ullendorff 1955 and Rose 1997).

The above so-called Cushitic sounds mentioned in Baye are almost found in all modern Ethio-Semitic languages. Hence, they alone cannot provide any proof for Amharic's pidgin past. The sounds *p* and *p'* probably entered Amharic from Greek via Ge'ez. They are clearly due to loanwords and have nothing to do with pidginization. The loss of some glottal sounds does not also favor the pidginization theory. Loss of glottal sounds is a common phonological process in languages. In fact, if we claim that it is a loss, it means that it is not a matter of pidgin. Note that also, some of the aforementioned glottal sounds such as *ħ* and *Ɂ* are found in a number of Cushitic languages although their distribution is restricted in Amharic. Thus, the non-existence of such sounds in present

51

Amharic cannot be explained by its mixing with Cushitic or any other language. In short, it cannot be due to pidginization. In general, Amharic phonology does not provide any support for the pidgin hypothesis.

4.5.4 On Morphology

Although Baye claims that Amharic has a number of non-Semitic affixes, he only cites *-äñña*. Nonetheless, this morpheme is found in some other modern Ethio-Semitic languages but not in Cushitic or any other non-Semitic languages of Ethiopia. As far as I know, nobody has ever claimed that Amharic is lacking Semitic morphology, despite some of its non-Semitic morphological patterns. "Amharic morphology has been generally less affected by the non-Semitic languages of Ethiopia and preserves much of the inherited Semitic structure, especially in the case of morphology of verbs" (Appleyard 2003: 235). Bender (1983: 42) also states that "enough morphology remains to make Amharic unquestionably Semitic: who would grant that a language could borrow so much in grammatical formatives?"

4.6 The Issue of Identity

In Ethiopia, people easily change their ethnic identity – intermarriage being one of the means.[66] Beside intermarriage, there are other practices in some ethnic groups that allow others to become members of their ethnic group. It is also common in Ethiopia for people who speak a dialect of the same language to refer to themselves with different names or consider themselves as distinct groups. For instance, the Wollayta, Gamo, Gofa, Dawro consider themselves distinct ethnic groups although their speech varieties are mutually intelligible. This is also true for the mainland Scandinavian languages, where the Swedes, Norwegians and Denies speak speech varieties that are only slightly changed. On the other hand, the converse could also be the case. For instance, in Ethiopia, the western and northern Gurage language speakers identify themselves by a single ethnic identity, namely Gurage, although the speech varieties that they speak are not mutually intelligible. In fact, these languages are also often collectively referred to by a single name: *Guragiñña*. Hence, the identity of the Amharic speakers discussed in chapter two cannot be considered to be supporting the pidgin hypothesis.

4.7 Summary

In this chapter, I have pointed out that Amharic's origin could not be

---

[66] Not only inter-ethnic marriage, but also inter-religious marriage has long been a common practice in the history of Ethiopia.

associated with the rise of the Zague dynasty, but that its place of origin must be somewhere in central Ethiopia. On this issue, Sergew (1972) has also pointed out a somewhat similar suggestion. According to Sergew (1972: 278), although Ethiopian tradition attributes the birth of Amharic to the period of the Zague dynasty, the language obviously originated at a much earlier date in the central part of Ethiopia among the Amhara people.

> During the Zagwé it [Amharic] seems to have acquired wider importance and was spoken at the imperial court. This explains why it was known in the beginning as Lisane Negus – the language of the Emperor. At that time the Amhara people were politically very active and ... occupied key administrative position as well as those of lesser rank.[67] Thus they had an opportunity to impose their language on others but their Semitic language in turn, was subject to the influence of the Hamitic languages, particularly in the areas of syntax and vocabulary (Sergew 1972: 278-279).

Despite Amharic being assumed to originate from a pidgin-creole, no one (including Bender 1983) denies its being Semitic. 75% of its core vocabulary is claimed to be Semitic. Its non-concatenative morphology is clearly of Semitic origin like the agreement markers of verbs and a number of other morphological features. Amharic's non-Semitic behavior mainly shows itself in its syntax. However, such non-Semitic syntactic features including the word order can hardly support the pidgin origin theory. The phonological features, too, do not support such a hypothesis. Moreover, the non-Semitic features in Amharic are found to a similar degree in the other modern Ethio-Semitic languages, and Amharic exhibits a number of common features with South Ethio-Semitic languages. As Hetzron (1972) points out such features are indications of a common origin.

In this chapter, in general, I have claimed that the pidgin origin hypothesis for the origin of Amharic is inconclusive. It neither has linguistic evidence on its side nor historical support. In fact, even Bender (1983), who takes this issue as his central point of investigation, did not claim that his proposed pidgin theory is conclusive. He rather suggests that detailed linguistic study is needed to affirm his proposed hypothesis.

---

[67] This specific period is suggested to be during the reign of king Lalibela (1140-1180) (see, for instance, Ayalew n.d.: 155ff.).

~ THE ORIGIN OF AMHARIC

To the best of our knowledge, no other linguist conducted research on the issue. Most recent works are simply echoing what Bender originally suggested as a topic for further research.[68]

Although there is no direct connection between the pidgin origin hypothesis and the origin of Ethio-Semitic, the pidgin origin hypothesis, as we have seen in chapter two, is based on the assumption that Ethio-Semitic languages were developed out of the South Arabian, SA, immigrant people. There is another hypothesis that considers Ethio-Semitic as an indigenous group living in their home of origin. Before we see the implication of the non-pidgin origin hypothesis towards the general history (and early spread of Amharic) and before I outline in full detail this alternative hypothesis, it seems crucial to examine the general assumptions about the origin of Ethio-Semitic first.

---

[68] In fact, as pointed out in chapter two, tradition has long asserted that Amharic was first a language spoken by soldiers and originated as a kind of mix (See, for instance Belay 1995 E.C: 130ff., Aleqa Taye 1914 E.C:8ff./1964 E.C: 40ff.).

Chapter Five: The Origin of Ethio-Semitic

5.1 Introduction

Theories about the origin of Ethio-Semitic, ES, can be categorized into two broad hypotheses. One is the migration hypothesis that proposes ES is an outcomer, i.e. brought by immigrants from South Arabia in the first millennium BCE, and the other is the non-migration hypothesis that proposes ES is an autochthonous language. The former hypothesis is a widely propagated hypothesis found in many historical and linguistic works. Recently, the latter hypothesis has been gaining ground.

The terms Semitic and Cushitic have their roots in the Bible. It seems that some are not clear about the various meanings of these terms. Besides their appearance in reference to ethnic groups or countries in religious and ancient historical documents, they are used in linguistic works in reference to language families. Understanding the various usages of such terms has a crucial role for the understanding of the origin of ES. Section 5.2 discusses the various usages of these terms. The subsequent parts of this chapter are organized as follows:

Section 5.3 presents the two different hypotheses on the origin of ES. Section 5.5 examines these hypotheses thoroughly. Section 5.4 discusses the place of ES within the genetic classification of languages. Section 5.6 outlines the probable date and place of origin of ES and its two major branches South Ethio-Semitic (SES) and North Ethio-Semitic (NES). It also proposes how these groups occupy their present location. Section

5.7 summarizes the major points discussed in this chapter.

5.2 The Terms "Semitic" and "Cushitic"
5.2.1 The Term "Semitic"

The derivation of the term Semitic is related to Shem of the Bible, one of the sons of Noah. It is used mostly in reference to a group of people such as the Arabs and the Hebrews who are thought to be descendants of Shem. However, this term also began to be used in reference to a group of languages spoken by quasi-racial groups, namely the Arabs, Hebrews, Armenians, and Abyssinians for the first time in the 18th century by Schlözer.

> This theory was based on the genealogy given in Genesis x, according to which both Aram and Arphaxad are made the children of Shem, and the further genealogy in Genesis xi, which makes Arphaxaed the ancestor of Abraham from whom were descended the Israelites and the Arabs who claimed to be the children of Ishmael.
>
> Closer scrutiny of these genealogies shows that the members are grouped simply according to political relations. Thus, Elam and Lud are noted in Genesis x, 22, as brothers of Asshur and sons of Shem: but the Elamies, Lydians, and Assyrians are not kindred races, and they are so grouped simply because they were united under Assyrian rule at the time when the genealogies were composed (O'Leary 1969: 2).

Moreover, the Abyssinians were not considered descendants of Shem in Genesis X. Probably due to this attitude, speakers of Semitic languages in Ethiopia were thought to have been founded by an immigrant Semitic group which intermingled with the locals; hence they are considered to be a quasi-racial group. Some scholars, such as Hetzron (1969:70, 1972: 23), even suggest that the Ethio-Semitic speakers, particularly the South Ethio-Semitic speakers, are Cushitic in origin.[69] As we will see in a

---

[69] "The speakers [what he calls the East Gurage speakers] are racially Cushites. The Semitic tongues were imposed on them by the cultural and military superiority of Semitic speakers, to a great extent Cushiticized themselves, that had come from the North in very early times" (Hetzron 1969:70). In his 1972 work, Hetzron repeated his suggestion: "SE is spoken by people of Cushitic stock" (Hetzron 1972: 23).

moment, this assumption seems to have greatly impacted the hypothesis on the origin of Ethio-Semitic.

Strictly speaking, it is very difficult to justify the usage of the term "Semitic" in reference to the language group which we know today by this name. It is also very difficult to justify its usage in reference to the racial groups as per the suggestion in Genesis X pointed out above. Moreover, in its contemporary reference to a racial group, the term "Semitic" is often used particularly to refer to the Jewish people. For instance, the often-used phrase "anti-Semitic" refers exclusively to the Jewish people.

Due to the aforementioned facts, one may think of inventing a more neutral term, especially with regard to the language group that the term "Semitic" refers to. However, rather than inventing a new term, as O'Leary (1969: 3) puts it, "it is practically more convenient to accept a term in general use". Hence, I have used in this work, as do other many linguists, the term Semitic, simply because it is convenient and it is one in common use.

5.2.2 The Term "Cushitic"

Although the term "Cushitic" in linguistics refers to one of the Afroasiatic language families that consists of languages such as Somali, Afar, Sidama, Oromo etc. spoken mainly in Ethiopia, Somalia, Djibouti, Eritrea and other Eastern African countries, this term has also a root in the Bible. In Genesis 10, 6 and 7, Cush is considered as a descendant of Ham. The Bible also used this term to refer to the country and the people south of Egypt that sometimes includes Sudan, Ethiopia, Somalia and Djibouti and at other times a more reduced area (Aba Gaspari n.d.: 9). For instance, in Genesis 2 and 13 the land of Cush was described as surrounded by the river Ghion. Indeed, as we know from historical documents, the term Cush was also one of the other names used by the Egyptians in ancient times to refer to mostly the land that immediately lies south of them and its inhabitants (Aba Gaspari n.d.: 5, Sergew 1972: 27). Note that also these Cushitic people also ruled Egypt in the first millennium BC.

We know from history that the ancient country referred to by Cush was not inhabited by the people who were speakers of a single language family that we know today by the name Cushitic. There were definitely other speakers. Among such other families, some could be the Nilo-Saharan speakers (see, for instance Bernal 2006). Hence, like the term "Semitic" the usage of the term "Cushitic" in reference to a language family does not fit with its ancient usage as a name of a country and the people who inhabited that country. It does not fully correspond either to the racial group that the Bible refers to nor the present group that speaks this language family. The current usage of the term "Cushitic" in reference to a language family in linguistics is, therefore, like the usage of the term Semitic discussed above; i.e. this term is simply applied because it is a convenient term in common use.

5.3 The Hypotheses on the Origin of Ethio-Semitic

Some works treat Proto-ES as a pidgin-induced language that resulted from a Cushitic and Semitic mixture where the latter is assumed to be brought by Semitic immigrants from South Arabia some time in the first millennium BC. Until recently, this hypothesis had not only been the most propagated one but also the generally accepted one: "In one form or another, the South-Arabian origin of Ethiopic, and of the Ethiopians, is today a generally accepted theory" (Drewes 1958: 115). However, some scholars, including Drewes himself, speculate that such an idea might be wrong primarily because of both the archaisms that the Ethio-Semitic languages have preserved and diversity that they have. I make in this section an overview of these different hypotheses.

5.3.1 The Migration Hypothesis

According to the migration hypothesis, a segment of the Semitic people migrated from South Arabia (SA) around 500 BCE and built a South Arabian type of civilization in the northern part of Ethiopia (including the present Eritrea) and later established the famous Axumite kingdom (cf. Ullendorff 1955, Leslau 1958a). Through the passage of time, some of them with a high rate of intermarriage with the locals moved to the central, eastern and southern parts of Ethiopia and created the languages which we know today as Ethio-Semitic.[70] The present Ethio-Semitic language speakers of Ethiopia are, therefore, suggested to be originally Cushitic speakers who later adopted the languages of the immigrant Semitic people from South Arabia who intermingled with them.[71] According to this theory, this is because the immigrant Semitic people had a superior culture to the natives (See, for instance, Ullendorff 1955,

---

[70] A recent account of such suggestion is found in Voigt (2005). "E.-S. (or Ethiosemitic, also Ethiopian Semitic) is a group of around 20 languages or dialects spoken in Ethiopia and Eritrea which go back to the language(s) of immigrants from South Arabia who settled in northern Ethiopia (partly now Eritrea) in the 1st millennium B.C." (Voigt 2005: 440).

[71] See, for instance, Hetzron (1972: 23).

THE ORIGIN OF ETHIO-SEMITIC

Budge 2001, Sergew 1972: 33ff.). Some such as Ullendorff and Budge are even harsh to the native Cushitic Ethiopians in characterizing them as uncivilized, barbaric, etc.: "the Semites found them Negro savages, and taught them civilization and culture" (Budge in Messay Kebede 2003: 5).[72]

---

[72] This type of suggestion seems to emanate not from scientific fact but from racist attitudes. Especially starting from the 19th century, racist outlooks emerged in Europe and gained ground in many fields. Those who promote the Arian supremacy not only spread the ideology characterizing African and non-Europeans in general as incapable of creating any civilization, but also they go as far to deny the Africans' Egyptian civilization and their enormous contribution to the later Ancient Greek civilization and to the world as a whole (see Bernal 1987, for an interesting discussion). We do not think people like Budge and Ullendorff will say something different, if they knew that the Semites were also native to Ethiopia, emigrating from no where. In fact, although Ullendorff suggests ES to be immigrant, he sometimes appears not to totally agree with this idea. However, he describes for instance the Oromo as contributing nothing for Ethiopian civilizations. He is, in fact, consistent in treating the Cushite as uncivilized. For instance, he characterizes the non-Semitic elements of Amharic and the claimed mixture of the Amharic speakers as follows: "the Semitized immigrants into Ethiopia have always been the virtually exclusive carriers of Ethiopian civilization and intellectual prestige. To this must now be added the political influence of Amharic as the official language of the Ethiopian Empire. *The socially superior minority has imposed its language by virtue of its prestige, while the majority has 'deformed' that language by virtue of sheer numerical impact*" (Ullendorff 1965: 5) *(italics is mine)*.

Map 2: Semitic migration as proposed by Sergew[73]

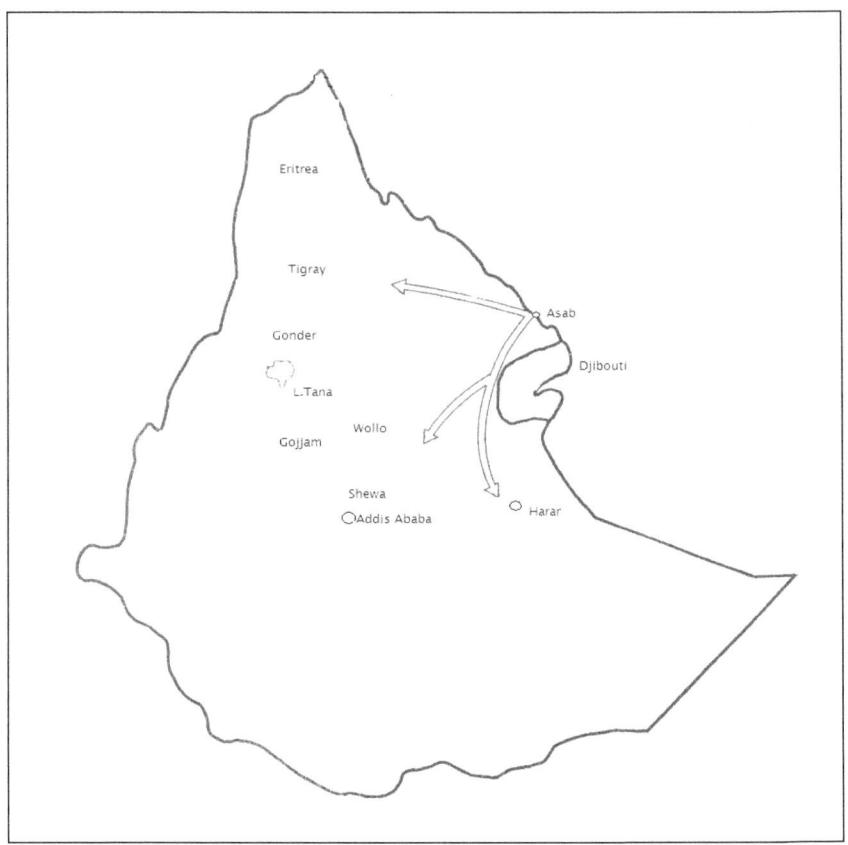

Some claim that the ancestral language of ES is Ge'ez which itself descended from Sabaean. This was almost the accepted theory until recently and replicated in many works outside the discipline of linguistics. See, for instance, Aba Gaspari G. Mariam's (n.d.) *Ethiopian History,* Last and Pankhurst's (1969) *A History of Ethiopia in Pictures,* Richard Greenfield's (1965) *Ethiopia: A New Political History,* and Claude Sumner's (1985) *Classical Ethiopian Philosophy.* Linguists like Ullendorff (1955) also considered Ge'ez to be the ancestor of modern Ethiopian Semitic languages. Leslau also suggests that, "the language of Ge'ez can be considered as representative of the Proto-Ethiopic type" (Leslau 1958b: 3). Recently, Voigt (2005) also advocates Ge'ez to be

---

[73] The map is adopted from Sergew (1972: 28). In Sergew, it is presented under the title Semitic migration and settlements. It is reproduced here with some modifications.

considered as either the ancestral or a representative language of the modern ES languages.[74] However, some other linguists such as Cohen (in Hetzron 1977: 18) and Houghton (1949: 10) considered only Tigre and Tigrinya as descendants of Ge'ez, leaving the other modern Ethio-Semitic languages aside. Leslau in a later work does not pursue his (1958b) suggestion quoted above that Ge'ez is the ancestral language of the modern Ethio-Semitic languages. He even does not take any position regarding the relation of Tigre, Tigrinya and Ge'ez; i.e. the North Ethio-Semitic languages: "In view of the fact that no thorough investigation has been made, the question of the relationship between Tigre, Tigrinya and Ge'ez remains open" (Leslau 1992: 564). Bender, Fulass and Cowley also mention that "the question of whether Giiz [Ge'ez] is the parent language or whether both Tigrinya and Giiz [Ge'ez] derive from some Proto-Ethiopic language or languages is not well definitely settled" (1976: 108). For some other linguists, however, the relation of Ge'ez, Tigre and Tigrinya is clear. For Fleming (1968) and some others, for example, Ge'ez and Tigrinya have more in common to each other than Tigre to Ge'ez or Tigrinya. According to Fleming, Tigrinya can be considered "a direct continuation of spoken Ge'ez" (1968: 363). Hetzron (1972, 1977), however, rejects such a suggestion: "Neither Tigre nor Tigrinna [Tigrinya] is descended from what we know as standard Ge'ez, as used in classical texts and codified by grammarians. Ge'ez contains a number of innovations with respect to Semitic not shared by Tigre and Tigrinna [Tigrinya]" (Hetzron 1972: 20).

Hetzron and Bender (1976: 25) also state that the assumed common ancestor of modern Ethio-Semitic languages could not be Ge'ez because there are features which are typical of Semitic found in the modern Ethio-Semitic, but not in Ge'ez. For instance, the negative element *'al(a) is not found in Ge'ez but is found especially in the South Ethio-Semitic languages.[75] Ge'ez has no trace of a main verb marker morpheme, a descendant of Semitic indicative markers. However, these

---

[74] "Both languages, [i.e. Tigre and Tigrinya], are roughly speaking, descendants of Ge'ez. More strictly speaking, they are the descendants of closely related daughter languages (or dialects) of Ge'ez" (Voigt 2005: 441). With regard to the origin of South ES Voigt suggests that "with the expansion of the Aksumite empire to the south and the resulting cultural dominance, Ge'ez (and later [Tigrinya]) dialects spread to the south of the plateau and emerged as new E.-S. languages. In contrast to the North E.-S. languages (…), these are called South E.-S." (Voigt 2005: 441).

[75] In fact, there is one exceptional case in Ge'ez with the verb *bo* 'there is' where its negative form is *'albo* 'there is not'.

elements are found in South Ethio-Semitic particularly in Soddo, and Gogot (Hetzron 1972) and traces are also found in the Southern Transversal and to some extent in some Western Gurage languages such as Muher, although their function in the latter two groups seems different (cf. Girma 2003). Ge'ez does not have the infinitive marker *m-* found in the modern languages, including Tigrinya, its closest relative. Hetzron (1977: 18) thus concludes that Ge'ez is neither the direct ancestor of the South Ethiopic languages nor of any other living tongue. According to Hetzron (Ibid) as there are a number of innovations in Ge'ez not found even in its closest relatives Tigrinya and Tigre, the modern languages can be considered more archaic.[76] Based on such facts, the modern languages of Ethiopia are assumed to have been spoken already when Ge'ez came into existence (cf. Hetzron and Bender 1976: 26).

On the other hand, the idea that Ge'ez was an Ethiopianized Sabaean is based on historical data that exhibit the Sabaean presence in northern Ethiopia.[77] On the other hand, when it comes to linguistic affinities as Rabin points out, 'it has never been shown that Ge'ez stands in a particular close relation to any specific branch of South Arabian' (Rabin in Hetzron 1977: 10).

As Drewes (1958) points out, the assumption that Ge'ez was a descendant of Sabaean was mainly based on the time differences between the Sabaean and Ge'ez inscriptions found in the northern part of Ethiopia. When such hypothesis proposed the earliest attested inscription of Ge'ez was dated to the 4th century ACE and the Sabaean inscription (in Ethiopia) to the 5th century BCE. However, recently found inscriptions of Ge'ez are dated to the 2nd and the first centuries AD bridging the gap between the earliest attested Sabaean inscription and the earliest attested Ge'ez inscription to only a few centuries. Moreover, there are two types of Sabaean inscriptions found in Ethiopia: one group with lots of Ge'ez influence and the other "pure" Sabaean. The latter are few in number and limited to earlier date whereas the former continued for some longer time. According to Drewes, this indicates that the former were written by the Ethiopians and that Ge'ez was a spoken language at the same time of the assumed migration of the Sabaean people. Drewes suggests that the Ethiopian were people most likely using Sabaean for writing purpose while using their own language, Ge'ez, for daily

---

[76] See also for similar suggestion Hetzron (1972), Hetzron and Bender (1976) among some others.
[77] This has to do especially with the existence of Sabaean monumental inscriptions in Ethiopia which happen also to be the earliest attested.

communication.

> The most likely interpretation is, in my opinion, that these inscriptions were made, not by south-Arabian immigrants, but by Ethiopians, who used Sabaean for their written language, often for religious purposes, but spoke Ge'ez in ordinary daily life. Ge'ez, their mother tongue, might easily have left its marks on the written foreign language, Sabaean. How easily this could have happened may be seen from the fact that, today, many of the Ethiopians who know Arabic, pronounce the Arabic "th" sound as "s" (Drewes 1958: 115).

Drewes (1958) convincingly argues that Ge'ez was a spoken language even before the attestation of the earliest Sabaean inscriptions in Ethiopia. The historically documented Sabaean cultural presence in North-Eastern Ethiopia, according to Drewes (1958, 1980) was, therefore, properly South Arabian influence in an area where Ge'ez was used already as a spoken language.

> It remains true that the two languages resemble one another, but we can no longer prove the South-Arabian origin of Ge'ez by referring to the presence of Sabaean inscriptions on Ethiopian territory. The inscriptions are proof of the close cultural contacts which existed between southern Arabia and Ethiopia in historical times. The origin of Ge'ez lies hidden in a period for which we have no written documents, before the Vth century B.C. (Drewes 1958:115).

On the other hand, some suggest that ES did not evolve out of Sabaean but out of closely related dialects. A recent advocate of this is Voigt (2005). According to Voigt, the South Arabian settlers brought with them "their own dialects and knowledge of Sabaic" (Voigt 2005: 440). However, Ge'ez and for that matter all the ES languages have preserved some archaic features that are not found in any of Epigraphic South Arabian languages (see, for instance Hetzron 1972). For instance, the assumed Proto-Semitic Imperfective verb form, i.e. an insertion of a vowel between the first two radicals, is found in ES but not in OSA. Mostly due to this fact, Voigt (1987) considers OSA to belong to Central Semitic rather than South Semitic leaving only MSA and ES in the South Semitic group. As Gragg states "it is not possible to derive Ethiopic Semitic from any attested form of Old South Arabian" (Gragg 1997:

242). As pointed out above, Sabaean and the other Epigraphic South Arabian languages, share some innovative features where ES preserved the archaic features. As can be seen also from the classification in the following section, in detail, Ge'ez (and for that matter any of the Ethio-Semitic languages) is neither the direct descendant of Sabaean nor any attested Epigraphic South Arabian language. Moreover, as pointed out above, it is not the ancestor of any living tongue either because there are a number of archaic features found in modern Ethio-Semitic languages but not in Ge'ez. Other recent studies on the suggested Sabaean cultural elements show also that Sabaean cannot be the ancestor of Ge'ez or any Ethiopian Semitic group. In general, Ge'ez is not a direct descendant of Sabaean or any other Epigraphic South Arabian language. Nor does it the ancestral language of the modern ES languages (see Hetzron 1972 for more discussion).

According to Girma (2001), if Ge'ez is not the parent language of Ethio-Semitic (and if the migration hypothesis is true), we have to assume either a number of migrations of Semitic languages from South Arabia to Ethiopia and separate pidginizations or to assume another unknown pidginized "Semitic" language to be the ancestral language of ES.[78] Different scholars in line with the migration hypothesis, indeed, have suggested both the above alternatives, although not all consider the level of mixture to go as far as pidgin. See, for instance, Fleming (1968) for the former who suggests that South-Ethiopian languages were derived from Arabia independently, and Palmer (1958), Hetzron (1972) and Ullendorff (1955) for the latter. In fact, for the latter two, all Ethio-Semitic languages can be assumed to have descended from a single but mixed Semitic speech varieties brought from South Arabia.[79]

From a purely logical point of view, it would be difficult

---

[78] This is because modern Ethiopian Semitic languages also share more Cushitic features than Ge'ez does (see Bender and Fulass 1978:5ff and Ferguson 1976). For instance, with regard to syntax it is suggested that "Cushitic, Omotic and Ethio–Semitic languages except Ge'ez share very similar syntactic features" (Bender and Fulass 1978: 5).

[79] Hetzron's (1972) position on this point is not clear. Although Hetzron seems in a position that favors the migration of several South Arabian languages/dialects to Ethiopia, in the conclusion part he sates that "there is no evidence that several South Semitic languages differing from one another were carried to Ethiopia" (Hetzron 1972: 122). In fact, unlike most Semitists who use the terms language and dialect interchangeably, especially when it comes to referring to the Ethio-Semitic speech varieties, Hetzron (1972) probably has used these terms with a clear distinction.

to imagine that it was a linguistically homogeneous group that Semiticized Ethiopia. Nevertheless, we can be sure that through constant intermingling, dialectal distinctions were neutralized ... and that all the Semitic languages of Ethiopia are descended from this Koine which, though probably without even becoming completely homogeneous, had ceased to reflect the ultimate dialectal divisions of South-Arabian. It is possible that the "mixer in this melting pot" was an early Cushitic (North Agew?) influence which provided this Africa dialect cluster with its first new characteristics, the first independent innovations that separated it from South Arabian. This Cushitic influence must have affected the dialect cluster before further splits took place (Hetzron 1972: 17-18).

Most of the scholars who suggest either various migrations and pidginizations or one or more migrations but a single pidginized (or non-pidginized) parent language as a source of Ethio-Semitic, are similar in their suggestion with regard to its place within the general Semitic classification. Most of these works assume that Ethio-Semitic languages are descendants of South Semitic. The most recent classification by Faber (1997) also puts ES under South Semitic as can be seen below:

Figure 3: Semitic classification according to Faber (1997)
Proto-Semitic
1. East Semitic
   - Akkadian, Eblaite
2. West Semitic
   A. Central Semitic
      – Arabic
      – Northwest Semitic
         • Ugaritic
         • Canaanite
           (Hebrew, Phoenician, Moabite, Ammonite, El-Amarna)
         • Aramaic
         • Deir-Alla
   B. South Semitic
      - Eastern
         • Soqotri
         • Mehri, Harasuusi, Jibbaali

- Western
    - Old South Arabian
    - Ethiopian

If Faber's classification were right, this would mean that Old South Arabian and Ethiopian descended from the same parent language which itself is a descendant of South Semitic, where South Semitic also descended from West Semitic and West Semitic, in turn, descended from Proto-Semitic. This kind of classification strongly supports the migration hypothesis. However, according to Hudson, assuming the Ethiopian Semitic autochthony, i.e. contra the migration hypothesis, Faber's family tree can be interpreted as follows:

> East Semitic separated from West Semitic, *which stayed home*; Central West Semitic separated from South West Semitic, *which stayed home;* Central split into Arabic and Northwest; South split into Eastern and Western, *which stayed home*; Eastern diverged into the Modern South Arabian languages; in Western South Semitic Ancient South Arabian separated from ES [Ethiopian Semitic], *which stayed home;* Ancient South Arabian diverged into Sabaean, etc.; and North ES separated from ES, *which stayed home* (Hudson 2002: 1768).

If the above idea of Hudson is true, it means that the Semitic people migrated to Asia at least four times. The crucial point here, however, is whether the grouping of Ethio-Semitic under South Semitic is an undisputed fact or mere speculation. I examine this point in the following section 5.4. Before we proceed to it, however, I first present the general assumption of the other hypothesis, referred to here as "the Non-migration Hypothesis" in section 5.3.2.

5.3.2 The Non-migration Hypothesis

Contra the migration hypothesis, more recent works consider that Ethio-Semitic languages are not immigrant but are spoken in their place of origin. Consider, for instance, the following from Hudson (1978):

> ES is an autochthonous group, the descendants of that group of Afroasiatic peoples which in pre-Semitic times separated from the other speakers of Afroasiatic language varieties in Ethiopia and, with the passage of time, developed the language characteristics which remain stamped on those languages which today we

know as Semitic (1978: 235).

The above suggestion is that not only ES but also Proto-Semitic and Afroasiatic originated in Ethiopia. The African origin of Semitic and Afroasiatic in general has been forwarded by some other scholars such as McCall (1998), Hudson (1977, 1978, 2002), Bender (1997), and Bernal (1987). It is worth quoting Bernal here, a person who contributed much to the understanding of the Afroasiatic people and languages vis-à-vis other distantly related language families such as Indo-European and their contributions for ancient civilization in Greece, Middle East and Africa (see for instance, his *Black Athena* that appeared in three volumes). Bernal (1987, 2006) specifically suggests that Afroasiatic had long established itself in the East African Rift Valley somewhere in southern Ethiopia or northern Kenya. For Bernal (1987), the break-up of the Afroasiatic languages can be dated to the 9th millennium BC. He explains how the various Afroasiatic people occupy their present location as follows:

> During the Ice Ages, water was locked up in the polar icecaps, and rainfall was considerably less than it is today. The Sahara and Arabian Deserts were even larger and more forbidding then than they are now. During the increase of heat and rainfall in the centuries that followed, much of these regions became savannah, into which neighboring peoples flocked. The most successful of these were, I believe, the speakers of proto Afroasiatic from the Rift. These not only had an effective technique of hippopotamus-hunting with harpoons but also possessed domesticated cattle and food crops. Going through the savannah, the Chadic speakers reached Lake Chad; the Berbers, the Maghreb; the Proto-Egyptians, Upper Egypt. The speakers of Proto-Semitic settled Ethiopia and moved on to the Arabian Savannah (Bernal 1987: 11).[80]

The following map, adopted from Bernal (1987: xxiv), shows the diffusion of Afroasiatic people/languages:[81]

---

[80] There is a slight modification in Bernal's later work, *Black Athena Volume III*, that appeared in (2006). We discuss Bernal's later modification and some other suggestions on Afroasiatic classification and origin in detail in section 5.6.

[81] The following Bernal classification assumes Afroasiatic to have nine

Map 3: The diffusion of Afroasiatic according to Bernal

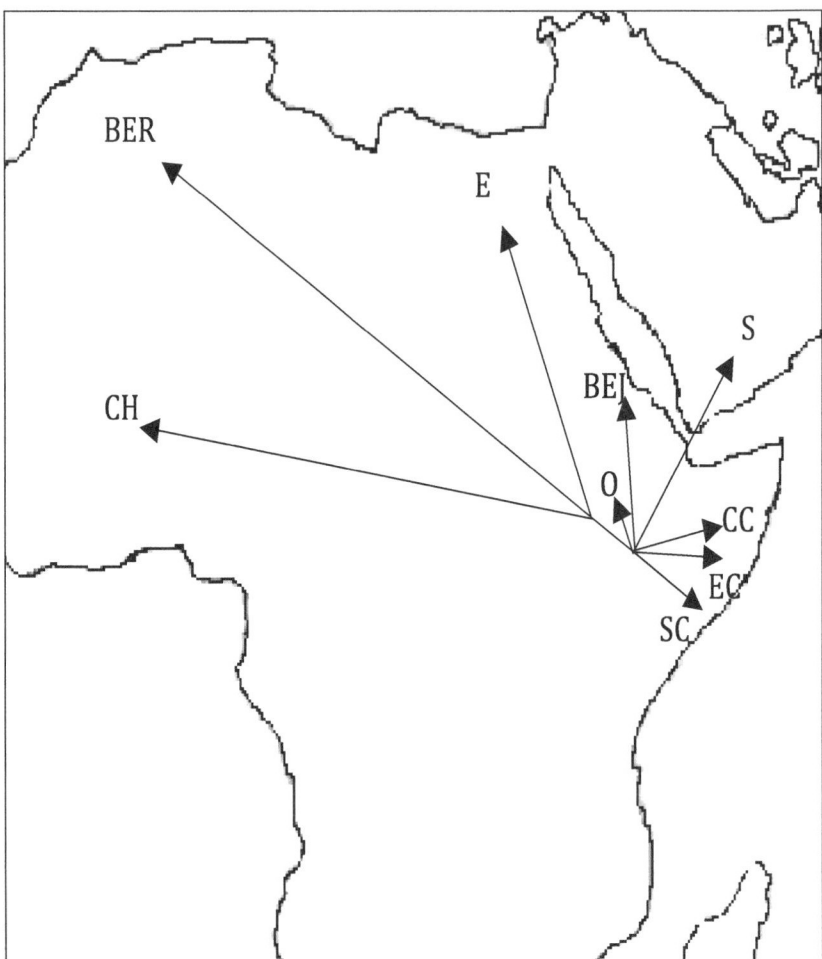

According to Bernal (1987: 12) the spread of Semitic speech from Ethiopia to Asia happened during the 6th millennium with the so-called Ubaid pottery. It first spread "to Assyria and Syria, to occupy more or less the region of South-West Asia where Semitic is spoken" (Bernal 1987: 12). See the following Map, which is also adopted from Bernal

---

language families. This is assuming that Beja (=Bej in the map) as well as the three major branches of Cushitic stand on their own, each as an independent family. Hence, in the map CC stands for Central Cushitic, EC for East Cushitic and SC for South Cushitic. The other abbreviations are as follows: BE= Berber, CH= Chadic, E=Egyptian, S=Semitic and O=Omotic.

(1987: xxvi).[82]

Map 4: *The diffusion of Semitic according to Bernal*

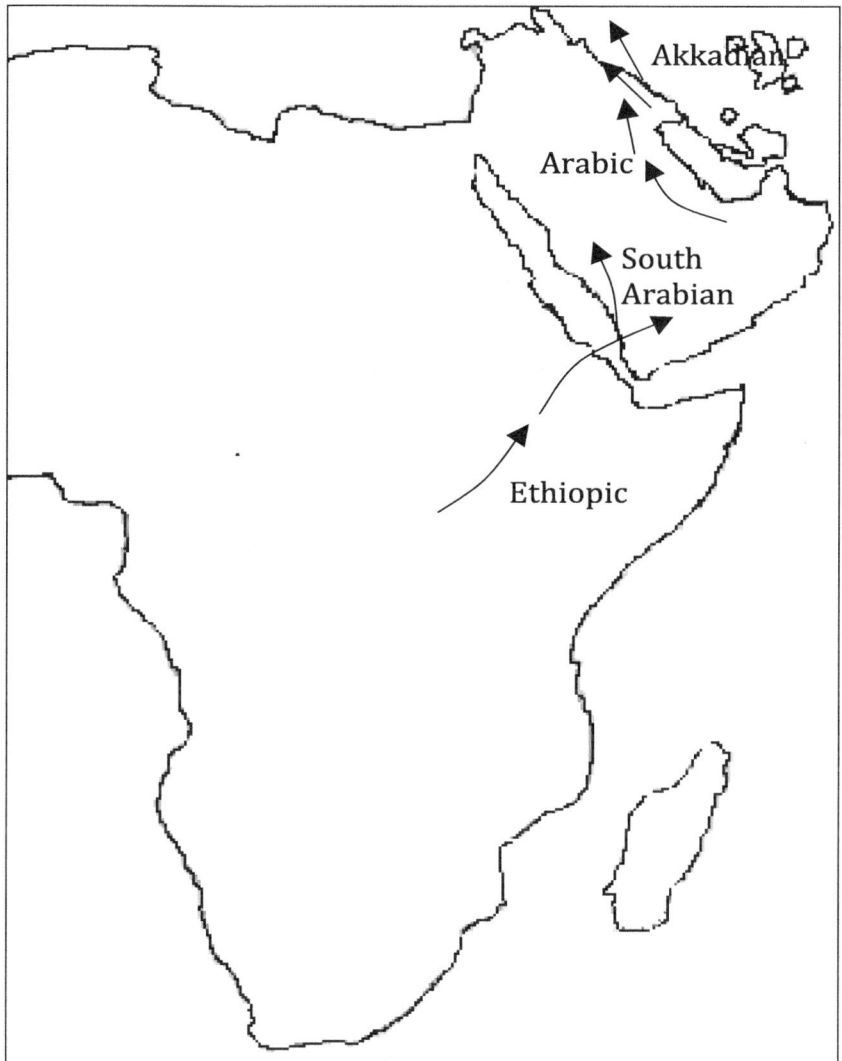

The proposal that Ethio-Semitic languages are descendants of a Semitic language or language groups brought by South Arabian immigrants in the middle of the first millennium BCE is mainly based on the presence of South Arabian cultural artifacts and Sabaean monumental inscriptions

---

[82] The map reproduced here with some modifications.

in the northern part of Ethiopia and the present Eritrea. This, in turn was mostly advocated by historians. However, as we have seen in section 5.3.1 Drewes (1958), who contributes much to the understanding of these monumental inscriptions, has already rejected such idea. Some historians, although a minority, have also suggested ES to be a non-immigrant group. For instance, Marcus (2002), although he has not denied the coming of Sabaean language into Ethiopia, interprets such presence on the contrary.

> Evidence is strong enough that Afro-Asiatic (Hamito-Semitic) group of languages developed and fissured in the Sudan-Ethiopian borderlands. There Proto-Cushitic and Proto-Semitic began their evolution. In Ethiopia, the Semitic branch grew into a northern group, today echoed in Tigrinya, and a southern group, best heard in Amharic. It simultaneously spread to the Middle East, whence, millennia later, it returned in a written form to enrich its cousins several times removed (Marcus 2002: 3).

Indeed, not only in recent works but also in some earlier works such as by scholars of the 19th century like Noldeke, it was reported that "the primitive seat of the Semites is to be sought in Africa" (Noldeke as cited in Hailu Habtu 1984: 14). I examine whether really there is any strong evidence to support such claim in section 5.5.

5.4 Classification of Semitic
5.4.1 Introduction

Blench (2006) points out that Yehuda Ibn Quraysh in the tenth century compares the phonology and morphology of Hebrew, Aramaic and Arabic. Ibn Quraysh's work is suggested to be the first appearance of comparative linguistic study in relation to any language family (cf. Blench 2006: 139-140 and the reference cited there). Job Ludolph in the seventeenth century has pointed out the relation of ES to other Semitic languages (see Ludolph 1682: 75ff.). Based on his informant Gregory, a native speaker of Amharic, Ludolph also mentioned the relation of some of the ES languages to each other. Ludolph specifically mentioned that Amharic is distantly related to Ge'ez where Tigrinya "comes the nearest related to" Ge'ez (Ludolph 1682: 79). According to Ludolph (ibid.) some of the southern languages such as Gafat are related to Amharic. Ludolph's suggestion corresponds to the current classification of ES into North ES and South ES – Tigrinya and Ge'ez belong to NES whereas

THE ORIGIN OF ETHIO-SEMITIC

Gafat and Amharic SES (see Chapter three). However, the first person who explicitly recognizes the kinship among Semitic languages, as Blench (2006: 140) points out, is Guillaume Postel (1538). The name "Semitic" for these related languages was first proposed by Schlözer (1781). The best classification of this language family with a well-developed methodology is attributed to our time specifically to Hetzron (1972, and subsequent works).

Although some consider grammatical features and lexical comparisons to support their claim, earlier classifications are based on geographic distribution and cultural importance of the various Semitic languages with no genetic implications (Hetzron 1972: 13, Faber 1997: 5). In this section we, therefore, discuss the classification of Semitic as proposed in Hetzron (1972, 1976, 1977) and Faber (1997). I particularly examine the evidence presented in these works in order to determine the position of ES within the general classification of Semitic.

5.4.2 An Overview of Semitic Classification

Hetzron's (1972, 1975) classification of the Semitic languages can be summarized as follows:

Figure 4: Hetzron's classification of Semitic

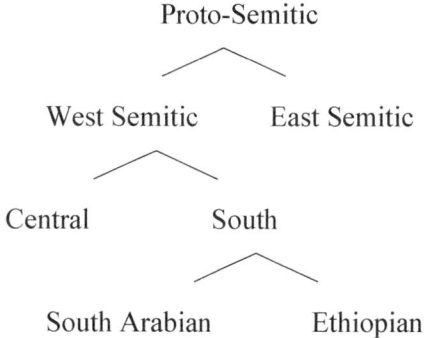

Hetzron's classification of Semitic as outlined in his monograph *"Ethiopian Semitic: Studies in Classification"* (1972) is based on the internal conjugations and affixation of verbal roots in the TAM-system. Accordingly, East Semitic is distinct with "an Imperfect of the *iqattVl*-type and a Perfect of the *iqtVl*-type – both prefix conjunctions, and a tenseless permissive with a suffix conjunction" (Hetzron 1972:15).[83]

---

[83] According to Hetzron, "this is the most archaic tense system in the Semitic languages" (1972:15) and, the *yVqatVl*-type could be the original Proto-Semitic

West Semitic is distinct from East Semitic as it uses a suffix–conjunction as past. According to Hetzron, this is an innovation of West Semitic, where its usage with no tense implication in East Semitic is retention from Proto-Semitic. The distinction between Central and South Semitic is with the innovation of a different Imperfective form in the former.[84] The Imperfective in Central Semitic has a *yVqtVl*-type which is assumed to be originally a Jussive form, whereas South Semitic has preserved the assumed original, i.e. Proto-Semitic, Imperfective like East Semitic, which is an insertion of a vowel between the first two radicals (Ibid.: 16). This means that South Semitic and East Semitic have the same Imperfective form, which is assumed to be an archaic form. South Semitic and Central Semitic have the same Perfective form with suffix-conjugations, but East Semitic is distinct from the two in using prefix-conjugations for the same purpose, which is also assumed to be an original form. The above-discussed TAM-system is summarized in the following table, which is adopted from Hetzron (1972: 16).

Table 2: Summary of the TAM-system in Semitic

	East	South	Central
Imperfective	*y*V*qatt*V(-)	*y*V*qat(t)*V(-)	*y*V*qtVl*-
Perfective	*y*V*qtVl*	*qat*V*la*	*qat*V*la*
Jussive	(*lu*)*y*V*qtVl*	*y*V*qtVl*	*y*V*qtVl*

In general, Hetzron's suggestion is that the TAM-system in East Semitic reflects the Proto-Semitic TAM-system. It is due to this that the usage of suffix-conjugations as past in West Semitic and the usage of *yVqtVl*-type as non-past in Central Semitic are considered in Hetzron as innovations, and hence, relevant for the aforementioned sub-grouping.

As pointed out above, Faber's (1997) classification, quoted in section 5.3.1 above, is mostly based on Hetzron's classification and can be considered a revision. For instance, the general classification of Semitic into East and West and the latter into South and Central is the same in

---

Imperfect (Ibid.: 16).

[84] In fact, as Hetzron points out in Geʻez "there is only one several of a prefix – conjugated perfect like that in East Semitic: in the root **bhl* 'to say', Imperfect *yəbəl*, perfect *yəbe*" (1972: 16)

Hetzron's and Faber's works. Though most of the differences between the two are minute, some are significant. One significant difference is that Hetzron considers ES to be directly branched from South Semitic, while Faber (1997) following Rodgers (1991), puts it along with Old South Arabian, i.e. Epigraphic South Arabian, and calls it Western South Semitic.[85] Another is that Faber considers some other grammatical features in addition to the internal conjugation of verbal roots. The verbal conjugations and the other grammatical features considered in Faber (1997) are summarized below. However, the summary mostly focuses on the assumed innovations that Faber (1997) and Hetzron (1972) suggest ES shares with specific groups of Semitic.

5.4.2.1 West vs. East Semitic

The main features suggested to be innovations of West Semitic after its separation from East Semitic are as follows:

- suffix conjugation as past tense (discussed above)
- Prohibitive marker *'al(a) 'Don't'

According to Faber, the negative particle *'al(a) 'Don't' "is attested throughout West Semitic, with the exception of Arabic, as a prohibitive or as a marker of main clause negation. The latter function appears to be a South Semitic innovation" (cf. Faber 1997: 8).

5.4.2.2 South vs. Central

After West Semitic separated from East, as pointed out above, Hetzron (1972) and Faber (1997) suggest that it separated into two branches named Central and South. The innovations in these two branches as given in Faber are summarized as follows:

Central

- pharyngealization as a secondary articulation
- prefix-conjugations with no vowel between the first two radicals for non-past
- within-paradigm generalization of vowels in prefix-conjugations
- generalization of -t- in suffix-conjugations verbs

---

[85] The other branch of South Semitic in Faber's classification is called Eastern South Semitic that represents the Modern South Arabian (MSA) speech varieties such as Soqotri, Mehri etc. (cf. section 5.3.1 above).

- development of compound negative marker *bal

South
- Generalization of -*k* in suffix conjugation verbs
- Generalization of *(')al* as verbal negative

5.4.2.3 Ethio-Semitic vs. Old South-Arabian

As pointed out above, among the minor differences between Hetzron's and that of Faber's classifications is that while Hetzron considers ES to be branched directly from South Semitic, Faber (1997: 11), following Rodgers (1991) considers it to be grouped with Old South Arabian (OSA) as Western South Semitic. According to Rodgers (1991), this group is characterized by the development of non-finite verb forms in serial verb constructions.

5.4.3 Examination of the Classification

In this section, I examine first the proposed grouping of OSA and ES together against MSA. Then I examine whether ES shares the suggested South Semitic and West Semitic innovations at all. Based on our examination, I try to see other alternatives suggested by some such as Murtonen (1967, 1969) and propose the most plausible place of ES in the overall classification of Semitic.

5.4.3.1 On the Grouping of Ethio-Semitic and Old South Arabian: On Western South Semitic Innovations

The only feature given in Faber to support the grouping of ES and OSA together as Western South Semitic is the use of non-finite verb forms in serial verb constructions (Faber 1997: 11). First, the use of converbs, i.e. non-finite verb form, in a serial verb construction in ES and OSA is considered to be an areal feature (cf. Ferguson 1976 and Bender 2003), and second, as Hetzron (1975:113) points out, although this phenomenon is common in ES, it is not widespread in OSA. Moreover, although serial verb construction is common in ES, not all ES use converbs or non-finite verbs for the same purpose. For instance, most of the so-called Gurage languages use finite verb forms for the same purpose, strengthening Ferguson's consideration of it as an areal feature. Hence, it is very difficult to consider the grouping of ES and Old South Arabian as opposed to Modern South Arabian as valid based on only serial verb constructions.

Besides non-finite verb uses in serial verb constructions, there are some features suggested in some other works such as Leslau (1943) to be common innovations of ES and Old South Arabian. However, such common features are examined in earlier works such as Murtonen (1967) and found to be not valid for such grouping. According to Murtonen (1967) the features which are assumed (for example by Leslau) to be shared by Ethiopic and Old South Arabian are found also in other groups. In terms of grammatical features, according to Murtonen; "ancient South Arabic [Arabian] is more closely related to (Northern) Arabic and North-West Semitic rather than Ethiopic" (Murtonen 1967: 74). Hetzron (1972, 1977) and Voigt (1987), who consider grammatical features for sub-grouping, also have not considered ES and OSA to form a distinct group within South Semitic. Voigt even claims that OSA speech varieties do not belong to South Semitic group. He considers OSA as Central Semitic leaving ES and Modern South Arabian as the only representative of South Semitic.

In fact, OSA and ES are distinct with the TAM-system. Recall that one of the core features suggested by Hetzron (1972) and adopted by Faber (1997) that distinguishes between Central and South Semitic is the preservation of the assumed Proto-Semitic Imperfective form, i.e. the insertion of a vowel between the first radicals, in the latter group. However, this form is only applicable to MSA and ES. OSA has only a single prefix verb form, which is originally assumed to be a jussive form like Arabic. When it comes to the TAM-system, OSA is closely related to Central Semitic than to ES and MSA languages. It is mostly due to this fact that Voigt (1987) considers OSA to belong to Central Semitic rather than South Semitic.

In a recent paper, Appleyard (1996) has also examined the relationship of Ethiopian Semitic and South Arabian languages. He found no conclusive evidence that ES and OSA form a group of their own within South Semitic. To the best of my knowledge, when it comes to grammatical features, no convincing evidence existed to support the above type of classification which groups ES and OSA together under Western South Semitic.

Besides the morphological and syntactic features, Murtonen's (1969) other phonology-based and lexicostatistics work also proves that the distance between Ethio-Semitic and Old South Arabian is much greater than was assumed before. Thus, the two cannot form a group.

> The other feature, however, viz., as far as Semitic languages are concerned, that South Arabic [Arabian]

> (particularly Soqotri) and South Ethiopic again stand widest apart on the scale, can hardly be interpreted as supporting such a theory, in any case not one in which Ethiopic is regarded as a direct descendant of ancient South Arabic [Arabian] (Murtonen 1969: 45).

Although Murtonen's suggestion above reveals that ES cannot be considered as a direct descendant of OSA, his work shows that OSA and ES do not form a specific group within South Semitic. Indeed, Faber (1997), who adopted the grouping of ES and OSA together as Western South Semitic from Rodgers (1991), does not seem to totally agree with this grouping as can be seen from her remarks below:

> Although virtually all discussions of Semitic sub grouping assume a single Ethiopian Semitic branch which later split into North Ethiopic and South Ethiopic, there is virtually no linguistic evidence for such a Common Ethiopian stage. Yet..., neither is there any evidence that the diverse forms attested in North and South Ethiopic do not reflect a stage of shared descent from South Semitic that is independent of Old and Modern South Arabian (Faber 1997: 12).

As can be inferred from Faber's and Murtonen's statements above, one of the problems in classifying ES under a specific branch of South Semitic is that there are too many diverse forms attested in the two branches of ES, i.e. SES and NES, and thus the classification does not reflect a common stage within South Semitic. I consider this issue further, as the relation of the two main branches of ES has large implications for the understanding of the position of ES in the general classification of Semitic with which we are dealing here.

5.4.3.2 On Proto-Ethio-Semitic: The Grouping of NES and SES

It has been long suggested that although the Semitic languages spoken in Ethiopia are grouped under one family named Ethio-Semitic, its two branches, i.e. North ES and South ES, do not show a common origin which lead scholars to divide them under a specific branch of South Semitic. For instance, although Fleming (1968) considers ES to be immigrant languages, he suggests that South Ethiopic and North Ethiopic may not come from a single Proto-Ethiopic language. According to Fleming, the South Ethio-Semitic group migrated independently from South Arabia. In fact, Hetzron (1972) who listed a number of pan-Ethiopian features does not claim that the grouping of the two branches of ES under one family is a settled issue. He rather suggests that although the distinction between NES and SES seems justified, the common origin of the two is a workable theory (Hetzron 1972: 22). Consider also the following from Blench (2006):

> The greatest diversity within Semitic is among the Gurage languages, spoken in southwest Ethiopia. Although the assumption is that the Ethio-Semitic languages form a single group, the relative uniformity of Amharic, Tigrinya, and others, in contrast to the variety of Gurage, is quite surprising. It may be that the Gurage languages have a different origin, either that they are a core Semitic group that stayed behind after the breakup of North Afroasiatic or they represent an earlier and different migration from Arabia (Blench 2006:157).

Note that here, Blench (2006) does not seem to agree entirely with the grouping of the Central South ES languages (and probably the whole Transversal South ES languages) along with the Gurage languages in one group. According to Blench "features that the Gurage have in common with the Amharic group would ... be the result of long interaction" (Blench 2006:157). Although this suggestion is questionable, it seems an undeniable fact that the diversity that exists between the NES and SES cannot be explained with the assumed common origin from South Semitic. For instance, the existence of a broken plural is one of the features that distinguish South Ethio-Semitic from North Ethio-Semitic, as it is found only in the latter group. However, this feature is also attested in SA (South Semitic) and Arabic (West Semitic). Although there is no consensus among all Semitists, it is indeed claimed that this feature is a Proto–Semitic one or even a Proto-Afroasiatic feature (see for relevant opinions and references Hetzron 1972: 15).[86] Although this may not be relevant for the genetic grouping of Semitic, the use of a pronoun as a copula like in Hebrew is only observed in NES, particularly in Tigre and Ge'ez (cf. Girma 2008), but not in SES. Main verb markers, which are suggested to be one of the archaic features, are only found in some SES languages, and not at all in NES. The negative marker *'al-, which is considered a South Semitic innovation (as a clausal negation) or, for that matter, a West Semitic innovation (as a prohibitive marker) is only found in SES but not in

---

[86] One of the three innovative features of Bender's (1997) proposed Central Afroasiatic group (that comprises Egyptian-Coptic, Macro-Cushitic: Cushitic, Semitic Berber) is indeed broken plural with an infix –a- in nominals.

NES.

5.4.3.3 On the Grouping of Ethio-Semitic and South Arabian: On South Semitic Innovations

Bender (1983: 44), quoting Hetzron, states that the features that mark Ethio-Semitic as a group and distinguish it from the rest of the South Arabian languages include the following:

- loss of the voiced velar fricative *s* found in both ancient and modern South Arabian languages,
- absence of the suffix-*n* as definite article,
- use of a prefix (Amharic *ind-*) before nouns meaning "like" and before verbs with the meaning "in order that" and,
- existence of compound verbs using the verb "to say", e.g. Amharic *zimm bel*!. Lit. quiet say, "Be quiet!".

The first two features listed above (that mark ES as a group and make it distinct from South Arabia) only make sense if we assume that ES really forms a group with the South Arabian languages. The remaining two features, in fact, do not only make ES distinct from SA but from any of the other Semitic branches. These features are not found in any Semitic language other than ES. Beside the aforementioned features, Hetzron (1972) and Voigt (2007) have also listed a number of pan-Ethiopian features. However, as we will see in a moment, such features are assumed to result due to contact mostly with Cushitic languages. For instance, the last two features quoted above, i.e. use of "verb to say" as a compounding verb and the use of a prefix as in Amharic *ind-* in both nouns and verbs, are argued to be the result of contact with the Cushitic languages of Ethiopia. Moreover, the distribution of most of the assumed pan-Ethiopian features is neither uniform in all ES languages nor found in all Cushitic languages. The Cushitic languages influence most likely occurred to the various ES languages independently. Such features are, thus, argued to be areal features, i.e. recent diffused features after the separation of the various Cushitic and Semitic languages of Ethiopia (see section 5.5 below). As these types of features do not show whether the grouping of ES with SA is appropriate, in this section, I shall only focus on examining the features that lead ES to be considered South Semitic, i.e. whether ES shares the suggested common innovations of South Semitic.

With regard to the grouping of ES and SA under South Semitic, Robert Hetzron states as follows:

> There is no doubt that Ethiopian Semitic and South Arabian constitute one branch of Semitic. One of the proofs is the territorially continuous (and not scattered) survival of a vowel between the first two radical consonants in the Imperfect, while the other prefix conjugation with a vowel between the last two radicals only fulfills the function of Jussive: Ge'ez *yəqäbbər/yəqbər* and Soqotri (Modern South Arabian) *iqóber/iqbér* .... This separates this branch from Arabic, with which it usually has been associated under the label "South Semitic" (1972:17).

Although Hetzron suggests that "there is no doubt of the grouping of Ethio-Semitic and South Arabian together", the crucial evidence that he gave in support for his classification, i.e. Hetzron 1972, is the form of Imperfect form vis-à-vis Jussive quoted above. This Imperfective form, i.e. an insertion of a vowel between the first two radicals which was considered crucial evidence for grouping ES and SA together, as we have seen above, is also crucial evidence that distinguishes Central and Southern Semitic from each other. Recall that, these Imperfective and Jussive forms found in South Semitic are suggested to be archaic Proto-Semitic features as they are also attested in Akkadian (East Semitic), however. Note that also, when it comes to the internal conjugations of verbs in the TAM-system, I have pointed out in the preceding section that unlike Hetzron's grouping, OSA is closer to Central Semitic than MSA and ES languages (see also Voigt 1987, Appleyard 1996). Hence, with regard to the TAM-system the only innovation in West Semitic happened in the Central group (following Voigt 1987 classification that puts OSA under the Central group), with the usage of prefix-conjugations with no vowel between the first two radicals for the non-past/imperfective. As innovations but not retentions are more relevant for sub-grouping, it means that the archaic Imperfective and Jussive forms found in ES and MSA cannot be taken as a good example for categorizing these groups together under South Semitic. It can equally be the case that ES and MSA separated from each other even earlier than the Central (following Voigt's 1987 grouping) departure, but both retain on these two archaic features independently. Hence, we must get other features to support grouping ES and SA together.

Recall that there are two more features which are assumed to be a South Semitic innovation, i.e. common to ES and SA. These are the usage of -k as a marker for the second person masculine in the perfective, and *'al as a clausal negative marker. The former, i.e. the second person masculine agreement marker -k, which is considered another common feature of ES and SA as a South Semitic innovation, is, in fact, added by Hetzron (1976). However, Hetzron further remarks that "unfortunately no second person forms of the past are attested in the limited corpus of Epigraphic South-Arabian" (1977: 10). On the other hand, Appleyard (1996) has mentioned two cases where this element is found in Sabaean, but not any trace in the other OSA speech varieties. With this feature, MSA and both ES groups, i.e. NES and SES, are positive. The distribution of this element as a second person marker in the perfective in these language groups can be summarized as follows:

Table 3: The distribution of -k in the so-called South Semitic languages

Perfective paradigm	OSA		MSA	ES	
	Sabaean	others		NES	SES
-k, as a second person marker	+	No information	+	+	+

The absence of evidence for the existence of -k in the OSA speech varieties, excluding Sabaean, does not necessarily mean that this feature cannot be considered for grouping OSA, MSA and ES, together. However, it cannot be considered as strong evidence on its own; there must be other uncontested features that strengthen such grouping. Moreover, even to consider this feature, i.e. –k, as supportive evidence, it must be the case that it is an innovation in the group in question, attested nowhere.

As pointed out above, OSA speech varieties do not exhibit one of the strong features that marks South Semitic, i.e. the $yi\text{-}qVt(t)Vl$-type Imperfective. The element –k as a second person marker in the perfective, therefore, cannot be considered as supportive evidence for grouping at least OSA along with MSA and ES. Nor can it be considered as strong evidence for the grouping of MSA and ES because it also exists in other branch of Semitic, i.e. outside South Semitic (Goldenberg 1977: 477-478).

Now, the only feature left among the aforementioned three common innovations of South Semitic is the usage of *'al as a negative marker.

This marker [*('al)] was generally retained in Central

Semitic as a prohibitive, but in South Semitic it was generalized as an indicative marker of negation. It is attested in Epigraphic South Arabian texts meaning 'not' and as a preverbal negative particle in Modern South Arabian and in Ethiopian Semitic; in Ethiopian Semitic, it occurs with a post-verbal *-m* in negative main clauses.[87] Thus, the change of *'al* from a prohibitive to a marker of sentential negation is characteristic of South Semitic (Faber 1997: 11).

The aforementioned feature is only true to SES, as the NES uses the assumed Proto-Semitic negative marker *'ayy-* (or its phonologically modified variants *'i*, in Ge'ez and Tigre and *'ay-* in Tigrinya).[88] The element *'ay-* and its phonological variants in NES are clausal negative markers. The suggestion that *'al* as a negative marker is an innovation of South Semitic does not, therefore, apply to NES. This, in turn, means that the usage of *'al-* as a negative marker does not make sense for the grouping of ES as a whole along with SA as opposed to Central.

The result of our examination of the so-called South Semitic innovations listed in Faber (1997) can be summarized in the following table:

---

[87] One should take Faber's claim cautiously, although not relevant to our present discussion. First, it is not the case that all ES use a post-verbal negative marker. For instance, languages such as Ge'ez, Tigre, Soddo, Selti, Wolane, Zay, Chaha, Muher, Gogot and Mäsqan have only a prefix negative marker. Second, the usage of *–m* as a post-verbal negative marker is only attested in three languages; namely Amharic, Harari and Gafat. This feature is probably a recent development of Amharic and later spread to Harari and Gafat, as it is not attested in Argobba, the closest relative of Amharic. Note that also Argobba shows a number of archaic features of Amharic.

[88] In fact, the negative element *'al* is also found in Ge'ez with only one verb *'al-bo* 'there is not' and Hetzron suggests that the element *'ay* is a later development in NES, i.e. a phonological variant of *'al*. However, this does not seem the case. First Hetzron does not provide any linguistic evidence convincing enough to support his claim. Second, the negative element *'ay* is also attested in SES as a prohibitive marker (for instance, Amharic *'ay* 'no'). Note that both negative elements are assumed to be archaic features and found almost in all groups of Semitic. What makes the choice of one of these elements over the other as relevant for sub-grouping is their widely distributed usage and the specific meaning that they carrry.

Table 4: South Semitic innovations

Features	Language groups			
	OSA	MSA	NES	SES
Two prefix conjugations	-	+	+	+
*al	+	+	-	+
-k	No information (Except Sabaean)	+	+	+

In sum, the element –*k* as a second person marker in the perfective cannot be considered strong evidence for subgrouping at all; the *yVqVt(t)Vl*-type Imperfective excludes OSA from the MSA and ES groups; and the usage of *'al* as a sentential negation excludes NES from the rest, i.e. SES, MSA and OSA. The entire major so-called "uncontested" grammatical features suggested by Faber (1997) for which ES (i.e. both SES and NES) is grouped under South Semitic along with South Arabian languages are, therefore, questionable and indeed inconclusive. As recalled from the discussion in Chapter 4 the date of separation between North Ethio-Semitic and South Ethio-Semitic needs a minimum of 5000 years. The diversity observed in the various ES languages which is greater than the rest of Semitic requires also such longer date (cf. Bender 1997). Beside the grammatical facts discussed above, such date of origin may indicate that Ethio-Semitic cannot branch from South Semitic, as the separation of South Semitic from the other group must take place at a later date than this. The only solution compatible with Faber's suggested features is to assume that the two branches of ES do not form a group and that only SES is a branch of South Semitic but not NES. OSA must also be excluded from the group. Before I examine this and other seemingly possible alternatives, I shall examine first the features suggested to be West Semitic innovations.

5.4.3.4 On the Grouping of Ethio-Semitic under West Semitic

Recall that one of the two features that separate West Semitic from East Semitic, according to Faber (1997), is the development of *'al(a)* 'Don't' as a negative/prohibitive marker in the former. The other feature

THE ORIGIN OF ETHIO-SEMITIC

suggested in Faber (1997) to be innovations of West Semitic that separate them from East Semitic is the usage of suffix conjugations for the past tense. As we have seen above, the former feature is only applicable to SES. Hence, among the "uncontested" features assumed to be a West Semitic innovation what is left for NES is only the use of pronominal suffix conjugations for the past tense.

If we strictly follow Hetzron's and Faber's suggested features for the sub grouping of the Semitic languages and try to determine the position of NES, the only possibility is to consider it as the first branch of West Semitic where South and Central branched later, that is, to consider NES as an archaic group of West Semitic. If this is the case, what makes the other West Semitic group different from NES is the innovation of *'al in the former. Setting aside the burden of the historical explanation, I shall examine this possibility in order to see whether it is a sound conclusion.

5.4.3.5 Further Examination/Examining the Alternatives

As we have seen in the above section, the grouping of ES as Western South Semitic is not plausible. Moreover, the grouping of ES (as a whole) and South Arabian together under South Semitic based on the TAM-system and the other grammatical features is not by any means conclusive. Hence, I have pointed out that the only possibility based on Hetzron's and Faber's suggested features is to take SES as a branch of South Semitic and NES as the first branch of West Semitic. This can be schematized as follows:

Figure 5: Tentative classification of Semitic

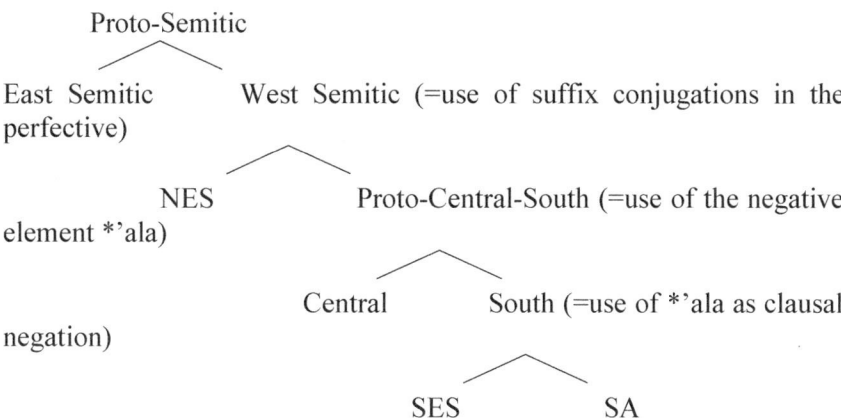

The above classification can also be interpreted as follows: it is NES which is closest to East Semitic. In fact, the grouping of ES as close to

East Semitic has been a long established suggestion. For instance, Haupt in his 1878 and 1887 works suggests "on the basis of some grammatical facts and some words common to both, a dialectal unity of Akkadian and Ethiopic within the group of the Semitic languages" (in Leslau 1944b: 53). Later Lambert (1921) also suggests "on the bases of some phonological and grammatical facts" that ES and Akkadian constitute one group within the Semitic language (ibid.).[89] If we examine the TAM-system further, NES seems even closer to East Semitic.

First, although MSA, SES, NES and Akkadian use an insertion of a vowel between the first two radicals in the imperfective, the latter two are distinct (from the former two) in geminating the penultimate radical. Second, as we can see from Hetzron's table quoted above, East Semitic has a prefix (*lV-*) as person marker in the Jussive. Although Hetzron did not mention it, the Jussive in NES (in fact in SES as well) is closer to East Semitic than to any other language groups as both have *(lV)yVqtVl-*type. Now the only feature left from Hetzron's (1972) set of features (i.e. the TAM-system) that distinguishes NES from East Semitic is the use of suffix conjugations as past in the former, like Central and South Semitic and prefix conjugations in the latter. In fact, although it is only one case, in Ge'ez and Tigre (two of the three NES languages), like in East Semitic, there is a prefix–conjugated perfective in the root √*bhl* 'to say', imperfective *yibil*, perfective *yibe* (as pointed out also in Hetzron 1972: 16 and Hetzron 1977: 15).

Table 5: Perfective, suffix conjugations and Jussive

Features	Language groups		
	Akkadian	NES	SES
Suffix conjugations *qVt(t)Vl*-type	tenseless	Perfective	Perfective
Perfective *yVqVtVl*-type	+	- (Except one verb in Ge'ez and Tigre)	-

The striking similarities between Akkadian and Ethiopian Semitic have intrigued linguists for some time now. It is in Akkadian and Ethiopian that phryngealized ejectives are found while the other Semitic languages

---

[89] See also Hetzron (1977: 13-14).

use emphatics. This means that the grouping of NES as close to Akkadian seems the best option. However, when we consider this possibility, we cannot think of grouping NES alone. SES shares with Akkadian almost the same features that NES and Akkadian share. Consider the following table, for instance:

Table 6: Akkadian and ES

Features	Language groups		
	Akkadian	NES	SES
Imperfective *yVqVttVl*-type	+	+	*yVqVtVl*-type
Jussive *(lV)yVqtVl*-type	+	+	+
Phryngealized ejectives	+	+	+

As can be seen from the above table, SES almost shares all the features except the non-existence of gemination in the Imperfective (in the basic verb types, i.e. Type A verbs).[90]

Recall that SES is grouped in South Semitic because of the use of *'al* as a negative marker. This feature is not, however, strong enough to support such grouping. Akkadian has *ul*, a somewhat similar negative element like West Semitic languages. The "uncontested" feature considered as relevant for Semitic classification is the internal conjugation of verbs. However, with regard to this, recall that OSA deviates from the other South Semitic languages but agrees with the Central group. If we categorize OSA based on this feature, following Voigt (1987) in the Central group, this classification makes the second person marker -*k* irrelevant for dividing South from Central. Furthermore the suggestion that the usage of the element *'al* as a sentential negative marker is a South Semitic innovation becomes unnecessary. Hence, grouping SES under South Semitic based on Faber's proposed features is not convincing.

---

[90] Note that in ES, except in Tigre and a few cases in Ge'ez, unlike the other Semitic languages Type B and Type C verbs are not derived from Type A verbs. These verbs have different roots and cannot be associated with specific meanings, such as intensity.

5.4.4 Proposed Position of ES

As we have seen above, the grouping of NES as West Semitic is only based on the use of suffix conjugation in the past/perfective. If this feature is found to be archaic, nothing is left in NES to be considered as West Semitic. In his examination of the Afroasiatic languages classification and origin Bender (1997) has grouped Egyptian, Cushitic, Semitic and Berber in one group as Central Afroasiatic as opposed to Chadic and Omotic. One feature that characterizes Central Afroasiatic language families, according to Bender, is the usage of the suffix conjugation for the past/perfective and the prefix for the non-past/imperfective. If this is the case, the usage of prefix conjugation for past tense could be an innovation in Akkadian. It may be the case however, that Proto-Semitic might have used both forms for the past. Akkadian formalized the prefix conjugation whereas NES, the latter with few traces only left as I pointed out above (cf. *yibe* in Ge'ez and Tigre). Let us examine the position of SES further again.

If suffix conjugations are retention from Proto-Semitic, what is left from Faber's (1997) suggested innovations that lead SES to be grouped under South Semitic is the use of *'al* as a negative marker. As pointed out above, this feature is not, however, strong enough to support this grouping. It is not only because Akkadian has *ul*, a somewhat similar negative element like West Semitic languages, and *al(a)* is reconstructed even as a Proto-Afroasiatic negative marker but also for other reasons. I will mention here only some complications.

One of the features mentioned above in Faber as a Central West Semitic innovation is the development of compound negative or prohibitive marker such as Hebrew *bli* 'without', Ugaritic/Phoenician *bl* 'not' and Arabic *bal* 'on the contrary' (Faber 1997: 9). However, Harari, a SES language, has *bilaay* 'without'. Although not with the element *b-*, other SES languages have also similar prohibitive marker; in the case of Amharic compounded with the preposition *k(ä)-* (or *y(ä)* in few cases) with the assumed Proto-Afroasiatic negative marker *al(a)* having the same meaning as in (*k/y)alä* 'without' like Central West Semitic.[91]

---

[91] Faber (1997) assumes that the source for Hebrew *bli* 'without', Ugaritic/Phoenician *bl* 'not' can be the assumed Proto-Afroasiatic negative marker *b* and either the assumed Proto-Semitic assertive marker *la* or the negative marker *la*. The element found in ES however, is clear that it is a preposition that combines with the negative marker *ala*; in the Harari case *b* plus *'ala* plus the other negative element, *'ay*. We are not quite sure whether

Moreover, although in limited constructions like in Central Semitic languages, the SES group uses the jussive form for the non-past as in *Yätim yıhid [Jussive] yät...* 'Wherever he goes' as opposed to *Yätim hedä [Perfective] yät...* 'Wherever he went' (Amharic). On the other hand, SES does not have a broken plural although this feature is common in Central and South Arabian languages. Interestingly, such a form is typical of NES. These complications may support Murtonen's (1967) suggestion that NES and SES might have diverged since Proto-Semitic times. Murtonen's type of suggestion seems also supported from the date of separation between North Ethio-Semitic and South Ethio-Semitic that I have pointed out already.

As we have seen above, the assumed innovative features used for subgrouping Semitic languages in Faber (1997) do not support in a straightforward manner the grouping of ES as a branch of South Semitic. If we continue classifying Semitic based on Faber's suggested features, bearing in mind our position with regard to the usage of suffix conjugation in the perfective, the best position that fits ES is to consider it either as a first branch of West Semitic or to group it along with Akkadian. However, what is common for Akkadian and ES in general are preserved archaic features; such grouping does not seem appropriate. The same is true with the other suggestion, i.e. with the consideration of ES as a first branch of West Semitic. The best position that seems fitting to ES is to consider it the first branch of Semitic as also suggested by some.[92] As far as the above examination is concerned, I am, therefore, inclined to proceed with this assumption unless convincing counter arguments are presented.

5.4.5 Conclusion

In this section, I have examined and suggested the best position that fits ES within the general classification of Semitic. However, I have not suggested what classification should be proposed for the other group and what features should be considered in the general classification of

---

the Hebrew *bli* can be analyzed in the same way like Harari. Note that here in Amharic although in some construction the assumed Proto-Afroasiatic negative marker *b is found, and *'ala is also used without the prepositions *k(ä)-* and *y(ä)-* with the same meaning 'without', no such combination is possible with the Proto-Afroasiatic negative marker *b (and the preposition *b(ä)-*).

[92] Recall that, Murtonen (1967) suggests ES to be considered as a direct descendant of Proto-Semitic. Bender (1997) among others also propagates a similar hypothesis. Girma (2001) also suggests a classification where Proto-ES is the first branched group of Proto-Semitic.

Semitic. Doing that is out of the scope of this work. Moreover, I do not think that I am in a position to do that. I leave such issue for the others who are more familiar with the Asian Semitic languages. But it seems clear that there is still a need to sit down, devise a better method and reexamine the internal classification of Semitic. Although innovations are best for sub-grouping, depending only on morphological features as what Hetzron (1972, 1975) suggests may not bring the true result with regard to Semitic classification. Moreover, as we have seen in the preceding sections, some of the suggested morphological innovations are found to be retentions. We may need to incorporate a wide area of issues such as phonological innovations, examination of vocabularies etc. as has been considered already by some such as Murtonen (1967, 1969) rather than leaving such issues aside.[93]

5.5 Examination and Discussion of the Hypotheses

As pointed out above, according to the migration hypothesis, the Semitic languages of Ethiopia are brought by South Arabian immigrants in the first millennium BC. This assumption in fact is based on the cultural presence of South Arabian elements in the northern part of Ethiopia (including the present Eritrea). Although such hypothesis is first suggested by historians, many linguists try to find some linguistic evidence to prove this assumption. However, as we have seen above, considering ES as a descendant of Old South Arabian or South Semitic in general is a disputed fact. In this section, I examine in detail whether there is any linguistic or non-linguistic evidence to support the migration hypothesis in general. As the lack of evidence does not necessarily mean that there is no migration at all, I also examine the arguments presented in support of the non-migration hypothesis.

5.5.1 The Position of ES in the General Classification of Semitic

With regard to the position of ES, as Hetzron (1977: 9) also points out "most Semitists agree that Epigraphic South-Arabian, Modern South-Arabian and Ethiopian display close affinity and should be classified as one branch of Semitic". Indeed, Hetzron's own classification and that of Faber quoted above also reflect such grouping. Moreover, as we saw from Hudson's interpretation of Faber's classification in section 5.3.1 above, not only those who promote the Semitic migration to Ethiopia but also some of those who consider them as indigenous consider ES to be a branch of South Semitic. There is some exception to this grouping,

---

[93] See also for relevant references Appleyard (1996).

THE ORIGIN OF ETHIO-SEMITIC

however. For instance, Murtonen (1967, 1969), who considers ES to be non-immigrant but found in its original habitat, suggested that Ethio-Semitic was probably a direct survival of Proto-Semitic and that its two branches, i.e. South Ethio-Semitic and North Ethio-Semitic, probably diverged since Proto-Semitic period. Murtonen further suggested that Soqotri (as a representative of Modern South-Arabian) should be considered as a separate branch of Semitic. The examination in Section 5.5 also shows that ES cannot be considered a descendant of South Semitic and for that matter a descendant of West Semitic. The only probable position that fits ES in the classification of Semitic is to consider it as the first branch of the family.

5.5.2 Date of Origin

The often talked-about migration date of South Arabian to Ethiopia is associated with the cultural presence of South Arabian in the northern part of Ethiopia (including present Eritrea). In most historical works, the migration is often claimed to have occurred not as a one-time act but as a continuous process starting from the middle of the first millennium BC and continuing to the full rise of the Axumite Kingdom at around 100 AD. However, according to Hetzron (1972) and Bender (1997, 2003), the grammatical and lexical differences exhibited in the various Ethio-Semitic languages cannot be assumed as a result of 2000 to 3000 years of separation (from Proto-ES).[94] It needs a longer span of time than this. This, however, does not mean that there has been no migration at all. It means only that ES cannot be considered to have migrated in the first millennium BC or at a later date. Indeed, some linguists such as Hetzron (1972) and Appleyard (1996) proposed this to be the case and that the great diversity observed in ES is due to a long contact with mostly the various Cushitic languages. Abraham Demoz (1978) objects for this kind of suggestion as follows:

> I would see little virtue myself in attempting as some have done to salvage the thesis of South Arabian origins for Ethiosemitic by proposing earlier periods of

---

[94] "Such diversity [i.e. the diversity seen among the modern Ethio-Semitic languages] - greater than that within the rest of Semitic- is not explainable in the "short chronology" of descent from Classical Ethiopic (Gi'iz), which died out in about the 8th century and was said to have given rise to modem Ethio-Semitic as the result of "military colonies" in southern Ethiopia as late as the 14th century (Bender 1997: 27-28).

migration than was heretofore assumed. If the evidence for migrations is flimsy for the earlier half of the first millennium B.C., it is simply non-existent for earlier millennia. To simply assume earlier migration would surely drag us deep into fanciful history (Abraham Demoz 1978: 14).

Be it fanciful or not, some continue to look for some historical support for an earlier migration of South Arabian into Ethiopia. Indeed, although hard to find strong historical evidence, some have already suggested that there were earlier migrations. For instance, Sergew (1972:34) has mentioned the existence of a local document which talks about Semitic civilization in Yeha that dates back some 4000 years attributed to South Arabian immigrants. According to the said document, Yeha itself was founded by South Arabian immigrants at year 1990 BC (Ibid.). Yayneshet (1962 EC: 4) has also mentioned a Semitic group called Heksos as migrated from South Arabia to Ethiopia at around 2000 BC. Hence, we need to look at some more points to consider whether ES migrated from South Arabia or not and whether it had a pidgin origin or not. I shall examine these points below.

5.5.2 On "Pidginization"

The pidgin theory is suggested not only to account for Amharic but also Ge'ez and/or Proto-ES. For instance, although Sergew claims that Ge'ez was not directly derived from Sabaean, he claims that it is originated out of a Cushitic language with the influence of Sabaean: "It [Ethiopic] is rather Kushitic in origin and after Sabaean influence; it started to develop as an independent language, Ge'ez" (1972: 33). Consider also the following statement from Gragg (1972):

> It [Ethiopic Semitic] is presumably derived from one or more forms of South Semitic brought from Yemen, probably in the first half of the first millennium BCE.... One may presume that Ethiopic Semitic evolved out of a South Arabian-based trade lingua franca. The substratum languages in this development presumably belonged to the Cushitic language family (Gragg 1997: 242).

According to Gragg (1997) and Sergew (1972), Ge'ez is a kind of pidgin language, although, for Gragg, it "maintains the level of morphological complexity inconsistent with any radical pidginization" (1997: 242). Since the ES languages show many non-Semitic features especially those of Cushitic, the pidginization theory seems to some a plausible hypothesis for the origin of Ethio-Semitic languages with Geʻez as their Proto-language. However, as discussed in section 2.3.1 above, the assumption that the ancestral language of the modern Ethio-Semitic languages is Geʻez, which itself descended from Sabaean, is proved not to be attractive (see also Appleyard 1996 and section 5.5 below).

Although Hetzron does not claim that Ethio-Semitic has a pidgin past, he claims that they are mixed with Cushitic languages and lists a number of pan-ES features most of which resulted due to such influence.[95] One of the unique ES features that Robert Hetzron mentioned is the use of "verb to say" (*√bhl) as a compounding item.

> Another extremely important pan-Ethiopian feature is the morphological behavior of the verb *hlw "there is" and its developments (allä, anä etc.). This verb is conjugated as a Perfect and can be augmented by subordinating morphemes used with the perfect. It usually has the meaning of the present. In spite of its shape, it can also have the subordinating temporal prefix "when" which, with every other verb, is limited to the Imperfect. In Geʻez, it can take the prefix ənzä, in Tigrəñña k-, in Amharic s- and in Gurage t- all meaning "when" and usually appearing before the imperfect. This is an extremely strong argument in favor of common origin (Hetzron 1972:18).

The other point mentioned in Hetzron to be a pan-Ethiopian feature, as a result of Cushitic influence, is the word order. All the modern Ethio-Semitic languages, i.e. except Geʻez, have a similar word order with Cushitic languages.[96] As Geʻez has preserved the Semitic syntax, it has been suggested that "the Cushitic influence affecting syntax came later and was independent in the different branches of Ethiopic" (Hetzron 1972:19).

According to Hetzron, the special behavior of the verb √bhl 'to say' "is most probably due to the Cushitic influence…, which affected the whole

---

[95] "It is impossible to say now how great a Semitic element becomes mixed with them at the same time as the new language was introduced. Thus, it is not surprising if the Cushitic speakers of this newly acquired language tried to level out irregularities in it" (Hetzron 1972: 23).
[96] In fact "the northernmost living language, Təgre [Tigre], is much less rigid in word order than the rest, and it may optionally have either the Semitic pattern or the Cushitic one" (Hetzron 1972: 19).

of Proto-Ethiopic" (Hetzron 1972: 18).[97] It is difficult to agree with Hetzron, however. Although verb-to-say compounds are common in Ethio-Semitic languages, not all Cushitic languages have such constructions. Furthermore, the productivity of verb-to-say compounds is not uniform in ES. For instance, in Ge'ez the distribution of these compounds is very minimal as compared to, for instance, Amharic and even its closest relative Tigrinya. It is an areal feature which spread to the languages after the major subdivisions of ES happened.

As we have seen above, for Hetzron, the Ethio-Semitic languages are distinct from the rest of Semitic mostly due to Cushitic influence. He does not claim ES to have a pidgin past. Indeed, the Ethio-Semitic languages cannot be considered as originated through the process of pidginization because unlike pidgin origin languages, ES maintains the basic core Semitic features.

Although Hetzron (1977) and Hudson (2002) have different opinions with regard to the origin of ES, both are the same in acknowledging the existence of core Semitic features in ES. According to Hetzron (1977), there are a number of archaic features found in Ethio-Semitic which, according to Hudson (2002: 1765), "often enable Proto-Semitic reconstruction on the ES alone".[98] This is hardly possible if Ethio-Semitic languages originated as a pidgin whether or not the superstratum was Semitic. Indeed it is due to the archaic features preserved in ES languages that Christian classified the group under "Old Semitic Languages" group and Haupt (1878, 1887) and Lambert (1920) along with Assyrian, i.e. Akkadian (in Leslau 1944b: 53, Hetzron 1977: 13-14). On the other hand, it is also true that ES is the highly influenced group (by Cushitic) among the other Semitic languages. The status of the Ethio-Semitic languages is as Bernal puts it: "The Ethiopian Semitic languages are ... more or less archaic and more or less influenced by neighboring Cushitic languages" (Bernal 2006: 87).

5.5.3 Diversity, Least-move and other Issues

5.5.3.1 Diversity and Least-move

As pointed out in chapter 2, section 2.3, according to Murtonen (1967),

---

[97] When used as a compounding item, this verb carries only grammatical features such as aspect and tense. It does not have semantic content.

[98] In fact, as we will see also in section 5.5 below, ES is one of the most archaic group of Semitic languages.

Hudson (1977, 1978 and 2002) and many others, ES (or any of its branches) cannot be considered as immigrant languages. According to Hudson (1977, 1978), ES cannot be considered as immigrant languages for the following basic reasons. First, it is generally believed that diversity indicates origin. That is, when there is a diversity of genetically related languages in a small place, it is most probably the case that the origin of the parent language (of those languages) could be that place. Although Voigt (2005: 440) considers ES to be immigrant languages, he claims that they amount to about 20 languages or dialects. Although Appleyard (1996: 207) advocates a similar hypothesis with Voigt, he suggests that ES is "the most complex and diverse branch of Semitic with its 20-plus languages". Bender also states that "the major Semitic languages of today are all found in Ethiopia, roughly from north to south: Tigrd (sic. [Tigre]), Tigrinya, and Amharic. There are several smaller languages: Harari and the various languages under the name Gurage" (Bender 2003: 23). Although the figure that 20 or 20-plus languages seems a little bit exaggerated, in Ethiopia, there are about 16 Semitic languages. That amounts to 80 percent of the living Semitic tongues (Hudson 2002). It is also true that the Ethiopian Semitic languages are the most diversified group of languages within Semitic (see also Blench 2006). For Hudson (1977, 2002), Bender (1997, 2003) and others, this clearly indicates that ES is an indigenous group of languages.

The second argument is as follows: Afroasiatic has at least six language families, namely Semitic, Omotic, Cushitic, Berber, Chadic and Old Egyptian. Only a few of the Semitic languages are spoken in Asia while the rest are spoken in Africa. Furthermore, of these six families three of them, namely Omotic, Cushitic and Semitic are spoken in Ethiopia. Note here also that Beja and Biraile, two languages of Ethiopia, formerly classified as Cushitic, are suspected to be separate additional, families.[99] If this is true, the number of language families in the Afroasiatic phylum will become eight and the language families spoken in Ethiopia will be increased to five. Following the "least-moves" principle, it is suggested that the origin of the Proto-Afroasiatic language/people is in Africa, especially Ethiopia, rather than Asia (cf. Greenberg 1971, McCall 1998, Girma 2001, Hudson 2002, Bender 1997, Bernal 1987, Blench 2006). Consider also the following statement from Murtonen (1991):

---

[99] See for similar discussion and relevant references McCall (1998: 139) and section 5.6 below.

> The fact that speakers of all the other language stocks of the Semito-Hamitic [Afroasiatic] phylum are indigenous to the eastern and northern parts of Africa strongly suggests that their last common home region was on that continent, presumably in the eastern rather than more western parts of it; the Semites would then have moved eastwards to their historical sites of habitation (Murtonen 1991: 1120).

As we have seen above, one of the strong arguments that supports the African origin is diversity. For Vycihl (1987), however, diversity may not indicate the origin of Afroasiatic languages:

> It would seem that the original home of the Hamito-Semitic languages was somewhere in Africa, as it is easier to conceive the migration of a single group from Africa to Asia than that of four [sic. at least five] groups from Asia to Africa. There are, however, two arguments in favour of an Asiatic origin. The first one is an anthropological and prehistoric, as we have not the slightest evidence of migrations from Africa to Asia. The second is linguistics, as all specific Hamito-Semitic features at their most complete are found in Semitic and not in the Hamitic groups (P. 109).

The anthropological and prehistoric "argument" of Vycihl is, in fact, considered as one of the strong arguments for those who promote the Asian origin (see, for instance Militarev 2000, 2003). This argument basically has to do with the existence of southwest Asian crops and stock in north Africa which is assumed as a spread of Natufian material culture and the genetic similarity between the Semitic people in Asia and that of northern Africa, particularly with Berbers (and the genetic mix exhibited mostly in the Ethiopian Semitic people, the Cushitic and Omotic people). For those who promote the Asian origin for the proto-Afroasiatic the genetic similarity was considered "as the result of a reflux from Asia to Africa" (Bernal 2006: 71). However, these two points are challenged in recent works. As Bernal (2006: 71) points out "southwest Asia was not the sole source of agriculture".[100] The genetic issue is now considered even as evidence on the contrary, i.e. as suggesting a movement of people from Africa to Asia.

---

[100] See also the discussion in this chapter on agriculture.

> The movement was really in the other direction; that is to say, that Asians and Europeans genetically resemble eastern and north Africans because they derive from these parts of the continent. Furthermore, not only have recent works shown skeletal evidence of Khoisan presence in Ethiopia but also some studies demonstrate a close genetic relationship between Khoisan and Oromo and Amharic-speakers of Afroasiatic in central Ethiopia. Suggesting to the authors a population continuum across Africa from south to east (Bernal 2006: 71-72).

As mentioned above, only part of the Semitic languages are spoken in Asia and based on the Ethio-Semitic languages alone, the Proto-Semitic features can be reconstructed (cf. Hetzron 1972). This means also that the other Vycihl's argument, "all specific Hamito-Semitic features at their most complete are found in Semitic", cannot be considered as supporting the Asian origin of the Afroasiatic phylum.[101] Note that here also, in almost all recent works Semitic is considered no more as a representative of the Afroasiatic phylum: "Semitic is not typical of Afrasian, but is a relatively recent offshoot of the BSCu [Berber, Semitic and Cushitic, which he calls Macro-Cushitic] branch of Afrasian" (Bender 1997: 25).

The association of Afroasiatic and Semitic origin with the Natufian material culture and the suggested genetic evidence cannot be considered as a strong argument for Asian origin.[102]

> The correlation with the Natufian culture of the Near East (Militarev 2000) fails the primary test of explaining the geography and internal diversity of African Afroasiatic. Although it is likely that many northern languages have been eliminated, it is still very hard to model the expansion of Afroasiatic on the assumption that it originated in the Near East (Blench 2006: 150).

As Bernal (2006: 72) points out, an Asiatic origin for Afroasiatic leaves unsolved the location of Omotic, which is now widely agreed not only to be separate branch of the phylum but also the earliest. The Omotic

---

[101] We will come back on the origin of Afroasiatic later in section 5.6.
[102] See Bernal (2006), Blench (2006) and Bender (1997, 2003) for more arguments and detailed discussions.

languages in their entirety are spoken in Ethiopia.[103]

As we have seen above, Vycihl's two "arguments" and, in general, arguments promoting the Asian origin are questionable. In fact, beside diversity and the least-move principle, there are other points that can be mentioned in support of the African origin of Semitic and Afroasiatic which I turn to now.

5.5.3.2 Other Issues

We know from historical records that Ancient Egyptians had trade contact since the beginning of their state with the people of Punt. The exact location of this land of punt, which was also referred to as *To Neter* 'God's Land' by the Egyptians, is not definitely known. However, currently it is generally believed that it is located south of Egypt that includes most parts of the present Ethiopia.

> Several modern authors ... have speculated as to whether Tigray or the Ethiopian-Sudanese borderlands, instead of Arabia or the Horn of Africa, may have been the legendary 'God's Land' of the ancient Egyptians. This land of Punt, producer of incense and other exotic treasures, where the pharaohs sent their ships, may at least have been one of the regions included at some time in the Aksumites' extended kingdom. Egyptian expeditions to Punt are known from as far back as Old Kingdom times in Egypt, in the third millennium BC, but the best-known report comes from the New Kingdom period, during the reign of queen Hatshepsut, in the fifteenth century BC. She was so proud of her great foreign trading expedition that she had detailed reliefs of it carved on the walls of her funerary temple at Dayr al-Bahri across the Nile from the old Egyptian capital of Thebes. The surviving reliefs show that the region was organised even then under chiefly rule, with a population eager to trade the recognisably African products of their lands with the visitors. Aksum is still today a sorting and distribution centre for the frankincense produced in the region, and it is not unlikely that the coastal stations visited by the ancient

---

[103] Note that Omotic was considered in earlier literature as a subfamily of Cushitic.

Egyptians acquired their incense from the same sources. Punt is suggested to have been inland from the Sawakin-north Eritrean coast ..., and, apart from the great similarity of its products with those of the Sudan-Ethiopia border region, an Egyptian hieroglyphic text seems to confirm its identity with the Ethiopian highland region by reference to a downpour in the land of Punt which caused the Nile to flood ... The inscription dates to the twenty-sixth Egyptian dynasty, and knowledge of Punt seems to have continued even into the Persian period in Egypt, when king Darius in an inscription of 486-5BC mentions, or at least claims, that the Puntites sent tribute .... One extremely interesting Egyptian record from an 18th Dynasty tomb at Thebes actually shows Puntite trading boats or rafts with triangular sails ..., for transporting the products of Punt, indicating that the commerce was not exclusively Egyptian-carried, and that local Red Sea peoples were already seafaring — or at least conveying goods some distance by water ... for themselves" (Munro-Hay 1991: 16).[104]

The Egyptians also claimed that they were relatives of the Puntites, with whom they traded. "These people [i.e. the Puntites] ... were regarded by the Egyptians as having the same origin as the Egyptians themselves" (Sergew 1972: 23). As Sergew (Ibid) further points out, the physical appearance of the Egyptians and that of the Puntites was almost identical (see also the picture below). If Afroasiatic originated in Asia, and the Egyptians descended from there, the latter wouldn't claim that they were descendants of the Puntites, and their physical appearance should have reflected more of the Arabian people than that of the Puntites.

---

[104] The page number of Munro-Hay (1991) given here and throughout this work are based on the electronic copy of the book available in the Internet.

Figure 6: The ancient Egyptian representation of their voyage to Ethiopia

(Adopted from Aba Gaspri n.d.: 6)

Besides the aforementioned historical fact, Murtonen provides another linguistic argument that supports the African origin of Afroasiatic and Semitic. Murtonen (1967), after his comparative vocabulary and grammatical studies suggests the horn of Africa to be the original homeland of Semitic.[105]

Note that in chapter four I have suggested that the diversity of the Ethio-Semitic languages needs a longer date than 2000-3000 years. Murtonen (1967) suggests this date often to be the period of Proto-Semitic. Bender (1997) has also proposed a similar hypothesis with Murtonen. For Bender and Murtonen the diversity that exists among the Ethiopian languages can only be explained if we assume ES as non-immigrant that continue to live in the original homeland of Proto-Semitic. On the other hand, Hetzron (1972) among some others has suggested the migration of ES to be before the first millennium BC. As the grouping of ES with South Arabian languages, which Hetzron strongly advocates, is controversial (cf. section 5.5), his proposed late migration of ES from South Arabia cannot be the case. In general, considering the Ethio-Semitic as immigrant languages is not a convincing theory any more as far as linguistics is concerned. Proto-ES can neither be considered to be created through a pidginization process nor can it (or any of its branches) be considered to be an immigrant language. As a matter of summarizing

---

[105] "Add the result of our vocabulary survey, according to which ancient South Arabic [i.e. Arabian] is more closely related to (Northern) Arabic and North-West Semitic rather than Ethiopic, and the fact that the syntax of sentences is also radically different in South Ethiopic from the state of things in the other languages studied, as well as from the rest of the Semitic family, although the present state of research and material available to the present did not allow investigation proper into the syntax. However, even what has been said above may be sufficient to prove that South Arabic, Soqotri, and the Ethiopic have been developing independently of each other since Proto-Semitic period, and that the connection between North and South Ethiopic also has been rather minimal from those days until less than a millennium ago and that at least some of the modern South Arabic languages do not derive from the epigraphically attested ancient South Arabic dialects. Moreover, the archaic feature of Tigre and Gurage can hardly be accounted for otherwise than on the supposition that they have been living apart from the rest of Ethiopic for long periods, and since ancient times, which hardly could have been the case, had they come together with the ancestors of present-day Ethiopians from South Arabia; Cushitic and Egyptian affinities also point to a permanent stay of most of Ethiopians on the African continent. We may therefore conclude our study establishing that the original home of the Semitic speaking nations was probably the Horn of Africa, and that they never formed quite close unity even in what is commonly called the Proto-Semitic period, but were partially isolated and also in contact with dialects from which some of the present-day Hamitic languages developed" (Murtonen 1967: 73-74, also quoted in Hailu Habtu 1984).

the aforementioned discussion, it is worth quoting Bender (2003).

> For those advocating the old orthodoxy [that] Semitic language and culture in Ethiopia are imports from across the Red Sea there has always been the embarrassing problem that Ethio-Semitic (E-S) languages have at least as much internal diversity as all the rest of Semitic. The proliferation of Ethio-Semitic was ascribed to descent from Classical Gi'iz, which died out in about the 8th century, and to the rise of "military colonies" in the South as recent as the 14th century, leaving a "short chronology" of only six to 12 centuries for the degree of diversification which is now seen (Bender 2003: 27).

Bender thus suggests that "Semitic may have originated in Ethiopia" (Bender 2003: 27). According to Bender (ibid), this suggestion "also makes the well-known special similarities between Ethio-Semitic and †Akkadian less mysterious". Indeed, most scholars of Afroasiatic have suggested that Afroasiatic and Semitic as well originated in Africa. It seems that those few who still continue promoting the Asian origin for Afroasiatic have more of an agenda than supporting their claims with strong linguistic evidence.

> The preconceptions of long-established traditions of scholarship in Egypt and the Near East are responsible for disagreements that have significant consequences for our understanding of its history. Most scholars of Afroasiatic (…) have argued for a structure that places the origin of Afroasiatic within Africa, with Omotic considered the primary branching. However, a significant minority place Semitic in primary position and conclude that Afroasiatic must have originated in the Near East (…). Debates like this have a strong ideological flavor; the association of Semitic culture with "high civilization" frequently marginalizes purely linguistic issues (Blench 2006: 143-144).

In the following section, I examine the non-linguistic issues, which were mentioned to support the Semitic migration to Ethiopia.

5.5.4 On the "Immigrant" Civilization

According to the migration hypothesis, the immigrant Semitic people did not only introduce their language to the local Cushitic speakers but also their highly civilized culture. They are claimed to be the founders of the

THE ORIGIN OF ETHIO-SEMITIC

Axumite kingdom, and the ones who introduced literacy, stone masonry, agriculture, etc. In general, they are considered to be responsible for every aspect of the ancient civilization that arose in Ethiopia. Consider, for instance, the following statement from a book on African history:

> The origins of the Axumite kingdom go back well into the first millennium B.C., when settlers from South Arabia and the Yemen introduced Semitic languages, building in stone, and literacy. They may also have been the first to introduce agriculture into this area ... – the only dates known to the present writer for cultivated grain from northern Ethiopia are of the sixth century AD (*The Cambridge History of Africa* 1978: Vol. 2, 262).[106]

There are at least three points that need critical examination here: the introduction of literacy, stone masonry and agriculture.

5.5.4.1 Agriculture

Gamst (1969: chapter 2) points out that although Ethiopia was not the only country that introduced agriculture, it had great contribution in adapting and distributing agriculture to the world. The production of fruits and cereals were assumed to be known amongst the Ethiopians before 3000 BC (cf. Gamst 1969, Marcus 2002). Bernal in volume III of Black Athena in chapter three under the section entitled "*The end of the Ice Age and the Agricultural Revolution*" discusses the matter in detail with the examination of various authoritative sources. He suggests that "southwest Asia and northern Africa appear to have been the earliest regions to go through the agricultural revolution" (Bernal 2006: 61). I quote Bernal at length:

> In southwest Asia and Lower Egypt, agriculture became based on wheat and barley, wild forms of which still grow in the hills of southwest Asia. For this reason, this region was assumed to be where these crops were first cultivated. From there they were thought to spread into the Nile Valley. Barely, however, could have been cultivated in Ethiopia even earlier. Although wild barleys are not found in Ethiopia, the country contains a far greater variety of domesticated barely than southwest Asia. Following the general principle that a crop would

---

[106] This kind of statements has more of a race prejudice background than factual evidence, as we will see in a moment.

101

have been first established in a region that now has the greatest diversity of that plant, some paleobotanists have suggested that barley was cultivated in Ethiopia before it was in southwest Asia. The wild Asian barley could be explained as "escapes" from domestic varieties.[107] ... Sorghums, millets and other crops were also cultivated in warmer regions of Ethiopia, possibly as early as the Seventh Millennium BCE, though most were domesticated in other parts of Africa (Bernal 2006: 61).

It is generally assumed that among the first plants domesticated in Ethiopia *enset* (*ensete edulis* "false banana"), *teff* (*Eragrostis tef*, family Gramineae),[108] chickpeas, and a number of oil plants can be cited (see Bernal 2006: 594, Marcus 2002: 3).[109] According to Marcus (2002: 3), Ethiopia was either the primary or the secondary point of dispersion by the cultivation of thirty-six distinct crops.

The assumption that use of the plow was introduced by South Arabian immigrants has also been challenged. As Marcus (2002: 3-4) points out, the cultivation of various food items with the plow by the Proto-Ethiopians is as old as agriculture itself which is some 10 millennia BP.[110] Munro-Hay also points out that "'words for 'plough' and other agricultural vocabulary are apparently of Agew origin in Ethiopian Semitic languages, indicating that the techniques of food- production were not one of the Arabian imports" (1991: 62).

As pointed out in section 5.5.3.2 above, there were trade exchanges (which included agricultural products) between the Egyptians and the Punt kingdoms long before the assumed migration of South Arabians. Although Punt's political boundary may not have included all of the present day Ethiopia, it is a fact that some of the present Ethiopian lands were part of the Punt kingdom and a lot of agricultural products besides

---

[107] Bernal (2006: 61) further remarks that "it would seem more likely, however, that both the southwest Asian and Ethiopian barleys derived from the barley harvested and possibly sown earlier in the Middle Nile".

[108] Teff is used to make *injera*, a pancake-like bread., which is a staple food of Ethiopia.

[109] See also Gamst (1969) and the references cited in Bernal (2006).

[110] "The great versatility of these cultivated foods enable Proto-Ethiopians to advance into the temperate plateaus and to clear the land, which they cultivated with the plow, a feature of the highlands as old there as agriculture itself" (Marcus 2002: 3-4).

silver and gold were brought from the interior lands of the present day Ethiopia (Aba Gaspri n.d., Sergew 1972, Munro-Hay 1991). As Marcus reports, this trading also continued when the Ethiopians came into contact with South Arabians: "Coming into contact with Sabaean traders, ... the Kingdom of Da'amat ... exchanged ivory, tortoiseshell, rhinoceros horn, gold, silver, and slaves for such finished goods as cloth, tools, metals, and jewelry" (Marcus 2002: 3-4). Therefore, not only was agriculture well known in Ethiopia but also were gold and silver mining two to three thousand years before the assumed migration of South Arabians. Accordingly, it is not possible to claim that agriculture was introduced by the so-called "Semitic immigrants" from South Arabia. As pointed out above, many who have studied this subject have claimed that Ethiopia is one of the first countries in the world that went through the agricultural revolution. Indeed, many who even claim that there was the migration of South Arabian and that the immigrants had superior civilization did not claim that the latter had introduced agriculture to Ethiopia.[111] This does not mean, however, that there was no South Arabian contribution to Ethiopian agriculture. As Marcus points out "the towns [in northern Ethiopia] featured adjacent, irrigated, intensive agriculture fed by the same type of reservoirs found in South Arabia. Farther away, traditional dry land agriculture was practiced best exemplified archeologically in the region around Axum" (Marcus 2002: 4).[112]

5.5.4.2 The Art of Building

The earlier historical studies that suggest the Axumite civilization originated due to South Arabian migration to Ethiopia have also been challenged. One of the major points in this regard are the obelisks at Axum which were assumed to have been made by an immigrant Semitic people since, the argument goes, the indigenous African people were not capable of such architectural works. However, critical studies reveal that the Axumite obelisks are indigenous works and do not have any parallel in South Arabia. This has been noticed in earlier time as well even among those who propagate the South Arabian migration and introduction of their "civilization" to Ethiopia. Consider for instance the

---

[111] Some, however, claim that they did introduce architecture. This is also questionable as we will see in a moment.
[112] Marcus further points out that "the use of both farming techniques created a vital synergy, one also evidenced in the high culture that developed" (Marcus 2002: 4).

following observation from Theodore Bent, the nineteenth century traveler:

> The great point of interest about the obelisks of Aksum is that they form a consecutive series, from these very rude unhewn stones up to the highly-finished and decorated obelisks, and it is highly probable that here we have the origin and development of the obelisk, side by side; high up in the valley they are all rough and unhewn, like the monoliths at Ava, placed in the ground at all angles, and in no way to be distinguished from the many rude stone monoliths which we find scattered all over the world (Bent 1896: 183-184).

The highly decorated obelisks with pseudo-doors and pseudo-windows look many storied castle.[113] These highly decorated obelisks probably are replicas of the actual palaces of the Axumite kings. Cosmas of the sixth century describes in his work "Christian Topography" that the Axumite king had a four-story building (as translated by McCrindle 1897). Munro-Hey (1991) has also noted this point:

> More probably, the stelae could have been exaggerated designs based on the Aksumite palaces; and here there is archaeological support, since the structure called the 'IW Building' partly cleared by the excavations of Neville Chittick..., included just such wood-reinforced walls.... Each ensemble must have formed very much the sort of thing mentioned by the sixth-century merchant Kosmas, who speaks of the 'four-towered palace of the king of Ethiopia'" (Munro-Hay 1991:107).

Although there is not any good reason to attribute South Arabian origin to the Axumite Obelisks, the presence of South Arabian cultural elements in Ethiopia is an undeniable fact. It has been noted that there is

---

[113] Bent after his visit to Axum in the 19th century describes the obliskes as follwos: "The highly-finished monoliths are nearly all of the same character, namely, representations of a many-storied castle. At the base are the altars, fitting beautifully on to the monoliths.... Then there is the sham door cut in the granite block, in one case with a lock and bolt, in another with a simple door-handle; above this we are left to imagine a lofty hall with a low story above it like an *entresol*. Between each of the stories and along the sides the beam ends are carefully cut, causing one to imagine that the original pattern of these monoliths was constructed of wood" (Bent 1896:184).

THE ORIGIN OF ETHIO-SEMITIC

a lot of mixture of the South Arabian and the Ethiopian culture not only with the techniques of agriculture that I discussed above but also with a number of other areas among which in the area of architectural works. For instance, Marcus points out about the famus women statues the early Axumite period as follows:

> The stiff forms of the heavily stylized seated figures, the characteristic placement of the hands on the knees, and the drape of the long chemise like garment may be based on South Arabian prototypes but are typically Axumite in realization (Marcus 2002: 5).

According to Marcus (ibid.) "the few examples of bas-relief portray men who are characteristically Ethiopian but rendered in poses that can be seen at sites from Egypt to Iran". Marcus (2002: 4) further points out that "the domination of the indigenous culture became more marked after the fourth century B.C. The fact is clearly apparent in surviving monuments, especially found at Yeha, Haoulti, Malazo, and elsewhere". For instance, ruins of a temple found at Yeha dated ca. 700 BCE is assumed to have Sabaean style architecture.

5.5.4.3 Literacy

The most advocated idea with regard to the origin of Ethiopic Script is associated with the South Arabian immigrants. The idea is that Ethiopic script evolved out of the Sabaean monumental script. It then went through many modifications: from line-shaped to curved, from the most attested order አቡጊዳ to ሀለሐመ,[114] and from non-vowel marking to vowelling where the latter is often thought as happened in the fourth century AD during King Ezana's period. However, most of these assumptions are challenged by recent findings.

First, recent studies suggest that the Ethiopic script is related to the cursive scripts found both in Ethiopia and the other side of the Red Sea. Hence, it is not a development of the monumental South Arabian script. "The mechanics of the change ... could have been through either intentional or accidental alteration. The script could have been inspired by an early importation, or even by a more recent inspiration subsequent to the period of the earlier inscriptions" (Munro-Hay 1991: 206). Drewes, one of the few authoritative scholars on these monumental

---

[114] In fact, the order called አቡጊዳ, which is similar to that of the Northwest Semitic order, is used interchangeably especially in the traditional church education.

inscriptions, suggests the following:

> While the evolution from cursive South Arabian writing to the Ethiopian alphabet, as far as reconstructable, was a gradual one, the change from Sabaean to Ethiopic as a written language was presumably abrupt. But it is difficult to determine, nonetheless, partly because of the brevity of the cursive inscriptions, partly because of the traces of the local language(s) in Ethiopian Sabaean generally, and in the later inscriptions in particular (Drewes 1980:35).

Second, the order ሀለሐመ, which was thought to be a later innovation by the Ethiopians and unique to the Ethiopic script, is found recently to be an archaic order (see Daniels 1997: 33 and the reference cited there). Third, the vowelling technique most probably was started long before Ezana's period as Ezana's predecessor Wazeba's silver coins contain a vocalized letter.

> The existence of one vocalised letter on certain silver coins of Wazeba, a predecessor of Ezana, may well indicate that the process of vocalisation was under way before Ezana, though the unvocalised Ge'ez inscription of Ezana has made it commonly accepted that the development of vocalisation occurred during his reign. Littmann (1913, IV: 78), Drewes and Schneider all suggest deliberate archaising; some of the letters, apart from lacking vowels, are of forms very much more ancient than those current for Ezana's time. ... It is of interest that almost no kings of Aksum in the subsequent centuries introduced vowelling on their coins, or when they did, it was only on a letter or two; and this long after vocalisation must have been current on other media (Munro-Hay 1991: 206).

Aba Gerima Gospels which were once assumed to be of the 11th or 12th centuries are now dated to many centuries back. Radiocarbon dating conducted at Oxford University Research Laboratory for Archeology for one of the manuscripts puts the date to 330-540 and for the other one 430-650.[115] I cannot rule out therefore the possible use of other not yet

---

[115] The Garima manuscripts are two from probably two writers as the handwriting are different. These illuminated manuscripts are found in the northern part of Ethiopia in a place called Abba Garima monastery named after the monk Abba Garima who came from Constantinople around the end of the

discovered media such as parchment which the Axumite might have used for keeping their records. The continuation of using unvowelled letters in coins and inscriptions long after even Ezana's vowelled inscription appeared may indicate that vowelling might have been employed on some media which are easy to craft letters such as parchment and papyrus whereas the unvowlled system used on monumental inscriptions and coins.

The earliest recorded inscriptional fragments found in Ethiopia dated to pre-Axumite times, i.e. to the kingdom of Da'amat/Da'amot (ca. 900 BC-500 BC). Although we do not know much about this kingdom, we have some information about it. The capital of the kingdom of Da'amat/Da'amot was around the current town of Yeha in the northern part of Ethiopia in Tigray region. This kingdom left its trace with a ruin of a temple (Figure 9), some artifacts, and inscriptions.

The inscriptions from the Da'amat period are monumental written in Sabaean although in some cases mixed in nature (see the discussion below). The writing in "pure" Ge'ez follows the Sabaean. The Sabaean is totally replaced by Ge'ez after the fourth century ACE.

> A fair number of inscriptions have been found dating from pre-Aksumite times and written in the Epigraphic South Arabian script, at such places as Yeha, Kaskase and Hawelti-Melazo. Some of these employ a form of the language which is apparently more or less pure Sabaic, while others, though contemporary, show linguistic features perhaps indicating that they were carved by Ethiopians. The use of the South Arabian script continued on into Aksumite times ... and as late as the reigns of Kaleb and W`ZB monumental inscriptions were still written in a version of this script, but using the Ge'ez language (Munro-Hay 1991: 206).

The earliest attested monumental inscription being in Sabaean may indicate the long presupposed suggestion that the Sabaean script was brought by the Sabaean or by immigrants who spoke other Epigraphic South Arabian dialects but used Sabaean for writing purposes. On the other hand, the continuation of the Sabaean script using Ge'ez as late as the 6th century, i.e. after the long period of the attestation of vowelling and the cursive script, may indicate that the Ethiopians were using the

---

fifth century of our era. These manuscripts are known to the world as the first illustrated Christian manuscripts.

Sabaean script especially in monumental inscriptions and the Ethiopic script (with the indication of vowel) in other media. Moreover, recall that Munro-Hay suggests that the mechanics of the change from cursive script to Ethiopic script is intentional or accidental alteration and the script could have been inspired by an early importation, or a recent one. However, the brevity of the Ethiopic script and the interference of Ge'ez even in the earlier Sabaean monumental inscriptions may indicate that the change from cursive script to Ethiopic script was intentional and it was most probably inspired by an earlier importation or it could even be a native one as, among a few others, Bruce (1813) and Ayele Bekeri (1997) suggest.

It is only in Ethiopia that the cursive script was developed in order to precisely mark of vowels. This act of brevity cannot be simply explained as an accidental change. It could have been the case that the Ethiopians were aware of other writing systems. Although to the best of our knowledge no earlier indigenous inscription is found used by Ethiopians, it seems that the Ethiopians were at least familiar with the Hieroglyphic, which was used by ancient Egyptians. The 18th century English traveler James Bruce, for instance, found an inscription in Ethiopia written with Heliographic. Bruce gave a detailed description of this valuable historical document as follows:

> The reader will see, that, in my history of the civil wars in Abyssinia, the king, forced by rebellion to retire to the province of Tigre, and being at Axum, found a stone covered with hieroglyphics, which, by the many inquiries I had made after inscriptions, and some conversations I had had with him, he guessed was of the kind which I wanted. Full of that princely goodness and condescension with which he ever honoured me, throughout my whole stay, he brought it with him when he returned from Tigre and was restored to his throne at Gondar.
>
> It seems *to me* to be one of those private Tots, or of the most curious kind. The length of the whole stone is fourteen inches, and six inches a broad, upon a base three inches high, projecting from the block itself, and covered with hieroglyphics. A naked figure of a man, near *six* inches, stands upon two crocodiles, their heads turned different ways. In each of his hands he holds two serpents, and a scorpion, all by the tail, and in the right

hand hangs a noose, in which is suspended a ram *or* goat. On the left hand he holds a lion by the tail. The figure is in great relief; and the head of it has that kind of cap or ornament which is generally painted upon the head of the figure called Isis, but this figure is that of a man. On each side of the whole-length figure, and above it, upon the face of the stone where it projects, are marked a number of hieroglyphics of all kinds. Over this is a very remarkable representation; it is an old head, with very strong features, and - a large bushy beard, and upon it a high cap, ribbed or striped. This I take to be the Cnuph, or Animus-Mundi, though Apuleius, with very little probability, says, this was made in the likeness of no creature whatever. The back of the stone is divided into eight compartments*, from the top to the bottom, and these are filled with hieroglyphics in the last stage, before they took the entire resemblance of leters. Many are perfectly formed; the. *Crux* Ansata appears in one of the compartments, and Tot in another. Upon the edge, just above where *it* is broken, is 1119, so fair and perfect in form, that it *might* serve as an example of calligraphy, even in the present times; 45 and 19, and same other arithmetical figures, are found up and down among the hieroglyphics.

This I suppose was what formerly the Egyptians called a book Or almanack; a collection of which was probably *hung* up in some conspicuous place, to inform the public of the state *of* the heavens, and seasons, and diseases, to he expected in the, course of them, as is the case in the English almanacks at this day. Hermes is said to have composed 36,585 books probably of this sort; or they might contain, the correspondent astronomical observations made in a certain time at Mereoe, Ophir, Axum, or Thebes, communicated to be hung up for the use of the neighboring cities. Porphyry+ gives a particular account of the Egyptian almanacks. 'What is comprised in the Egyptian almanacks,' says he, 'contains but a small part of the Hermaic institutions; all that relates to the rising and setting of the *moon and planets, and*, and of the stare and their influence, and also some advice upon diseases.'

THE ORIGIN OF AMHARIC

> It is very remarkable, that, besides my Tot here described, there are five or six, precisely the same in all respects, already in the British Museum; one of them, the largest of the whole, is made of sycamore, the others are of metal. There is another I am told, in Lord Shelburne's collection; this I never had an opportunity of seeing; but very particular attention seems to have been paid to make all of them light and portable, and it would seem that by these having been formed so exactly similar, they were the Tots intended to be exposed in different cities or places, and were neither more or less than Egyptian almanacks (Bruce 1813: Vol. II: 332-335).

As already mentioned above, the ancient Egyptians claimed to be both relatives and descendants of the Puntites. In addition, they also conducted trade with them.[116] Although the exact location of the land of Punt is uncertain, as pointed out earlier, most recent works propose that it covered most of Ethiopia and this land had not only trade exchanges with the Egyptians but also had its very own civilization and probably ruled by kings. Although only few hieroglyphic inscriptions were found in Ethiopia, we cannot, therefore, rule out the idea of the ancient Ethiopians familiarity at least with hieroglyphics.[117]

On the other hand, as Daniels (1997: 24) among many others points out "the Ethiopic script was ... the first Semitic script to notate vowels consistently, and it does so in a way unique within the Semitic sphere" (Daniels 1997: 24). Moreover, as pointed out above, Ethiopic script might not be developed out of the South Arabian monumental inscriptions. However, this does not mean that Ethiopic script does not have any relation to the Sabaean script. This is not only because the cursive script was found both in Ethiopia and South Arabia but also it is because both scripts can be traced back to a single source.

> It [Ge'ez] was written in characters descending from the same parentage as the script now called Epigraphic South Arabian, but more cursive in form; the modern

---

[116] The trade between the Egyptians and Ethiopians goes even back to pre-dynastic period. For instance, pre-dynastic Egyptian used to bring Obsidian from Ethiopia.

[117] Bedside the above remark Bruce strongly asserts this assumption (See Bruce for more, in the 1813 edition, Vol II: Chapter III).

Ethiopian alphabet is the only survivor of this script today. Its development required that certain letters employed in dialects of South Arabian were omitted and others added as necessary. A number of early texts and graffiti from Ethiopia are themselves in a cursive form of the old South Arabian script (Munro-Hay 1991: 206).

Consider these two scripts below where the Ge'ez script is given with its first order, which is also assumed to be its ancient unvoweled form:

THE ORIGIN OF AMHARIC

Table 7: South Arabian and Ge'ez scripts

South Arbian	Ge'ez
Y	ሀ
ገ	ለ
Ψ	ሐ
⅋	መ
⸸	ቀ
⊙	ወ
⸲	ሠ
⸱	ረ
⊓	ሰ
✕	ተ
⸲	ስ
⸲	ከ
५	ነ
⸲	ኘ
⸲	ጸ
⸲	
◆	ፈ
⸲	አ
○	ዐ
⊟	ፀ
⸲	ገ
⸲	ደ
⸲	
⊡	ጠ
⸲	ሐ
⸲	
⸲	የ
⸲	
⸲	
	ጸ
	ፐ

As can be seen above, the Ge'ez script has 26 basic characters where two of them, i.e. symbols for /p/ and for /p'/ indicated in the last lines, are unique to it. The Sabaean script, on the other hand, has 29 characters.

Although there are some differences between the two scripts it is clear that both are related.[118] These scripts are closer to each other than any of them has to the other Semitic scripts.[119]

I have pointed out that the Ethiopians most probably were aware of other writing systems (for instance, hieroglyphics) before the arrival of the Sabaean script. I have also pointed out that although both the Ge'ez and Sabaean scripts can be assumed as developed from a single source, the former may not be the source for the latter. Although many recent works do not agree with the idea, for James Bruce and a few others the Ethiopic script is considered to be the first alphabetical script of the world out of which the Hebrew for instance developed. Bruce has some interesting arguments for this claim (see the appendix).

On the other hand, whether it was the Sabaean immigrants who introduced literacy to Ethiopia or whether they only brought their own script and introduced it to the already literate society, the undeniable fact is that at the time of the suggested Sabaean migration, the language Ge'ez existed in Ethiopia as it can be inferred from even the earliest Sabaean inscriptions which are supposed to have been written when the Sabaean reached Ethiopia: "The earliest inscriptional fragments appear to be in Sabaean, but a closer perusal suggests an amalgam, with features that can derive only from Ge'ez, a local Semitic language" (Marcus 2002: 4). Drewes (1980) also points out this fact as follows:

> The language of the Sabaean inscriptions from Ethiopia is distinguished from South Arabian Sabaean ... by a number of features which are undoubtedly due to the interference of the local language or languages. Certainly, these features are not shared by all inscriptions. In some they are significantly absent and these texts - all written in monumental South Arabian and dating from the V and the IV century B.C., according to Pirenne's Paléograohie - can be ascribed to immigrant Sabaeans. But the majority of the Sabaean inscriptions from Ethiopia must be attributed to Ethiopians, who used 'Sabaean as a written language only (Drewes 1980: 35).

---

[118] The Sabaean, i.e. Old South Arabian, script is considered a branch of Proto-Sinaitic alphabet.
[119] For discussion on the various Semitic scripts, see Daniels (1997).

In sum, although the South Arabians might have brought their writing system at the suggested period, i.e. either around 5th century BCE or much earlier, the first Ethiopic script is not a development of the monumental South Arabian script. Second, it may not be the case that the Sabaeans introduced literacy to Ethiopia. Third, and last, it is logical to conclude that Ge'ez and other Semitic languages in Ethiopia existed before the first attestation of Sabaean inscriptions.

5.5.4.4 Summary

The attribution of the Ethiopian Semitic languages and the earlier Axumite civilization to the South Arabian immigrants has been questioned increasingly in recent works. Levine (1974) writes that,[120]

> [Semitic] groups of immigrants have hitherto been thought of as constituting the core population of northeastern Ethiopia in antiquity and have been credited with introducing into Ethiopia a cultural complex that included Semitic language, the art of writing, architectural technology, the practice of irrigation and Sabaean religious and political symbolism. Since, however, there is no clear evidence that any of these cultural traits appeared in South Arabia earlier than on the Ethiopian plateau, and since ... Semitic language now appears to have been spoken in Ethiopia as early as 2000 B.C., that conception deserves to be modified (Levine 1974: 31).

Messay Kebede (2003) in a recent paper goes further and challenges the entire notion of deriving every aspect of Ethiopian civilization from South Arabian immigrants. Messay Kebede on this point states the following:

> South Arabia did not have a superior civilization to the native Ethiopians. Such things as state formation, class stratification, advanced agricultural techniques, written language, grandiose architectural designs were already present in Ethiopia, better still, were unknown on the Arabian side of the Red Sea (Messay Kebede 2003: 16).

Indeed, the challenge to the migration hypothesis has already been made

---

[120] Levine's (1974) work, called "Greater Ethiopia", was translated into Amharic in 2002 and is available now for the wider Ethiopian public.

by a number of recent studies. Munro-Hay points out that "there were undoubtedly some South Arabian immigrants in Ethiopia in the mid-first millennium BC, but there is ... no sure indication that they were politically dominant" (Munro-Hay 1991: 63). It is worth quoting Munro-Hay here further:

> Evidently the arrival of Sabaean influences does not represent the beginning of Ethiopian civilization. For a long time different peoples had been interacting through population movements, warfare, trade and intermarriage in the Ethiopian region, resulting in a predominance of peoples speaking languages of the Afro-Asiatic family. ... [The Ethio-Semitic speaking] and other groups had already developed specific cultural and linguistic identities by the time any Sabaean influences arrived (Munro-Hay: 1991: 57).

Messay Kebede notes that "whatever resemblances one finds between Aksum and South Arabia, they are the products, not of South Arabians colonizing the native peoples of Ethiopia, but coming to Ethiopia in search of better opportunities" (2003: 17).[121] This seems indeed the standard assumption also among most historians including those who propagate the Ethiopian Semitic group as immigrant. Consider, for instance, Sergew (1972), whose book is undoubtedly one of the seminal works that brought together a number of historical documents on the history of ancient Ethiopia up to the Zague dynasty:

> For demographic and economic reasons, the people of South Arabia started to migrate to Ethiopia. It is hard to fix the date of these migrations, but it can be said that the first immigration took place before 1,000 B.C.
>
> Most probably the forerunners of the migration were merchants of the Sabaean kingdom. After they had

---

[121] "The assumption makes sense in view of the rise of Aksum to great prosperity and influence. Some such opportunity can attract immigrants from the other side of the Red Sea, who then brought their gods and wherever they settled left their names and inscription... Moreover, the assumption that these resemblances are due to Ethiopian influences cannot be discarded when the absence of historical documents attesting to the political and military domination of South Arabians is contrasted with the availability of evidence showing that 'South Arabia was under actual Ethiopian domination several times during its history'" (Messay Kebede 2003: 17).

> studied the climate as well as the economic conditions of Ethiopia, these people advised their countrymen to emigrate. Of course the process was long and gradual and the motive was utilitarian and political in character. The idea was to settle and live peacefully in the "new world" which had been discovered by merchants (Sergew 1972: 26).

Given the fact that the civilization in South Arabia was inferior to the one flourishing in Axum, and that the Axumites were ruling over South Arabians several times (which last for centuries) but not on the contrary, and given the proximity of Egypt and the civilization at Meroe to Axum/Ethiopia, the assumption that the Axumite civilization or its predecessor had a South Arabian origin brought by immigrant people does not make sense at all.[122] Although questioning the migration hypothesis increased recently, there are earlier writers who rejected such idea. As a matter of concluding this section, it is worth to quote Henry Salt from the 19th century who looked for a corroborative account in South Arabian lore and questioned the Ethiopian Semitic group as descendants of South Arabian immigrants.

> The Abyssinians, or the Axomites (as they were called by the Romans) are descended from a race of the aboriginal inhabitants of Africa, composed of native Ethiopians who became in the course of time mixed with settlers from Egypt, and that they do not exhibit any claims to an Arabian descent... The history of the Abyssinians, their buildings, written character, dress, and the description of them given in the earliest Arabian and Byzantine writers, all tend to prove them a distinct race from the Arabs (Salt in Hailu Habtu 1984: 6-7).

Indeed, as Hailu Habtu (1984: 7) points out, "one of the pillars of the theory of the Semitic/Sabaean origin of Axumite civilization is presumably the introduction of Semitic languages by the South Arabian settlers in the first millennium B.C." which can no more proved from the linguistics side as we have seen in the preceding sections.[123]

---

[122] Meroe was destroyed later by the Axumites.
[123] However, some still insist that the modern Semitic languages of Ethiopia are descended from Ge'ez and Ge'ez is the result of South Arabian immigrants. See for instance, Voigt (2005).

5.6 An Outline of the Origin and Diffusion of Ethio-Semitic

In the preceding section, I have suggested that ES cannot originate out of South Arabian immigrants in the first millennium BCE for a number of reasons. I have also pointed out that most recent works suggest Afroasiatic as having originated in Africa. Although most authors place the birthplace of Afroasiatic in southern Ethiopia, not all suggest this to be the case. The same is true with Semitic birthplace. While some consider it to be central Ethiopia where the present Gurage languages are spoken, some suggest the northern part of Ethiopia. Still some others suggest northeastern Africa somewhere in Egypt and there are as well other suggestions. These different suggestions with regard to the birthplace of Semitic and Afroasiatic mostly emanate from the treatment of the internal classification of the Afroasiatic phylum. For instance, Bender (1997) classifies the Afroasiatic phylum as follows:

Figure 7: Bender classification of Afroasiatic

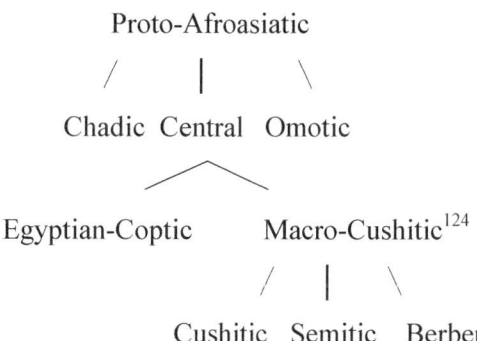

According to Bender, the "original location of *Afrasian language was in the area of the Blue-White Nile confluence (modern-day Khartoum)". Bender suggests that around 10,000 BP an "explosion" moved Chadic to the west, Omotic to the east, and a bit later Egyptian to the north, leaving Macro-Cushitic behind (Bender 1997 as summarized in Bender 2003: 26). According to Bender, around 8,000-7,000 BP a second "explosion" had moved Berber to the northwest and Cushitic and Semitic to the east into Ethiopia (Ibid.). The following map is from Bernal (2006) who represented Bender's diffusion of Afroasiatic:

---

[124] According to Bender (1997), see also Bender (2003: 29), Macro-Cushitic would have six or seven branches namely Berber, Semitic, Beja, Agew, Highland East Cushitic, Lowland East/South Cushitic and with the possibility of including Indo-European.

Map 5: The diffusion of Afroasiatic languages according to Bender

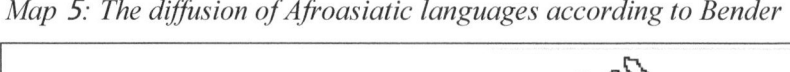

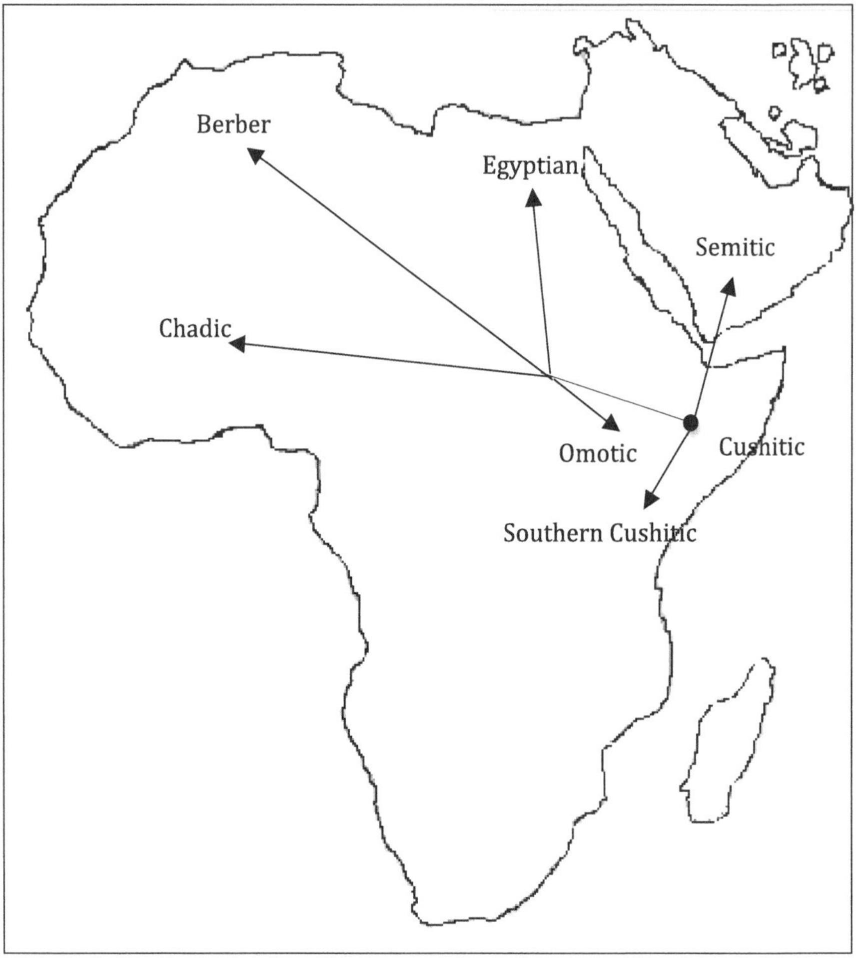

Unlike Bender, some others, such as Blench (2006), Bernal (2006) and Ehret (1995) suggest the homeland of Afroasiatic languages to be the southern part of Ethiopia. Blench adopted Ehret's (1995) internal classification with some modification. Based on that, Blench suggested that "Proto-Afroasiatic must have been spoken in Ethiopia, in approximately the same area where Omotic is spoken today. Omotic is highly internally diversified, and there is no hint that Omotic speakers have ever been located elsewhere than their present homeland" (Blench

2006: 150).[125]

Map 6: The diffusion of Afroasiatic languages according to Blench (2006)

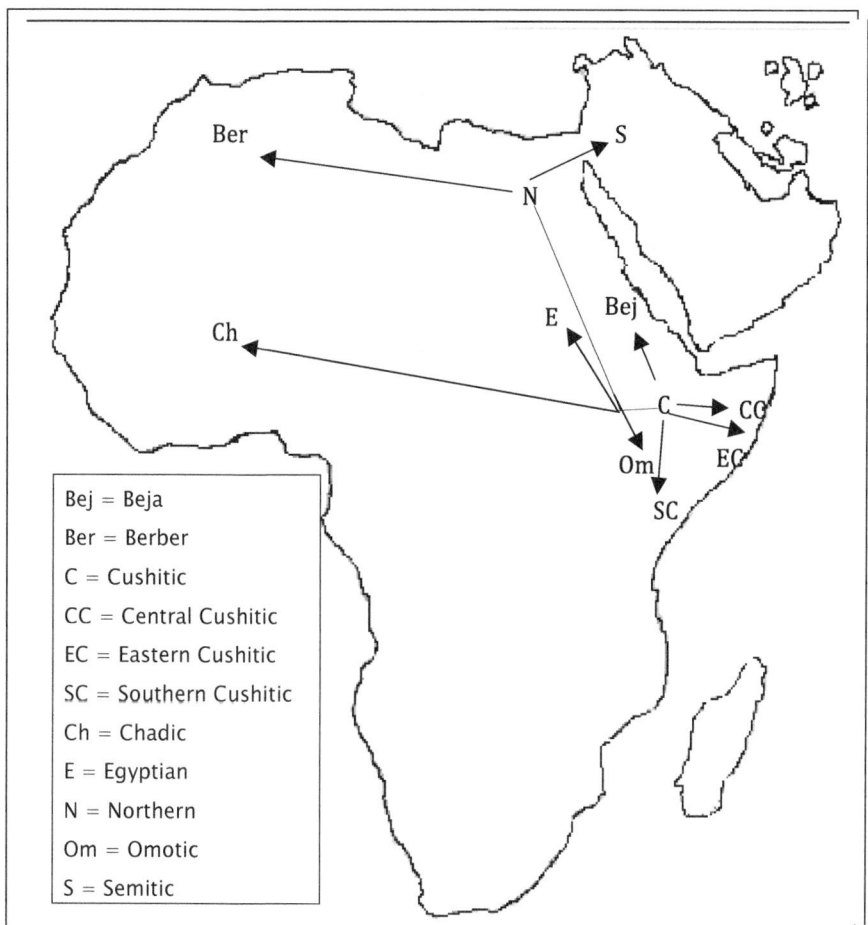

Most linguists, who suggest either Southwest Ethiopia or Khartoum for the origin of Afroasiatic, claim that the Semitic languages must have originated in Ethiopia probably in the place where most South Ethio-Semitic languages are spoken today. Some however suggest that the Semitic family might originate either in the northern part of Ethiopia or

---

[125] See Blench (2006: 150ff.) for the details of his proposal of the dispersal of the various families of Afroasiatic with chronology.

in the south Arabian on the other side of the Red Sea. For instance, Bernal proposes both alternatives at different times.

> In 1980 I maintained that Semitic had emerged in the region where South Ethiopic Semitic is spoken today. I am less certain of that today. I now think it more likely that Semitic originated either in the Ethiopian province of Tigre or the present Eritrea or in Yemen and the Hadramawt, where many different Semitic languages have been spoken in the past and, in the east of the region, still are today (Bernal 2006: 82).

With this later assumption, Bernal points out as follows:

> I believe that Semitic spread both south and north, south to its present range in Ethiopia. The great diversity of South Ethiopic Semitic languages indicates that this process must have been long before the convention date of the First Millennium BCE. Semitic also expanded north through what is now the Arabian desert, but which in the Tenth or Ninth Millennia BCE was savanna. Semitic speakers then went on into the Levant where their material culture appears to have merged with the new southwest Asian agricultural societies into the pre-pottery Neolithic Natufian (Bernal 2006: 82-83).

Although Bernal suggests two different alternatives, he remarks also that both options are within the realm of speculation and cannot be securely established (Bernal 2006: 82). Whatever one suggests, the ancient presence of Ethio-Semitic on African soil now becomes an undeniable fact. ES could not have been brought by South Arabian immigrants by the mid first millennium BCE. In this section, I outline the diffusion of the Ethio-Semitic languages.

As discussed above, the Semitic family and the Afroasiatic phylum in general are assumed to have originated in Ethiopia, if not in Africa. It is suggested more convincingly that the Ethio-Semitic languages are spoken in their home of origin. Hudson, who consistently propagates the indigenousness of ES on the Ethiopian soil, recently suggests for its diffusion as follows:

> Assuming an Ethiopian or Northeast African home for Semitic's Afroasiatic source language, and such homeland as well for Semitic itself ..., we can as easily begin our historical interpretation in Central Ethiopia,

and proceed from there, thus. The Semitic Proto-language arose in Ethiopia. After groups of these Semitic speakers separated and moved into South Arabia and beyond, the Ethiopian Semites separated into northern and Southern groups (Hudson 2000: 79).

As we will see in a moment, I am inclined to believe along with Hudson that ES separated in the central part of Ethiopia where the present Gurage languages are spoken. However, for the reason discussed in the preceding sections and chapters, I assume that the separation between NES and SES happened during an earlier time, probably at the time of proto-Semitic.

As pointed out in chapter three, Ethio-Semitic languages are divided into northern and southern groups. Although this grouping is geographical, the division has strong linguistic support (See, for instance, Hetzron 1972). The North Ethio-Semitic languages are mainly spoken in the northern part of Ethiopia (and the present Eritrea). The South Ethio-Semitic languages at present are spoken in the southern and central parts of Ethiopia. It is plausible to assume that the North Ethio-Semitic languages diverged from their parent Proto-North ES somewhere in the north, Tigray or Eritrea. In the same way, it seems plausible to assume that South ES diverged somewhere in the south, most probably in the Gurage area since most of the South ES languages are spoken in the south, especially in the Gurage Zone,.

If the above suggestion is the case, there are at least three possibilities for the origin of Proto-ES, i.e. the parent of Proto-South and Proto-North. One possibility is that Proto-ES originated either in the south or north. If we assume north, it means that Proto-South moved to the south after separating from its parent language in the north.[126] Conversely, if we assume the latter, NES must have moved to the north, after being separated from its parent in the south. The other possibility is that Proto-ES originated in the central part of the country (or any other place) and then one group moved to the north and became the parent of NES. Similarly, the other group moved to the south and became the parent of SES.[127] With this assumption, it could be the case that one group remained in the place where Proto-ES was but later ceased to be spoken as we have no evidence of such separate language group. However, it is more plausible to pursue the third assumption that Proto-ES developed in

---

[126] This is in line with Bernal (2006).
[127] This can happen after both developing their own distinct features.

the South, most probably around the present Gurage land. This is for the following reasons:

First, among the 16 or so Semitic languages found in Ethiopia, only three of them are found in the north. Most SES languages that are rich in diversity are found in the Gurage Zone.[128]

> It is quite surprising that in a compact territory, with no serious geographical obstacles preventing contact between neighboring tribes, a group of so closely related languages exhibits so much surface differentiation. There is now a great deal of contact between the tribes, so that no isolationism may explain it, unless the present situation is a later development, and there used to be more clannish separatism in the past (Hetzron 1977: 6).

Second, when we consider the date of origin, SES (Proto-SES) could be considered as a "grandfather" to NES. As I have pointed out in the preceding chapter, Proto-NES may not be older than 3000 years. However, Proto-SES dates back 4000 to 5000 years.[129]

---

[128] As diversity indicates origin, the least-moves principle favors south.
[129] Note that the separation between NES and SES must have taken place before 3000 years.

Map 7: The birthplace of ES and its two branches

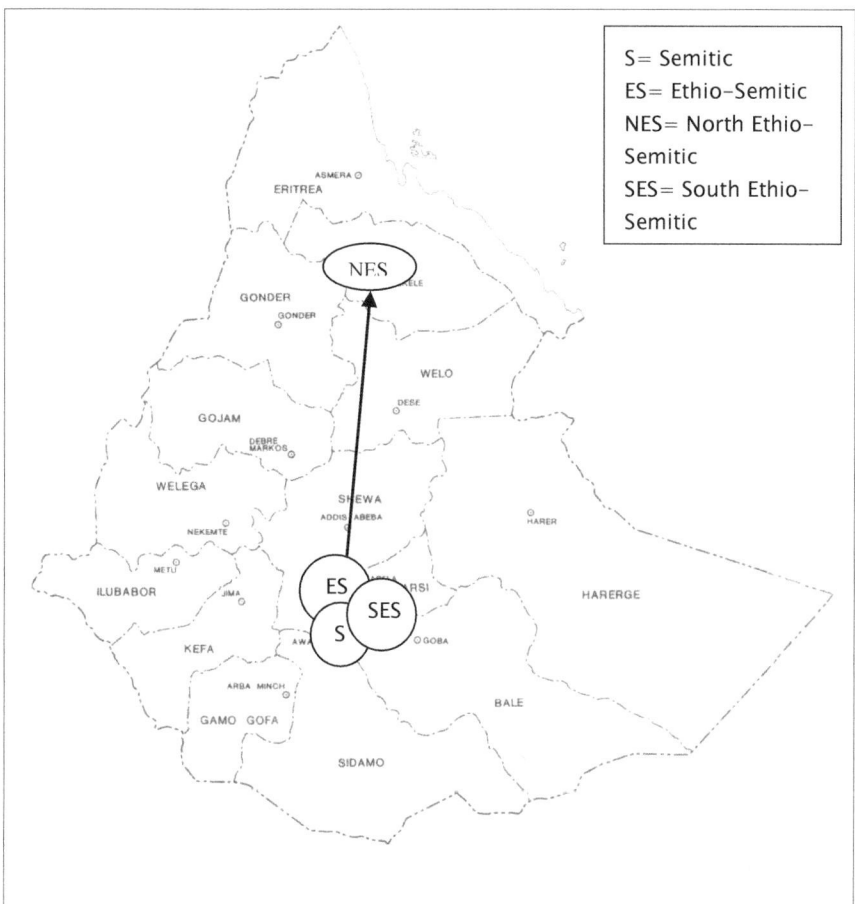

As previously mentioned, North ES is the least diversified and contains only three languages namely Ge'ez, Tigre and Tigrinya. As we have seen in Chapter three, South ES are divided into Transversal and Outer. The Outer SES is the largest group containing †Gafat and the North Gurage languages, i.e. Soddo, Gogot and Mäsqan, and the Western Gurage languages; Muher, and the three tense group Ezha, Chaha, Gumer, Gura, Ennemor (from the Central Western Gurage) and Geyto, Endegeñ, Ener, †Mesmes (from Peripheral Western Gurage). Except Gafat, which is extinct, all are exclusively spoken in the south, particularly in the present Gurage Zone. Hence, we can assume that the Proto-Outer SES place of origin is like that of its parent Proto-SES in the south. It can, in fact, be considered a direct descendant/ survival of Proto-SES that resides in its place of origin. It is also plausible to assume that Transversal SES originated in the south since most of these languages are spoken there.

Map 8: The diffusion of ES

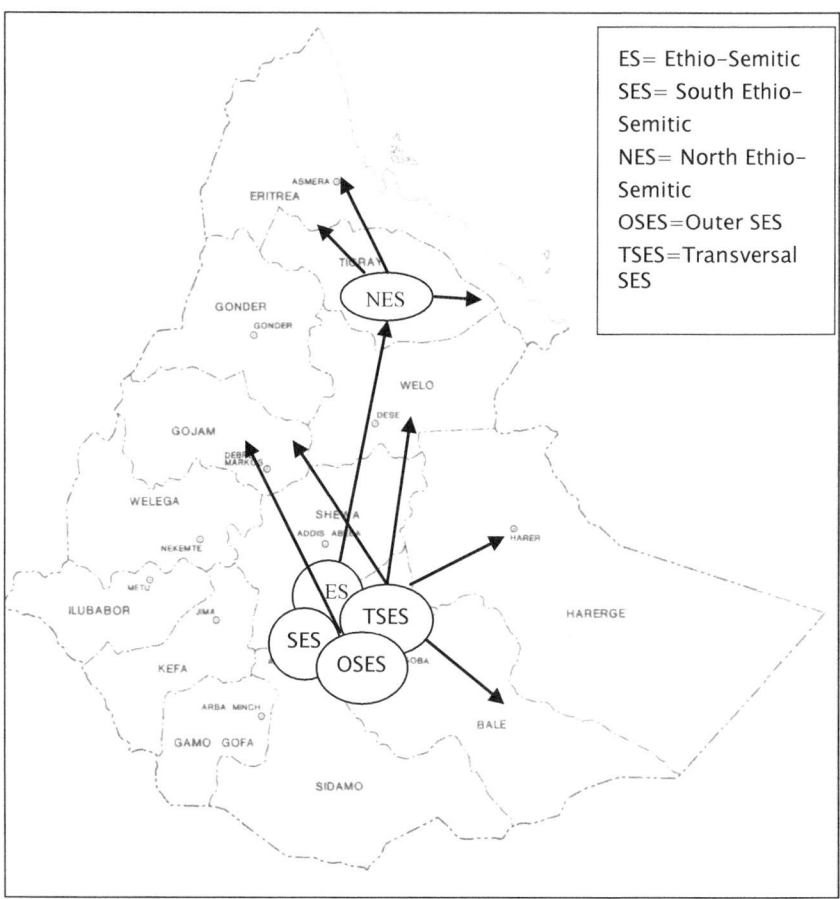

The only arrow in the above map stretched from OSES to Gojjam is to indicate Gafat, an extinct and only known language spoken outside the Gurage Zone.[130] The Transversal SES languages distribution is, in fact, not the same with Outer SES (see also the following chapter).

5.7 Summary

The migration hypothesis was built not purely on linguistic evidence but

---

[130] In fact, the now extinct Mesmes, a Peripheral Western Gurage speech variety, was spoken outside the present Gurage Zone but in nearby areas.

also with distorted historical assumptions. As we have seen in section 5.3.1, in earlier works, it is suggested that the South Arabian immigrant people brought their civilization: introduced agriculture, the art of writing and stone masonry. It is also suggested that these immigrant people were the ones who founded the Axumite kingdom. However, although there was undoubtedly cultural contact between the two sides of the Red Sea, this suggestion is found to be mere speculation. Although, as Irvine (1978: 43) remarks, examining this issue is the problem of historians rather than linguists, a birds-eye-view examination in section 5.3.2 shows that the Axumite civilization is an indigenous one and agriculture was known to Ethiopians well before the supposed migration date. There is a lack of seriously convincing historical evidence that satisfactorily proves ES was brought by South Arabian immigrants. Hetzron (1972) did an impressive work on the classification of ES and the Semitic languages in general based on shared morphological innovations. Yet, as Hudson (2000) interestingly observes, Hetzron pursued a "South Arabian source for ES, which he adopted from historians and archeologists - who, nevertheless, may now refer to Hetzron for linguistic support of their own claims" (Hudson 2000: 78). This observation of Hudson indeed reflects the general truth.

As Hetzron (1977) and Ullendorff (1965) also point out, it is only until very recently that ES received the full attention of general Semitists.

> In the universities, and in academic study generally, the Ethiopian languages have almost invariably been approached from the *ensemble* of Semitics. True, some of the modern tongues have been notably, others even profoundly, influenced by their Cushitic (i.e. Hamitic-Ethiopian) substrata, but none has yet lost its essentially Semitic character, its original identity. The Ethiopian languages constitute an important link in the chain of the Semitic tongues. They often produce evidence and corroboration where these have been lost in the other languages (Ullendorff 1965: 4).

Consider also Hetzron:

> The Ethiopian branch of Semitic has often been treated as a stepchild of general Semitics. Treatises of comparative Semitic have been making some mention of Ge'ez, but very little of the modern languages. This branch has been, overtly or by implication, represented

> as a deformed, even degenerate outgrowth of Semitic, of anecdotal interest. Yet on the one hand, it should be recognized that Ethiopian Semitic has given less of some of the "typical" traditional Semitic features than, say, Modern East Aramaic (Modern Syriac). ... On the other hand, more importantly, the modern Semitic languages of Ethiopia have been shown to provide new evidence and insights for a reconstruction of Proto-Semitic.... One may state without hesitation that Ethiopian constitutes a well-integrated branch of Semitic, interesting both by its original developments and by the archaisms it has preserved (Hetzron 1977: 9).

The status of ES as a Semitic language was controversial especially in earlier literature, mostly due to both the influence of neighboring languages and the archaic features they preserved. In fact, the treatment of ES as a Semitic language was not very attractive, especially in earlier literature. Questioning the Asian origin brought strong condemnation from Semitists.

> Questioning the Near Eastern origin of Afroasiatic is almost a taboo subject among scholars with a Semitic or Egyptological background. But, researchers based in the more diverse African branches concluded long ago that its most likely homeland was in sub-Saharan Africa, more specifically in southwest Ethiopia, the present location of its most fragmented branch, Omotic, and the "center of gravity of Cushitic (Blench 2006: 150).

In this chapter, I have examined and rejected the migration hypothesis, in general, for the following basic reasons:

- Linguistic facts, i.e. grammatical features and lexicon;
- Date of origin, i.e. chronological issues;
- Diversity of languages and least-move principle; and
- Historical and cultural facts

The examination on linguistic features in this work and in other recent linguistic researches favors that not only Ethio-Semitic but also Proto-Semitic and its ancestral language Afroasiatic originated in Africa, if not in Ethiopia. It seems that the non-Ethio-Semitic languages moved from Ethiopia to Asia and the other Afroasiatic language families, i.e. Berber, Chadic and Old Egyptian to northern Africa.

As far as linguistics is concerned, the migration hypothesis for ES, which is a base for the pidgin origin hypothesis, is not an acceptable theory. Accordingly, neither from the linguistic nor from the historical points of view, does the pidgin theory for the origin of Amharic make sense. Instead, a convincing hypothesis will assume Amharic descended linearly from a South-Ethio-Semitic language but not a pidgin. This is not a new suggestion: "Judging from the Amharic spoken today, it is clearly an Ethio-Semitic language and could have developed out of the proposed proto-Ethio-Semitic" (Meyer 2006: 117). Amsalu (1976 EC) and Appleyard (2003) among others also advocate for a similar hypothesis. However, as pointed out in the introductory chapter of this work, none of these works has taken the subject seriously and elaborated their points. They are merely suggestions and not fully worked out assertions. In the following chapter, I pursue this hypothesis, i.e. non-pidgin origin hypothesis, and outline not only the origin of Amharic but also its spread in detail, especially during its early years.

Chapter Six: An Outline of the Origin of Amharic

6.1 Introduction

In chapter 4, I examined the widely propagated pidgin hypothesis, concerning the origin of Amharic and argued that the hypothesis was not convincing. The evidence presented in support of it shows on the contrary that Amharic most probably originated as non-pidgin. Moreover, I have argued that Amharic or Proto-Central SES, i.e. Proto-Amharic-Argobba, could not have been developed around the Bashilo River in the place known as Amhara.[131] If this assumption is true, then questions regarding where and when pre-Amharic developed, and how it spread, especially early on needs explanation. In this chapter, therefore, I first outline in section 6.2 where and when Amharic along with its parent language, i.e. Proto-Central SES, originated. In section 6.3 I discuss the expansion of primarily the Proto-Central group. In section 6.4, I discuss a few points on the usage of the term Amhara in reference to an ethnic group.

6.2 Place of Origin of Amharic/Proto-Amharic-Argobba

According to Appleyard (2003: 233) "it is difficult to be precise about the origin of Amharic, arising as it must have done during the centuries preceding the 13th centuries and in a region on the southern fringes of the old Aksumite heartlands". Appleyard specifically suggested as follows: "The original home of Amharic is obviously to be found in the lands

---

[131] We will not repeat the arguments for this claim here.

covered by the name Amhara, a somewhat flexible term in its application at different periods, but the earliest occurrences of the name refer to the area east of Abbay between the Bashilo and Weleqa rivers" (Ibid.). Meyer (2006), like Appleyard (2003), claims that Amharic's origin is somewhere in the lands covered by the name Amhara around the Bashilo River. Meyer's and Appleyard's suggestion is similar with Bender's (1983). For Appleyard (2003: 233), this suggestion is for the following reasons:

> The fact that Amharic's closest relatives are now spread in isolated pockets from Harar in the east to Zay in the south (Argobba and the remaining East Gurage languages Silte, Inneqor, Wollane) further suggests that these represent the fragments of what was likely to have been a more continuous band of closely related Semitic languages and dialects before the ethnic upheavals following the incursions of the Oromo in the 16th century.

It may be the case that Amharic got its name from the place known as Amhara, as Appleyard (2003), Bender (1983), Levine (2003) and many others have suggested. However, as discussed in chapter four, it is difficult to assume that pre-Amharic or Proto-Amharic-Argobba originated in the Amhara province in north-central Ethiopia. It seems a fact as Appleyard and many others suggest that the lands from Harar in the east to Zay in the south and to Wällo in northeast and further north to Shoa and beyond might have been occupied by closely related Semitic languages and dialects (most probably by the TSES varieties) before the Oromo expansion in the 16th century. However, this cannot be considered strong evidence for the claim that Amharic originated in the Amhara province. It may rather indicate that it originated further south.

In the preceding chapter, I suggested that Transversal SES originated in the south most probably in the present Gurage Zone like that of its parent Proto-SES and its sister Proto-Outer SES. As mentioned earlier, this group is composed of Central and Southern Transversal SES. The former contains Amharic and Argobba whereas the latter Harari, Zay, Wolane, and Silte (with its varieties). In the Southern Transversal Group, except Harari, all are found not far from the place where most of the Outer SES languages are spoken. The Central group contains the most widely spoken language. Its people lived and still lives in a wide area stretching from Bale in the south to Eritrea in the north and to Harar and Afar regions in the east (refer to my discussion of the Argobba settlement in chapter 4). It seems very likely, therefore, that the Southern Transversal group was developed in the same place as its parent Transversal South Ethio-Semitic. It is plausible to suggest that it is after developing its own feature that part of Transversal South Ethio-Semitic speakers moved further east giving rise to Harari and further south giving rise to Zay whereas the remaining group stayed at home, and giving rise to the speech varieties that we know today as Silte, Wolane, Inneqor etc.

Before part of the Southern Transversal language speakers, i.e. Harari and Zay, moved to the east and south respectively, the Central presumably diverged and moved to the northeast.[132] This means that the Central TSES, i.e. Proto-Amharic-Argobba, originated somewhere in the south, probably a little further northeast to its parent South ES. This place could be somewhere in Yifat, probably around Gedem. The point here is whether this assumption can be supported by other facts? Indeed, it can. First, this assumption makes a lot of sense when we examine the settlement of Argobba (cf. chapter four). I assume that Argobba is a direct survival of Central SES, as it preserved more archaic features than Amharic. In terms of ethno-genesis, "Gedem Goze is often claimed by the Argobba as one of their original homelands" (Abebe 1992: 84).[133] On the other hand, "Mänz is considered one of the core Amhara areas. It is traditionally seen by the Amhara as the place of their (የአማራ ምንጭ *yä'amara minč'*)" (Reminick and Sokolinskara 2007: 753). Gedem is neighboring one of the districts of Mänz in the east. Hence, both the Amhara, at least those of the central Amhara people, and the Argobba oral traditions trace their origin to almost the same place.

I schematize the diffusion of TSES discussed above as follows:

---

[132] One group from TSES may have even moved further east to Harar/Dire Dawa at the same time or before the two, CTSES and STSES, diverged and gave rise to the people that we know in history as Harla. Although we have some information about this people, we do not know much about their language, in fact. However, it is most likely the case that the Harla were another group of TSES, but see Banti (2005).

[133] See also among others Ahmed (1999 E.C.) and Fauvelle-Aymar and Hirsch (2011) and the reference cited there.

Map 9: The diffusion of TSES[134]

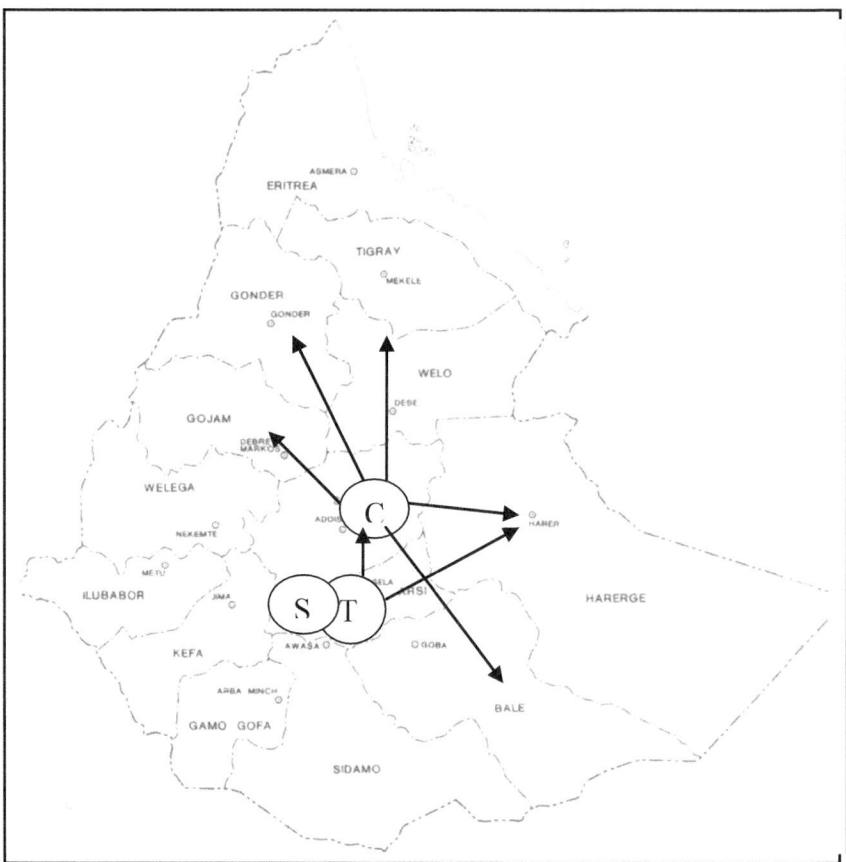

Now back to our crucial point, where and when did Amharic diverge from Argobba? In other words where did Amharic develop its own feature?

As mentioned above, according to Hetzron (1972) and some others, Amharic and Argobba became distinct around the 10th or 11th century A.D. However, as recalled from our discussion in chapter four, during the war in the early medieval period between the Christian kingdom and the Muslim Sultanate, i.e. the Yifat Sultanate, the 14th century Arab historian Al 'Umari reported that both were speaking the same language. If this is true, then, the two must have become distinct at a later date.

---

[134] S = South Ethio-Semitic (SES), T = Transversal SES, C = Central Transversal SES (see for further abbreviations Appendix I).

When we consider the minimal difference of these languages, it seems that they were mutually intelligible till three to four centuries ago.

On the other hand, we know from history that the Argobba adopted the Islamic religion at least in the 9th century, while the "Amhara" in the north adopted Christianity much earlier time.[135] Although this appears to be the fact, the two were in contact besides having different religions. The question is where did Amharic diverge from Argobba, i.e. at which particular place did Amharic develop its own feature? Moreover, is it possible at all to attribute a particular place of origin for Amharic independent from Argobba?

I suggest that Amharic and Argobba became distinct languages not because of geographical differences but because of religious differences. Accordingly, Amharic's place of origin cannot be different than that of Proto-Central, i.e. the parent of Argobba and Amharic's place of origin. Note that during the early medieval period, the Mänz were Muslims and fought against Amdä Seyon (1314-1344) (Pankhurst 1997, Reminick and Sokolinskara 2007). It is later that the Mänz became Christians.

On the other hand, those who resisted the acceptance of Christianity and remained Muslims alienated themselves from their Christian neighbors not only in terms of religion but also in terms of language as the speech variety that they spoke developed on its own and became a distinct language known as Argobba. This also shows once again that Amharic and Argobba developed as distinct speech varieties not due to geography but religion.

6.3 The Spread of Amharic

The spread and expansion of Amharic can better be captured taking the 13th century as a dividing point.[136] The spread of Amharic before the 13th century is not much known. On the other hand, though much has been written about the later period, it is out of the scope of this monograph to go into details about this period. Hence, my discussion of this period is

---

[135] This took place probably since the adaptation of Christianity as a state religion in the 4th century. In a number of ancient documents, places in Gonder, particularly Semen Mountains, Gojjam and Wollo were mentioned as part of the Axumite Empire. See for instance Cosmas's Christian Topography of the six century.

[136] Although there is no consensus when Amharic became a language of administration, i.e. whether it was during Lalibela (1140-1180) or later during Yikuno Amlak (1270-1285), it is generally believed that Amharic's golden time came starting with the reign of the latter in the thirteenth century.

restricted to a minimum. For a more elaborate discussion of this late period see, among some others, Cooper (1976) and Amsalu Akilu (1976 EC.).

6.3.1 The Expansion of Amharic before the 13th Century

In the above section, I have suggested that Proto-Central SES developed its own feature in the central part of Ethiopia probably around Gedem, and that Amharic and Argobba became distinct languages later than the "Amhara kings" took power from the Zague dynasty. I have also pointed out above that Amharic or a pre-Amharic like language was in existence in the north during the Axumite period. As the settlements of Argobba and Amhara reveal, it seems plausible to assume that Proto-Central SES, after developing its own feature, moved to the east as far as Harar and to the south as far as Bale and to the north as far as Eritrea. The movement of this people can be assumed to be an expansion in a way similar to the Oromo expansion that happened later in the 16th century. I elaborate this expansion a little more.

After Proto-Amharic-Argobba developed its own feature somewhere in the Central Shoa, one group might have moved to the eastern and central parts of Ethiopia occupying the lowland areas of Shoa and Wällo. The group that moved to eastern Shoa might be the one that continued to move eastwards to Harar via the Great Rift Valley. Pockets of Argobba settlements still exist all the way to Harar; for instance in Mätähara, Awash, Asäbot and Korämi.

> As a result of the connection between the Argobba and Wälashma and the fortunes of the Muslim sultanates which developed in north-eastern Shoa between 1270-1415, there is evidence indicating that the present Argobba of Shoa and Wällo are remnant population of the sultanate of Ifat (Abebe 2003: 333).

This does not mean, however, that the group that moved to Wällo and Harar migrated in the 13th century although some suggest this to be the case (see for instance Taddese 1992 for the suggestion of late Argobba migration to Harar).

> The oral traditions of the group "Southern Argobba" (Harar region) refer their origin to a migration which would have taken place from Ifat and the southern part of Wallo. The "Western Argobba" of Ifat and southern Wallo … refer their origins … to the installation of Arab settlers who would have seemingly migrated to Ethiopia either

during the time of the Prophet, or during the time of the exile of the Umayyad family in the 8th century A.D. (Fauvelle-Aymar and Hirsch 2011: 37).

The Makzumite family which migrated from Arabia is believed to have established the first Muslim sultanate in Shoa around the 9th century (see among many others, Ahmed 1999 EC and Abebe 1992). Although the Argobba popular oral tradition claims the involvement of Arabic in the development of the Argobba language, there is no linguistic proof that indicates such pidgin-induced past. As discussed in chapters three and four, Argobba is closely related to Amharic and both descended from the same Proto-language which itself was a descendant of South Ethio-Semitic. Although this is the case, the oral tradition mentioned above may also be considered as an indication of the expansion of the Argobba group eastwards at an earlier date. As Argobba did not linguistically originate from Arabic, the expansion of the Argobba to different places might have taken place even before the 13th century. As can be recalled from the discussion in chapter four, the linguistic divergence between Argobba and Amharic took place at a much later date. Hence, such expansion could be regarded as the expansion of the pre-Amharic-Argobba linguistic group.

THE ORIGIN OF AMHARIC

Map 10: The spread of Proto-Amharic-Argobba before the 13th century

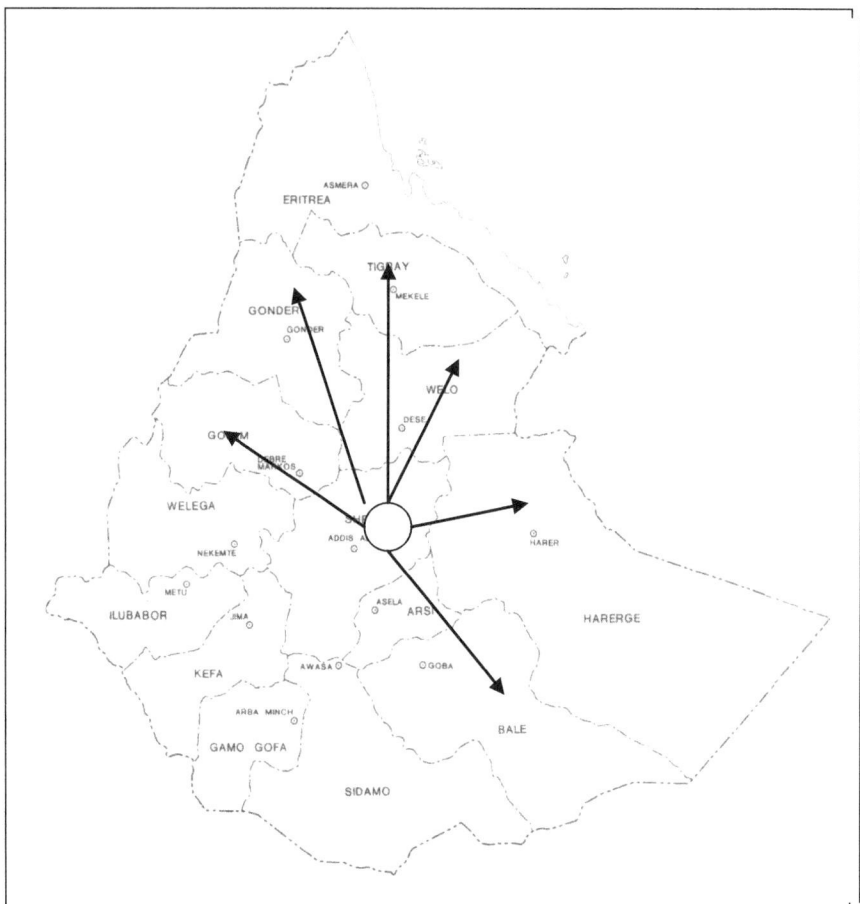

The above map is meant only to show the diffusion of Proto-Amharic-Argobba. The arrows indicate the movement of this group to various regions of Ethiopia and do not necessarily mean that each group moved separately. For instance, it could be the case that only one group moved north to Gojjam, then continued to Gonder, Tigray and Eritrea. The land occupied by such group around the 13th century can be hypothetically mapped as follows:

AN OUTLINE OF THE ORIGIN OF AMHARIC

Map 11: The land occupied by Amharic-Argobba speakers around the 13th century

Before the aforementioned expansion, another group of the Central South Ethio-Semitic-speakers might have first occupied the central and north-central highlands. From there, it moved north as far as Eritrea (see Map 10). I have laid out in chapters two and four the evidence for the expansion of a pre-Amharic-Argobba group to the far north. As the reader might remember, there are names similar to Amharic in the list of the Axumite kings starting from the beginning of the 8th century. The first expansion of a pre-Amharic-Argobba to north could have taken place, therefore, probably starting from the beginning of the sixth century or the seventh century.[137] When the Axumite Empire was

---

[137] We cannot establish for sure the specific date. However, it seems that it was

weakened and the administrative power shifted to the Zague dynasty in Lasta, i.e. Agew Midir, Amharic or pre-Amharic was already spoken in nearby localities such as the Amhara Province. Because the Amharic speakers also started to take ranks in the administration of the Zague rule, and especially in the late Zague period when King Lalibela (1140-1180) preferred them in his administration, Amharic was elevated to that of a language of administration and given a nickname "Language of the King" (cf. Sergew 1972: 278, Ayalew n.d.: 155ff.). As this kingdom and Christianity were like a hand-in-a-glove and the people who resided south of the Christian kingdom adopted Islam and established their own Muslim kingdom, the elevation of Amharic or pre-Amharic to that of a language of administration gave rise to two historical facts. First, the speech variety spoken in the Christian kingdom started to become distinct from the speech variety spoken by the Muslims. Put differently Amharic and Argobba began to diverge and develop into distinct dialects. Second, it gave Amharic the opportunity to expand and spread further. Indeed, the best opportunity for Amharic's development and expansion for a later period truly started with the reign of Yikuno Amlak (1270-1285) from Amhara province that took power from the Zague dynasty and moved the center from Lasta to his province.[138]

6.3.2 The Spread of Amharic after the 13th Century

In the above section, I have suggested that the first major occasion that helped the spread of Amharic over a large area began from the sixth or the seventh century ACE by the Central South Ethio-Semitic group, i.e. long before Amharic and Argobba became distinct languages on their own. I have suggested that the best opportunity for Amharic's development and expansion for a later period truly started with the reign of Yikuno Amlak (1270-1285) who moved the center from Lasta to the Amhara province. Although the center of power moved from place to place with successive governments, it remained mainly in the Amharic-speaking territories and most of the emperors, except Emperor Yohannis VI (1872-1889), were Amharic speakers.[139] This definitely helped

---

before the rise of Islam.

[138] The promotion of Amharic as a language of administration and the successful expansion of the Christian kingdom over a large area which started especially with the reign of Yikuno Amlak (1270-1285) can, therefore, be considered as the main factor for the aforementioned two facts, i.e. the development of Amharic as a distinct language, and its expansion and development over a large area.

[139] Indeed, Emperor Yohannes IV as well was also using Amharic as his

Amharic to strengthen its position as the language of administration. However, the second major expansion that helped Amharic to spread further in new areas can be assumed only to have taken place starting from the end of the 19th century with the reign of Menelik II. The major role played for such spread was the expansion of his territory further to the southern and eastern parts of the country with the introduction and establishment of a government school system, media, a new administrative system and towns.

Recently, Meyer and Richter (2003) have conducted a research on the usage of Amharic in various towns of Afar, Amhara, Gambela, Oromia, Somali, and SNNP regional sates and major cities such as Addis Abeba, Harar and Dire Dawa. Based on their findings, Meyer and Richter (2003: 40) conclude that Amharic is used as lingua franca in every town of Ethiopia and estimated that about 80 percent of the total population of the country speaks it. Amharic was promoted to be used as the only medium of instruction in all Ethiopian Schools in 1956. During this period all administration, court cases etc. continued to be conducted in Amharic. Moreover, various printing presses were established. Various types of writings also started to appear in Amharic. These helped Amharic to develop as a written language.[140]

6.5 A Few Points on Amhara

In most cases, rather than talking (or investigating) the genealogy of a community, it is much easier to talk about the genealogy of a language although there are shortcomings in the various methods of the latter. A certain community may give up its language entirely and take up a different language of another community. With the passage of time, we may not even know whether such total language shift had occurred or not. Even at present, language shift is a frequent occurrence in multilingual nations. According to UNESCO's report, every 15 days on average one language is disappearing from the surface of the earth. In Ethiopia also, there are languages which are extinct, of which we have some information and can trace back in our history. We can imagine that lots of languages to have already been extinct without leaving any trace of their existence in this country. Currently, about 20 of the Ethiopian languages are listed as endangered. Some of them, such as Anfilo and Biraile (alternatively known as Southern Omo and Onogota

---

language of administration like his predecessor Theodore.
[140] For more information see Cooper (1976), Meyer and Richter (2003) among many others.

respectively), are going to be extinct within a few years, at most within a decade or two as only very few elderly people (not more than 10 in each case) speak these languages.

The extinction of languages, however, does not necessarily mean the extinction of its speakers. Language extinction rarely happens along with the extinction of its people. Language extinction mostly occurs alone without its speakers, when its speakers adopt the language of other people. Due to language shift, speakers of the same language at a given period of time may not share the same origin and history. In multilingual countries, the origin and history of a language, therefore, may not always be the origin and history of all its speakers. Ethiopia, a multilingual country of 86 or so languages that are in state of extreme language contact and shift in its history, is no exception to this.

As discussed in chapter four, the term Amhara started to be used as an ethnic appellation very recently. Even with this usage, the people referred to Amhara cannot be considered an ethnic group but rather a social group (Chrenetsov 1993, Levine 1974). On the other hand, I have claimed that it would be better to consider Amharic to be a direct descendant of a Semitic language not developed out of a pidgin-induced process. The question here is how these two suggestions can be compatible.

Meyer (2006: 131), who suggests a non-pidgin origin to Amharic, states that "the existence of the Amharic language in early times does not necessarily imply that there was also a clearly definable ethnic group, the Amhara, who spoke this language". This statement of Meyer's is, however, controversial.

As pointed out above, although, in a multilingual country like Ethiopia, the origin and history of a language may not always be the origin and history of all its speakers, it is unlikely the case that the origin of a language does not imply the origin of the people who speak it. A language cannot originate without speakers unless the language is artificial. Amharic cannot be an exception to this. If the suggestion made in this work that Amharic was descended from a Semitic language is true, it means that there was definitely an ethnic group who spoke this language. However, it may not be the case that either such ethnic group was the ancestor of all the current Amharic speakers nor even known by the term Amhara. In fact, as the various Amharic-speaking groups such as Wällo, Yifat, Tägulät and Mänz, identify themselves with their specific region as in Wälloye, Yifate, Tägulte, and Mänze respectively, and as the term Amhara started to be used in reference to a specific ethnic group very recently, it is difficult to suggest that the earlier ethnic group who spoke Amharic or pre-Amharic identified itself with the term Amhara. Meyer's statement, therefore, can only be true in the sense that the earlier Amharic speakers, i.e. the first ethnic group of Amharic speakers, might not have been known by the term Amhara. There is no known historical documentation that reveals the name by which the earlier ethnic group was referred. However, the most important question is not by which name the earlier Amharic or pre-Amharic speakers were referred. It is rather why the present Amharic speakers cannot be considered an ethnic group or rather why they do not feel to be so. The answer seems clear when we consider the historical makeup of the present group referred to as Amhara.

After Amharic was promoted as a language of administration in the Christian kingdom, the soldiers who were from different ethnic groups started to speak it. Amharic became not only a spoken lingua franca in the royal court and the Orthodox Church but also in the military.[141] The identity of the Amharic speakers, therefore, became the identity of the Christian kingdom. In other words, being an "Amhara" became being an Ethiopian and a Christian (cf. chapter four).

The 15th century Arab historian Maqrizi in his work "The Book of the True Knowledge of the History of the Moslem Kings in Abyssinia" mentions that Yifat, one of the seven Muslim Sultanates which belongs to Abyssinia used to speak the same language as that of the language spoken by the Christian kingdom. He refers to this language as the Abyssinian language, which is most likely Amharic (Maqrizi as translated by Huntingford 1955: 8).[142] However, Maqrizi does not refer to Yifat as Amhara. Maqrizi used the term Amhara interchangeably to refer to the Christians who belong to the highland Christian kingdom and sometimes to the soldiers of the Emperor. We know from history that the Ethiopian Emperors from very early on used to have solders from

---

[141] Because Amharic continued to serve as a language of administration, a number of non-Amharic speaking people started to speak it in some cases as their native language. As pointed out in both this chapter and chapter four, most of the Amhara especially those who live in Gojjam, some parts of Wello and Gonder were Agew and a number of former speakers of other Cushitic and Omotic languages became Amharic speakers.

[142] As pointed out in chapter four Al 'Umari of the 14th century has also reported the same thing.

various ethnic groups (Sergew 1972, Taddese 1972).[143] Being an Amhara, therefore, did not necessarily mean speaking Amharic and vice-versa. It can be assumed that it is due to such facts that the identity of the earlier Amharic or pre-Amharic speaking group gradually lost ground. For a detailed and interesting discussion of this sort, i.e. the origin and historical make up of the so-called Amhara, see Chernetsov (1993) and Heran (1994).[144]

6.6 Summary

I have suggested in this chapter that the first major expansion that helped the spread of Amharic over a large area took place most probably starting from the beginning of the 6th century or the 7th century ACE by the Central South Ethio-Semitic group, i.e. long before Amharic and Argobba became distinct languages on their own. The end of the 12th century, i.e. Lalibela's period, saw Amharic as a language of administration.[145] The time afterwards, especially after the restoration of the Solomonic dynasty in the 13th century, helped Amharic to develop as an administrative language. The second major expansion of Amharic in new areas, however, only took place starting from the 19th century with the reign of Menelik II.[146] Amharic's major development as a written language also began in the 20th century.

Amharic's period as *"Lisane Niguss"* up to Menelik II can only be interpreted as helping Amharic strengthen its position as a language of administration. Amharic started to be employed on regular basis for administration purposes during the reign of Menelik II: "Amharic has long been used as the administrative language of the Ethiopian Christian highlands. Not until Mənilək II became emperor in 1889, however, was Amharic regularly employed for administration purposes" (Nornitsin 2003: 239). This does not mean that Amharic did not expand before the reign of Menelik II.

---

[143] As pointed out in chapter four, Chernetsov (1993) reports that some people with different ethnic identity and having no or little knowledge of Amharic refer to themselves as Amhara – to mean that they are Ethiopian.

[144] See also for further discussion the reference cited there.

[145] Note that the first king of the Zague dynasty Mära Tekle-Haymanot has an Amharic or Amharic-like name where Mära, the first part of his name, is neither Ge'ez nor Agew but Amharic.

[146] The first expansion, which can be assumed to be the expansion of pre-Amharic, i.e. pre-Amharic-Argobba, took place from central to north, east and south whereas the second was from the central to the south, west and to all the newly integrated territories within the Ethiopian Empire.

As is known from history, most of the inhabitants of Gojjam, Gonder and Wällo were Agew speakers. We know also from history that among the early kings from the Solomonic dynasty, Emperor Amdä Seyon (1314-1344) and Emperor Zär'a Ya'qob (1434-1468) expanded their territory further to the south and east more than any of their predecessors did. Zär'a Ya'qob had also settled his soldiers on newly conquered territories. However, we do not have any evidence for the spread of Amharic beyond Shoa, Wällo, Gondar and Gojjam, i.e. in all places occupied by Amdä Seyon (1314-1344) and Zär'a Ya'qob (1434-1468).

On the other hand, the 16th century Oromo expansion might have also had an adverse effect not only on Amharic but also on many other languages. A number of areas inhabited by Amharic and other language speakers were occupied by the Oromo speakers. For instance, the eastern and northeastern parts of Shoa, some parts of Arsi, a number of areas in Bale and the lands all the way from eastern Shoa to Harar were occupied once by the Argobba speakers. Hence, Amharic might have also been spread by the early medieval Solomonic monarchs to new unknown areas but lost to the Oromo in the 16th century.

In this chapter, I have also suggested Amharic's place of origin to be somewhere in the central part of Ethiopia and its date of origin to be much earlier than the start of the Zague dynasty. However, our suggestion is not novel in all respects. Sergew (1972: 278ff.) has also suggested Amharic to have originated in the central part of Ethiopia among the Amhara and made somewhat similar suggestions regarding its place and manner of origin, although he is not specific on the latter.

Chapter Seven: The Development of Amharic as a Written Language

7.1 Introduction

Amharic was used in various sectors of the government since it became known as *Lissanä Nigus* 'language of the king'. However, until very recently it was Ge'ez that enjoyed the status of a written language. The first known written documents in Amharic are lyrics praising the deeds of emperors Amdä Seyon (1314-1344), Dawit (1375-1404), Yishaq (1413 -1430), Zär'a Ya'qob (1434-1468), and Gälawdewos (1540 - 1559).[147]

Around the end of the 16th century and the beginning of the 17th, foreign missionaries used Amharic for religious purposes (Amsalu 1976 EC, Kane 1975). During this period, we see also some documents written in Amharic instead of Ge'ez by people from the Ethiopian Orthodox Church in defense of their religion. Amharic started replacing Ge'ez as a written language for official purposes during the period of Emperor Theodore II (1855-1865). However, Amharic developed as a standard written language only very recently. Even during Menelik's period,

---

[147] These first-known Amharic written materials are referred to variously. They are sometimes referred to as (imperial) songs, as lyrics and sometimes as poems. In this work, we have used these terms interchangeably without giving any theoretical status for our usage.

Amharic was used on a regular basis in various administrative sectors and almost every written activity of the administration was done in this language, including the establishment of the first Amharic newspaper in 1900 EC. Yet, it was not really a well-developed written language. Amharic writings both in quantity and quality increased specially after the first quarter of the 20th century. Today we find Amharic writings on almost every subject.

In the following section, I outline the development of Amharic as a written language. Going into a thorough discussion on Amharic writing is beyond the scope of this work. For an elaborate discussion on the subject, the reader is advised to consult Kane (1975) and Amsalu Aklilu (1976 EC). Also, for a comprehensive discussion on the development of specific genres see Balashova (2003) and the references cited there for Amharic drama, Kane and Nosnitsin (2003) for an overview of Amharic traditional historical writings, and Asfaw Damte and Denis Nosnitsin (2007) and the references cited there for novels.

In section 7.3 I discuss the Amharic script from a historical perspective. I particularly try to figure out when the Amharic script was developed, how it was transferred from generation to generation, i.e. how it was studied especially in earlier times, and what kind of changes that it made. Section 7.4 summarizes the discussion made in the preceding sections.

7.2 An Overview of the Development of Amharic Writing

It is very difficult to assume that the first Amharic written work appeared in poem-form. However, as pointed out above, the first written document known to this date is that of a song praising the deeds of Amdä Seyon (1314-1344).

ሐርበኛ፡ ዓምደ፡ ጽዮን፡፡	line=(L.) 1
መላላሽ፡ የወሰን፡፡	
ወኸ፡ እንደመስን፡	
መላላሽ፡ የወሰን፡፡	
ከወጅ፡ ዜብዳርን፡፡	L. 5
ይውረድ፡ አድርገኸው፡ ትግሬውን፡፡	
ከወጅ፡ ዜብዳርን፡፡	
ከገንዝ፡ ጠጠን፡፡	
ምን፡ ቀረኸ፡ በወሰን፡፡	
ከድያ፡ አመኛን፡	L. 10
ምን፡ ቀረኸ፡ በወሰን፡፡	
ከባሊ፡ አሊን፡፡	
ከደዋሮ፡ ጌደራን፡፡	
ከፈጠጋር፡ ዜላርድን፡፡	

ኬፋት፡ አምበልአበከርን፨   L. 15
ከግድም፡ የዊሳይን፨
ከአንጎት፡ ገን፡ አሞራን፨
ከአገው፡ አቤት፡ አገርን፨
ከትግሬ፡ ነገደ፡ ክርስቶስ፡ ይውረድ፨
አደረግኸው፡ ገንዙን፨   L. 20
እንዲሰራ፡ ዳውነውን፨
ማን፡ ቀረከ፡ በወሰን፨
አላጸፋኸው፡ ፊቱን፨
አላስማረኸው፡ ልጅ፡ ምሽቱን፨
ከጎጀም፡ ገን፡ ኽምርን፨   L. 25
ከጋፋት፡ አወላሞን፨
በዳሞት፡ ሞት፡ ለሚን፨
ማን፡ ቀረከ፡ በወሰን፨
ያላስጸፋኸው፡ ፊቱን፨
ያላስማረኸው፡ ልጅ፡ ምሽቱን፨   L. 30
ሐርበኛ፡ ዓምደ፡ ጽዮን፨
መላላሽ፡ የወሰን፨
ዓምደ፡ ጽዮን፡ ስም፡ ይዘራ፨
በወጅ፡ እስከ፡ በጥርአሞራ፨
ቃራ፡ ይነሰንስ፡ ቃራ፡ እንደ፡ ጭራ፨   L. 35
በወንዶች፡ ገረገራ፨
በሐድያ፡ እስከ፡ ጉዴላ፨
በባሕር፡ እስከ፡ ኤርትራ፨
ዓምደ፡ ጽዮን፡ ስም፡ ይዘራ፨   (Bruce 88)

Beside the above lyric in the 14th and 15th centuries, recall that, we have other lyrics to praise the deeds of emperors Dawit (1375-1404), Yishaq (1413 -1430), and Zär'a Ya'qob (1434-1468).[148] Besides these royal songs, other written Amharic texts of this early period until the 16th century are rare.[149] Goldenberg (1976: 131), quoting Desta Tekle Wold (1970), reported that an old text about the biography of *ič'äge* Täklä-Haymanot (died in 1313) is found written in Amharic. I cannot attest the existence of this document for the time being, although I have to admit that my effort in obtaining such document has not been satisfactory. On the other hand, there is no evidence that those imperial songs were even written down in the time of their alleged composition although it seems to be the case that they were.

---

[148] These poems are attached in the appendix.

[149] In the Ge'ez grammar manuscript of the 15th century (could be 16th century) found at Gunda Gunde, there are some Amharic and Tigiryna vocabularies. In Metshafe Mistre Semay wemidir of the 15th century, the few non-Ge'ez vocabularies are that of Tigrinya (Brook Abdu, P.C.).

THE ORIGIN OF AMHARIC

There are various versions of the imperial songs that praise the deeds of the emperors. No version of such documents is found that dates back to the time of their composition. The earliest of the manuscripts found to date is the one found in England referred to as Bruce88 of the Bodleian Library at Oxford. Guidi (1889) has presented this manuscript in "Le canzone geez-amariña in onore di Re Abissini". Guidi (1889) has noted some differences that he came across with *Manuscript Eth 143* of the Bibliotheque Nationale Paris. Some other variants are also found at Rüpell collection in Frankfurt am Main. The other popular variants are found in a manuscript called ታሪከ ነገሥት 'History of Kings' which is thought to have been collected by the order of Dejzamach Hailu, a son of Dejazmach Eshete, in the year 1777 (EC) when Emperor Iyasu (also known by the name Birhan Seged) was crowned (Tekle-Tsadik 1951:100).

Nosnitisn (2003: 238) and some others suggest that those imperial songs were first composed orally and written down in a much later date, probably in the 16th or 17th century. It seems very plausible that such lyrics were composed by Azmaries orally and performed in the royal court as Richter (1997) also suggests.

> Songs of praise are elements which are deeply rooted in the Ethiopian literary tradition and have survived until recent times, especially in the highland region of Gondar. Hymns of praise or panegyric songs are usually produced and performed by *azmaris,* the professional singers and accompanied by traditional instruments such as *bägäna, masinqo* or *krar.*
>
> We know neither the authors of the songs nor the concrete circumstances of their presentation at the royal court - our single witness is the text itself. But we may assume that these songs originally were produced and performed in a manner similar to that which is still alive in the tradition of the *azmaris* (Richter 1997: 545).

Although it seems the case that the royal songs were composed orally most probably by *azmaris*, it is very difficult to agree with Nosnitisn (2003: 238) and similar suggestion that they were written in the 16th or 17th century. First, some of the songs are too long; for instance in the Emperor Dawit's case two songs contain 57 and 61 lines each (see section 7.3) and in the song for Emperor Yishaq's more than 170 lines (see the appendix).[150] Second, most of the imperial lyrics are mixed with Ge'ez. They have a number of Ge'ez vocabularies which are foreign to the ordinary Amharic speakers. For instance, in the song for Yishaq's, we find a number of Ge'ez vocabularies.[151] Third, some of them have poor literary quality that does not seem to be easily remembered and transmitted orally from generation to generation.[152]

Due to the above three points, I am inclined to believe that at least some of the imperial lyrics were written down from the beginning.[153] I also assume that besides those lyrics, Amharic was probably used in writing in this early period for limited purposes. This assumption is based on two historical accounts.

First, according to the 15th century Arab historian Maqrizi, recall that Zayla, the Muslim region which belongs to the country of Abyssinia, had seven kingdoms, namely Yifat (in Maqrizi term Awfat), Dawaro, Arababni, Hadya, Sharha, Bali, and Darah (Maqrizi as translated by Huntingford 1955: 7). In these kingdoms of Zayla "there are several dialects; in fact, more than fifty can be counted, all of which are written in Abyssinian letters" (Ibid: 11). As pointed out already, Maqrizi mentions that the people of Yifat, one of the kingdoms of Zayla, "speak Abyssinian language, though there are some who speak Arabic" (Ibid.: 8). It is unlikely that all the 50 or so languages were used in writing at the time of Maqrizi report. However, it is most likely the case that at least some of them including Amharic-Argobba, referred to as Abyssinian language, were used for writing purposes.[154]

Note that also Maqrizi reported that Emperor Sayf Ar'ad, known also as Newaye Kirstos, (1344-1372) charged Ali, king of Yifat, "by written letters, to set his son over a certain district of Jabarta" (Ibid: 13). If there

---

[150] In fact, these long songs could have been composed by different poets and brought together later. However, even with such possibility, it is very difficult to assume that it was written down at a much later date for the reasons mentioned below.

[151] Note that Ge'ez was not a spoken language during that time. It was only known by those who had good education in it.

[152] We are not implying here that oral poetry has superior quality over all written ones.

[153] The earliest known copy of the imperial lyrics is found in a manuscript called Bruce 88 found in Oxford. The manuscript is assumed to be written between the end of the 16th century and the beginning of the 17th century.

[154] Note that Yifat was the strongest of the Muslim kingdoms especially in the 14th and 15th centuries.

was letter exchanges between the Muslim Sultanates and the Christian Kingdoms, it is unlikely that, the Muslim kings of these Ethiopian tributary regions used to write in Ge'ez, as Ge'ez was strongly associated with Christianity. Since they were using the Ethiopic alphabet and spoke the same language as the language spoken in the Christian kingdom, it is most likely the case that the letters were written in Amharic-Argobba.

Second, the most glorious period in Ge'ez literature came when the Amharic-speaking kings took power.[155] In other words, Ge'ez developed its glorious literature by the Amharic speakers or when Amharic was used for a broader communication. Starting from the 13th century, not only translated works but also original compositions of religious Ge'ez texts flourished (see, among many others, Amsalu Aklilu 1976). In the church schools, the teaching of Ge'ez was conducted through Amharic medium. As I will discuss in detail later, Amharic was used for making comments in the margins of Ge'ez manuscripts and in some cases providing glossaries on the translation of Ge'ez and Arabic words. Although such writings are not attested before the 16th century, the practice may have begun earlier.

As pointed out above, there might be some Amharic texts which have been lost for various reasons. However, we can be sure that Amharic was not employed in writing in various sectors. Moreover, what we can infer from those imperial songs is that Amharic was not developed well as a written language in those periods.[156] In fact, what we can also infer from Ludolf's comments about Gregory is that the writing of Amharic was not developed even in the seventeen century. Gregory, who was a native speaker of Amharic and well-educated in the Church, had the same difficulty writing Amharic as he did speaking in Ge'ez (Ludolph 1682: 77ff.).

In the 16th and the 17th centuries, we find other written sources in Amharic. This is often thought as initiated by foreign missionaries especially by the Portuguese to preach their Catholic faith. During this period, we see also some documents written in Amharic instead of Ge'ez by people from the Ethiopian Orthodox Church in defense of their religion (Amsalu 1976 EC, Kane 1975). There are at least two important

---

[155] Note that, this period is particularly the period long after Ge'ez ceased to be a spoken language.
[156] For an interesting analysis of the imperial songs, see Gezahegn (2004). See also Praetorius (1879), Richter (1997) and Littmann (1944).

manuscripts that can be safely dated back to 16th century. These are ትምሕርተ ሀይማኖት *Timhirte Haymant* 'Teaching of the Faith', discussed by Cowley (1974) and a manuscript about Mary who anointed Jesus' feet also discussed by Cowley (1983).[157]

From 16th to 18th centuries, we see more texts in Amharic. Works such as አንቀፀ አሚን *anqäsä amin*, ጠቢበ ጠቢባን *t'äbibä t'äbiban*, ስነ ፍጥረት *sinä fit'rät*, ምሥጢረ ፅግያት *mistirä s'igyat*, were translated from Ge'ez into Amharic by the Ethiopian Orthodox Church scholars "to make them accessible to the common ecclesiastics and useful in the public anti-Catholic polemics and to promote the Orthodox faith" (Nosnitisn 2003: 238). Other well-known works considered to be an original Amharic text of this period includes ነገረ ሀይማኖት *nägärä haymanot* (Nosnitisn 2003: 238).[158] A German missionary translated the Gospel of John into Amharic. It was published in 1647 (Amsalu 1976 EC). A manuscript called ይህ፡ መጽፍ፡ የሚጠቅም፡ መድኃኒት፡ የሚነግር፡ ነው 'This Book Tells of Useful Medicine' was assumed to be written between the years 1682-1706 (Nosnitisn 2003: 239). Ludolph published an Amharic grammar and lexicon in 1698. Various magical treatises such as ምሥጢረ ዳዊት mist'irä dawit 'Mystery of the Psalter' were also produced in the 17th and 18th centuries (Nosnitisn 2003: 239).

Amharic writing also appears in the form of what is known as *andemta*-commentaries often written on the margins of originally Ge'ez texts. Although the oral tradition of such commentary is thought to be as old as the restored Solomonic dynasty, it is very difficult to be precise when exactly such practice started to be written down. Although much of such marginal notes can be dated to the 17th and 18th centuries, we have such commentary in the 15th century manuscript EMML 2117 (Nosnitisn

---

[157] According to Cowley (1974) Timhirte Haymant can be dated as the 16th century manuscript. With regard to the manuscript about Mary who anointed Jesus' feet Cowley (1983) suggests that in some respects it "represents a very slightly more archaic stage than TH [Timhirte Haymant]" (1983: 21). However, it seems that in many respects the former is more archaic than Timhirte Haymant. Hence, it is reasonable to consider the manuscript about Mary as a 16th or a pre-16th century manuscript. Getatchew (1980) has made a comment on Cowely's analysis of Timhirte Haymanot. Both Amharic texts are the most valuable works for the study of Old Amharic. We have considered these manuscripts in the examination of Old Amharic grammar in the following chapters. We have also attached these texts in the appendix.

[158] See Getatchew (1979 b) for the analysis of an Amharic text of this sort from the early seventeenth century.

2003: 239).[159] Whether such commentary is as old as the manuscript itself is hard to tell, indeed.

Beside *andemta*-commentaries, Amharic glossaries are found in some texts. Leaving aside the 17th century work of Ludoplh's Amharic grammar, Ge'ez-Amharic glossaries (often referred to as *sewasew*, which, of course, include also grammar and rhetoric), were also very common since at least the 16th century (see Getatchew 1970 for the analysis of some such glossaries).

Although Amharic continued to be used in various forms of writing, it started replacing Ge'ez as a written language for official purposes from the period of Emperor Theodore II (1855-65), when he ordered the use of Amharic to write his chronicle for the first time and used it himself to write letters in his official activities. Indeed, Shale Selassie, King of Shoa from 1813-1847, also used Amharic in his official letters. In this period, Theodore's chronicle writer Däbtära Zeneb has written a short book which is still cited for its literal quality.[160]

In this 19th century, some historical books such as የቴዎድሮስ ታሪh "The History of Theodore' written by Däbtära Zeneb and የዓለም ታሪh ከፍጥረት ጀምሮ እስከ ዘመናችን ድረስ "History of the World from the Creation to Our Time' by Isenberg published in 1842 appeared in Amharic. He also published a book on spelling and reading and on geography in Amharic in 1841. The British and Foreign Bible Society in London also published in 1824 a diglot Giiz-Amharic edition of the Four Gospels (Pankhurst 1976: 311). "Giiz and Amharic versions of the New Testament and an Amharic Old Testament followed" (Ibid).

Yohannes IV continued using Amharic as the official language of the Ethiopian empire. Amharic progressed significantly as a written language during Menelik II. Menelik established among others the first government school and the first newsletter both in 1908. He introduced European style administration with the establishment of several ministerial offices. All these required activities in writing. Due to this, a number of Amharic writings appeared in various fields, including the first "novel" called ልብወለድ ታሪh *libb wäld tarik* which later came to be known as ጦቢያ *t'obia* by Afework Gebereyesus in 1908. A number of other texts have also published in this century (see Amsalu 1976 EC, and Kane 1975 for more). However, as pointed out in the introduction

---

[159] Ethiopian Manuscript Microfilm Library, Addis Ababa.
[160] For samples of this text, see the appendix.

section of this chapter, Amharic developed as a standard written language only very recently.

Although Amharic was employed in writing in various fields in the Menelik II period and continued afterwards, it was still in its infancy even in the first quarter of the 20th century. Consider the following three sample official writings of the first quarter of the 20th century taken with their translation from Eadie's (1924) collection published in the book "An Amharic Reader":[161]

---

[161] We have attached additional samples of the Amharic writing of this period, i.e. the beginning of the 20th century, in the appendix.

THE ORIGIN OF AMHARIC

Text One

ያዋጅ፡ ቃል፡፡

አቢጋዝ፡ በያገርሀ፡ ሌባና፡ ቀማኛ፡ ጠብቋ፡ በገሌ፡ አገር፡ ሰው፡ ተቀማ፡ የሚሉ፡ የሰማኍ፡ እንደ፡ ሆነ፡ አቢጋዙ፡ ነው፡ የሚከፍለው፡፡

ጌታ፡ የሌለሀ፡ ስራ፡ ፊት፡ ላቢጋዝ፡ እሰጠሁት፡ ከተማ፡ ገብተህ፡ ተቀመጥ፡፡ አገር፡ ቤት፡ ሆነህ፡ ባላገር፡ አታውከ፡፡

ከዚህም፡ ቀደም፡ በሰንበት፡ ስራ፡ እንዳይሰራ፡ ክልክል፡ ነው፡ አሁንም፡ በሰንበት፡ ስትሰራ፡ የተገኘህ፡ ትወረሳለህ፡፡

ማር፡ ያለህ፡ ልኩን፡ ላቢጋዝ፡ ስጥቼሀለሁና፣ በዚያ፡ ማርህን፡ አግባ፡ ማር፡ የሌለህ፣ ገራዳ፡ አራት፡ ብር፡ ሽበታ፡ ሶስት፡ ብር፡ ጭሰኛ፡ ሁለት፡ ብር፣ እረኛ፡ አንድ፡ ብር፡ ስጥ፡ ማር፡ እያለህ፡ ግን፡ ብር፡ እሰለሰጉት፡ ብለህ፣ ማርህን፡ ሸጠህ፡ የተገኘህ፡ እጥፍ፡ ማር፡ ከፈል፡ ገራዳም፡ ሆንህ፡ እንደ፡ ሸበታ፡ ሶስት፡ ብር፡ አውጣ፡ ገራዳም፡ ሸበታም፡ ጭሰኛም፣ እረኛም፡ ቀፎህን፡ ስቀል፡ ቢቸግርህ፡ ነው፡ እንጂ፡ ግብርህ፡ ማር፡ ነውና፡ መልከኛም፡ የማር፡ እሽት፡ አትንካ፡፡

ወደ፡ ፊት፡ ለሚሰራው፡ ስራ፡ ሁሉ፡ እንደ፡ ጥንቱ፡ ደሚናህን፡ ይዘህ፡ ስራ፡፡

ከዚህ፡ ቀደም፡ ካገር፡ አገር፡ ተዛውረህ፡ እንጂ፣ አዲስ፡ አገር፡ አላወጣህምና፣ ኰቤ፡ ባሳና፡ አትብላ፡ ብዬ፡ ባዋጅ፡ ነገርኩህ፡ አሁን፡ ብሰማ፣ ክድኃው፡ ተቀብለኸው፡ ተገኘኍ፡ ይኸን፡ ካዋጅ፡ በላይ፡ የበላኸውን፡ ገንዘብ፣ ለድኃው፡ መልስ፡፡

ወደ፡ ፊትም፣ አቢጋዛና፡ ደሚና፡ ከተደበላለት፡ በላይ፡ አልፎ፣ መልከኛ፡ የድኃውን፡ ገንዘብ፡ እንዳይላበት፡ ጠብቁ፡ አልፎ፡ የተበባበትን፡ ገንዘብ፡ ድኃው፡ ለናንተ፡ ነግሮአችኍ፡ ሳታስመልሱለት፡ ስራውና፡ [sic. ስራን]፡ ትቶ፡ ለኔ፡ የጮኸ፡ እንደ፡ ሆነ፡ ጥፋቱ፡ የናንተ፡ ነውና፡ ገንዘቡን፡ ትክፍላላችኍ፡፡ እናንተ፡ ግን፡ ከዚያ፡ ከወሰደበት፡ ሰው፡ ትቀበላላችኍ፡፡ ባለገርም፡ ለደሚናህና፡ ላቢጋዝሀ፡ ሳትንገር፣ ወደኔ፡ አትምጣ፡፡

በሶስቱ፡ ዓመት፡ በአል፡ የፍየል፡ እንደ፡ ጥንቱ፣ ሁለት፡ ሁለት፡ ብር፡ ተቀበል፡፡

፷፫ሐምሌ፡ ፳፱፻፳፮፡ ሐረር፡፡

The words of the proclamation

You Abagazes! Be on the watch for thieves and brigands in your respective countries. If I hear that people have been robbed in such and such a province, 'tis the Abagaz who will pay them.

You who have no master and are without employment! enter the town that I have given to the Abagaz and live there. Do not stay in the villages and worry the farmers.

Before this also it was forbidden that work done on Sunday and now if you work on Sundays and are found you will be deprived (of your property).

You who have honey! I have given the measure to the Abagaz and put your honey in that. You who have not honey! (being) a "garada" give $4, a "shibata" $3, a householder without land $2, and a herdsman $1. But if you having honey say, "I will give dollars" and sell your honey and are found, pay double quantity of honey. You who being a garada pay the same taxes as a "Shibata". Garadas, Shibtas, Chisaññas and Shepherds! Hang up your beehives. Your tribute is honey, even though it may inconvenience you.

And You "Malkaññas"! don't touch the new honey. In future, as formerly, work with your "Damina" for all the work which is being done.

You before this wandered from province to province, but you did not get a new country. I told you by proclamation not to misappropriate dues. Now if I hear that it has been found that you have received it from the poor, return to them the property that you have "eaten" over and above the proclamation.

And for the future you the Abagaz and Damina! Be careful that the Malkaññas having exceeded what has been assigned to him, does not "eat" the money of the poor. The poor having told you what has been exhorted in excess, if he leaves his work and complains tome, before you cause it to be given back to him, the loss is yours; you will pay the money. You, however, will receive it from that person who took it from him. And you farmer! Don't come to me before you have spoken to your Damina and Abagaz. As formerly receive 2 dollars in lieu of goats on the 3 yearly festivals.

13th Hamle 1905. Harar.

Text Two

ምክር

አሁን፣ በከተማው፣ ፈንጣጣ፣ ገብታ፣ ሰውን፣ እንደምትፈጅ፣ ታያላችሁ። ይኸችንም፣ በሽታ፣ ካገር፣ ለማጥፋት፣ በከተማ፣ ያለው፣ ሰው፣ አዋቂም፣ ልጅም፣ ከከብት፣ ሃኪም፣ ዘንድ፣ ወይም፣ ከሆፒታል፣ እየኼደ፣ ይከተብ።

ለመከተቡም፣ ዋጋም፣ አያስፈልግ፣ ጊዜም፣ አያስፈታ፣ ካምስት፣ ደቂቃ፣ ይበልጥ፣ አያቆይ።

አሁንም፣ ለራሳችሁና፣ ለልጆቻችሁ፣ የምታስቡ፣ ሰዎች፣ ሁሉ። ሳታስከትቡ፣ ቀርታችሁ፣ ሰው፣ ቢሞትባችሁ፣ በስንፍናችሁ፣ መሆኑን፣ እወቁ።

መጋቢት፣ ፪ቀን፣ ፲፱፻፬ዓመተ፣ ምሕረት፣ አዲስ፣ አበባ፣ ከተማ፣ ተፃፈ።

ነጋድራስ ኃይለ ጊዮርጊስ

የንግድና የውጭ ጉዳይ ሚኒስተር

Advice

You see how smallpox having entered the town destroying the people. For exterminating this evil disease out of the country, let the people who are in the town - adults and children - go and vaccinated either at the veterinary surgeon's or at the hospital.

To be vaccinated no charge is required and it does not cause loss of time; it does not detain one more than five minutes.

Now all you people who think for yourselves and for your children, if you fail to have the vaccination done, and any one dies know that it is owing to your laziness.

2nd Maggabit 1904 A.M. Written at the town of Addis Ababa.

Nagadras Haile Giyorgis

Minister for Commerce and Foreign Affairs

Text Three

የኢትዮጵያ መንግስት።

የርሻና የመስሪያ ሚኒስቴር።

ማስታወቂያ።

በመጀመሪያ፡ ጀንሆይ፡ ይህነን፡ ያዲስ፡ አበባን፡ ከተማ፡ ለመስራት፡ የቆረቆሩ፡ ጊዜ፡ መሬቱ፡ ባዶ፡ ምንምን፡ ዛፍ፡ የሌለበት፡ ነበር። ነገር፡ ግን፡ ለጊዜው፡ እንዲደምቅና፡ እንዲያምር፡ ላይን፡ ማረፊያ፡ እንዲሆን፡ ተብሎ፡ በቶሎ፡ እሚያድግ፡ ይህነን፡ እካሊብቶስ፡ አስመጡ፡ እንጂ።

የጀንሆይ፡ አሳብ፡ ግን፡ ላገራችን፡ ለሕዝቡ፡ የሚጠቅም፡ ፍሬው፡ የሚበላ፡ እንጨቱም፡ ስራ፡ የሚይዝ፡ ጥቅም፡ ያለውን፡ ሁሉ፡ እያስመጡ፡ ለማስተክል፡ ነበር። ይኸውም፡ ይታወቅ፡ ዘንድ፡ በያይነቱ፡ አስመጥተው፡ መፈተናቸው፡ አልቀረም፡ ከተፈተነውም፡ ሁሉ፡ አንድ፡ ዓይነት፡ አልጠፋም። ሁሉም፡ ጥንት፡ ከተገነበት፡ ከሀገሩ፡ የበለጠ፡ እየሆነ፡ በቅጺል፡ ለምቷል፡ እንጂ።

ይህነውም፡ በትልቁ፡ ዓይነት፡ ኮክ፡ ቡቱት፡ በሐሩ፡ ዛፍ። በጽጌ፡ ረዳ፡ በሲጥራ፡ ተረዱት፡ እንዚህንም፡ የመሰሉ፡ ብዙ፡ ዛፎችና፡ ተክሎች፡ አሉ። እኛም፡ ይህነን፡ ዓይተን፡ ነው፡ ጥቅም፡ የሌለውን፡ ዛፍ፡ አሳንስን፡ ጥቅም፡ ያለባቸውን፡ እናብዛ፡ ማለታችን።

ቴትም፡ የሚባለው፡ የሐር፡ ዛፍ፡ ፍሬው፡ ይበላል፡ ቅጠሎም፡ የሐር፡ ትል፡ ማርባት፡ ለወደደ፡ ሰው፡ ዋና፡ ነገር፡ ነው። ይህም፡ ባይሆን፡ ደግሞ፡ ቅጠሉን፡ ለላምና፡ ለበሬ፡ ለበግና፡ ፍየል፡ ቢያበሉት፡ እጅግ፡ ያወፍራል። ግንዱም፡ ሲቆረጥ፡ ለስራ፡ ይሆናል፡ ብዙ፡ ገንዘብ፡ ያወጣል፡ ቁመቱም፡ በልክ፡ ነው።

እንደዚህ፡ ያለውን፡ ጥቅም፡ ያለበትን፡ ዛፍ፡ ለማልማት፡ ነው፡ ልዑል፡ ያልጋ፡ ወራሹም፡ ያስቡት። ይህ፡ እካሊብቶስ፡ ግን፡ የሚበላውን፡ አታክልትና፡ መሬት፡ ከማጥፋት፡ በቀር፡ ምንም፡ ምን፡ ጥቅም፡ የለውም። ባጠቤ፡ ምንጯ፡ ያለ፡ እንደሆነ፡ የደርቀዋል፡ የጉድጓዱንም፡ ውሃ፡ ሁሉ፡ ስፉ፡ እየሳበ፡ እየጠጣ፡ አይረቀው። እንጨቱም፡ ሥራ፡ አይይዝ፡ ፍራውም፡ አይበላ፡ አሁንም፡ በየቦታው፡ እካሊብቶስ፡ ያለው፡ ሁለት፡ እጁን፡ ይንቀል፡ አንዱ፡ እጅ፡ ይቆይ። በተነቀለው፡ ፈንታ፡ ጥቅም፡ የሚገኝበትን፡ የዛፍ፡ ግልገል፡ እንስጣለን።

መጋቢት፡ ፳፪ቀን፡ ፲፱፻፳፮ዓመተ፡ ምሕረት፡ አዲስ፡ አበባ፡ ከተማ፡ ተፃፈ።

157

Minister of Agriculture of Ethiopia

Notice

At first, at the time when the Emperor founded this city of Addis Ababa, the soil was void and had no trees whatsoever. But he imported this quickly-growing Eucalyptus tree so that it might be beautiful and agreeable and pleasant to the sight. The Emperor's intention however was to import and have planted all those useful (trees) that are useful to our country and nation, whose fruit is edible, and whose wood is useful. To find this out (lit. so that this may be known) he imported (trees) of every kind, and did not omit to test them (lit. their being tested did not lack). From all that were tested not one kind failed to grow, but all grew and flourished better than in the country where they were originally found.

They (i.e. the people of Abyssinia – or the Emperor Menelik) were assured of this by the large kind of plum tree; by the mulberry, the silk tree; by the rose tree; by the "Sitre". There are also many trees and plants which resemble these. And we having seen this, it is our intention to make less the trees which are useless and to increase those which are of use (lit. let us increase).

And the silk tree which is called mulberry, its fruit is edible. Its leaves are the chief requisite for persons who wish to breed silkworms. Leaving this out of the question (lit. if this be not), if people give the leaves to eat to cows, oxen, sheep, and goats, they (i.e. leaves) make them very fat. The trunk also being cut each year will be of use. It brings in much money and is of moderate height.

H.H. The Heir Apparent thought that a tree which has such advantages should be cultivated. This Eucalyptus however has no use with the exception of destroying the plants and earth which it eats. If there be a spring in the vicinity, it dries it up, and sucking and drinking the bottom of wells it dries up the water. Its wood is no use and its fruit is not eaten. And now in every place let him who has Eucalyptus pull up 2/3 of it and let 1/3 remain. In place of what has been pulled up, we will give trees which possess advantages.

Maggabit 12th, 1905 A.M. Written at the town of Addis Ababa.

THE DEVELOPMENT OF AMHARIC AS A WRITTEN LANGUAGE

As can be seen from the above three sample writings, see also the appendix, Amharic was not really a well-developed written language even at the beginning of the 20th century. Punctuation marks and spelling are hardly standardized; the language employed is more of a spoken language; etc. Amharic made real progress during the Haile Selassie I period. It developed as a standard written language especially after the restoration of Haile Selassei's power in 1941. In the last half of the 20th century, we have seen the production of literary works of high quality such as ከአድማስ ባሻገር Kä'admas Bashagär (by Bealu Girma) and ፍቅር እስከ መቃብር Fiqir iskä Mäqabir (by Hadis Alemayehu).

Currently, Amharic is used in various fields. However, the writing of Amharic especially in the hard sciences is not yet satisfactory. Scientific articles even in the field of social science often are written in English. However, works such as አጥቢዎች *at'biwoc* 'mammals' (2000 EC) of Solomon Yirga in the field of biology and Baye Yimam's የአማርኛ ሰዋሰው 'Amharic Grammar' (2000 EC) written with concepts of modern linguistics prove that Amharic is now ready to be employed in any field or for any task.

7.3 The Amharic Script

There is no question that the Amharic script developed out of the Ge'ez script. The Amharic script differs from the Ge'ez script in that it has some additional symbols for the sounds not found in Ge'ez. The additional symbols found in the basic chart are called traditionally Arabi. The first order of these letters is ፐ, ሸ, ጀ, ገር, ቸ, ቈ and ኸ. The current Amharic script is as follows:[162]

---

[162] The transcription given below for each letter is based on current usage.

THE ORIGIN OF AMHARIC

Table 8: Basic Amharic characters

1st order C+ä[163]	2nd order C+u	3rd order C+i	4th order C+a	5th order C+e	6th order C+ɨ	7th order C+o	Transcription (Representation of the consonants)
ሀ /ha/	ሁ	ሂ	ሃ	ሄ	ህ	ሆ	h
ለ	ሉ	ሊ	ላ	ሌ	ል	ሎ	l
ሐ /ha/	ሑ	ሒ	ሓ	ሔ	ሕ	ሖ	h
መ	ሙ	ሚ	ማ	ሜ	ም	ሞ	m
ሠ	ሡ	ሢ	ሣ	ሤ	ሥ	ሦ	s
ረ	ሩ	ሪ	ራ	ሬ	ር	ሮ	r
ሰ	ሱ	ሲ	ሳ	ሴ	ስ	ሶ	s
ሸ	ሹ	ሺ	ሻ	ሼ	ሽ	ሾ	š
ቀ	ቁ	ቂ	ቃ	ቄ	ቅ	ቆ	q
በ	ቡ	ቢ	ባ	ቤ	ብ	ቦ	b
ተ	ቱ	ቲ	ታ	ቴ	ት	ቶ	t
ቸ	ቹ	ቺ	ቻ	ቼ	ች	ቾ	č
ኀ /ha/	ኁ	ኂ	ኃ	ኄ	ኅ	ኆ	h

---

[163] There are few exceptions to this. Some mark in their first order the mid-low vowel /a/ instead of the mid-central /ä/. In those cases, the first order and the fourth order will have the same reading. We indicate such exceptions below in each case. C stands for a consonant.

አ /a/	ኡ /u/	ኢ /i/	ኣ /a/	ኤ /e/	እ /ɨ/	ኦ /o/	(Vowels)[164]
ከ	ኩ	ኪ	ካ	ኬ	ክ	ኮ	k
ኸ	ኹ	ኺ	ኻ	ኼ	ኽ	ኾ	x
ነ	ኑ	ኒ	ና	ኔ	ን	ኖ	n
ኘ	ኙ	ኚ	ኛ	ኜ	ኝ	ኞ	ñ
ዐ /'a/	ዑ	ዒ	ዓ	ዔ	ዕ	ዖ	ʔ
ወ	ዉ	ዊ	ዋ	ዌ	ው	ዎ	w
ዘ	ዙ	ዚ	ዛ	ዜ	ዝ	ዞ	z
ዠ	ዡ	ዢ	ዣ	ዤ	ዥ	ዦ	ž
የ	ዩ	ዪ	ያ	ዬ	ይ	ዮ	y
ደ	ዱ	ዲ	ዳ	ዴ	ድ	ዶ	d
ጀ	ጁ	ጂ	ጃ	ጄ	ጅ	ጆ	ğ
ገ	ጉ	ጊ	ጋ	ጌ	ግ	ጎ	g
ጠ	ጡ	ጢ	ጣ	ጤ	ጥ	ጦ	t'
ጨ	ጩ	ጪ	ጫ	ጬ	ጭ	ጮ	č'
ጰ	ጱ	ጲ	ጳ	ጴ	ጵ	ጶ	s'
ጸ	ጹ	ጺ	ጻ	ጼ	ጽ	ጾ	s'
ፐ	ፑ	ፒ	ፓ	ፔ	ፕ	ፖ	p'

---

[164] Although in limited contexts, this character is used to represent the glottal stop /ʔ/ as in አአምሮ ʔaʔmɨro 'mind'. In Old Amharic, as in Tigrinya and Geʻez, ዐ represents the pharyngeal voiced fricative /ʕ/ and አ the glottal stop /ʔ/.

161

ፊ	ፈ	ፌ	ፋ	ፎ	ፍ	ፆ	f
ፐ	ፑ	ፒ	ፓ	ፔ	ፕ	ፖ	p
ቨ	ቩ	ቪ	ቫ	ቬ	ቭ	ቮ	v

Not including the above chart, there are some symbols. Among them is ኧ /ä/ that represents the mid-central vowel. There are also five basic characters for labiovelars with five orders each often listed in the Amharic (and Ge'ez) alphabet charts.

Table 9: Labiovelars

C^w+ä	C^w+i	C^w+a	C^w+e	C^w+o	Bare consonants
ቈ	ቊ	ቋ	ቌ	ቍ	q^w
ኈ	ኊ	ኋ	ኌ	ኍ	h^w
ኰ	ኲ	ኳ	ኴ	ኵ	k^w
ዀ	ዂ	ዃ	ዄ	ዅ	h^w
ጐ	ጒ	ጓ	ጔ	ጕ	g^w

In addition to the above characters, all of the fourth orders of the basic characters, except for /v/ in Table 6, can either add the horizontal line (_) on the foot of the characters or a similar line on the top. Those characters are understood as C^w+a, where C^w here stands for any consonant. The former applies for most of the characters as in ሏ /l^{w}a/, ሓ /h^{w}a/, ሷ /s^{w}a/ etc. whereas the latter only for few cases such as ሯ /r^{w}a/, ፏ /f^{w}a/ and ማ /m^{w}a/. Even this later case is often alternatively replaced with the lower horizontal line (_) in uniformity with the majority as in ሟ /m^{w}a/ and ፏ /f^{w}a/.

There are some points that I need to address here. When was the Amharic script created? How was it transmitted from time to time and what kind of changes did it make? I raise these questions, because we do not know much about the way the Amharic script was studied until the introduction of a government school system in the 20th century.

7.3.1 Date of Origin of the Amharic Script

As already mentioned, we have the first written document that goes back to the fourteenth century, i.e. a lyric for Amdä Seyon (1312-1342/1314-1444). In this lyric, see section 7.2 above, we have the symbols such as ኘ, ሽ, ጀ, ጠ, ጨ and ኸ as in ሐርበኛ (L.1), መላላሽ (L. 2), ከወጀ (L. 4), ዝን (L.10), ጭራ (L.35), and አላጸፍኸው (L.23) respectively. These symbols are not those of Ge'ez. There are two lyrics praising the deeds of Dawit (1375-1404) in Bruce 88 manuscript. These lyrics are among the oldest Amharic written materials. Fortunately, in both lyrics too, we have the symbols which are not those of Ge'ez. In fact, all of the seven unique Amharic symbols, i.e. ኘ, ሽ, ጀ, ጠ, ቸ, ጨ and ኸ, are found in these lyrics for Dawit. Consider these lyrics below:

Lyrics for Dawit

I

አንት፡ ልጅ፡ የብስማግ።	Line (=L.) 1
ለምን፡ ጸላኸ፡ የኛን፡ ፍቅር።	
ምሽት፡ ስጥተነኸ፡ ዊዛር።	
አከል፡ ስጥተነኸ፡ ሐመር።	
ሰፊ፡ ስጥተነኸ፡ ሀገር።	L. 5
ለምን፡ ጸላኸው፡ የእኛን፡ ፍቅር።	
ድላ፡ ተመተር።	
ሐአባትኸ፡ አገር።	
ቢጸባ፡ መስቀል።	
ይስሐቅ፡ ደረስ፡ ስትል።	L. 10
እንደ፡ አግዓዘን፡ ደምብር።	
እንደ፡ ቀኁር፡ ብረር።	
ጎልቆኸን፡ ቀጻር።	
ልጅ፡ ምሽትኸን፡ ዘዝር።	
ድላ፡ ተመተር፡ ሐአባትኸ፡ አገር።	L. 15
ዝን፡ እንግዴ፡ የሰማ፡ ነገር።	
አንበሳ፡ ዳዊት፡ ተኳር።	
ይበላ፡ አልጸፈጠው፦ እኸል።	
ይጠጣ፡ አልጸፈጠው፦ ቅምብር።	
ገነኑ፡ ቢሉ፡ ገበር።	L. 20
በሽንገ፡ አሉ፡ ሰፈር።	
ስንቱን፡ እቀኁጻር።	
የሐላባ፡ ገበር።	
የጣይቶ፡ ገበር።	
የላቦላ፡ ገበር።	L. 25
የጌደብ፡ ገበር።	
ስንቱን፡ እቀኁጻር።	

የጉዴላ፡ ገባር፡፡
ሲፈክር፡ ነበር፡፡
ስንኳ፡ ለአምሓራ ጌር፡፡   L. 30
ሰማይ፡ ቢከነበል፡፡
እናቆም፡ ሲሉ፡ ነበር፡ በጾር፡፡
ሲፈክሩ፡ ነበር፡፡
አጠፋዋቾ፡ ለከር፡፡
ደርሶ፡ በስንገ፡ ሠፈር፡፡   L. 35
አጠፋዋቾ፡ ለዝከር፡፡
ሬሳቾ፡ በእሳት፡ ሐረር፡፡
አንበሳ፡ ዳዊት፡ ትኩር፡፡
አሉ'ክ፡ ንገብር፡፡
በአባት'ክ፡ የነበር፡፡   L. 40
ፈረስክን፡ ናቀባለ፡፡
በቅሎ'ክን፡ ናቀብል፡፡
አንጥፋ፡ ለዘር፡፡
አንበሳ፡ ዳዊት፡ ትኻር፡፡
ቢደበና'ክ፡ መገን፡፡   L. 45
ቢፈረስ'ክ፡ መገን፡፡
በሪም'ክ፡ መገን፡፡
በመሽት'ክ፡ መገን፡፡
በሕፃናት'ክ፡ መገን፡፡
አማስለ'ክ፡ አትፍጀን፡፡   L. 50
እኛስ፡ ፈቃደኛነን፡፡
እንስጥ፡ መንግሥት'ክን፡፡
ፈረስ'ክ፡ የተፈተን፡፡
ወርቅ፡ የተመዘን፡፡
ሐበት፡ ቂራጥ፡ ብለን፡፡   L. 55
ናድርስ፡ መንግሥት'ክን፡፡
አማስለ'ክ፡ አትፍጀን፡፡

II

ገነን፡ በደል፡ እሳት፡፡
ጽርሐ፡ ንግሥት፡ ታቦት፡፡
እንደ፡ ተከስዋት፡ በእሳት፡፡   L. 60
አስሐረረዋቾ፡ እርሱም፡ በእሳት፡፡
አንበሳ፡ ዳዊት፡፡
ሐሶ፡ ተሸንጉርት፡፡
መለኩሴ፡ እንዲያገስ፡ በሰዓት፡፡
ደርሶ፡ አወረደባቾ፡ የሴፍ፡ መዓት፡፡   L. 65
ተጋየሱ፡ ጊስት፡፡
ትለለቾ፡ አበቡት፡፡
ሐምል፡ ወፍራ፡ የዳዊት፡፡
የግራ፡ ቀኝ፡ ባልታት፡፡

በደብር፡ እላችኑ፡ መለኩስት። L. 70
በከተማ፡ ያላችኑ፡ ሕፃናት።
ማን፡ ተዋጋችሁ፡ አቄት።
ንጉሥ፡ በክረምት፡ ሲዘምት።
ወርኅ፡ የሌለ፡ ሲሉ፡ አለጕለት።
አለሰኔና፡ ግንቦት። L. 75
እንቲገቡ፡ ይወጹበት። አንበሳ፡ በድል፡ እሳት።
አለመለስ፡ አለዋት።
ድላ፡ ዝመት።
ማርያም፡ ትኁንሕ፡ እናት።
ሚካኤል፡ ይኁንኽ፡ አባት። L. 80
የከተሉኸ፡ ሠራዊተ፡ መላእክት።
ተነሣ፡ በተሳት። ጨማ፡ ሳይል፡ በቀልቀኣለት።
ሐርቡን፡ ሳይል፡ ኸተት።
በቅሎ፡ ሳይል፡ ለዓቀበት።
ፃርማን፡ ሲወርዱ፡ ቀኣልቀኣለት። L. 85
ጎሸ፡ ተገኛ፡ በረት።
ናንየቾ፡ ለአቄት።
ለም፡ አስመስሎ፡ የተጕለት።
የገድ፡ መዘመሪያችነት።
ጸርማን፡ በተሳት። L. 90
ሐዋሽ፡ መርማን፡ በጽዋት።
ለዝያቾ፡ ለወብራ፡ አገዊት።
ስታዝን፡ የተውነዋት።
ድላ፡ ተመለስ፡ ብስራት።
ስታዝን፡ የተውነዋት። L. 95
የሐዋሽነት፡ ምላት።
አላሰርገፈኝም፡ አባቀኣልት።
አላሰፈታንም፡ ወገረት።
ድላ፡ ተመለስ፡ ብስራት።
አብሰራ፡ ያብስረዋት። L. 100
ምንም፡ አልኁነም፡ በለዋት።
ስታዝን፡ የተውነዋት።
የወቢ፡ ምምላት።
አላሰርገፈም፡ አባቀኣልት።
አላሰፈታንም፡ ወገረት። L. 105
ድላ፡ ጔቶ፡ ንገር፡ መላኽት።
ምንም፡ አልኁነም፡ በለዋት።
ለዚአች፡ ለወብራ፡ አገዊት።
ምንም፡ አልኁነም፡ በለዋት።
አንበሳ፡ ዳዊት። L. 110
ጽርሐ፡ ንግሥትነ፡ ታቦት።
እንደተከዕሰዋት፡ ታበእሳት።

አሳረርዎች፡ እርሱም፡ በእሳት።
ደርሱ፡ አወረደባች፡ ዮሴፍ፡[165] መዓት።
ሐሰ፡ ተሸንጉርት።   L. 115
መለኩሴ፡ እንድያገስ፡ በተሳት።
አወረደባች፡ ዮሴፍ፡ መዓት።
አንበሳ፡ ዳዊት። (Bruce 88)

As can be seen above, all the non-Ge'ez symbols are found in the songs for Dawit. Consider for ኛ, for instance, የ(እ)ኛን (L. 2 & L. 6) and ቆኛ (L. 69); for ሽ, ምሽት (L. 3), ምሽትክን (L. 14), ጎሽ (L. 86), ሐዋሽ (L. 91) and የሐዋሽነት (L. 86) (L. 21); for ጅ, ልጅ (L. 1 & L. 14) and አትፍጀን (L. 50 & 57); for ጨ, ጨማ (L. 82); for ጋ, በሽንጋ (L. 21), ጋን (L. 16 & 58) and መጠመሪያችነት (L. 89); for ች, አወረደባች (L. 117), ለዝያች (L. 92), and አጠፋዎች (L. 34 & 36); and for ኸ, ጸላኸው (L. 6), ጎልቆኸን (L. 13), እኸል (18), and በደበናኸ (L. 45).

Although I argue that the imperial songs might have been written down at the time of their composition, whether they originally were written with different symbols is hard to tell. As I have pointed out in section 7.2, we have documents written in Amharic from the sixteenth century. As can be seen from texts attached in the appendix, we have the "unique" Amharic symbols in this period. Although the date for imperial songs are not exactly known and other Amharic writings only date back to the 16th century, it seems to be the case that the Amharic script was created at a much earlier date than the 16th century.

As pointed out above, Maqrizi mentions that besides the Christian kingdom, the Muslim kingdoms of Ethiopia had fifty plus dialects as early as the fifteenth century were written with the Ethiopic script, with what Maqrizi refers to as the Abyssinian script.

> They [i.e. the 50 plus dialects spoken in the seven Muslim kingdoms of the Zayla region of Abyssinia] write from right to left, and use 16 letters. Each letter has 7 forms, which brings their number to 112, except for six other letters which stand by themselves and have nothing in common with any of the 16 letters we have spoken of. The vowels are joined to the consonants and are not separated from them (Maqrizi as translated by Huntingford 1955: 11).

---

[165] This word does not make sense in this context. Its original form most probably is የሴፍ 'of sword', as appeared in L.65. See also Gezahegn (2004).

THE DEVELOPMENT OF AMHARIC AS A WRITTEN LANGUAGE

The script that Maqrizi mentions is definitely the Ethiopic script but it does not seem that it was modified to properly suit each of the respective languages. However, there are some problems with Maqrizi's account. First, the figure he gave is unreliable. The Ge'ez script has 26 basic characters, not 16 and Amharic has seven additional basic letters which have seven orders like the others (cf. Table 6). It is unlikely that only 16 letters with their basic orders were used to write those languages since not only Amharic but most other Ethiopian languages also require more symbols than described by Maqrizi. Second, as pointed out above, it is very difficult to assume that all the 50 plus languages were put into writing at that time. However, it is most likely the case that, some of them or at least what Maqrizi calls the Abyssinian, i.e. Amharic-Argobba (the language of Yifat) were written down. Consider the following remark from the eighteenth century English traveler James Bruce:

> None of the many other languages (i.e. other than Ge'ez), spoken in Abyssinia, have characters for writing them. But when the Amharic was substituted, in common use and conversation, for the Geez, after the restoration of the Royal Family from their long banishment in Shoa, seven new characters were necessarily added, and these apparently were invented by the scribes, but no book was ever yet written in any other language except Geez. On the contrary, there is an old law in this country, handed down by tradition only, that whoever should attempt to translate the Holy Scripture into Amharic, or any other language, his throat should be cut after the manner in which they kill sheep, his family sold to slavery, and his house razed to the ground; and, whether the fear of this law was true or feigned, it was a great obstacle to me in getting those translations of the Song of Solomon made, which I intend for specimens of different languages of those distinct nations (Bruce 1813: 341- 342).

As Bruce remarks, some of the additional symbols were probably used at least at Maqrizi's time. It might be also the case that some of the symbols used for writing Amharic might have been created even earlier than the 13th century, at least during the Zague dynasty to write foreign words in Ge'ez.

Based on the information from an Amharic native speaker and well-educated Church scholar called Gregory, Ludolph (1682) explained how

167

THE ORIGIN OF AMHARIC

the study of Ge'ez was conducted in Ethiopia in the following way:

> They (the Europeans) are contented only with a vocabularie wherein according to several classes, the Ethiopic words are explained in the Amharic dialect. They call it a ladder, in imitation of the Arabians, who call such a kind of book, a (u) Great Scale or Ladder. The more unskillful seek for such words therein which they do not understood in the Ethiopic; but there are very few that speak Ethiopic [Ge'ez] in Ethiopia itself (Ludolph 1682: 78-79).

Note that, Ge'ez writings flourished with the restoration of the Amharic-speaking Solomonic dynasty in 1270 when Ge'ez had already long ago ceased to be a spoken language. Note that also the emperors used Ge'ez for sending messages in their official correspondence, not only with foreign countries but also with the various governors of the local regions until the mid 19th century. See for example Maqrizi's account for such exchange of letters between the emperors and the governors of the Yifat sultanate as early as the 14th and 15th centuries. Although we do not have many documents about the Zague period, we know that the emperors then were devoted Orthodox Christians and continued using Ge'ez not only for religious purposes but also for official correspondence. Since Agew, the main lingua franca of the Zague dynasty, and Amharic have sounds which are not found in Ge'ez, the additional symbols needed to write Amharic were probably created during this time.

Getatchew (1970:70) observes from a 16th century manuscript where "the palatals are not developed". As pointed out in the preceding section, it was a common practice to write *andemta*-commentaries in Amharic on the margins of Ge'ez manuscripts. Nevertheless, no such commentaries are found written in Amharic before the 16th century. Even if this is the case, we do find words containing "Amharic" symbols in other Ge'ez writings of the 16th century and earlier. For instance, in Aba Bahrie's work on Oromo Ethnography, we have words such as ጁዳ, ጨረቃ, ጿሌ, ጨሪ, and ሰያፍ. These and a number of other words in Bahrie's work contain Amharic symbols (Getatchew Haile 1997EC: 63ff.). Note that also the title ičʼäge was given to Abunä Tekle-Haymanot of the 13th century. It is importatnt to note that also the pre-15th century famus author of various religious books was referred to as Abunä Giorgis Zägasäčʼ. In the documents that I consulted in both cases, they have the symbol for /č/. Moreover, in the 16th century manuscript known as Timhertä Haymanot 'Teaching of the Faith' all the basic Amharic letters are found. See, for instance in the appendix, for ጨ /č'/, ቢጨምር (Plate II, column 2, line 5); for ሽ /š/, ይሳው (Plate I, column 2, line 20); for ች /č/, ማየች (Plate I, column 1, line 20); for ኽ /x/, የሸኽ (Plate I, column 3, line 19) etc. The unavailability of the palatals in the 16th century work that Getatchew referred to above is most probably due to the unfamiliarity of the scribe with the Amharic symbols. However, note that, Bahrie's original copy is not yet found. The documents that Getatchew and others referred to are later copies with a varied degree of differences (Getatchew 1997 EC). Moreover, I have to admit that the documents that contain some of the Amharic symbols such as ጨ and ጰ mentioned above are not original copies. However, even with lack of authentic documents from earlier centuries, from the reasons discussed so far, it seems that the Amharic script or at least some of its "unique" symbols developed probably in the 13th century or earlier as pointed out above. However, note that, in an inscription which is suggested to be written in the eighth century the word that seems to contain the palatal ሽ is written as መንገሳ mängäsa (instead of መንገሻ mängäsha). As Sergew (1972: 198) remarks, this is because ሽ "had not been developed at that time".

7.3.2 Development/Changes in the Amharic Script

When we examine earlier manuscripts such as those of the sixteenth and the seventeenth centuries, there were some symbols, which were shaped differently. Some have already noticed these facts in certain manuscripts. For example, Getatchew Haile (1979a) has examined the 17th century manuscript, EMML 1943, f.3v, and notes the following reagarding the shape of some letters: "The horizontal line of the symbols of palatalized consonants, and more especially of those which are placed on an added carrier, is not obvious, e.g. ኗ as in ኛርንኗ " (Getatchew 1979a: 233). Getatchew further notes that "the form of the sixth order of ች is not known, instead the third order is used, e.g. ወለጄ... It is not clear in what order ጀ in ጀሐር is" (Ibid 234). Getatchew (Ibid.) also observes in the same manuscript two representations of the fifth form of ገ; ጌ and ጔ as in ጌተፎ and ጔተከሞ. Getatchew claims that the latter form "is probably a mistake". It is difficult to agree with some of Getatchew's comments made above, however.

In the 17th century Amharic alphabet given in Ludolf (1682) the third form of ገ is represented as ጔ where the current third form is used as the sixth order. The letter ጌ is not mentioned in Ludolf's alphabet (see Figure 14 below). Second, although the top horizontal line of the palatalized consonants in most cases is missing in the text that

Getatchew referred to, it is not always like that. Consider, for instance, the following usage of /ña/ in [Amharic]. In fact, this same letter was written at different places differently in transcribing the same word. Consider this symbol from the same manuscript that Getatchew refers to in the last word of the second line below and compare it with the one quoted above:

ዳግም ፡ ዕጣነ ፡ ሞገር ።
አግለ ፡ ክሎስ ፡ ሣሮቡ ፡ የሣርበ𝑛 (Getatchew 1979a: 230)[166]

Third, although Getatchew mentions that the order of the letter ਸ is not clear, at another point following Cowley he suggests that it is most probably the first order. This might be the case for the particular case that Getatchew mentioned. However, this does not mean this symbol is used as the first order in all its occurrences in OA. As can be seen from the following chart of the 19th century, it is listed as the sixth order.[167]

Figure 8: The Amharic additional symbols

CARACTÈRES ADDITIONNELS EN AMARIÑÑA.

ሸ ša	ሹ šu	ሺ si	ሻ ša	ሼ še	ሽ și	ሾ šo
ቸ ca	ቹ cu	ቺ ci	ቻ ca	ቼ ce	ች ci	ቾ co
ኘ ña	ኙ ñu	ኚ ñi	ኛ ña	ኜ ñe	ኝ ñi	ኞ ño
ከ ka	ኩ ku	ኪ ki	ካ ka	ኬ ke	ክ ki	ኮ ko
ዠ ja	ዡ ju	ዢ ji	ዣ ja	ዤ je	ዥ ji	ዦ jo
ጀ ja	ጁ ju	ጂ ji	ጃ ja	ጄ je	ጅ ji	ጆ jo
ጨ ça	ጩ çu	ጪ çi	ጫ ça	ጬ çe	ጭ çi	ጮ ço

PRINCIPALES CONSONNES À DIPHTONGUES USITÉES EN AMARIÑÑA.

ሏ ሟ ሯ ሷ ሿ ቧ ቷ ቿ ኋ ዟ ዯ ዷ ጧ ጯ ጿ ፏ
lua mua rua sua šua bua tua cua nua zua yua dua ṭua çua ẓua fua

The usage of the letter ਸ as sixth order is very common until mid-20th century. See, for instance, the collected correspondence letters of Alfred

---

[166] Note that this is the handwritten copy that Getatchew (1979a) made. See for the photocopy of the original in the appendix in his article.
[167] The chart is from Abbadie (1859: VII).

Ilg published by Bairu Tafla (2000). Even in the 19th century this symbol was used interchangeably with the one used currently, ሸ. For instance, Littmann (1902) in the published version of the chronicle of Emperor Theodore II written by Aleqa Zeneb (1902) used this symbol stating that from the original manuscript the letter "ሸ has been replaced by its second form ኰ" (Littmann 1902: VII). In Afework (1905) too the sixth order is given as ኰ in the list of Amharic alphabet and used throughout the book. The Amharic alphabet in Guidi (1901) Amharic-Italian dictionary and Guidi (1892) Amharic grammar and Armbruster (1908) also listed ኰ as the sixth order. In the 17th century alphabet given in Job Ludolph (1682: 7) too, it is listed as the sixth order.

THE ORIGIN OF AMHARIC

Figure 97: The Amharic Alphabet from Ludolph (1682)

Hoi	υ	ha	υ·	hu	ዝ	hi	Ν	ha	ሃ	he	υ	he	ሆ	ho
Lawi	ለ	la	ሉ	lu	ሊ	li	ላ	la	ሌ	le	ል	le	ሎ	lo
Haut	ሐ	ha	ሑ	hu	ሒ	hi	ሓ	ha	ሔ	he	ሕ	he	ሖ	ho
Mai	መ	me	ሙ	mu	ሚ	mi	ማ	ma	ሜ	me	ም	me	ሞ	mo
Saut	ሠ	se	ሡ	su	ሢ	si	ሣ	sa	ሤ	se	ሥ	se	ሦ	so
Rees	ረ	re	ሩ	ru	ሪ	ri	ራ	ra	ሬ	re	ር	re	ሮ	ro
Sat	ሰ	sa	ሱ	su	ሲ	si	ሳ	sa	ሴ	se	ስ	se	ሶ	so
Kaf	ቀ	ka	ቁ	ku	ቂ	ki	ቃ	ka	ቄ	ke	ቅ	ke	ቆ	ko
Bet	በ	be	ቡ	bu	ቢ	bi	ባ	ba	ቤ	be	ብ	be	ቦ	bo
Tawi	ተ	te	ቱ	tu	ቲ	ti	ታ	ta	ቴ	te	ት	te	ቶ	to
Haun	ኀ	ha	ኁ	hu	ኂ	hi	ኃ	ha	ኄ	he	ኅ	he	ኆ	ho
Nahas	ነ	na	ኑ	nu	ኒ	ni	ና	na	ኔ	ne	ን	ne	ኖ	no
Alph	አ	a	ኡ	u	ኢ	i	ኣ	a	ኤ	e	እ	e	ኦ	o
Qaf	ከ	qa	ኩ	qu	ኪ	qi	ካ	qa	ኬ	qe	ክ	qe	ኮ	qo
Wawe	ወ	we	ዉ	wu	ዊ	wi	ዋ	wa	ዌ	we	ው	we	ዎ	wo
Ain	ዐ	a	ዑ	u	ዒ	i	ዓ	a	ዔ	e	ዕ	e	ዖ	o
Zai	ዘ	za	ዙ	zu	ዚ	zi	ዛ	za	ዜ	ze	ዝ	ze	ዞ	zo
Jaman	የ	je	ዩ	ju	ዪ	ji	ያ	ja	ዬ	je	ይ	je	ዮ	jo
Dent	ደ	de	ዱ	du	ዲ	di	ዳ	da	ዴ	de	ድ	de	ዶ	do
Geml	ገ	ge	ጉ	gu	ጊ	ghi	ጋ	ga	ጌ	ghe	ግ	ghe	ጎ	go
Tait	ጠ	te	ጡ	tu	ጢ	ti	ጣ	ta	ጤ	te	ጥ	te	ጦ	to
Pait	ጰ	pa	ጱ	pu	ጲ	pi	ጳ	pa	ጴ	pe	ጵ	pe	ጶ	po
Zadai	ጸ	tza	ጹ	tzu	ጺ	tzi	ጻ	tza	ጼ	tze	ጽ	tze	ጾ	tzo
Zappa	ፀ	tza	ፁ	tzu	ፂ	tzi	ፃ	tza	ፄ	tze	ፅ	tze	ፆ	tzo
Af	ፈ	fa	ፉ	fu	ፊ	fi	ፋ	fa	ፌ	fe	ፍ	fe	ፎ	fo
Psa	ፐ	pa	ፑ	pu	ፒ	pi	ፓ	pa	ፔ	pe	ፕ	pe	ፖ	po

A. *Angl ou Gall* i *Ital* a *longum* c *clar* e *obscur* o *Long*

THE DEVELOPMENT OF AMHARIC AS A WRITTEN LANGUAGE

As pointed out above the usage of the letter ጀ as the sixth order is common for a number of centuries. This does not mean that Getatchew's observation is wrong. It seems a fact that ጀ is also used as a first order as can be inferred from Cowley's (1974) remark in words such as ጀመረ. It is also true that ጅ is used as the sixth order in the aforementioned text. The interchange use between ጅ and ጀ is evidenced by Getatchew's examples.

An alternative form for ጀ with two horizontal legs in the bottom, ጄ, is also found in many manuscripts (see for instance the imperial lyrics in the appendix). Armbruster (1908) although lists ጀ as the sixth order in the Amharic alphabet chart, he states that ጄ and ጅ also used alternatively as the sixth order. Isenberg also provided the Amharic alphabet chart in both his dictionary (1841) and grammar (1842) and has ጄ as the sixth order. On the other hand, there seems to be another alternative list of characters for the representation of /ž/ in OA. For instance, Praetorius (1879: 17) lists the following symbols where the first order and the sixth order have very similar shape:

ጀžā ጄ ጇ ጀ ጅ ጀ ጄ

173

∂ THE ORIGIN OF AMHARIC

From the above list it is difficult to differentiate between the first order and the sixth order symbols. It seems that the same symbol is used to represent both "orders". In the manuscripts we have the following examples: መጀመሪያ 'first' and ጀመረ 'he started, began' (Praetorius 1879:17) where ጀ is used as the first order.

In general, there are some differences between the current alphabet and the alphabet given in Job Ludolph (Table 14). Among such differences, the sixth order of /ž/ discussed above is the one. Currently it is written as ዥ. The symbol for the affricative ejective /č/ is also different from what is used at present. In its current usage, this sound with its seven forms is represented as ጨ, ጩ, ጪ, ጫ, ጬ, ጭ, and ጮ.[168] In fact, even in recent years there are some changes especially with some diphthongs as pointed out in the preceding section and as can be seen in Abbadie's chart above. However, generally speaking, the majority of the symbols in the 17th century Amharic alphabet we saw above are the same with today's alphabet. Although there are some changes in some of the symbols, such changes cannot be considered as unusual. If we consider even the English alphabet, we see some changes after the introduction of the printing press. Now, the question is how Amharic kept its alphabet for such a long time almost unchanged without the existence of any known formal education to study Amharic?

7.3.3 The Study of Amharic Script

Until the introduction of a government school system in the beginning of the 20th century, religious institutions, namely the Orthodox Church, the Quranic and the missionary schools, provided the main education. Although Maqrizi, in the 15th century, mentions that the then Muslim

---

[168] Note that, however, the 16th century manuscript known as Timherte Haymanot 'Teaching of the Faith' has the same symbol for /č/ as what we have today. This is unlike what is given in Ludolph. It might be the case that as late as the 17th century, probably both forms, i.e. the current symbol and that of the one given in Ludolph, were used interchangeably. Different forms are also observed with other characters. For instance, the other 16th century manuscript about Mary who anointed Jesus' feet of the Jerusalem version published by Cowley (1983) has the bar subscript, i.e. a horizontal underline on the foot of the character, for /ñ/ instead of the superscript as used currently. Consider the following few examples:

(i) a. ለእኚ
    b. ያልኸኙ (Cowley 1983:4)

sultanates of Ethiopia used the Ethiopic script for writing local languages, we do not have any evidence that the Quranic schools (which are the main, probably the only, centers of education for Muslims at that time and until the introduction of a government school system) used to teach the Ethiopic script. As is the case for other Muslims, Arabic is a holy language for Ethiopian Muslims, and "is considered to be inseparable from the study of Quran and Islamic literature in their primary sources" (Haile-Gabreil 1976: 349). On the contrary, the local languages were written with the Arabic script. Such works came to be known as Ajem.

The Orthodox Church schools are the oldest and were established since the fourth century (Hail-Gebereil 1976: 349). However, we do not have any evidence that Amharic was taught in the Ethiopian Orthodox school system in earlier days. Amharic, in fact, was taught probably for the first time, in the missionary schools. The first missionary schools were assumed to have established by the Jesuits around the beginning of the 17th century.

> By 1617, the Jesuits at Fermona had a seminary with sixteen Portuguese children and two sons of noblemen, and were giving instruction in their own houses to an unspecified number of local children; the missionaries had in addition a seminary with thirty-four youngsters in Dembea and a school for thirty-five children in Gojjam. The students were taught to read and write in both Portuguese and Amharic, into which latter language one of the fathers had already translated a treatise on the alleged doctrinal errors of the Ethiopians as well as sundry religious texts (Pankhurst 1976: 310).

The missionaries, in fact, taught Amharic wherever they established schools, even in areas where Amharic was not spoken as a first language. According to Pankhurst, the Roman Catholic Lazarists established schools in the 1870s and 1880s among other places in Keren. They ran a mixed school and orphanage and "a boys' school at Akrur in Akele Guzay Province where 20 children were taught to read and write both in Amharic and Tigrinya" (Pankhurst 1976: 314). Both places are in Eritrea. In this same former region of Ethiopia, Italians taught to the locals among others Amharic, as early as the 1890s (Pankhurst 1976: 314).

A missionary named Isenberg also wrote the first known Amharic textbook. Isenberg along with another missionary named Krapf also ran a school for boys in Shoa in the 1830s (Pankhurst 1976: 311). However, it is very difficult to assume that it is due to the missionary schools that Amharic kept its script for such a long time, i.e. transmitted from one generation to the next. First, we do not have any evidence of the existence of such missionary schools before the 17th century anywhere in Ethiopia. Because of religious strife, the missionaries were sent back to their homes. Since the middle of the 17th century, for around two centuries, no foreign missionary schools were operation in Ethiopia. Therefore, the only institution in place for the transmission of the Amharic script, if not its teaching, was the Orthodox Church.

As pointed out in the preceding chapters, from the beginning of at least 1270 "Amharic acquired authority as the language spoken inside the royal court (*lissanä nigus*), as the medium of preaching and teaching in the ecclesiastical milieu and as the lingua franca of the large part of the Ethiopian highlands" (Nosnitisn 2003: 238). Note that also during this period Ge'ez was no longer a spoken language. As pointed out in section 7.2.1, and see also for an earlier account Ludolph (1682), the teaching of *sewasew* (that is grammar, rhetoric and vocabularies)[169] and *andemta-*commentaries (i.e., Amharic comments on a Ge'ez manuscript) were common practices. Although we do not have any evidence of the Amharic written commentaries and the Ge'ez-Amharic glossary that Ludolph mentions written before the 16th century, I have suggested that the Amharic script (or more appropriately the additional symbols needed for writing Amharic) most probably was created in the 13th century or earlier. From the discussion so far, it seems logical to suggest that the additional symbols needed to write Amharic most probably were studied along with the Ge'ez script, since the 13th century.

Note also that when the first government-operated school was opened in 1908 in Addis Ababa and later in the same year in Harar, "schooling was open to any one who could read and write Amharic" (Pankhurst 1976: 315). The requirement of knowing how to read and write Amharic in order to enroll in secular schools continued until recently. As there were no modern pre-schools, the learning of the Amharic alphabet in pre-school times was in churches or in private, mostly taught by church scholars. This may also indicate that such practice is an ancient one.

---

[169] These are mostly Ge'ez-Amharic glossaries.

7.4 Summary

Amharic came to be known as *Lissane Niguss* 'language of the king' either during the Zague dynasty or during the reign of Yikuno Amlak (1270 - 1285) who claimed to be a descendant of the biblical King Solomon and the legendary Queen Sheba (Aleqa Taye 1914 EC/1964 EC). As pointed out in the preceding chapters, however, some suggest that Amharic had already been in use at the imperial court before the 13th century during the Zague dynasty (1137-1270) and that the term *Lissane Niguss* in reference to Amharic goes well back to this period (Sergew 1972: 278-279). We have mentioned in the preceding chapters that the usage of Amharic as lingua franca most probably started in the 9th century. This latter date corresponds with the fall of the Axumite kingdom and the end of Ge'ez as a language of verbal communication. One of Ge'ez's golden times in writing, however, corresponds with the rise of Solomonic dynasty in the 13th century. Unfortunately, we have not found any record of Amharic written material dated to this or earlier centuries. Recall that James Bruce of the late 18th century in his travelogue reported the existence of an old traditional law which condemns the writing of Amharic. Whether due to the existence of such law or not, we do not find many manuscripts written in Amharic until the late 19th century. Unfortunately, there are not many old manuscripts in Amharic.

The earliest attested manuscript dates back to the 14th century, which appears in the form of lyrics. Its dating is controversial. Some claim that it was written later although its content is definitely that of the 14th century as it is created in praise of the great Emperor Amdä Seyon (1314-1344). More Amharic writings are found in the late 16th century when missionaries started to convert the locals in the vernacular language. This prompted the Ethiopian Orthodox scholars to respond in Amharic to defiance of their religion. When the European missionaries were expelled in the 17th century, Amharic writings continued by the Ethiopian Church scholars.

As we have seen in this chapter there are some Amharic writings that include magical scrolls in the 17th and 18th centuries. Good progress in the Amharic written tradition, however, was made in the 19th century with the reestablishment of relations with European countries, whose missionaries preferred to write and teach in Amharic, and with the reign of Emperor Theodore II (1855-1868) who used Amharic for official correspondences.

◊ THE ORIGIN OF AMHARIC

The first written materials so far found are the royal lyrics. There might be some Amharic texts lost for various different reasons. However, what we can infer from Ludolph's comments about Gregory is that written Amharic was not developed even in the seventeenth century. Gregory who was a native speaker of Amharic and well-educated in the Church found it just as difficulty to write in Amharic as it was to speak in Ge'ez (Ludolph 1682: 77ff.).

As Cowely (1967) clearly remarks, there were certain spelling variations as recently as the 1960s, meaning that the writing was hardly standardized.[170] As we can see from the sample texts of the early 20th century discussed in this chapter (see also the appendix), the language was more of a spoken language. Punctuation marks are not standardized. It seems that only three punctuation marks; namely, *hulät nät'ib* (:), *dirrib säräz* (፤) and *'arat nät'ib* (።), were used at that time.

With regard to the Amharic script there were problems with standardization. Even in its current usage, there are some symbols such as ሀ, ሐ, and ኀ which no longer mark distinct phonemes. These all represent a single phoneme /h/, as Amharic lost through time the respective sounds (see the next chapter). Moreover, since Amharic took all the Ge'ez characters as they are, the symbols ሠ and ሰ (which do not have different phonemes in Amharic) stand for the single phoneme /s/. Standard Amharic writing also does not mark gemination.[171] Apart from these, as Cowley (1967: 1) also points out, the Amharic script from its inception is approximately phonetic.

In this chapter, I have raised some points on the origin and development of the Amharic writing as well as its script. It is almost impossible to undertake a very detailed analysis of this subject here. Nor is the intention of this work to perform such a thorough discussion. This topic alone would require volumes of its own work.

---

[170] See for the effort made to standardize the Amharic script by the Haile Selasse government, the report in Journal of Ethiopian Studies (1970), Vol. VIII:1; 119-134.
[171] See Bender, Head and Cowley (1976) and Cowley (1967) among many others on this point.

Chapter Eight: A Grammatical Sketch of Old Amharic[172]

8.1 Introduction

This chapter examines old Amharic manuscripts with regard to the diachronic grammar of Amharic. There are three core points which I would like to address in this chapter. As discussed in the preceding chapters, it is widely entertained that through a pidgin-induced process (a) Amharic lost the core pharyngeal and glottal Semitic phonetic features (Baye 2000 EC); (b) the syntax of Amharic became uncharacteristic for a Semitic language (Bender 1983, Baye 2000 EC) and (c) its morphology acquired properties of Cushitic languages (Baye 2000 EC). In chapter four, I have argued that such assumption is far-fetched. To examine further the validity of such suggestion, I will mainly examine here the grammar of Old Amharic based on its early manuscripts of the 16th and pre-16th centuries.

Besides the panegyrics of Amdä Seyon (1314-1344), Dawit (1375-1404), Yishaq (1413-1428), Zär'a Ya'qob (1433-1467), Gälawdewos

---

[172] This chapter is a slightly modified version of my own paper entitled "A Grammar of Amharic from Pre-17th Century Manuscripts" in Sy, Habib. (ed). *Africa the Cradle of Writing*. Paris: L'Harmattan. I thank Daniel Abera, Ronny Meyer, Kassahun Chekole and Hailu Habtu for their comments on the earlier version of this chapter. I also thank Habib Sy for both the encouraging and stimulating discussions we had.

(1540-1559),[173] there are two important manuscripts that can be safely dated back to the 16th and pre-16th centuries. As discussed in the preceding chapter, these are Timhirte Haymant 'Teaching of the Faith' and a manuscript about Mary who anointed Jesus' feet. My argumentation in this work is mainly based on these oldest Amharic manuscripts. There are other manuscripts of this period. For instance, Getatchew Haile (1970) brought to our attention a manuscript which can be dated to the same period containing a glossary of Arabic with a translation into Ge'ez and Amharic.[174]

The manuscript about Mary who anointed Jesus' feet discussed by Cowley (1983) appeared also in Ludolf (1698a&b). The version in Ludolf, however, is shorter than what Cowley found in the Jerusalem collection of Ethiopian manuscripts. Cowley's (1983) discussion includes both versions of the manuscript. The manuscript is referred to as Fragmentum Piquesii and abbreviated as FP in Cowley. I will use Cowley's abbreviation and call this manuscript FP.[175] I focus on the Jerusalem version of the manuscript as it is more complete than the one discussed by Ludolf. Unless stated otherwise, FP refers only to the Jerusalem manuscript as it appeared in Cowley (1983). Following Cowley (1974), I will refer to Timhirte Haymant as TM.

My aim here is to examine the grammar of Amharic as reflected through the aforementioned manuscripts. It is not my intention to look at the historical changes that Amharic made through different periods although I may make an occasional remark here and there. I will continue refering to the language of this period as Old Amharic, OA, although this term is used in some works in reference to pre-20th century Amharic. I use the term modern Amharic, MA, for the language spoken today without

---

[173] For the imperial songs, I often use Guidi (1889) for ease of reference. However, I cross checked with the earliest manuscript, i.e. Bruce 88, for any cited examples here and alternatively used also Bruce 88. The collection of the imperial lyrics as found in Bruce 88 appeared in the appendix.

[174] Getatchew Haile discusses two manuscripts which he dated to the 16th and 17th centuries. However, he mostly used the one from the 16th century. I also will consider some examples from Getatchew Haile (1970) although it remained unclear to which of the two manuscripts a particular example belongs. There are also no copies of the original texts given in an appendix.

[175] As Cowley notes, Ludolf got the manuscript from his friend Ludovicus Piques who found it "among Ethiopic folios of Seguier's library" (Cowley 1983: 1). It is due to this that the manuscript is referred to as Fragmentum Piquesii. Ludolf made use of the text in his grammar and dictionary and appended a short fragment of it in his grammar work (see Ludolf 1698:59).

giving any theoretical status to my usages.[176, 177]

8.2 Phonology

The general assumption with regard to Ethiopic letters which are also used for writing Amharic is that ሐ and ዐ represent the pharyngeal fricatives /ħ/ and /ʕ/ respectively, አ the glottal stop /ʔ/ and ሀ the glottal fricative /h/.[178] However, it is unclear what the phonetic representation of ኀ was in Ge'ez. In Tigrinya, ኀ is just an alternative representation of the voiceless pharyngeal fricative ሐ /ħ/. However, this form most probably was representing the velar fricative /x/ in Ge'ez, which in the modern languages is written with ከ (see also Dillmann 1899/1907:16). Getatchew (1970: 61) observes that "a word is written with ኀ because it is very often closer to ከ than to ሀ. A good example would be አኁን "now" (today normally spelt አሁን) which is sometimes written አኹን". In FP, out of four occurrences of this same word, i.e. axun, only one is written with ኀ (see the attached manuscript in the appendix). The other three words use ከ instead. This usage of ኀ for /x/ is probably a result of Ge'ez influence. We cannot rely on this matter with regard to its usage in OA, however. OA has ከ which is undeniably phonetically closer to /ħ/ since they share place of articulation. ከ is clearly used as /x/ as can be seen, for instance from ከተተ *xität* DL, L83 (Bruce 88) which is currently pronounced as ከተተ *kität*. In some words ሐ is used instead of ከ. For instance, the MA preposition ከ /kä/ is sometimes written with ሐ in OA as in ሐዳኚ *xi-dañña* to-judge 'to a judge' FP, (Cowley 1983:10) and (16) ሐአባትከ አገር *x-abbat-ix agär* from-father-2mspos country 'from the land/country of your father' DL, L8, L15 (Bruce 88). This same preposition is also written with ኀ as recent as the 19th century as can be seen from D'Abbadie's (1881: 3) dictionary ኀ-ገበያ ነበርኩ *xi-gäbäya näbbär-hu* in-market was-1ss 'I was in the market', ኀ-ታች *xi-tačč* from-below 'down'. This kind of confusion is found in a number of Ge'ez texts

---

[176] A similar naming and abbreviation are used in Cowley (1983).

[177] To establish a clear theoretically categorization of the various periods of Amharic, one needs to examine carefully the grammar and lexicon of the language as exemplified in different periods. For such comparison, there are valuable sources on Amharic grammar such as Ludolf (1698), Isenberg (1842), Praetorius (1879), Armbruster (1908), Leslau (1995) and Baye (2000 EC) that one should consider. See also Little (1974) and the works cited here-and-there in this chapter for some discussion on the historical grammar of Amharic.

[178] We are using here and throughout this chapter the first order of the Ethiopic alphabet to represent consonants. For further issues on transcription, see "Notes on Transcription" in the appendix.

as well. The mixing of the symbols has most probably to do with the writer's poor knowledge of the alphabet. Such mixing can be found in a single manuscript. For instance, consider from DL, L79 ት኉ንሕ and L80 ይ኉ንኸ (Bruce 88) where ኉, ሕ and ኸ seem representing the same sound. The first radical of the verb "become" is pronounced as /k/ in Geʿez /k/ or /x/ in Tigirnya. It is plausible to assume that ኉ in the above examples represent /x/. The second person marker alternates in MA between /k/ and /h/ depending on the preceding sound. The form in OA in the above examples can also be assumed as representing /x/. These two examples can therefore be transcribed as t*i-xun-ih 2fss-become$_{Impf}$-2msNSA* and t*i-xun-ih 2mss-become$_{Impf}$-2msNSA*.

As pointed out above, the current usage of ዓ in Tigrinya is an alternate to ሐ. In OA, except few cases, its usage seems also related to ሐ rather than to ኸ. Consider, for instance, ዓንጌቴ 'my neck' FP (Cowley 1983: 7) and ሐንጌት 'neck' YL, L. 37 (Guidi 1889: 55). The same word 'neck' is written in the former with ዓ and in the latter with ሐ. It is logical to suggest in these two cases that both represent the same sound, most probably the pharyngeal fricative /ħ/ as in Tigrinya. Hence, these two words can be transcribed as follows:

(1) a. ዓንጌቴ FP (Cowley 1983: 7)
    ħaŋgät-e
    neck-1sposs
    'My neck'
   b. ሐንጌት YL, L. 37 (Guidi 1889: 55)
    ħaŋgät
    'Neck'

The present form in (1) is አንጌት *angät* 'neck' with the loss of the initial consonant /ħ/. The alternation of ሐ and ዓ in old Amharic is, in fact, very common as can be seen also in (2) with the perfective verb 'see'. It is logical to assume that ሐ and ዓ in these examples represent the same sound /ħ/.[179]

---

[179] Note that there seems to be a phonological change between pharyngeal and glottal sounds. Such change, however seems only to occur during derivations as evidenced by the following Shonke Argobba example: ሐለቅ *halläq* 'he ended' vs. ማህለቅ *mahläq* 'to end, ending'. *halläq* is a perfective verb with a default third masculine singular subject agreement whereas *mahläq* is an infinitive which, in Argobba and other Ethio-Semitic languages, is a verbal noun corresponding to the English gerund rather than to the infinitive.

(2) a. ጎዩ TM, Plate II, Column 2
ḥay-u
see_perf-3pls
'They saw'
b. የሐየኽ YL, L. 11 (Guidi 1889: 54)
yä-ḥay-ä-x
RM-see_perf-3mss-2mso
'that/who saw you'

From the example in (2b), it is important to consider the usage of the symbol ኽ, which I transcribe as /x/. ኽ in this example is the second person masculine singular subject agreement marker (2mss) as can be seen also from the morphological gloss.[180] Although in current Amharic this sound is pronounced /h/, I assume that the 2mss marker ኽ in (2b) is /x/. The change from OA /x/ to MA /h/ is caused by phonological conditioning. Hence, in OA it is safe to assume the pronunciation of ጎ often to be the same as ሐ.[181] Considering this to be the case, I investigate the phonemic features of this and other sounds which are not found in MA or are marginal in § 8.2.1. A few words on the historical loss of such phonemes and phonological processes made before their loss will be discussed in § 8.2.2.

8.2.1 Phonemic features

Modern Amharic is known for lacking the pharyngeal sounds ሐ /ħ/ and ዐ /ʕ/ and the glottal sound አ /ʔ/ which are typical of Semitic languages. Baye (2000 EC) even considers this as a support of Bender's claim of Amharic's pidgin past. I have challenged this assumption in the preceding chapter, based on among other factors, the existence of such phonemes in Argobba[182] and in historical Amharic itself as recent as 18th century.[183] The manuscripts considered here also show the existence of

---

[180] Note that, as pointed out above ኽ has an allomorph /k/ in MA.

[181] The inconsistency of spelling has to do with the scribe's knowledge of the alphabet as it is found in some cases in a single manuscript. For instance, in TM we have በተሐየው Plate II, column 3, የሚትሐይን plate III, column 3 and ጎዩ Plate II, Column 2 (cf. 2a above).

[182] This is true especially with the Shonke-Tollaha variety of Argobba (cf. Wetter 2011, Demeke 2011). Argobba is a closely related language to Amharic and was assumed to be its dialect.

[183] The pharyngeal constants have been lost in the 19th century. For instance, Isenberg (1842) claims that the distinction is totally lost in Amharic in his time: "In the present Amharic [i.e. mid 19th century], ሀ: ሐ and ጎ are pronounced alike, like *h* in horse, and are often exchanged for አ:, thus entirely dropping the

such sounds in Old Amharic.

There seems to be no difference between ሐ and ኀ in OA. As pointed out above, both in most cases represent the pharyngeal sound /ħ/. In MA no existence of this pharyngeal sound is found. Despite that, the reduction of this and other pharyngeal consonants may have started even at an earlier time. /ħ/ is found almost in every word position in the manuscripts investigated here.[184] Consider the following where it exists at the initial position in all manuscripts under consideration:[185]

(3) a. ሐርበኛ ዓምደ ጽዮን AL, L.1 (Guidi 1889:62)
    ħarbäñña ʕamdä sˈɨyon
    Warrior Amdä Seyon
    'The warrior Amdä Seyon'
  b. ሐፍሶ YL, L. 5 (Guidi 1889:55)
    ħafs-o
    scoop up/gather$_{gerund}$-3mss
    'After gathering, scooping up'
  c. ሐንዘት ZYL, L2 (Guidi 1889:55)
    ħanžät
    'intestine'
  d. ሐርብ GL, L9
    ħarb
    'military force'
  e. ሐንድ TM Plate III, Column 2 (Cowley 1974)
    ħand
    'One'
  f. ሃጣዕ (Getatchew 1970: 72)
    lose$_{perf}$.3mss
    ħatˈaʕ
    'He did not find (it), he lost'
  g. ሐጸበችው FP (Cowley 1974:11)
    ħasˈsˈäb-äčč-iw
    wash$_{perf}$-3fss-3mso
    'She washed it'

---

aspiration" (Isenberg 1842: 6).
[184] See also for a brief discussion on this and the other pharyngeal and glottal sounds Cowley (1974 and 1983).
[185] The translation given here may not exactly correspond to their contextual meaning in their original text.

h. ሐረረ DL, L. 36 (Guidi 1889:59)
harrär
burn_perf.3mss
'It burned'

A number of occurrences of this pharyngeal sound /ħ/ in the medial position of a word are also attested, as in መሓላ *mähala* 'promise' DL, L.17 (Guidi 1889:62), ጠሐለው· *t'ähal-ä-w fail_perf-3mss-3msNSA* 'he made him fall, he lost it' GL, L. 23 (Guidi 1889:60), ለአምሐራ *lä-ʔamhara* 'for Amhara' DL, L.29 (Guidi 1889:59), በመስተሐየት *bä-mästihayät* 'by mirror, glass' FP, (Cowley 1983: 5), and የየሐዝ *yä-yähaz RM-catch_perf.3mss* 'he who caught' YL, L. 111 (Guidi 1889: 58). /ħ/'s occurrence in word-final position is also attested. Consider for instance በፍልሕ *bä-filih* 'by hot-iron' YL, L. 51 (Guidi 1889:55), ንስሐ *nisiha* 'confession' FP, (Cowley 1983: 6), and እቃሕ *ʔiqah* 'goods, materials, things' (Getatchew 1970: 73).

In the examination of the FP manuscript, Cowley (1983: 21) states with regard to the opposition between አ /ʔ/ and ዐ /ʕ/ that they are lost in the majority of words. The imperial songs do not have many of these sounds either. However, we find in these manuscripts the retention of አ /ʔ/ and ዐ /ʕ/ in a sizeable minority of words in all positions.[186] For the pharyngeal ዐ, at the initial position we have examples such as ዓይን *ʕayn* 'eye' YL, L.8 (Guidi 1889:54), ዓዋቂ *ʕawaqi* '(a) wise (man)' FP, (Cowley 1983:10), and ዐለት *ʕilät* 'day' FP, (Cowley 1983: 6); at the medial position, ሣዕርን *saʕir-in* grass-Acc 'grass' TM, Plate III, Column 4, ከሰብዓቱ *kä-säbʕat-u* from-seven-def 'from the seven' (Cowley 1983: 4), ጓር ጿዓር *gäʕar s'äʕar* 'wailing (and) agony' (Cowley 1983: 6), በዓልቴት *bäʕaltet* 'Madame' ZYL, L.8 (Guidi 1889: 63), ማዕበሉ· *maʕbäl-u* wave/storm-def 'the wave, storm' YL, L.13 (Guidi 1889: 54), and ሩብዕት *rabʕit* 'after after tomorrow', *i.e.,* the 4th day from today' (Getatchew 1970: 4);[187] and, at word final position, ቁጥዓ *qutʕa* 'anger' GL, L13 (Guidi 1889:65), መልክዕ *mälkiʕ* 'face, color, feature', መብልዕ *mäbliʕ* 'food' FP, (Cowley 1983: 4), ተጽኑዕ በላጋራ *tä-s'inuʕ balagara* from-fierce enemy 'from bad enemy' TM, Plate II, Column 1, ይቀንዕ *yi-qäniʕ 3mss-be.eager_Impf* '(was) eager' ZYL, L.52 (Guidi 1889:64), ትልዕ *tilʕ* 'warm', and ተኛዕ *täññaʕ sleep_perf.3mss* 'he slept'

---

[186] Note that, as in the case with ሐ and ኀ, there is a confusion also in the usages between አ and ዐ in usages. Such confusion is found sometimes in the same manuscript and with the same word. For instance, /ʕ/ is written with አ as in ንበልአኹ መሓላ *nibälʕaxu mähala* (DL. L. 17, Guidi 1889:62) and as ዐ in አንበልዓም መሓላ *ʔannibälʕam mähala* (DL, L. 22, Guidi 1889:62) where in both examples *bälʕa* 'to eat' is the same imperfective verb.

[187] A slightly different form exists in Argobba (see Demeke 2011).

(Getatchew 1970: 71).

It is very difficult to tell whether the glottal stop አ /ʔ/ is found in OA at the initial position or not, as the symbol that represents it also indicates vowel word-initially. Hence, forms such as እቃሕ 'goods' (Getatchew 1970: 73) can possibly be either /ʔiqah/ or /iqah/ without the glottal stop. Similarly, አርአጅ 'a kind of a polecat, skunk' (Ibid.) can be /ʔarʔaj/ or /arʔaj/. However, we have a number of cases that proves its existence in Old Amharic. For instance, in the latter example, the medial አ must be /ʔ/, or a representation of a consonant, since a sequence of vowels is not allowed.[188] Moreover, we have plenty of examples that show its existence in word medial and final positions as in - *Medial Position* - ከበአስን *kä-bäʔas-ä-n if-bad$_{perf}$-3mss-1plo* DL, L.17 'if (things) affected us, if (things) go wrong for us' (Guidi 1889: 62), ከክፍአት *kä-kifʔat from-evil* 'from evil' FP, (Cowely 1983: 7) and ዘአግ *zäʔag-ä rust$_{perf}$-3mss* 'it did rust' (Getatchew 1970: 77); and - *Final Position* - ተመታእ *tä-mättaʔ passive-hit$_{perf}$-3mss* 'he was hit' YL-III, L. 3 (Guidi 1889: 58), እንዲእ *ʔindiʔ* 'there is no knowledge' MA እንጃ *ʔinga* (Getatchew 1970: 74), ቀንእቶ *qänʔit-o*[189] *jealous$_{perf}$-3mss* 'he was being jealous' TM, Plate II, Column 3, and መጽላእትን *mäsʼlaʔit-n*[190] *hate-Acc* 'hate' TM, Plate II, Column 1.

Although still in use, the glottal fricative /h/, like አ /ʔ/ does not seem to be used as what it appeared in OA. Below are few OA examples of ሀ /h/ not more found in MA.

(4) a. ሄት FP, (Cowely 1983:6)
    het
    'Where'
   b. ያበራሁ FP, (Cowely 1983:8)
    y-abärrah
    RM-light$_{perf}$-2mss
    'You, who (made the blind) see'

---

[188] Note that the glottal stop is not totally lost in MA. We have some words that preserved this sound such as mäʔat 'disaster, a lot', maʔqäb 'sanctions', maʔkäl 'central' etc.
[189] The -t in qänʔito is not part of the root. The root only consists of q, n and ʔ - √qnʔ.
[190] The -t in this example as well is not part of the root. The form is in the infinitive, i.e. a verbal noun in Amharic, marked by the prefix mä-. The root is √sʼlʔ.

c. ሀየኩ ZYL, L. 47 (Guidi 1889: 64)
   hayä-hu
   see_perf-1ss
   'I saw'
d. ሀባይ ZYL, L. 48 (Guidi 1889: 64)
   habay
   'Lair'

The current form of (4a) is የት yät, (4b) ያበራ y-abärra, (4c) አየሁ ayähu, and (4d) አባይ abay. The current form of (4a) is different from its old form not only with the loss of /h/ but also with the addition of the glide followed by the mid central vowel. The deletion of /h/ when followed by the vowel /e/ does not always seem to result in /yä/. For instance, in the glossary given by Getatchew (1970: 65) we have ኄሊ where in MA it is ኤሊ 'tortoise'.[191] In general, the loss of glottal and pharyngeal sounds however in many cases leaves a trace.

8.2.2 Phonological process

Cowley (1983: 21) on the examination of FP remarks that "in a few forms, the vowel which would have been in final position is retracted and attached to the penultimate consonant ..., or even attached to the penultimate consonant as well as remaining in final position".[192] This statement is only partially true. Among the examples that he gave, it only applies to ስሚዕ and የተፈጉዑም. The /-i/ in ስሚዕ sämiʕ 'listen (you.f)!' is a feminine agreement marker which appears as a suffix in the imperative verb form, as in ስበሪ sibär-i 'break-2sfs' 'break (you.f)!' ፈልጊ fällig-i search-2sfs 'search (you.f)!' etc. The final /-u/ in የተፈጉዑም yä-tä-fägguʕ-u-m is a suffix agreement for third person plural subject. The /u/ found inside the stem is an allophone of /ä/ caused by feature spreading where the base form is *yä-tä-fäggäʕ-u-m. Cowley's other examples do not support the assumption that the vowel found following the penultimate consonant in the above examples is retracted from the final position. We do not have any evidence for the existence of such or any other vowel in the final position.

The verbs that Cowley gave are in the perfective aspect with a third person masculine singular subject. If Cowley's explanation were right, such forms would have /a/ as a third person masculine singular subject

---

[191] ኄት could be a complex form; the preposition element /x-/ plus yät. More data is needed to confirm this.
[192] Cowley (ibid.) gave for the former ስሚዕ, ያበሩህ, ያረታዕ and ያነጽሕ, and for the latter የተፈጉዑም.

agreement marker.[193] However, this does not seem to be the case. First, we do not have any evidence of such usage in its history. Second, as we will see in the next section, it is difficult to assume that the form /a/ is a Proto-form of Transversal or even the Central Transversal group that comprises only Amharic and Argobba because, among others, Argobba of the Shonke-Tollaha variety do not have it. Third, Old Amharic has two forms when the subject is 3mss in the perfective verb. One is a zero morpheme as in Shonke-Tollaha and the other is /-ä/ as in MA. This can be observed even from the same clause from which Cowley (1983) picked his examples.

(5) በእንተ ፍቅረ ሰብእ ዕውር ያበራህ ሐንካስ ያረታዕ ለምጽ ያነጻህ መጻንዕ ያሽዓረ በ፴፰ ዓሙቱ ከተሐመመ ሙት ያነሣ የርኅብን ያጸገበ በጢቄት ነገር 'For love of man, who made the blind see, who straightened the lame, who cleansed the leper, who cured the paralytic in his 38th year after he became sick, who raised the dead, who satisfied the hungry with a small thing' FP, (Cowley 1983: 8 & 16).

Among the eight verbs found in (5), three of them, ያሽዓረ y-a-šäʕar-ä RM-transitivizer-cure$_{perf}$-3mss 'who cured', ከተሐመመ kä-tä-ḥammäm-ä from-passive-sick$_{perf}$-3mss 'from became sick', and የርኅብን yä-rḥab-ä-n RM-hungry$_{perf}$-3mss 'who were hungry', are marked with /-ä/, whereas ያበራህ y-a-bärrah RM-transitivizer-light$_{perf}$.3mss 'who made (the blind) see', ያረታዕ y-a-rättaʕ RM-transitivizer-straigthen$_{perf}$.3mss 'who straightened', ያነጻህ y-a-näsˀsˀaḥ RM-transitivizer-raise$_{perf}$.3mss 'who raised', and ያጸገበ y-a-sˀäggäb RM-transitivizer-satisfy$_{perf}$.3mss 'who satisfied' are not. The existence of an overt Agr in ያነሣ y-a-nässa RM-transitivizer-raise$_{perf}$.3mss 'who raised (the dead)' is not clear as it lost the final radical. Hence, the final /a/ in y-a-nässa could be the 3mss Agr or part of the stem. In addition to ያበራህ, ያረታዕ and ያነጻህ, the form ያጸገበ appears without a suffix vowel, i.e. the 3mss agreement, exactly like what we have in Shonke-Tollaha variety of Argobba. As we will see in the following section, this lack of overt 3mss Agr in the perfective is one of the characteristics of OA. The point now is; what is the reason that we find /a/ following the penultimate radical instead of the perfective marker /ä/ in ያበራህ, ያረታዕ and ያነጻህ? When we examine these data closely, it is clear that the vowel /a/ is an allophone of /ä/ caused by the following consonant.[194] This assimilation can be formalized with the following

---

[193] In fact, the Shagure, Shoa Robit and Aliyu Amba varieties of Argobba as well as Harari, a language also closely related to Amharic, use /-a/ for such agreement. MA uses the mid central vowel /ä/ for the same purpose.

[194] The underlying forms of these verbs are *y-a-bärräh, *y-a-rättäʕ and *y-a-

calssical phonological rule.

(6) /ä/ → /a/ /- pharyngeal
             - glottal

The assimilation proposed in (6) is a well-known phonological process in a number of languages. I assume that it is after this phonological process took place that the loss of such consonants did occur historically as the form in MA is ሰማ sämma, በራ bärra, ረታ rätta and ነፃ näs's'a. The phonological change of /ä/ → /a/ should be seen as a historical one. In Pre-Amharic /ä/ most probably existed. I illustrate this proposal taking all the above examples with the perfective form as follows:

Table 10: Phonological process with pharyngeal and glottal sounds

Root	Pre-Amharic	Old Amharic	Modern Amharic	Gloss
√smʕ	sämmäʕ	sämmaʕ	sämma	'he heard'
√brh	bärräh	bärrah	bärra	'it was lighted'
√rtʕ	rättäʕ	rättaʕ	rätta	'he won'
√nsʼh	näsʼsʼäh	näsʼsʼah	näsʼsʼa	'it was clean'

Supportive evidence to the above claim comes from the varieties of Argobba, Amharic's closest relative. Consider the following, for instance:[195]

---

näsʼsʼäh.
[195] For comparison, the MA cognates to the Argobba words are given in the Table below.

189

Table 11: Varieties in Argobba

Root	Shoa Robit Argobba	Aliyu Amba Argobba	Shonke-Tollaha Argobba	Modern Amharic	Gloss
√lht'	lähat'-a	lahat'-a	lähat'	lat'-ä	'he peeled'
√lhlh	lähaläh-a	lalah-a	lähaläh	lala-Ø	'it became lose'

As can be seen in Table 10, the Argobba varieties illustrate properties of the different periods of Amharic. The Shonke-Tollaha and the Shoa Robit varieties are more archaic than OA. The Aliyu Amba variety on the other hand corresponds exactly to OA.[196]

The change of /k/ to /x/ is common in modern Ethio-Semitic languages such as Tigrinya and Argobba. Change of k to *x → h is also attested in MA due to phonological conditioning. However due to the limited data, I could not figure out what causes the change of k to x. In some cases, it seems that it is changing without any reasonable phonological environment. For instance, the form ከብት käbt 'cattle, wealth' is alternatively written as ኸብት xäbt. In fact, both exist in the same manuscript, sometimes in sequential sentences as can be seen from the following FP text ኸብቴን *xäbt-e-n wealth-1sposs* 'my wealth' and ከብትዋን *käbt-wa-n wealth-3fposs-Acc* 'her wealth'.

(7) ገረድዋን ጸራቺ እስቲ ያን ኸብቴን ጉሉን አንጭ አለቸዋት ያለውን ከብትዋን በሙሉ አመጻቸላት, FP
 'She called her maid and said to her "So, then, bring all that wealth of mine!" She brought to her, in full, all her wealth that there was' (Cowley 1983: 9&17)

What is interesting from a diachronic point of view with particular reference to *käbt* and *xäbt* is that both exist in MA having two different meanings as can be seen below.

---

[196] In a number of cases, in fact, the Shonke-Tollaha Argobba shows more archaic feature than OA and the rest of the Argobba varieties as well.

(8) MA
  a. ከብት
    käbt
    'cattle'
  b. ሀብት
    habt
    'wealth'

The phonological process and semantic shift on *käbt* which took place historically can be schematized as follows:

Table 12: Semantic and phonological changes of ከብት *käbt*

Pre-Amharic	OA	MA
käbt 'wealth, cattle' →	1. käbt 'wealth, cattle' →	käbt 'cattle'
	2. xäbt 'wealth, cattle' →	*häbt → habt 'wealth'

From the phonological side, there are two processes done sequentially in time in the above data: change in manner of articulation and place of articulation. The change of the voiceless velar stop /k/ to its counterpart fricative /x/ is done in OA. This change is neither total nor can it be assumed as caused by assimilation as the retention of the former /k/ still exists. On the other hand, the velar fricative x further changed to the glottal fricative /h/. This latter glottal sound further gave part of its behavior, which is particularly lowering of the tongue, to the following vowel /ä/. Hence, /ä/ is changed to its lower counterpart /a/ by progressive assimilation. This change is schematized in the rule based theory as follows:

(9) x → h then ä → a /h- .

The change of /k/ to /x/ also existed in other contexts, as with the preposition /kä-/. I repeat those examples in (10) below for ease of reference.

(10) a. ሕዳኝ (Cowley 1983:10)
   xi-dañña
   to-judge
   'to a judge'
 b. ሐአባትህ አገር DL, L8 (Guidi 1889: 58)
   x-abbat-ih agär
   to-father-2mspos country
   'to the land/country of your father'

As pointed out above x(ä)- is found as an allomorph of the preposition kä- at least until the 19th century (see D'Abbadie 1881:3). In some regional dialects, both allomorphs do still exist side by side although standard Amharic uses only kä-.

The loss of the pharyngeal and glottal sounds had already begun in the 16th century, and probably in earlier centuries. In some cases, we find a loss of one sound and retention of another even in a single word. Consider, for instance, ይራራን in (11):

(11) ይራራን ኤልን, FP (Cowley 1983:10&18)
   yi-rarrah ʔell-ä-n
   3mss-be.merciful$_{impf}$ Aux-3mss-interrogative.particle
   'Will he not be merciful?'

The word in (10) is identical with the Shoa Robit Argobba one as can be seen in (12a), but the most complete form of this word occurs in Shonke-Tollaha Argobba (cf. 12b). As mentioned before, the latter speech variety has preserved all the pharyngeal and glottal sounds.

(12) a. ራረሀ (Shoa Robit Argobba)
     rarräh-a
     be.merciful, kind, compassionate(perfective)-3mss
  b. ረሀረሀ (Shonke-Tollaha Argobba)
     räharräh
     be.merciful, kind, compassionate(perfective).3mss
     Both: 'He was compassionate, merciful, kind'

The OA word in (11) corresponds to the Shoa Robit form in (11a) as both lost the second radical. The Shonke-Tollaha item in (12b) shows a more archaic form from both the OA's word in (11) and the Shoa Robit's in (12a). This is true for a number of other cases. This is also a good support for the suggestion that the divergence between Amharic and Argobba took place much earlier than the 15th or 16th century. As pointed out in chapter four it might have taken place beginning from the 9th

century when most of the Argobba people embraced Islam.

In Amharic some gerunds and infinitives use to have an epenthetic element -*t* which is not part of the root as in *bälla* 'he ate' vs. *mäblat* 'to eat, eating', and *bälto* lit. 'after he has eaten'. It was generally believed that the loss of pharyngeal and glottal sounds at word final position triggered the appearance of this -*t* as it is restricted to words that lost final radicals. It seems that however, the appearance of the element -*t* existed before the loss of such sounds as can be seen in the following example with the root √*wgʕ* 'fight'.

(13) ወግዬ DL, L.11 (Guidi 1889:62)
 *wägʕit-e → wägʕičč-e
 fight$_{ger}$-1spos

Although it is difficult come to any decisive conclusion, I found a word in OA - አርግናና ʔirginna-na 'and oldness', FP, (Cowely 1983: 7) with /g/ where its current form in MA is አርጅናና ʔirǧinna-na with /ǧ/. It seems that the verb form arräǧ- 'become old' is also a later development in Modern Amharic as many derived forms are also with /g/ as in *aroge* 'old' arogit 'an old women' but not with /ǧ/. However, due to the limited data, it is difficult for me to conclude whether the change of /g/ to /ǧ/ is a wide spread phenomenon in historical Amharic.[197] There are a number of other phonological processes which I leave for future work.

8.3 Morphology and Syntax
8.3.1 Agreement

In the perfective aspect most Ethio-Semitic languages use /-ä/ as a third person subject agreement marker. However, the Aliyu Amba, Shoa Robit and Shagura varieties of Argobba as well as Harari - use /-a/ for the same purpose, although their distant relative Geʻez use /-ä/ in the same way Amharic does. It is interesting that the Shonke-Tollaha variety which is similar to OA in terms of its phonological features discussed in the above section and also with regard to 3mss Agr of the perfective verb. This dialect of Argobba does not have a visible morpheme for the identification of the third person masculine singular subject word-finally. This seems also the case with OA. Consider the following:

---

[197] As Meyer pointed out to me (p.c), velar to palatal is observed in Gunnän Gurage languages. In MA and the other modern Transversal languages this type of palatalization does not occur, however.

193

(14) a. ሞት አል FP, (Cowely 1983:5)
   mot ʔall
   death exist.3mss
   'there is death' lit. 'death exists'
 b. የኖር YL, L. 51 (Guidi 1889:56)
   yä-nor
   RM-live_perf.3mss
   'he who lived'
 c. ኀጣዕ (Getatchew1970: 72)[198]
   ħatʼtʼaʕ
   miss_perf.3mss
   'He did not find (it), He did not recognize, etc.'
 d. ሬሳቾ በእሳት ሐረር DL, L. 35 (Guidi 1889: 59)
   resa-ččo bä-ʔɨsat ħarrär
   body-3plposs by-fire burn_perf.3mss
   'their bodies burned by fire'
 e. ወረዎር GL, L. 14 (Guidi 1889: 65)
   wäräwwär
   throw_perf.3mss
   'He threw'

Although the verb of existence in the third person singular cases often appears in FP in its bare form, in few occasions we find it with /-ä/ as in (15).

(15) a. እንዴህ ያለ FP, (Cowley 1983: 10)
   ʔɨnd-eh y-all-ä
   like-this RM-exist-3mss
   'like this'
 b. ከኔ የበአስ ኀጥዕ ማን አለ FP, (Cowley 1983: 11&19)[199]
   kä-ne yä-bäʔas-ä ħatʼʕ man ʔall-ä
   from-me RM-be.bad_perf-3mss sin who exist-3mss
   'who is a worse sinner than I?'

In FP, in few other cases we find also /-ä/ as in ያን የአኽል ከብት ቢሐይ ደነገጠ *ya-n yäʔaxɨl käbt b-i-ħay dänäggäsʼ-ä* that-Acc much wealth when-3mss-see_impf startle_perf-3mss 'when he saw that much wealth, he was startled' FP, (Cowley 1983: 9 &18). In FP, we find not many cases of /-ä/'s occurrence. This is true especially with matrix verbs. In embedded clauses, we often find /-ä/ as in (15b) ከኔ የበአስ ኀጥዕ *kä-ne yä-bäʔas-ä ħatʼʕ*

---

[198] MA አጣ.
[199] Interesting here is the form of ኀጥዕ where MA uses ሀጢያተኛ.

A GRAMMATICAL SKETCH OF OLD AMHARIC

and (5) የርኅበን ያጸገበ *yä-räxab-ä-n y-a-s'äggäb* RM-be.hungry$_{perf}$-3mss-Acc RM-satisfy$_{perf}$.3mss 'who satisfied the hungry'. However, this cannot be considered an obligatory case since we find embedded clauses without it as in ይኽን ያላዓወቅ እንደሆን *yix-n y-al-ʕawwäq ʔindä-xon* this-Acc RM-neg-know$_{perf}$.3mss if-be.3mss 'if he did not know this' FP, (Cowley 1983: 10).[200] In TM, however, the form /-ä/ existed in the majority cases. On the other hand, in the Imperial songs almost all perfective verbs agreeing with a 3sm subject do not have /-ä/. In this respect, the Imperial songs are more archaic than TM and FP.[201]

It might be the case that Proto-Central SES, i.e. Proto-Amharic-Argobba, had a zero morpheme for third person singular subject marker in the perfective aspect as in Shonke-Tollaha. The current use of /-ä/ in Amharic for this purpose might be an innovation after its separation from Argobba. As it is clear from the OA data, the use of /ä/ is very limited in pre-17th century manuscripts. Except few optional cases such as *kasa izih näbbär(-ä)* K. here was-3mss 'Kasa was here' and *kasa izih indä-hon(-ä)* K. here if-was-3mss 'if Kasa were here' in MA /ä/ is needed. This obligatory occurrence is however definitely a later development. The usage of /a/ in the Shoa Robit-Aliyu Amba dialect of Argobba should also be considered a later development after the two dialects of Argobba separated. I illustrate this historical fact of the third person masculine singular subject marker in the perfective verb in what Hetzron (1972) calls Central Transversal South Ethio-Semitic group as follows:

(16) 3mss agreement marker in the perfective verb

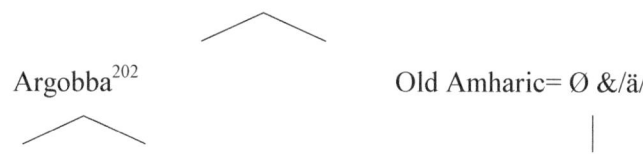

Proto-Amharic-Argobba/Proto-Central Transversal SES = Ø

Argobba[202]   Old Amharic= Ø &/ä/

Shonke-Tollaha= Ø   Shoa Robit-Aliyu Amba = /a/   MA = /ä/

The third person object feminine agreement element is also different from the current one. In MA it is *-at* as in *fälläg-Ø-at* want$_{perf}$-3mss-3fso 'he wanted her'. In OA the form is *-wat* as it is revealed in all the

---

[200] What is important here is that we find both in a single manuscript.
[201] I could only manage to find a single case in the song of Dawit which is ተገኘ tä-gäññ-ä passive-find$_{perf}$-3mss 'it was found' DL, L. 27 (Guidi 1889: 60).
[202] Note that this applies to word final positions. Like MA all the Argobba varieties take, /-ä /as 3mss marker when there is an object marker.

195

manuscripts investigated here. Consider the following few examples:

(17) a. አለቻዎት FP (Cowely 1983:5)
   ʔalä-äččä-wat
   say-3fss-3fso
   'she said to her'
   b. የተውነዋት DL, L. 34 (Guidi 1889: 60)
   yä-täw-nä-wat
   RM-leave-1pls-3fso

Most of the agreement morphemes that are extant from OA are similar to MA. However, I do not have the whole list of these elements as the data is limited. However, the agreement elements given in Ludolf (1698a:12) are almost identical to MA. The only difference is a minor phonological change on the second person singular which is /-k/ after a consonant in MA but /x/ in Ludolf's work. On the other hand, Cowley (1974:604) states that "where the 3m.s. Object suffix to verbs is infixed, it is *-uw-*, instead of MA -äw as in ይቀብሩዋል (... for MA ይቀብረዋል)". However, this interpretation does not seem to be the case. The form ይቀብሩዋል is what is known as impersonal construction.[203] This kind of constructions still exists although not as common as in the Gurage languages and OA (See Section 8.3.6 below). Forms such as -ዋቸው, -አቸው and -አኝ are also observed for third person plural object markers. The variation between the latter two seems to be a problem related to spelling standardization.

8.3.2 Tense

Except the western Gurage languages that have three tenses, the remaining Ethio-Semitic languages have a two-way distinction of tense: past vs. non-past. In most of these languages the past tense is marked by the bare perfective verb whereas the imperfective verb denotes non-past either in its bare form or with an auxiliary. The latter is commonly referred to in the descriptive literature as compound imperfect.

In MA the imperfective form must add the auxiliary /all/ to mark non-past in affirmative matrix clauses. This is, in fact, also the case with Harari and related languages and considered as one of the innovations of the Transversal group. In OA both the bare imperfective and the compound imperfective are found in matrix clauses denoting non-past.

---

[203] Cowley in his other work as well, i.e. (Cowley 1983), mistakenly treated this kind of forms as agreement with third plural subject and often translates it, as "they...', which is wrong. The subject of such construction is an expletive pro which can be translated in English as 'one'. See section -8.3.6 below.

Consider first the bare imperfective constructions in (18):

(18) a. ይልሐጽ YL, L. 8 (Guidi 1889:54)
yɨ-llɨhas'
3mss-passive.peel$_{impf}$
'he will peel'
 b. ቢስማሙ ይሻል FP, (Cowley 1983:10)
b-i-smam-u yɨ-š-šal
if-3pls$_i$-agree$_{impf}$-3pls$_i$ 3mss-passive-be.better$_{impf}$
'it will be nice if they agree'
 c. አብ ከቡን ይመስል TM, Plate V, Column 1
ʔab kɨbäb-u-n yɨ-mäsl
Father circle-def/poss-Acc 3mss-be.like$_{impf}$
'Father is like its circle' (Cowley 1974: 600)[204]
 d. ይነሰንስ AL, L. 4 (Guidi 1889:63)
yɨ-näsännɨs
3mss-sprinkle$_{impf}$
'he will sprinkle'
 e. ማን ይሐይኽ ገጽ በገጽ YL, L. 49 (Guidi 1889:55)
man yɨ-ḥay-ɨx gäs' bä-gäs'
who mss-see$_{impf}$-2mss face by-face
'Who can (dare) look at you face to face?'

All the clauses in (18) are ungrammatical in MA due to the lack of the auxiliary -*all*. We also find the so-called compound imperfective in OA in the same way that we find them in MA as can be seen in (19) where in (19a) the form የአንሰላታል and ያመልጣል have the auxiliary -*all* and can be understood respectively as follows: *yä-ʔansi-llät-all 3mss-reduce$_{impf}$-Aux* 'it will be reduced' and *y-amält'-all 3mss-escape$_{impf}$-Aux* 'he will escape'.

(19) a. ነገር ዓዋቂ ተሰው የተጻላ እንደኖን ሕዳሬ ሳይደርስ ቀድሞ ቢታረቅ እዳውም የአንሰለታል ከዳኝነትም ያመልጣል
'If a person of experience has quarreled with another, his debt will be reduced for him, and he will escape from judgment, if he is previously reconciled, before he reaches the judge'. FP, (Cowley 1983:10 &19)
 b. ይነሳል TM, Plate VII, Column 2
yɨ-näss-all
3mss-rise$_{impf}$-Aux
'it will rise'

---

[204] For the contextual meaning of this and all other examples, please consult the respective references.

Although we find both forms, i.e. bare and compound imperfective forms, in OA the distribution among the manuscripts under investigation is not uniform. The usage of bare imperfective in TM is very rare. The majority in FP are also compound imperfective forms. On the other hand, we do not find compound imperfective, i.e. imperfective plus the auxiliary -*all* in any of the imperial lyrics.[205] It is hard to arrive to any conclusion against the suggested Proto-Transversal innovation of the so-called compound imperfective in the main clauses, however. First, the imperial songs are poems where lots of freedom of usage is allowed. Second, we do not have many imperfective forms in those lyrics. For instance, from the longest lyric of all, i.e. YL, I found only two occurrences of imperfective in matrix clauses both, in fact, without the auxiliary -*all*.

8.3.3 Sentential Negation

Amharic has a negative concord where matrix clause negation appears with pre-verbal and post-verbal negative elements. However, the post-verbal negative marker is sensitive to the type of clause and mostly asserts polarity. In old Amharic, the post-verbal negative marker seems optional even in main clauses as can be seen in (20).

(20) a. ከሰብዓቱ ኀጢያት ምንም አይጏደለዋት FP, (Cowley 1983: 4)
    kä-säbʕat-u ħat'iyat minim ʔay-gʷaddäl-ä-wat
    from-seven-def sin nothing neg-miss$_{perf}$-3mss-3fso
    'She lacked nothing from (all) the seven sins'
  b. አላስማረኸው ልጇ ምሽቱን AL, L. 24 (Guidi 1889: 62)
    ʔal-as-marräx-ä-w liǧǧä mišt-u-n
    neg-caus-surrender$_{perf}$-3mss-3msNSA child wife-his-Acc
    'You did not make surrender his children and wife'
  c. አልጸፋጠው DL. 19 (Guidi 1889: 58)
    ʔal-s'affät'-ä-w
    neg-taste$_{perf}$-3mss-3msNSA
    'He did not like (it)'

In most cases, we find the post-verbal negative marker in OA in a similar way that we find in current Amharic. Consider the following:

---

[205] There is one questionable case in DL, however. This form is ትለለች, which seems having the auxiliary -all with a feminine subject agreement. However, in another version of the same manuscript, this word is replaced by ተከለት and the one with ትለለች does not give sense in its context.

(21) a. አይከተልም FP, (Cowley 1983:8)
   ʔay-yɨ-kättäl-m
   neg-3mss-follow_perf-neg
b. አልኮነም DL, L. 43 (Guidi 1889:61)
   ʔal-hʷän-ä-m
   neg-be/become-3mss-neg
c. አልገዛዎችም, YL, L. 96 (Guidi 1889:57)
   ʔal-gäzz-a-wacco-m
   neg-rule_perf-3mss-3plo-neg
d. አይኖረውም, TM, Plate v, column 1
   ʔa-y-nor-äw-ɨm
   neg-3mss-have-3mso-neg

Note that, like MA most Ethio-Semitic languages have pre- and post-verbal negative markers in matrix clauses. However, from both northern and southern language groups there are some languages that do not have at all post-verbal negative markers (Girma 2003: chapter five). OA shows both forms in matrix clauses. However, the usage of the post-verbal negative marker is attested in the Transversal group to which Amharic belongs and could be an innovation in this group. If this is the case, the existence of a negative verb in the matrix clause in OA without the post-verbal negative marker is retention in a similar way with the bare imperfective in main clauses discussed above.

For the negation of the verb *all- exist_perf-* 'to exist' we found in FP ኤለው *ʔelläw* 'he did not have' FP (Cowely 1983: 7) where MA has የለውም *yälläwim*. In FP we find also ኤለን *ʔellä-n* with the interrogative particle *-n* where again in MA it is የለም *yälläm* 'there is not' with a rising intonation, if it is an interrogative clause. However, in Getatchew we find the post-verbal negative marker *-m* as well in this irregular verb as in ኤለም *ʔelläm* 'there is (are) not' ኤለኝም *ʔelläññim* 'I do not have' (1970: 72). The negation of the present tense copula is also somewhat different from what we have in MA and can appear with or without the post-verbal negative marker *-m*.

(22) a. ምግባራችን አይዶል FP (Cowely 1983:10)
   mɨgbar-accɨ-n ʔaydol
   moral-1plposs-Acc is.not
   'it is not our deed/character'
b. አይዶለውም TM, Pate II, Column 4, & Plate III, column 4
   ʔaydoläwɨm
   'It is not'

199

The form አይዶል or አይዶላም 'is not' existed as recent as the 20th century and even heard currently in some dialects.[206] However, the form አይዶላውም found in TM still exists in MA but with different meaning - 'it did not concern him'.

8.3.4 Relative clause constructions

In MA the relative clause is marked by *yä-* in the case of perfective and *yämm-/imm-* in the case of imperfective.[207] In this regard, there is some difference between MA and related languages. In most Gurage languages, RM is found only with perfective verbs. In Argobba the situation is a little bit complicated where imperfective may or may not appear with RM. In OA although the relative markers appear in the same way like MA, bare imperfective is also found in relative clauses. Consider the following:

(23) a. በዜህ   ብታ   ያመልጡዋል
        bä-zeh bita   y-amält'-uw-all
        by-this alone   3pls$_i$-escape$_{impf}$-3pls$_i$-Aux
        አይምሰልሽ   ነፍሴ FP, (Cowley 1983: 6)
        a-yi-msäl-iš   nɨfs-e
        neg-3mss-think$_{impf}$-3fso soul-1sposs
   'My soul, by this alone does not think that one can escape'[208]
   b. ያነዱ   አይሻእ FP (Cowley 1983: 5)
      y-anädd-u   ʔa-yi-šaʔ
      3pls$_i$-ignite$_{impf}$-3pls$_i$ neg-3mss-need$_{impf}$
   'It does not need one who ignites (it)'

Note that (23a&b) are internally headed RCs. Although not the preferred one, in MA we have also bare imperfective in internally headed RC as in *[RC käne tamälč'i] aymsäliš* 'do not think that you can escape from me'. In some cases, probably dialectal, the bare imperfective may also be used in other type of RCs as in the popular saying *tiläbsäw yälat tikänanäbäw amarat* 'one who does not have (a basic dress) to wear wished (for a shawl) to wrap up with'. In this case, though the head noun is not overt, it can be assumed as external one as in *tiläbsäw [N] yälat ikänanäbäw [N] amarat* where the phonologically null N can be overtly filled by *libis* 'clothes, dress' and 'shawl, cloak' as the translation shows. This kind of structures in MA are however very rare. This seems also the case in OA

---

[206] See Getatchew Haile (1970: 74) for some discussion about this form.
[207] In both cases the relative marker (RM) is prefixed to the relativized verb.
[208] The form ያመልጡዋል is an impersonal construction and the translation here is slightly modified from Cowley (1983: 13).

as we do not often find these types of RCs, i.e. bare imperfective relativized verb. In this regard, it seems that MA and OA do not have any differences.

In the case of negative RC in OA, besides the bare imperfective form that we saw in (23b), it has *yä-* as in (24).

(24) a. ዛቢያው ያይታወቅ ዕፅ YL, L. 48 (Guidi 1889:55)
zabiya-w y-a-y-t-awäq ʕis'
ax.handle-3msposs RM-neg-3mss-know$_{impf}$ wood
b. ረብኅ ያይኖረው ሐዘን TM, Plate VIII, Column 1
räbxa y-a-y-nor-äw ħazän
benefit RM-neg-3mss-have-3mso sorrow
'A pointless sorrow', lit. 'a sorrow that does not have benefit'

As can be seen in (24), RM in the imperfective is the same as the one we find in the perfective. This type of construction is very common in OA and probably existed through the 19th century as it is reported in Praetorius (1878). See also Getatchew (1970: 79-80). However, in MA (be it in the negative or affirmative) either *yämm-* or *imm-* should appear but not *yä-* in the imperfective RC. The origin of the *-mm-* part of the relative marker of the imperfective aspect is controversial. Praetorius (1878:274) suggests its source to be a complementizer in subordinating clauses. Hetzron (1973), on the other hand, suggests that it originated from the negative post-verbal element *-m* which he also claims to be identical to the contrastive focus marker *-m* not only in terms of phonetic shape but also in terms of function. For him *-mm* is needed in the imperfective relative but not in the perfective because there is a need to be specific in time for the latter. According to Hetzron (1973:9) *-mm-* might be first used in restrictive relative clauses but extended later to all imperfective RCs. It later was trapped under *yä-* and hence became part of the relative marker. Hudson (1983) raises the possibility of *-mm-* in the imperfective relativized verb as a nominalizer and the perfective verb form being claimed to have a nominal origin. If we assume relativaization as a sort of nominalization, and if the assumption that perfective has a nominal origin is right, the consideration of *-mm-* as a nominalizer can be justified. This however raises many questions, which are difficult to answer. However, Hudson did not pursue this assumption. He rather suggests that this element might have originated from the indefinite/interrogative pronoun.

In modern Amharic RC precedes its head noun. We find similar structures in Old Amharic as we can see from the example in (25) where the head noun ሞት 'death' follows its qualifier RC ዕረፍት የሌለው 'that does not have rest'.

(25) ዕረፍት የሌለው   ሞት   ቢለምኑ
    ʕiräft yälelläw   mot   b-i-lämmɨn-u
    rest that.doesn't.have death if-3pls$_i$-plea$_{impf}$-3pls$_i$
    አይገኝ, FP (Cowley 1983: 6 & 13)
    ʔa-y-gäññ
    neg-3mss-find$_{impf}$
    'which has no rest, in which if one plead for death, it will not be found' [209]

In MA having the head noun at phrase initial position is totally out. In OA beside the above alternative structure, we find also the head preceding RC. Consider (26) for instance:

(26) a. አለ እኹንም ብርድ አስሐትያ ገላ የሚቆርጥም፣
    ʔall-ä ʔaxun-ɨm bɨrd ʔashatya gäla yämm-i-qorätʼtʼɨm
    there.is-3mss now-too cold ice body RM- 3mss-shrivel$_{impf}$
    ጥርስ የሚያንቀጠቅጥ, FP (Cowley 1983: 6 &13)
    tʼɨrs yämm-iy-anɨqätʼäqqɨtʼ
    tooth RM-3mss-tremble$_{impf}$
    'There is cold (and) ice, which shrivels the body, which makes the teeth tremble'
  b. ያን ነጋዴ ዕፍረት ያለውን, FP (Cowley 1983:9&18)
    ya-n nägade ʕifrät y-all-ä-w-ɨn
    that-Acc trader unguent RM-exist-3mss-3msNSA-Acc
    'That trader who has unguent'

The head-initial pattern we have seen in this section is not restricted to complex noun phrases. Genitive phrases, and simple and complex clauses also show this pattern in OA. I discuss this issue further in the following section.

8.3.5 Word Order

Except Geʿez all Ethio-Semitic languages are SOV languages like other Afroasiatic languages in Ethiopia. Proto-Semitic on the other hand is assumed to have VSO order. It is not clear when the modern languages of Ethio-Semitic shifted to SOV. The complexity arises also out of the following circumstance. Though Tigre and Tigrinya are a part of the same northern group with Geʾez, they have an SOV order like that of the

---

[209] The translation is a little bit modified here.

southern group. Although it is possible to assume that SOV order is an innovation of the southern group exclusively and that Tigre and Tigrinya shifted on an individual basis, the facts in OA does not support such suggestion. Little (1974) pointed out that Amharic could probably have had a VSO order. Bach (1970) claims that Amharic is a VSO language. Girma (2003) suggests that Amharic sentence structure can easily be derived by applying the same kind of technique that applies to derive VSO languages based on the examination of relative clauses and genitive constructions from the then prominent transformational grammar theory point of view. According to Girma (2003) although MA is an SOV language, its derivation does not follow the derivation of the well-known SOV languages such as Japanese. As pointed out in chapter four, Amharic clearly shows a VSO pattern in its intermediate derivation.

Although most of the aforementioned works are done from theoretical perspectives and based on synchronic data, the manuscripts investigated here exhibit VSO order. This may indicate that SOV in Modern Ethio-Semitic is a recent innovation that took place in individual languages.[210] As we have seen above, in OA RC follows its head as in VO languages, which is totally impossible in MA. In this section, we will explore some more examples on ordering differences between MA and OA in both simple and complex clauses. Consider first the following complex clause from FP(Cowley 1983: 4&11).

(27) ነበረች   ሕንድ   ሴት   ፅኑዕ   መልክዓም
 näbbär-äčč   hand   set   s'inuʕ   mälkiʕa
 was-3fss   one   woman determined   comely
 ሕንድ   አይጓደላዋት   ከጥርስ
 hand   a-yi-g^wädäl-ä-wat   kä-t'irs
 one   neg-3mss$_i$-lack$_{impf}$-3mss$_i$-3fsNSA from-tooth
 ከዓይን   ከከናፍር   ከአነጋገር   ከእጅ   ጻት
 kä-ʕayn   kä-känafir   kä-ʔanägagär kä-ʔiǧǧ   s'at
 from-eye   from-lips   from-speech   from-hand finger
 ከእግር   ጻት
 kä-ʔigir   s'at
 from-foot   toe

'There was a woman, determined, comely, from whom nothing was lacking, from tooth, from eye, from lips, from speech, from finger, from toe'

---

[210] If this is the case, the current pattern should be considered as an areal feature which has no relevance for genetic sub-grouping.

If we examine the example in (26) piece by piece we have first VSO matrix clause ነበረች ሐንድ ሴት 'there was a woman' lit. 'A woman was there/existed'. The adjective also follows the head noun ሐንድ ሴት ፅኑዕ መልክዓም 'A beautiful courageous woman' as does RC: ሐንድ ሴት ፅኑዕ መልክዓም ሐንድ አይጓደለዋት 'a beautiful courageous woman who has everything (lit. complete in everything)'. The internal constiuents of the RC also follows the verb: ሐንድ አይጓደለዋት ከጥርስ ከዓይን ከከናፍር ከአነጋገር ከአጅ ጻት ከአግር ጻት 'from whom nothing was lacking, from tooth, from eye, from lips, from speech, from finger, from toe'.[211] Head-initial pattern in general is very common in OA. Consider also (28) where the verb comes at the initial position in all the three examples:

(28) a. ንጽሕፋለን በጥቂቱ ቸርነቱን
nɨ-s'ɨħf-all-än bä-t'qit-u čärnät-u-n
1pls-write$_{impf}$-Aux -1pls by-small-def goodness-his-Acc
የእግዚአብሔርን ለእኛ ያደረገልን, FP (Cowley 1983: 4&11)
yä-ʔɨgziʔabɨher-n lä-ʔɨñña y-adärräg-ä-llɨn
of-God-Acc to-us RM-3mss$_i$-do$_{perf}$-3mss-1plNSA
'We write in brief the goodness of God, which he did for us'
b. ሃዩ ርኁነቱን, FP (Cowley 1983 4&11)
ħɨy-u rɨruħnät-u-n
see$_{perf}$-3pls mercy-his-Acc
'See his mercy!'
c. ነአምናለን እስከ ለዓለም TM, P. III, C. 4
nä-ʔamɨn-all-än ʔɨskä lä-ʕaläm
1pls-belive$_{impf}$-Aux -1pls until to-world
'We believe for ever'

In (28a) besides VO order of the matrix clause, the relative clause follows the head noun and the "possessum" ቸርነቱን precedes the "possessor" የእግዚአብሔርን and the verb precedes all other constituents. This pattern is totally out in MA. In (28b&c) as the subject is pro, we

---

[211] Note that, (27) does not contain the entire clause as it appeared in the manuscript. The complex noun phrase has two more RCs which all follow the head noun ሴት 'woman' as can be seen in (i) which is taken from FP, (Cowley 1983: 4&11).
(i) ነበረች ሐንድ ሴት ፅኑዕ መልክዓም ሐንድ አይጓደለዋት ከጥርስ ከዓይን ከከናፍር ከአነጋገር ከአጅ ጻት ከአግር ጻት የጸጋዋ ነገር ብዙን ያይጓደል ወርቁ ብሩ ቀማሱ ያን ጉሉ በዝሙት የገዛች
'There was a woman, determined, comely, from whom nothing was lacking, from tooth, from eye, from lips, from speech, from finger, from toe, the matter of whose wealth was abundant, from whom gold, silver, clothing was not lacking, who purchased all that by fornication'.

A GRAMMATICAL SKETCH OF OLD AMHARIC

cannot be sure about its position. However, in both clauses the object follows the verb, which is not the case in MA. Besides VSO in OA manuscripts, we have SVO as in (29):

(29) a. እንዳገኘ የሚናገር ይኰነናል
    ʔind-agäññ   yämm-i-naggär yi-k*änän-all
    as-find$_{perf}$.3mss RM-3mss-talk   3mss-condemn$_{perf}$-Aux
    በደይን, FP
    bädäyn
    judgment
    'The one who speaks improperly will be condemned by judgment' (Cowely 1983:5&13)
b. በዓርብ ዕለት ፈጠረ ሰውን የኍሉን አባት TM, P. III, C. 1
    bä-ʕarb   ʕilät säw-n   yä-xulu-n   ʔabbat
    by-Friday day man-Acc/focus   genitive-all-Acc/focus   father
    'On the day of Friday, He created man, the father of all' (Cowley 1974:599)

Beside (28), we have a number of other structures where the verb takes medial position as in (29).

(29) a. ርኁነው ጌታቸንስ (Cowley 1983: 4)
    riruħ-näw g\ʷeta-ččuni-s
    mercy-is Lord-his-Acc-topicalizer
    'As for our Lord, He is merciful!'
b. ያን   የአኽል   ጽፍጥ መብልዕ ይረብሐሽና   ጽዋዓ
    ya-n y   yä-ʔaxil č'iffit' mäbliʕ yi-räbħa-š-inna s'iwaʕa
    that-Acc RM-equal tasty food 3mss-profit$_{impf}$-2fso-and coup
    ሞት   ሳለ   መሪር, FP (Cowely 1983:6&14)
    mot   s-all-ä   märir
    death   while-exist-3mss bitter
    'Shall so much tasty food indeed profit you, while the coup of death is bitter?'
c. እንዴት ተቀጠፈው ይኸን በሞት, FP (Cowely 1983:7&14)
    ʔindet ti-qät'äf-i-w yi-hon bä-mot
    how 2fss-cut$_{impf}$-2fss-focus/3mso 3mss-be by-death
    'How shall you be spoiled in death?
d. እንዴት ትኾነው ይኸን እራቁትሽን
    ʔindet ti-hon-äw yi-hon ʔiraqut-š-in
    how 2fss-be-2fss-focus 3mss-be naked-2fsposs-Acc
    ያቆሙሽ ጊዜ በእልፍ አእላፋት መላእክት ፊት, FP (Cowely 1983:7&14)
    y-aqom-u-š gize bä-ʔilf ʔaʔilafat mälʔikt fit
    RM-stnad$_{perf}$-3pls-2fsNSA time by-thousands angels face

205

'How shall you be at the time when they stand you naked in front of myriads of angels?'

In (29a) what we have is Adjective-Copula-Subject. We do not know in fact whether this order is the unmarked one or a focus structure. In current Amharic we have also similar structure, but for pragmatic purpose. However, in the other examples (i.e. 29b-d), the verb is not final. In (29b) the adjective መሪር follows the verb ይረብሐኝና. Note that, this adjective is part of the subject ጽዋዓ ሞት which is in construct state.[212] In (29c) the prepositional phrase በሞት follows the "compound" verb ተቀጠፈው ይኸን and (29d) the RC follows the compound-like verb ትኾነው ይኸን. In this same example, the prepositional phrase በእልፍ አእላፋት መላእክት ፊት also follows the relativized verb.

Putting the embedded clause after the main clause is possible in MA, but only for emphasis. We find a similar structure in OA although it is not clear whether it is the marked or unmarked order. For instance, (29b) above has the matrix clause preceding the subordinate clause.

The usage of VSO and SVO orders and the general order pattern of VO languages that we just saw in this section in OA clearly indicate that the complete shift to OV is a recent development in Amharic. It is most probably the case that the change of VO to OV in the other South Ethio-Semitic languages also occurred on individual bases recently. For this claim however, we need to examine the properties of each language in the group.

8.3.6 Impersonal constructions

Experntial verbs in most literature on Ethiopian languages are referred to impersonal verbs. These verbst take impersonal objects as grammatical subjects. The logical subject, often the experiencer, ends up as a grammatical object as in (30).

(30)   ine-n wiha t'ämmañ
        I-Acc water thirst$_{perf}$-3mss-1sNSA
        lit. 'water made me thirst', 'I am thirsty (of water)'.

I am not referring to the above type of clauses as impersonal constructions here. I am referring to impersonal constructions of the type found in the so-called Gurage languages. In these languages almost every verb has an impersonal construction where the grammatical subject is often an expletive pro. This form is rare in modern Amharic,

---

[212] It can be considered as modifying ጽዋዓ alone.

however. What is interesting is that this impersonal construction is common in Old Amharic.[213] Consider the following:

(31) a. ከተአሰረም ያመልጡዋል
ka-tä-ʔassär-u-m y-amält'-uw-all
from-passive-be.bound$_{perf}$-3ps-foc 3pls-escape$_{impf}$-3pls-Aux
ተሸሽጎም ይትገጡዋል
tä-šäšig-o yi-t'ḥat'-uw-all
passive-be.hidden$_{ger}$-3mss 3pls-not.be.find$_{impf}$-3pls-Aux
አይምሰልኽ, FP (Cowley 1983: 7&14-15)
ʔa-yi-msäl-ix
neg-3mss-seem$_{impf}$-2msNSA
'Do not think that one will escape if he is bound, or being hidden, will fail to be found'

b. እዳ በእዳ ሲጨምሩ ይኖሩዋል, FP (Cowley 1983: 5)
ʔida bä-ʔida s-i-č'ä-mir-u yi-nor-uw-all
debt upon-debt while-3pls-add$_{impf}$-3pls 3pls-live$_{impf}$-3pls-Aux
'One will remain spending his time adding debt upon debt'

c. ሐርሶ ይቀብሩዋል TM, Plate VI, Column 4
ḥars-o yi-qäbr-uw-all
plough$_{ger}$-3mss 3pls-bury$_{impf}$-3pls-Aux
'After ploughing, one buries it' (Cowley 1974: 601)

The constructions in (31) are different from experiential verb constructions. First, these constructions, as pointed out above, are constructed from any verb. Second, their subject can only be an expletive pro hence the term impersonal.[214] On the other hand, experiential verbs, which are often referred to as impersonal verbs (in the descriptive literature on Ethiopian languages) often take an impersonal object as a grammatical subject where the logical subject becomes a grammatical object. These verbs, which include psychological verbs, however, like any transitive verb, mark their direct object for the accusative Case. The verb can also be passivized as in *tä-t'ämma-hu passive-thirsty$_{perf}$-1ss* 'I am thirsty'. Note that, in impersonal constructions the expletive subject is identified by a third person plural agreement and always attached to the main verb. However, in the "regular" verb construction, if there is the

---

[213] This is true especially to FP. In the other manuscripts investigated in this work, I found very few cases of impersonal construction. This, however most probably is because of the nature of the texts.
[214] Note that Cowley (1983) does not seem aware of it. He did not mention such construction at all. In most cases, he also translated such structures with third person plural subject pronoun, i.e. they.

auxiliary *-all*, the third plural suffix Agr attaches to it; not to the main verb. Consider (32) from MA:

(32) a. ይሮጡዋል እንደ ሀይሌ (Impersonal)
yɨ-rot'$_{impf}$-uw[215]-all ɨndä hayle
3pls-ran-3pls-aux like Haile
'One should run like Haile'
b. እንደ ሀይሌ ይሮጣሉ
ɨndä hayle yɨ-rot'$_{impf}$-all-u
like Haile 3pls-ran-3pls-aux
'They run like Haile'

As can be seen in the above data beside the positional difference of the suffix Agr, the order of constituents between the impersonal and its counterpart regular verb constructions is different. In the impersonal construction in (32a) the verb comes first. Although MA is a head final language, in the impersonal construction in general a head initial pattern is preferred.[216]

8.3.7 Copular constructions

The present tense copular clauses, in current Amharic are constructed by the present tense copula *n-* 'be'. An examination of ancient manuscripts on this issue results in a number of constructions – a similar one as in MA (cf. 33), without any visible copula as in Ge'ez (cf. 34),[217] or with the element *-t* as in Highland East Cushitic (cf. 35).[218]

(33) a. ልጅነቱም ዕቡብ ነው TM Plate III, Column 4
lɨǧǧɨnät-u-m ʕɨs'ub näw
sonsship-3sposs wonderful is
'His sonship is wonderful' (Cowley 1974: 599)
b. ርኁነው· ጌታችንስ (Cowley 1983: 4)
rɨruħ-näw geta-ččɨnɨ-s
mercy-is Lord-his-Acc-topicalizer
'As for our Lord, He is merciful!'

---

[215] Note that *w* in *-uw* is inserted due to a hiatus.
[216] This could be an indication of Amharic's VSO past and therefore a retention. However, it could be for pragmatic reasons. Further research is needed to claim beyond doubt.
[217] Note that, Ge'ez has a pronoun copula.
[218] Highland East Cushitic languages have the element *-t* in copular construction but used for focusing purpose (see Crass et al 2005).

(34) a. ክፉ	ምግባርሽን	ሲሰሙልሽ በዚያ
kifu	migbarr-iš-n	s-i-säm_impf-u-lliš
evil	deed-3fsposs-Acc	when-3lss-hear_impf-3pls
ዱለት	የሚያሳፍር (Cowley 1983: 7)
dulät	yämm-iy-asafr_impf
assembly	RM-be.shameful_impf
'When they hear concerning your evil deeds in that assembly, it causes (you) shame (lit. it is a shame (for you)'

b. ወይ	ስጋዬ	በላሽ	ጠጣሽ
wäy	siga-ye	bäla-š	t'ät't'a-š
alas	flesh-my e	at_perf-2fss	drink_perf-2fss
አምሐርሽ		ሰብሃሽ	ለመለምሽ
ʔamḥar-š		säbḥa-š	lämälläm-š
be.beautiful_perf-2fss	be.plump	thrive_perf-2fss
ለምስጥ ሌላስ ሙአያ	ኤለው (Cowley 1983: 7&14)
lä-mist' lelas muʔaya	ʔelläw
to-terminate other function has.not
'Alas, my flesh, you ate, you drank, you became beautiful, you became plump, you thrived – for the terminates; it has no other function'

(35) a. ኩነኔ ዘለዓለም በርሳቾት TM, Plate III, Column 2
k^wunäne	zäläʕaläm	bä-risaččo-t
condemnation	for.ever	by-they-_t_
'Everlasting condemnation is upon them' (Cowley 1974:599)

b. የጥሐሉዋት	የመነኑዋት	ነፍስ
yä-t'ḥal-u-wat	yä-männän-u-wat	näfs
RM-throw_perf-3pls-3fso	RM-reject_perf-3pls-3fso	soul
ይኸት ቦታዋ (Cowley 1983: 6&13)
yih-t bota-wa
this-_t_ place-3fspos
'For the soul which they threw out, which they rejected, this is her place'

c. የሰይጣንነም　　　　　　　ቸብቸበውን　　　ደግሜ
   yä-säyt'an-nä-m　　　　　čäbčäbo-w-ɨn　　dägɨmm-e
   of-Satan-Acc-focus　　　neck-3msposs-Acc　again-1sposs
   እቆርጸው･　　አኁን　ጊዜውት (Cowley 1983: 11&19)
   ʔɨ-qorsʼ-äw　　ʔaxun　gize-w-t
   1ss-cut_{impf}-3mso now　time-3mposs-*t*
   'And now it is the time that I should again cut the neck of Satan'

In a number of South Ethio-Semitic languages the current copula is similar with the one that we have today in Amharic, i.e. *n-*. However, in Harari it is *t-*. Interesting enough, however, in both cases the agreement element identifying the semantic subject is the one that is used to identify objects in regular verb constructions. There is always a question as to when really the copula *n-* is developed. The general assumption is that it was an innovation of Proto-South Ethio-Semitic (with a questionable explanation left for the Harari case just mentioned). The case we have seen above seriously questions such assumption. The use of *n-* as a copula is limited to some constructions in OA.

There is a controversy with regard to the status of the element *-t* found in copular clauses of the sort in (34). While Goldenberg (1976) considers it a copula, Getatchew (1979b) does not. In support of its copular status, Cowley (1983) presents some more examples. According to Goldenberg it is always found post nominal in OA and "similar t-copulas are widespread among the South-Ethiopian languages: in Gafat, Gurage (Kəstanəñña, Muxer, Goggot, Chaxa, Zway) and Sidamo" (1976: 136). A closer examination of the element in the suggested languages does not support Goldenberg's claim, however (cf. Crass et al 2005, Girma 2012). For instance the usage of *-t* in Zay is not a common phenomenon and instead the usage of copular constructions is with the element *n-*. Even the element *-n*, which is most commonly found in copular constructions in Zay, is considered a focus marker (cf. Meyer 2002). Goldenberg's treatment of the element *t* as a copula in Soddo, i.e. Kəstanəñña, is also questionable (cf. Crass et al 2005). The case with Sidama is the same. The element *-t* is, in fact, found in all Highland East Cushitic languages but with a function of focus, although some considers it to be a copula. This is not to deny the usage of the element /t/ as a copula in any of the Ethiopian languages, however. The usage of this element as a copula is, in fact, attested in Harari. However, the Harari *-t* inflects for agreement markers. This is not the case in OA.

Getatchew (1970) suggests that the element *-t* could be a redundant element as in the one found in honorific form *näwo(t)* 'you(polite) are'.

However in his later work, i.e. Getatchew (1979b), he proposes that the element *-t* can be a definite marker: "The possibility that it marks a certain degree of definiteness of the possessed noun phrase cannot be excluded" (Getatchew 1979b:120-121). In a later work he also suggests the same thing: "After spending so much time in defining the role of this particle [ት], I am inclined to believe that it is a certain type of a definite article, the same article that appears with a relative verb in the plural, e.g. የሄዱት "the ones who left" (Getatchew 1983: 168). Getatchew also brings forth some more examples from the 18th century manuscript where its existence may not be directly interpreted as a copula. Among his examples, it appears along with the copula *näw* as in ይህት ነው *yih-t n-äw this-t be$_{pres}$-3mss* 'this is' (Getatchew 1983:167). I therefore suggest that the element *-t* was a focus marker in OA and never developed as a copula in the history of Amharic. See Girma (2012) for detailed discussion.

The form of the negative copula in OA is slightly different than MA. In OA it is aydoll. Currently, this form is used in the case of statements as aydälläm 'it is not' and in the case of interrogatives aydäll 'is it not?'. The source of this suppletive negative form is mysterious. However, it might be developed from *dollä* 'concern' as in ምን ዶላህ *min dolläh* 'what concerns you?' which still exists in regional dialect. See also Cowley (1983:25) for a similar suggestion.

8.4 Summary

We have seen in this chapter that OA had preserved all the pharyngeal and glottal sounds which are assumed to be typical features of Semitic languages. These glottal sounds also existed in the 17th and 18th centuries Amharic. Perfective verbs may appear with a zero morpheme in the case of third person singular subject like the Shonke-Tollaha variety of Argobba. Impersonal constructions were also common like the Gurage languages. Imperfective matrix clauses may appear without an auxiliary. The post-verbal negative marker was not always found in matrix clauses. Copular constructions may or may not appear with a copula. Nominal heads may or may not precede their qualifiers. VSO, SVO and SOV pattern were also attested. OA in general had a mixed word order. Although such mixed order does not favor a treatment of OA as a VO language, it is a strong indication that Pre-Amharic might be a VO language. All these unique features of OA indicate that most of the un-Semitic features that Amharic show at present are recent developments. (This might be also the case with the other modern Semitic languages of Ethiopia.) This once again puts aside the doubt of Amharic's Semitic origin.

Although recent works challenge the most advocated idea that Ethiopian Semitic languages are the result of a pidgin-induced process, works still continue to operate within this traditional notion as pointed out in chapter 5. The crucial Semitic features found in OA will give rise to more questions than answers to those who still stick to the traditional much propagated assumption of a Semitic language migration from South Arabia some time in the middle of the first millennium BCE as a source of Ethio-Semitic. The Semitic features that we have seen in OA are difficult to explain with a pidgin-induced and "migration" theory. On the other hand, although it is just from one language, the Old Amharic grammar (containing more critical Semitic features than MA) that we saw in this chapter reinforces the plausibility of our suggestion in chapter five, which is advocated by scholars like Hudson (1977, 1978) and Murtonen (1967), that Ethio-Semitic is an autochthonous group.

Chapter Nine: Concluding Remarks

As we have seen in chapter two, Bender (1983), Baye (2000 EC.) and some others claim that Amharic originated as a pidgin around the Bashilo River. For Bender (1983) and Bender and Fulass (1978), Amharic began its pidgin process in the 4th century and developed into a distinct language around the 14th century. I have argued, however, that Amharic cannot be considered created through a pidgin-stage process. It is rather a linear descendant of a Semitic language. Its changes are merely changes natural to any language.

As we have seen in chapter eight, Old Amharic has more Semitic features than contemporary Amharic. For instance, OA has the glottal and pharyngeal consonants found in other Semitic languages. The VSO pattern is also attested in OA. All these and the other Semitic features discussed in chapter eight are not found in MA. The lack of these features in MA is one of the main reasons for advancing a pidgin hypothesis. Since the loss of these features happened at a later date, i.e. long after it started serving as lingua franca, the theory porposing a pidgin-induced origin for Amharic is extremely unlikely.

Moreover, despite the fact that Amharic has non-Semitic features, Modern Amharic still has suffcent grammatical features and also basic lexical items in order that it be considered a linear descendant of a Semitic language. The close relation that Amharic shows with the South Ethio-Semitic languages also strengthens this suggestion. The non-

Semitic features that MA exhibits, therefore, are not due to pidgin-induced origination but due to a later influence. Given the fact that Amharic has served as lingua franca in the multilingual Ethiopian nation for more than a millennium, the Cushitic and Omotic features that it exhibits are natural and, accordingly, to be expected.

As it is difficult to conceive of Argobba independently from the origin of Amharic, and as the settlement of Argobba also reveals, I have further suggested that Amharic may not have originated in the north-central part of Ethiopia around the Bashilo River in the Amhara province. One possible hypothesis is rather to assume that Amharic originated somewhere in the central part of Ethiopia along with Argobba. It may be the case, however, that Amharic got its name from the place known as Amhara, as suggested also by others.

The implication of the non-pidgin hypothesis on the spread of Amharic as outlined in chapter six is that there were at least two major expansions; the first by pre-Amharic speakers or more appropriately by a Central SES group, i.e. Proto-Amharic-Argobba speaking group, and the second by the Amharic speaking group starting from the end of the 19th century with the reign of Menelik II. Proto-Amharic-Argobba, after it developed its own features, moved to the east as far as Harar and to the south as far as Bale and to the north as far as Eritrea. This first expansion especially to the north probably took place at the beginning of 6th or 7th century. When the Axumite Empire was weakened and the administrative power shifted to the Zague dynasty in Lasta, i.e. Agew Midir, Amharic or pre-Amharic was already spoken in nearby localities such as the Amhara Province. Because Amharic speakers also started to take top positions in the administration of the Zague rule, Amharic was made the administrative language and nicknamed the "Language of the King". This happened particulary during Lalibela's period (1140-1180) (cf. Sergew 1972).

Indeed, the best opportunity for the development and expansion of Amharic truly started at a later period with the reign of Yikuno Amlak (1270-1285) from Amhara province. He took power from the Zague dynasty and moved the capital from Lasta to his province Shoa where Amharic was predominantly spoken. The second major expansion occurred with the reign of Menelik II in late 19th century, wherein Amharic begun to be used regularly as the language of administration and also further developed into a written language.

References

Abbadie, Antoine D'. 1859. *Catalogue Raisonne de Manuscrits Ethiopens.* P. VII. Paris.

Abbadie, Antoine D'. 1881. *Dictionnaire de la langue Amariñña.* Paris: F. Vieweg.

Abebe Kifleyesus. 1992. The Dynamics of Ethnicity in a Plural Polity: Transformation of Argobba Social Identity. Doctoral Dissertation: Northwestern University.

Abebe Kifleyesus. 2003. Argobba Ethnography. In Siegbert Uhlig (ed.). *Encyclopedia Aethiopica.* Vol. 1 (A-C). Wiesbaden: Harrassowitz, 332-334.

Abraham Demoz. 1958. The Peculiarities of the Gonderine Amharic. *Ethnological Bulletin.* 4: 11-14.

Abraham Demoz. 1978. Ethiopian Origins: A Survey. In *Abbay.* 9: 12-14.

Afework Gebreyesus/Avefork G. J. 1905. *Grammatico della Lingua Amarica.* Rome.

Afework Gebereysus. 1908. ልብወለድ ታሪክ. Rome.

Ahmed Mohamed Ebrahim. 1999 EC. በኢትዮጵያ የማከዙማይትና የሃሺማይት ወላስማ ስርወ-መንግስት ስልጣኔና ታሪክ፤ የአርነባ ህዝብ የመነሻና የማንነት ግንዛቤ። Addis Ababa: (n.p.).

Amsalu Aklilu. 1976 EC. የአማርኛ ስነ-ፅሁፍ ታሪክ. Ms. Addis Ababa: Addis Ababa University.

Appleyard, David. 2003. Amharic: History and dialectology of Amharic. In Siegbert Uhlig (ed.) *Encyclopedia Aethiopica.* Vol. 1 (A-C). Wiesbaden: Harrassowitz, 232-234.

Appleyard, David. 2004. Some Thoughts on the Origin of the Amharic Object Marker -.ን -[Ə]n. In Boll, Verena et al. (eds.) *Studia Aethiopica: In Honour of Siegbert Uhlig on the Occasion of his 65th Birthday*. PP. 291-301. Wiesbaden: Harrassowitz Verlag.

Armbruster, C. H. 1908. *Initia Amharica: An Introduction to Spoken Amharic*. Cambridge: Cambridge University Press.

Asfaw Damte and Denis Nosnitsin. 2007. Libb Wälläd. In Siegbert Uhlig (ed.) *Encyclopaedia Aethiopica*. Vol. 3 (He-N). PP. 532-534. Wiesbaden: Harrassowitz Verlag.

Ayalew Sisay. (n.d). የአገው ሕዝቦችና የዛጉዌ ሥርወ መንግስት ታሪክ *(The History of the Agew People and the Zague Dynasty)*. Addis Ababa: Commercial Printing Press.

Ayele Bekeri. 1997. *Ethiopic: An African Writing System*. Lawrenceville: The Red Sea Press, Inc.

Bach, Emmon. 1970. Is Amharic an SOV Language?. *Journal of Ethiopian Studies*. 8: 1; 9-20.

Bairu Tafla. 2000. *Ethiopian Records of the Menilek Era: Selected Amharic Documents from Nachass of Alfred Ilg 1884-1900*. Wiesbaden: Harrassowitz.

Balashova, Galina. 2003. Amharic Literature: Amharic Drama. In Siegbert Uhlig (ed.) *Encyclopaedia Aethiopica*. Vol. 1 (A-C). PP. 243-246. Wiesbaden: Harrassowitz Verlag.

Banti, Giorgio. 2005. Harla. In Siegbert Uhlig (ed.). *Encyclopaedia Aethiopica*. Vol. 2 (D-Ha). P. 1034. Wiesbaden: Harrassowitz Verlag.

Baye Yimam. 2000 EC. *የአማርኛ ሰዋሰው (Amharic Grammar)*. 2nd Edition. Addis Ababa: Birhanina Selam Printing Press.

Belay Gidey Amha. 1995 EC. *አህሱም*. Addis Ababa: N.P.

Bender, M. L, Hailu Fulass and Roger Cowley. 1976. Two Ethio-Semitic Languages. In Marvin L. Bender et al (eds.). *Languages in Ethiopia*. PP. 99-119. Oxford: Oxford University Press.

Bender, M. L, Sydney W. Head and Roger Cowley. 1976. The Ethiopian Writing System. In Marvin L. Bender et al (eds.). *Languages in Ethiopia*. PP. 120-129. Oxford: Oxford University Press.

Bender, M. L. and Hailu Fulass. 1978. *Amharic Verb Morphology: A Generative Approach*. East Lansing: Michigan State University.

Bender, M. Lionel et al (eds.). 1976. *Languages in Ethiopia*. Oxford: Oxford University Press.

Bender, M. Lionel. 1983. The Origin of Amharic. *Journal of Ethiopian Languages and Literature*. 1; 41-50.

Bender, M. Lionel. 1997. Upside-down Afrasian. In *Afrikanistische Arbeitspapiere*. 22: 19-40.
Bender, M. Lionel. 2003. Northeast Africa: A Case Study in Genetic and Areal Linguistics. *APAL*. 1: 21-45.
Bernal, Martin. 1987. *Black Athena: The Afroasiatic Roots of Classical Civilization. The Fabrication of Ancient Greece 1785-1985.* Volume 1. London: Free Association Books.
Bernal, Martin. 2006. *Black Athena: The Afroasiatic Roots of Classical Civilization. Vol. III, The Linguistic Evidence.* London: Free Association Books.
Bent, Theodore. 1896. *The Sacred City of the Ethiopians* (New Edition). London, New York, and Bomday: Longmans, Green and Co.
Blench, Roger. 2006. *Archeology, Language, and the African Past.* London: AltaMira Press.
Bruce 88. Ethiopian Manuscript. Oxford: Bodleian Library.
Bruce, James.1790. Travel to Discover the Source of the Nile (In 5 volumes). Edinburgh. (Bruce, James.1813. Travel to Discover the Source of the Nile. Third Edition: Corrected and Enlarged. In 7 volumes. Edinburgh: Gorge Ramsey and Company.)
Budge, Sir E. Wallis. 2001. *The Queen of Sheba and Her Only Son Menyelek*. London: Kegan Paul.
Chernetsov, Sevir B. 1994. On the Origins of the Amhara. *St. Petersburg Journal of African Studies*. 1: 97-103.
Cohen, Marcel. 1958. The Amharic Language. *Ethiopian Observer*. 2:3; 101-103.
Committee Report. 1970. የአማርኛ ፊደል ሕግን እንዲጠብቅ ለማድረግ የተዘጋጀ ሪፖርት ማስታወሻ. *Journal of Ethiopian Studies*. 8:1; 119-134.
Cooper, Robert L. 1976. The Spread of Amharic. In Marvin L. Bender et al. (eds.) *Language in Ethiopia*. 289-324. London: Oxford University Press.
Cooper, Robert L. and Ronald J. Horvath. 1976. Language, Migration and Urbanization. In Marvin L. Bender et al. (eds.) *Language in Ethiopia*. 191-212. London: Oxford University Press.
Cowley, Roger. 1967. The Standardisation of Amharic Spelling. In *Journal of Ethiopian Studies*. 5: 2; 1-8.
Cowley, Roger. 1974. A Text in Old Amharic. In *Bulletin of the School of Oriental and African Studies*. 37: 3; 597-607.
Cowley, Roger. 1983. Ludolf's Fragmentum Piquesii: An Old Amharic Tract about Mary who Anointed Jesus' Feet. *Journal of Semitic Studies*. 28:1; 1-47.

Crass, Joachim et al. 2005. *Copula and Focus Constructions in Selected Ethiopian Languages*. ULAP: Leipzig.

Crummey, Donald. 2003. Čäwa. In Siegbert Uhlig (ed.) *Encyclopedia Aethiopica*. Vol. 1 (A-C). Wiesbaden: Harrassowitz, 704.

Daniels, Peter T. 1997. Scripts of Semitic Languages. In Robert Hetzron (ed.). The Semitic Languages. PP. 16-45. London and New York: Routledge.

Demeke, Girma A. and Ronny Meyer. 2008.The enclitic -mm in Amharic: Reassessment of a "multifunctional" morpheme. In *Linguistics*. 46–3, 607–628.

Desta Tekle-Wold. 1970 EC. ዐዲስ ያማርኛ መዝገበ ቃላት. Addis Ababa: Artistic Printing Press.

Dillmann, August. 1899. Carl Bezold (ed.), Jams A. Crichton (trans.) 1907 (translated edition). *Ethiopic Grammar*. London, Amsterdam: Philo Press.

Drewes, A. J. 1958. The Origin of the Semitic Languages of Ethiopia. *Ethiopian Observer. 2: 3; 113 - 115.*

Drewes, A. J. 1980. The Lexicon of Ethiopian Sabaean. *Raydān*. 3: 35-54.

Eadie, J. I. 1924. *An Amharic Reader*. Reprinted in 2000 with an Amharic and English introduction by Hailu Habtu. Addis Ababa: Zamra Publishers.

Ehret, Christopher. 1988. Social Transformation in the Early History of the Horn of Africa: Linguistic Clues to Developments of the Period 500 BC to AD 500. In Taddese Beyene (ed.) *Eighth International Conference of Ethiopian Studies.* Volume I. 639-651. Addis Ababa: Institute of Ethiopian Studies.

Ehret, Christopher. 2011. *History and the Testimony of Language*. Berkeley: University of California Press.

Ethiopian Languages Academy. 1989 EC. መዝገበ ቃላት ትግርኛ ብትግርኛ. Addis Ababa: Commercial Printing Press.

Ethiopian Languages Research Center. 2005. Ethiopian Languages. Addis Ababa: Addis Ababa University Press.

Faber, Alec. 1997. Genetic Subgroupings of the Semitic languages. In Robert Hetzron (ed.). *The Semitic Languages*. 3-15. London: Routledge.

Fauvelle-Aymar, François-Xavier and Bertrand Hirsch. 2011. Muslim Historical Spaces in Ethiopia and the Horn of Africa: A Re-assessment. *Northeast African Studies*. 11: 1; 25-54.

REFERENCES

Ferguson, C. A. 1976. The Ethiopian Language Area. In M. L. Bender, J. D. Bowen, R. L. Cooper and C. A. Ferguson (eds.). *Languages in Ethiopia*. 63–76; London: Oxford University Press.

Fleming, Harold. 1968. Ethiopic Language History: Testing Linguistic Hypotheses in an Archeological and Documentary Context. *Ethnohistory*. 15: 353- 388.

Gamst, C. Fredrick. 1969. Translated by ባየ ቧላ ላቀው።1993 EC. *ቅማንት፤ አረማዊ-አሪታዊ ኢ.ትዮጵያዊ ጎሳ።* Birhanina Selam Printing Press.

Gaspri Gebre-Mariam (Aba). (n.d.). *Ethiopian History (text in Amharic)*. Addis Ababa: Shewa Printing Press.

Getatchew Haile. 1970. Archaic Amharic Forms. *Proceeding of the third International conference of Ethiopian studies. Addis Ababa:* PP. 61-80.

Getatchew Haile. 1974. The Copula ነው (näw) in Amharic. *Proceedings of the Fourth International Conference of Ethiopian Studies. PP 139-154.*

Getatchew Haile. 1979a. Panegyrics in Old Amharic, EMML 1943, f.3v. In *IOS.* 9: 228-237.

Getatchew Haile. 1979b. Some Archaic Features of Amharic. *Proceedings of the Fifth International Conference of Ethiopian Studies.* Section B, Chicago; PP. 111-124

Getatchew Haile. 1980. Some Notes On 'A Text In Old Amharic' Of Roger Cowley. In *Bulletin of the School of Oriental and African Studies*. 43: 3,578-580.

Getatchew Haile. 1983. Old Amharic Features In A Manuscript From Wollo, Segert, S. and A. J. E. Bodrogligeti (eds.). *Ethiopian Studies Dedicated to Wolf Leslau on the Occasion of His Seventy fifth Birthday*. pp. 157-169. Wiesbaden: Harrassowitz.

Getatchew Haile. 1997 EC. የአባ ባሕርይ ድርሰቶች አርሞዎችን ከሚመለከቱ ድርሰቶች ጋራ. Addis Ababa: N.P.

Getatchew Haile. 2005. Ge'ez Literature. In Siegbert Uhlig (ed.). *Encyclopaedia Aethiopica*. Vol. 2 (D-Ha). PP. 736-741. Wiesbaden: Harrassowitz Verlag.

Gezahegn Getatchew. 2004. የግዕዝ ተጽዕኖ በመጀመሪያዎቹ የአማርኛ ግጥሞች ላይ. The First International Symposium on Ethiopian Philology. 107-129.

Girma A. Demeke. (to appear). An Examination of Amharic Grammar from Pre-17th Century Manuscripts. In Sy, Habib (ed.). *Africa: Cradle of Writing*.

Girma A. Demeke. 2001. The Ethio-Semitic Languages: Re-examining the Classification. *Journal of Ethiopian Studies.* 34: 2; 57- 93

Girma A. Demeke. 2003. The Syntax of Ethio-Semitic. Doctoral Dissertation: University of Tromsø.

Girma A. Demeke. 2008. Copula Construction in Ge'ez and Tigre. In Ronny Meyer, Andreas Wetter and Joachim Crass (eds.). *Copula and Focus Constructions in Ethiopian Languages.* Köln: Rüdiger Köppe Verlag.

Girma A. Demeke. 2011. *Argobba-Amharic Dictionary.* Addis Ababa: Merwa SO Publishers.

Girum Tefera. አማርኛ የተወለደው አክሱም ነው፤ የአማርኛ ወረርሽኝ. አዲስ አድማስ. Amharic Weekly Newspaper. 9: 487, Ginbot 22, 2001 EC.

Goldenberg, Gideon. 1968. Kəstanəñña: Studies in a Northern Gurage language of Christians. *Orientalia Suecana.* 17: 61-102.

Goldenberg, Gideon. 1976. A Copula ት in Old Amharic. *Israel Oriental Studies.* 6: 131-137.

Goldenberg, Gideon. 1977. The Semitic Languages of Ethiopia and Their Classification. *Bulletin of the School of Oriental and Africa Studies.* 40:3; 461-507.

Gragg, Gene. 1997. Ge'ez (Ethiopic). In Robert Hetzron (ed.). *The Semitic Languages.* 242-260. London: Routledge.

Greenberg, J. H. 1971. African Languages. In Anwar Dil (ed.). *Language, Culture, and Communication.* Stanford: Stanford University Press.

Greenfield, Richard. 1965. *Ethiopia: A New Political History.* London: Pall Mall Press.

Guidi, Iganzio. 1892. *Grammatica Elementare della Lingua Amariña.* 2ª Edizione. Roma: Accademia dei Lincei.

Guidi, Ignazio. 1889. "Le canzoni geez-amariña in onore di Re Abissini. In *Della Reale Accademia dei Lincei.* CCLXXXV1, Serie Quarta: *Rendiconti* V;51-66.

Guidi, Iganzio. 1901. *Vocabolario Amarico-Italiano.* Roma: Istituto Per L'oriente.

Haile-Gabreil Dagne. 1976. Non-Government Schools in Ethiopia. In M. Lionel. Bender, et al (eds.). *Languages in Ethiopia.* PP. 339-370. Oxford: Oxford University Press.

Hailu Habtu. 1984. Preliminary Notes on Ancient Ethiopian History. Ms.; New York.

Heran Sereke-Brhan 1994. Ethiopia: A Historical Consideration of Amhara Ethnicity. In Marcus, Harold and Grover Hudson (eds). *New trends in Ethiopian Studies: papers of the 12th International Conference of Ethiopian Studies*. 742-774. Lawrenceville: Red Sea Press.

Hetzron, Robert. 1969. Two Notes on Semitic Laryngeals in East Gurage. *Phonetica: International Journal of Phonetics*. 19:2; 69-81.

Hetzron, Robert. 1972. *Ethiopian Semitic Studies in Classification*. Cambridge: Manchester University Press.

Hetzron, Robert. 1973. The Element -mm- in the Amharic Verbal System. *Annali*. Vol. 32:1-10.

Hetzron, Robert. 1975. Genetic Classification and Ethiopian Semitic. In J. and T. Bynon (ed.). *Hamito-Semitic*. Pp. 103-127. The Hague: Mouton.

Hetzron, Robert. 1976. Two Principles of Genetic Reconstruction. In *Lingua*.38: 89-104.

Hetzron, Robert. 1977. *The Gunnan Gurage Languages*. Napoli: Instituto Orientale di Napoli.

Hetzron, Robert and Marvin L. Bender. 1976. The Ethio-Semitic Languages. In M. Lionel Bender et al (eds.). *Languages in Ethiopia*. Oxford: Oxford University Press.

Houghton, Herbert P. 1949. *Aspects of the Amharic Verb in Comparison with Ethiopic*. Second Edition. Northfield, Minnesota: Mohn Printing Company.

Hudson, Grover. 1977. Language Classification and the Semitic Prehistory of Ethiopia. *Folia Orientalia*. 18: 119 -166.

Hudson, Grover. 1978. Geolinguistic evidence for Ethiopian Semitic prehistory. *Abbay* 9: 71-85.

Hudson, Grover. 1983. Evidence of the Nominal Origin of the Perfect in Amharic. In Segert, S. (ed.). *Ethiopic Studies Presented to Wolf Leslau*. PP. 236-242. Wiesbaden: Otto Harrassowitz.

Hudson, Grover. 1994. Agaw Words in South Ethiopian Semitic? In *New Trends in Ethiopian Studies*. Papers of the 12th International Conference of Ethiopian Studies. 1261- 1269.

Hudson, Grover. 1996 (ed.). *Essays on Gurage Languages and Culture. Dedicated to Wolf Leslau on the Occasion of His 90th Birthday*. Wissebaden: Otto Harasswotiz.

Hudson, Grover. 2000. Ethiopian Semitic Overview. *Journal of Ethiopian Studies*. 33: 2; 75- 86.

Hudson, Grover. 2002. Ethiopian Semitic Archaic Heterogeneity. In Baye Yimam et al. (eds.) *Proceedings of the 14th International Conference of Ethiopian Studies, November 6-11, 2000, Addis Ababa*. Addis Ababa: Institute of Ethiopian Studies, 1765-1776.Hussien Mohamed et al. 2006. Sociolinguistic Survey among Ethnically Argobba Communities. *ELRC Working Papers*. 2:4; 415-454.

Hudson, Grover. 2010. South Ethiopian Semitic pronoun reconstruction. Sergio Baldi, (ed.), *Studi Magrebini VI*, 137-150. Naples: Università degli Studi di Napoli.

Hudson, Grover. 2011. Amharic Rs Pronouns. *In* Luca Busetto, Roberto Sottile, Livia Tonelli & Mauro Tosco (eds.). *He Bitaney Lagge: Studies on Language and African Linguistics in Honour of Marcello Lamberti*. Milano: Qu.A.S.A.R. S.R.L.

Hudson, Grover. (to appear). Some Agaw Non-loanwords in Ethiopian Semitic. In McCollum, Adam (ed.). *Festschrift for Getatchew Haile*.

Huntingford, G. W. B. 1965. *The Glorious Victories of 'Amde Seyon, King of Ethiopia*. Oxford: Oxford University Press.

Hussien Mohamed et al. 2006. Sociolinguistic Survey among Ethnically Argobba Communities. *ELRC Working Papers*. 2:4; 415-454.

Irvine, A. K. 1978. Linguistic Evidence on Ancient Ethiopia: the Relationship of early Ethiopian Semitic to Old South Arabian. In *Abbay*. 1: 5; 43-48

Isenberg, Charles William. 1841. *Dictionary of the Amharic Language*. London.

Isenberg, Charles William.1842. *Grammar of the Amharic Language*. London.

Kane Ge'ez-Amharic Grammar. (A manuscript of the 18th century. Ms. No. 196)

Kane, Thomas Leiper and Denis Nosnitisn. 2003. Amharic Literature: Traditional Historical Writing in Amharic. In Siegbert Uhlig (ed.) *Encyclopaedia Aethiopica*. Vol. 1 (A-C). PP. 240- 243. Wiesbaden: Harrassowitz Verlag.

Kane, Thomas Leiper. 1975. *Ethiopian Literature in Amharic*. Wiesbaden: Harrassowitz.

Lapiso G. Delibo. 1982 EC. የኢትዮጵያ ረጅም የሕዝብና የመንግስት ታሪክ፡ Addis Ababa: Commercial Printing Press.

Last, Geoffry and Pankhurst, Richard. 1969. *A History of Ethiopia in Pictures*. Addis Ababa: Oxford University Press.

Leslau, Wolf. 1944a. The Position of Gafat in Ethiopic. *Language.* 20: 2; 56-65.
Leslau, Wolf. 1944b. Vocabulary Common to Akkadian and South-East Semitic (Ethiopic and South-Arabic). *Journal of the American Oriental Society.* 64: 2; 53-58.
Leslau, Wolf. 1945. *Gafat Documents: Records of a South-Ethiopic Language.* New Haven, Connecticut: American Oriental Society.
Leslau, Wolf. 1958a. The Languages of Ethiopia and their Geographical Distribution. *Ethiopian Observer.* 2: 3; 116 - 121.
Leslau, Wolf. 1958b. *The Verb In Harari (South Ethiopic).* Berkeley, Los Angeles: University of California Press.
Leslau, Wolf. 1969. Toward a Classification of the Gurage Dialects. *Journal of Semitic Studies.* 14: 96 - 109.
Leslau, Wolf. 1992. *Gurage Studies: Collected Articles.* Wiesbaden: Otto Harrasowitz.
Leslau, Wolf. 1995. *Reference Grammar of Amharic.* Wiesbaden: Harrassowitz Verlag.
Leslau, Wolf. 1997. *Ethiopic Documents - Argobba: Grammar and Dictionary.* Wiesbaden: Harrassowitz Verlag.
Levine, Donald N. 1974. *Greater Ethiopia.* Chicago: University of Chicago Press.
Levine, Donald N. 2003. Amhara. In Uhlig, Siegbert (ed.) *Encyclopaedia Aethiopica.* Vol. 1 (A-C). Wiesbaden: Harrassowitz, 230-232.
Little, Greta D. 1974. Approaches to Amharic Historical Syntax. PhD Dissertation; University of North Carolina.
Littmann, Enno. 1902. *The Chronicle of King Theodore of Abyssinia.* New York: Charles Scribner's Sons, Leipzig: Otto Harrassowitz.
Littmann, Enno. 1944. Altamhansches Glossar: *Der Wartschatz in den „Canzoni Guz-Amariña". RIVISTA DEGLI STUDI ORIENTALI.* 20: 473-505-
Ludolf, Hiob/Ludolph, Job. 1682. *A New History of Ethiopia.* Reprinted with Introduction in 1982 by Sasor Publisher.
Ludolf, Hiob/Ludolfo, Iobo. 1698a. *Grammaticæ Linguæ Amharicæ.* Francofurti ad moenum/Frankfurt am Main: J. D. Zunnerum.
Ludolf, Hiob/Ludolfo, Iobo. 1698b. *Lexicon Amharico-Latinum.* Francofurti ad moenum/Frankfurt am Main: J. D. Zunnerum.
Maqrizi. (as translated by Huntingford in 1955). The Book of the True Knowledge of the History of the Moslem Kings in Abyssinia. Ms. Addis Ababa: Addis Ababa University/IES Library.

Marcus, Harold G. 2002. *A History of Ethiopia (Updated Edition)*. Berkeley: University of California Press.
McCall, Daniel F. 1998. The Afroasiatic Language Phylum: African in Origin, or Asian? *Current Anthropology*. 39: 139 - 144.
McCrindle, J. W. 1897. *Christian Topography of Cosmas*. London: Bedford Press.
Mersie Hazen Welde Qirqos. 1935 EC. *የአማርኛ ሰዋስው*፡፡ አዲስ አበባ፤ አርትስቲክ ማተሚያ ቤት፡፡
Messay Kebede 2003. Eurocenterism and Ethiopian Historiography: Deconstructing Semitization. In *International Journal of Ethiopian Studies*. PP.1-19.
Meyer, Ronny and Richter, Renate. 2003. *Language use in Ethiopia from a network perspective. Results of a sociolinguistic survey conducted among high school students*. Frankfurt: Peter Lang.
Meyer, Ronny. 2002. 'To be or not to be': Is there a present tense Copula in Zay? In Baye Yimam et. al. *XIVth International Conference of Ethiopian Studies*. Vol. 3: 1798- 1808. Addis Ababa: Addis Ababa University Press.
Meyer, Ronny. 2006. Amharic as Lingua Franca in Ethiopia. *Lissan: Journal of African Languages and Linguistics*. 20:1/2; 117-132.
Muhamed Meded Ahmed and Jewhar Muhamed Meded. (n.d.). *የአርጎብኛ ቋንቋ መማሪያ*፡፡ Addis Ababa: Bedir Printing Press.
Munro-Hay, Stuart. 1991. *Aksum: An African Civilization of Late Antiquity*. Edinburgh: Edinburgh University Press.
Murtonen, A. 1967. *Early Semitic: A Diachronic Inquiry into the Relationship of Ethiopic to the Other So-called South- East Semitic Languages*. Leiden: E. J Brill.
Murtonen, A. 1969. *Early Semitic II: Lexico- and Phonostastical Survey of the Structure of the Semitic Stock of Languages with Special Reference to South Semitic*. Melboune: University of Melbourne.
Murtonen, A. 1991. On Proto-Semitic Reconstructions. In Alan S. Kaye (ed.). *Semitic Studies: In Honor of Wolf Leslau*. Volume II; 1323 -1336. Wisebaden: Otto Harrassowitz.
Nosnitsin, Denis. 2003. Amharic Literature: Beginning of Amharic Written Tradition. In Siegbert Uhlig (ed.) *Encyclopaedia Aethiopica*. Vol. 1 (A-C). PP. 238-240. Wiesbaden: Harrassowitz Verlag.
O'leary, de Lacy. 1969. *Comparative Grammar of the Semitic Languages*. Amsterdam: Philo Press.

Palmer, F. R. 1958. Comparative Statement and Ethiopian Semitic. In *Philological Society*. 119-143. Hertford: Stephan Austin & Sons, Ltd.

Pankhurst, Richard. 1976. Historical Background of Education in Ethiopia. In M. Lionel Bender, et al (eds.). *Languages in Ethiopia*. PP. 305-323. Oxford: Oxford University Press.

Pankhurst, Richard. 1997. *Ethiopian Borderlands: Essays in Regional History from Ancient Times to the end of the 18th Century*. Lawrenceville: The Red Sea Press, Inc.

Praetorius, Franz. 1879. *Die amharische Sprache*. Halle.

Reminick, Ronald A. and Evgenia Sokolinskara. 2007. Mänz. In Siegbert Uhlig (ed.) *Encyclopaedia Aethiopica*. Vol. 3 (He-N). PP. 752-754. Wiesbaden: Harrassowitz Verlag.

Richter, Renate. 1997. Some Linguistic Peculiarities of Old Amharic Texts. *Ethiopia in Broader Perspective*. Vol.1. Pp. 542-551.

Rodgers, Jonathan. 1991. The Subgrouping of the South Semitic languages. In Alan S. Kaye (ed.). *Semitic Studies: In Honor of Wolf Leslau*. Volume II; 1323 -1336. Wiesbaden: Harrassowitz.

Rose, Sharon. 1997. Theoretical Issues in Comparative Ethio-Semitic Phonology and Morphology. Doctoral Thesis: McGill University.

Salt, Henry. 1816. *A Voyage to Abyssinia*. Philadelphia: M. Carey; Boston: Wells & Lilly.

Sergew Hable Sellassie. 1972. *Ancient and Medieval Ethiopian History to 1270*. Addis Ababa: Haile Sellassie I University.

Solomon Yirga. 2000 EC. አጥቢዎች. Addis Ababa: The Ethiopian Wildlife and Natural History Society.

Sumner, Claude.1985. *Classical Ethiopian Philosophy*. Addis Ababa: Commercial Printing Press.

Taddese Tamrat. 1972. *Church and State in Ethiopia: 1270-1529*. Oxford: Oxford University Press.

Taye Gebre-Mariam (Aleqa). 1889 EC. መፅሐፈ ሰዋስው፡፡ ግንኩሉ፤ ሚስዮን ማኅተሚያ፡፡

Taye Gebre-Mariam (Aleqa). 1914 EC. *የኢትዮጵያ ሕዝብ ታሪክ*. Asmara: Swedish Mission. /1964 EC. *የኢትዮጵያ ሕዝብ ታሪክ* (with additional introductory remarks by Taddese Tamrat)፡፡ Sixth Edition. Addis Ababa: Central Printing Press.

Tegegne Teka. 1998. Amhara Ethnicity in the Making. In Mohamed Salih and John Markakis (eds.). *Ethnicity and the State in East Africa*. PP. 116-126. Uppsala: Nordisk Afrikainstitutet.

Tekle-Tsadik Mekuria. 1951. የኢትዮጵያ ታሪክ፤ ከአፄ ይኩኖ አምላክ እስከ ልብነ ድንግል።። 2ኛ መፅሐፍ።። Addis Ababa: Tesfa Printing Press.
The Cambridge History of Africa, Volume 2: From c. 500 BC to AD 1050. Cambridge: Cambridge University Press.
Tsehaye Teferra. 1979. Reference Grammar of Tigrinya. Ms. Washington, D.C.; Georgetown University.
Ullendorff, Edward. 1955. The Semitic languages of Ethiopia: A Comparative Phonology. London: Taylor's Foreign Press.
Ullendorff, Edward. 1965. The Challenge of Amharic. An Inaugural Lecture; Delivered on 28 October 1964; School of Oriental and African Studies: University of London. Pp. 1-22.
Voigt, Rainer. 1987. Classification of Central Semitic. In *Journal of Semitic Studies*. 32: 1-21.
Voigt, Rainer. 2005. Ethio-Semitic. In Siegbert Uhlig (ed.). *Encyclopedia Aethiopica*. Vol. 2 (D-Ha). PP. 440-444. Wiesbaden: Harrassowitiz Verlag.
Voigt, Rainer. 2007. North vs. South Ethio-Semitic. 16th International Conference of Ethiopian Studies. Ms.
Vycihl, W. 1987. The Origin of the Hamito - Semitic Languages. H. Jungraithmayer and W. Mullur (eds.). *Proceedings of the 4th International Hamito-Semitic Congress*. 109-121. Amsterdam: John Benjamin's Publishing Company.
Wagner, Ewald. 1997. Harari. In Robert Hetzron (ed.). *The Semitic Languages*. 486- 508. London: Routledge.
Wetter, Andreas. 2003. Languages and Identity among the Argobbas. Identités Composées. Dynamiques Linguistiques et Religieuses en Afrique. Université Paris 1.
Wetter, Andreas. 2010. *Das Argobba: Eine deskriptive Grammatik der Varietät von Shonke und T'ollaha*. Kölen: Rüdiger Köppe Verlag.
Zelealem Liyew. 2003. *The Kemantney Language. A Sociolinguistic and Grammatical Study of Language Replacement*. Köln: Rüdiger Köppe.
Zeneb (däbtära). 1924 EC. መጽሐፈ ጨዋታ ስጋዊ ወመንፈሳዊ. (Written in 1857 and Published in 1924). Addis Ababa: Goh Tsibah Printing Press.

Appendices

This part of the work has three appendices. The first appendix contains the abbreviations and transcriptions used in the main body. Appendix II contains James Bruce's argument about the origin of the Ethiopic script and the third Amharic texts from different periods.

Appendix I. Abbreviations and Transcriptions

1.1 Abbreviations

1 = 1st person
2 = 2nd person
3 = 3rd person
Acc = Accusative
Agr = Agreement
AL = A lyric for Amdä Seyon
Aux = Auxiliary
Caus = causative marker
CTSES = Central South Ethio-Semitic
DCM = Declarative Clause marker
Def = definite
DL = A lyric for Dawit
EC = Ethiopian Calendar
ES = Ethio-Semitic
Ethio = Ethiopian
F = feminine
Foc = focus
FP = Fragmentum Piquesii
GL= A lyric for Gälawdewos
Imp = imperative

Impf = imperfective
L. = Line
M = masculine
MA = Modern/current Amharic
MSA = Modern South Arabian
Neg = negative marker
NES = North Ethio-Semitic
NSA = Non-subject agreement marker
O = object
OA = Old Amharic
OSA = Old South Arabian
OSES = Outer South Ethio-Semitic
OV = SOV
Pass = passive (marker)
Perf = perfective
Pl = plural
Poss = possessive marker
RC = Relative clause
RM = Relative clause marker
S = singular, or subject
SA = South Arabian
SES = South Ethio-Semitic
SOV = Subject-Object-Verb
SVO = Subject-Verb-Object
TAM = Tense, Aspect and Mood
TM = Timhirte Haymanot "Teaching of the Faith'
TSES = Transversal South Ethio-Semitic
VO = SVO, VSO
VSO = Verb-Subject-Object
YL = A lyric for Yishaq
ZYL = A lyric for Zär'a Ya'qob

1.2 Notes on Transcriptions

Ethiopic writing can be categorized as phonetic writing. However, it marks neither gemination of consonants nor vowel lengthening. The Amharic letters are syllabograms. Each letter has seven orders also called forms that correspond to the seven vowels that Amharic and a number of the other Ethiopian Semitic languages have. Except those symbols that represent pharyngeal and glottal sounds, the first order of each letter contains the vowel /ä/. In the transcription of an OA word we tried to be as accurate as possible with inferring its possible pronunciation from current usages and from the pattern in sisterly languages. Transcription is made using IPA. However, the mid central vowel is represented by /ä/ following the Ethiopian linguistic tradition.

Appendix II: Bruce on the Origin of Ethiopic Script

As we have pointed out in chapter five James Bruce and few others suggest that the Ethiopic script is the first alphabetical script of the world where the Hebrew for instance developed out of it. Bruce's suggestion cannot simply be rejected as he has some interesting arguments. We provide Bruce's explanation below for ease of reference.

> "It is thought by some, that the first alphabet was Ethiopic, founded on hieroglyphics, and afterwards modeled into more current, and less laborious figures, for the sake of expedition in business. Mr. Fourment is so much of this opinion, that he says it is evident the three first letters of the Ethiopic alphabet are hieroglyphics yet, and that the beta resembles the door of a house or a temple. But, with great submission, the doors of houses and temples, when first built, were square at the top, for arches were not known. The beta must have been taken from an earlier example than this, the doors of the first Troglodytes in the mountains, which were rounded, and gave the hint for turning the arch, when architecture advanced nearer to perfection.

> "Others are for giving letters a divine original: they say they were taught to Abraham by God himself; but this is no where vouched, though it cannot be denied, that it appears from Scripture there were two sorts of characters already known to Moses, when God spoke to him on Mount Sinai. The first two tables, we are told, were wrote by the finger of God, in what character is not said; but as Moses received them to read to the people, so he surely understood them. But, after he had broken these two tables, and had another meeting with God on the mount on the subject of the law, God directs him specially not to write in the Egyptian character or hieroglyphics, but in the current hand used by the Ethiopian merchants, like the letters upon a signet; that is, he should not write by a picture representing the thing; for that the law forbids, and the bad consequences

of this were evident; but he should write the law in the current hand, by characters representing sounds (though nothing else in heaven or on earth), or by the letters that the Ishmaelites, Cushites, and India-trading nations on the continent, had long used in business for signing their invoices, engagements, &c. and this was the meaning of being like the letters of a signet.

"Hence, it is very clear, that God did not invent letters, nor did Moses, who understood both characters before the promulgation of the law upon Mount Sinai, having learned them in Egypt, and during his long stay, among the Cushites and Shepherds in Arabia Petrea. Hence it would appear also, that the sacred character of the Egyptian was considered as profane, and forbid to the Hebrews, and that the common Ethiopic was the Hebrew scared character, in which the copy of the law was first wrote. The text is very clear and explicit: "And the stones shall be with names of the children of Israel, twelve according to their names, like the engravings of a signet; every one with his name, shall they be according to the twelve tribes." Which is plainly, You shall not write in the way used till this day, for it leads the people into idolatry; you shall not represent Judah by a lion, Zebulun by a ship, Issachar by an ass couching between two burdens; but, instead of writing by pictures, you shall take the other known hand, the merchants' writing, which represents sounds, not things; write the names Judah, Zebulun, Issachar, in the letters, such as the merchants use upon their signets. And, on Aaron's breastplate of pure gold, was to written, in the same alphabet, like the engravings of a signet, HOLINESS TO THE LORD.

"These signets, of the remotest antiquity in the East, are worn still upon every man's hand at this day, having the name of the person that wears them, or some sentence upon it, always religious. The Greeks, after the Egyptians, continued the other method, and described figures upon their signets; the use of both, as far we know, has been always common in Britain.

"We find afterwards, that, instead of stone or gold, for

APPENDIX

greater convenience Moses wrote in a book; 'And it came to pass, when Moses had made an end of writing the words of this law in a book, until they were finished'.

"Although Moses certainly did not invent either, nor any character, it is probable that he made two, perhaps more, alternations in the Ethiopic alphabet as it then stood, with a view to increase the difference still more between the writing then in use among the nations, and what he intended to be particular to the Jews. The first was altering the direction, and writing from right to left, whereas the Ethiopian was, and is to this day, written from left to right, as was the hieroglyphical alphabet †. The second was taking away the points; which from all times, must have existed, and been, as it were, a part of the Ethiopic letters invented with them, and I do not see how it is possible it ever could have been read without them; so that, which way soever the dispute may turn concerning the antiquity of the application of the Masoretic points, the invention was no new one, but existed as early as language was written. And I apprehend, that these alterations were very rapidly adopted after the writing of the law, and applied to the new character as it then stood; because, not long after, Moses was ordered to submit the law itself to the people, which would have been perfectly useless, had not reading, and the character been familiar to them at that time.

"It appears to me also, that Ethiopic words were always separated, and could not run together, or be joined as the Hebrew, and that the running the words together, must have been matter of choice in the Hebrew, to increase the difference in writing the two languages, as the contrary had been practiced in the Ethiopian languages. Though there is really little resemblance between the Ethiopia and the Hebrew letters, and not much more between these and the Samaritan, yet I have a very great suspicion the languages were once much nearer akin than this disagreement of their alphabet promises; and for this reason, that a very great number of words are found throughout the Old Testament, that have really no root, nor can be derived from any Hebrew origin, and yet all have, in the Ethiopic, a plain, clear, unequivocal origin, to and from which they can be traced without force or difficulty" (Bruce 1813, Vol. II: 335-340).

Appendix III: Sample Amharic Texts

This part of the appendix contains the Amharic written materials from different periods. The first section contains additional imperial songs. The latest of these lyrics is composed in praise of Gälawdewos (1540-1559). The second section contains two of the 16th century most important manuscripts for the study of the grammar of Old Amharic – Timhirte Haymanot 'Teaching of the Faith' and Fragmentum Piquesii, the text about Mary who anointed Jesus' feet. The third section has extract texts from one of Däbtära Zeneb's famous work, and three letters from the 19th century. The fourth section has some sample texts of different genres from the early 20th century.

3.1 Imperial Songs

The imperial songs below of the first Amharic texts are mainley from a manuscript referred as Bruce 88, found at Oxford, Bodleian Library. This manuscript is assumed to be the earliset manuscript that contains the imperial lyrics written between 1592 and 1605 (Huntingford 1965:38). These lyrics are cited in a number of works such as Guidi (1889), Tekle-Tsadik (1951E.C.) and Amsalu Aklilu (1976 EC). As pointed out earlier Tekle-Tsadik used a different manuscript called Tarike Negest which is a late copy than Bruce 88. There are some differences between the copies. Some of them have been noted in Guidi (1889).[219] Just for comparative consideration, we have presented below a lyric for Amdä Seyon from Tekle- Tsadik as Bruce 88 is given in chapter seven. We have given below a typed and photocopy of Bruce 88 as the photocopy is sometimes difficult to read.

3.1.1 Amdä Seyon (1314-1344)

ሐርበኛ፡ ዓምደ፡ ጽዮን።	L. 1
መላላሽ፡ የወሰን።	
ወሁ፡ እንደመስን፡ መላላሽ፡ የወሰን።	
ከወጅ፡ ዜብይዴናን፡ ከገንዝ፡ ጠጠን።	
ምን፡ ቀረህ፡ በወሰን፡ ኪድያ፡ አመኖን።	L. 5

---

[219] Gezahegn (2004) has also made a brief remark on the differences between some of the copies.

ምን፡ ቀረህ፡ በወሰን፡ ከባሊ፡ አሊን፡
ከደዋሮ፡ ኃደረን፡ ከፈጠጋር፡ ዜላርድን፡
ከኢፋት፡ አምበል፡ አቦከርን፡
ከግድም፡ የዊሰይን፡
ከአንጎት፡ ጎን፡ አሞራን፡   L.: 10
ከአገው፡ ቤት፡ አጌርን፡
ከትግሬ፡ ነደ፡ ክርስቶስ፡ ይውረድ፡
አደረግኸው፡ ገንዙን፡
እንዲሠራ፡ ደውጀውን፡
ማን፡ ቀረህ፡ በወሰን፡   L. 15
አላጸፋኸው፡ ራቱን፡
አልአስማረከኸው፡ ልጅ፡ ሚስቱን፡
ከጎኛም፡ ጆን፡ ከምርን፡
ኪጋፉት፡ አወላሞን፡
በዳሞት፡ ሞት፡ ለሚን፡   L. 20
ማን፡ ቀረህ፡ ከወሰን፡
ያላጸፋኸው፡ ራቱን፡
ያላስማረከኸው፡ ልጅ፡ ሚስቱን፡
ሐርበኛ፡ ዓምደ፡ ጽዮን፡
መላላሽ፡ የወሰን፡   L. 25
ዓምደ፡ ጽዮን፡ ስም፡ የዘራ፡
በወጅ፡ እስከ፡ በጥርአሞራ፡
ቃራ፡ ይነስንስ፡ ቃራ፡ እንደ፡ ጭራ፡
በወንዶች፡ ገንገራ፡
በሐድያ፡ እስከ፡ ጉዴላ፡   L. 30
በባሕር፡ እስከ፡ ኤርትራ፡
ዓምደ፡ ጽዮን፡ ስም፡ የዘራ፡ (Tekle-Tsadik 1951 EC: 100-101)

3.1.2 Emperor Yishaq (1413-1428) (from Bruce 88)

1.
ገፀ፡ ዝን፡ ይስሐቁ፡ ገጽ፡   L.1
የአርያም፡ ይመስል፡ አንቀጽ፡
እሳት፡ ይመስል፡ ብቁጽ፡
ከመ፡ መዳልው፡ ልጽሉጽ፡
ገጹ፡ እንድ፡ ያስደነግጽ፡   L.5
እስራኤላዊ፡ መደንግፀ፡
ዓይን፡ ቀራንቱን፡ ቢገልጽ፡
ማን፡ የሐዮክ፡ ገጽ፡ በገጽ፡
ዓይን፡ እንደ፡ ሎሚ፡ ይፈረጽ፡
ገላው፡ እንደ፡ ሽንጉርት፡ ይልሐጽ፡   L.10
የሐየክ፡ ገጽ፡ በገጽ፡
እሳት፡ ይመስል፡ ዝን፡ ተራራ፡ ጊዞ፡ ሲልጽ፡
ማዕበሉ፡ ሲቆረጽ፡
እንድ፡ ያስደነግፀ፡

❦ THE ORIGIN OF AMHARIC

ዝን፡ ይስሐቄ፡ ገጽ፡፡	L.15
አንበሳ፡ ይመስል፡ ዝን፡ ፍሪዳ፡ ኒዞ፡ ሲጋየጽ፡፡	
ማዕከለ፡ ገዳውን፡ ሲፈጻፍጽ፡፡	
ጋማውን፡ ሐገለጽ፡፡	
እንድ፡ ያስደነግዕ፡፡	
እንዲአት፡ ታስደነግጽ፡፡	L.20
ጎሽ፡ ከፈላው፡ ሲወጽ፡፡	
ዳር፡ በቀንዱ፡ ሲገልጽ፡፡	
እስትንፋሱ፡ ቢቄረጽ፡፡	
ደንግያ፡ በእግሩ፡ ሲፈልጽ፡፡	
እንድ፡ ያስደነግዕ፡፡	L.25
እንዲአት፡ ታስተደነግዕ፡፡	
ደንግያ፡ በቁኝልቀኝላት፡ ሲሮጽ፡፡	
እርስ፡ በእርሱ፡ ሲፋለጽ፡፡	
እንድ፡ ያስደነግዕ፡፡	
እንዲአት፡ ታስተደነግዕ፡፡	L.30
ኮከብ፡ ትመስል፡ ዝን፡ በጽሩ፡ ሰማይ፡ ሲሮጽ፡፡	
ወደ፡ ምዕራብ፡ ሲሠርዕ፡፡	
ገጽኁ፡ እንድ፡ ያስደነግዕ፡፡	
ሲሬ፡ ሥራዊ፡ ይመስል፡ ዝን፡፡	
ሐምበል፡ አልብሱ፡ ረመጽ፡፡	L.35
ጉድን፡ በሪም፡ ሲፈጻፍጽ፡፡	
ሐንገት፡ በሰይፍ፡ ሲቄርጽ፡፡	
ገጽኁ፡ እንድ፡ ያስደነግዕ፡፡	
ዝን፡ ይስሐቄ፡ ገጽ፡፡	
ምልአት፡ ይመስል፡ ዝን፡፡	L.40
ሳፍ፡ ለሳፍ፡ ካንፈርዓጽ፡፡	
ወርካ፡ ከስሩ፡ ነቅሎ፡ ሲያሮጽ፡፡	
እንድ፡ ያስደነግጽ፡፡	
ገጽኁ፡ የዝን፡ ይስሐቄ፡ እንድ፡ ያስደነግጽ፡፡	
ዝን፡ ይስሐቄ፡ ገጽ፡፡	L.45
ፈረስ፡ ሰሮ፡ ሲጋየጽ፡፡	
ሰለጢን፡ ኒዞ፡ የግብጽ፡፡	
ዛብያው፡ ያይታወቅ፡ ዕዕ፡፡	
ማን፡ ይሐይኸ፡ ገጽ፡ በገጽ፡፡	
ወምበዬ፡ ጠፋ፡ ለደምጽ፡፡	L.50
ዓይን፡ በፍልሕ፡ ሳታፈረዕ፡፡	
እጅ፡ ቡብልሕ፡ ስትቄርዕ፡፡	
ጥቡብህ፡ የግብዕ፡፡	
ኃይልኸ፡ የሕንዕ፡፡	

II.

ዝን፡ ይስሐቄ፡ ትኩር፡፡	L.55
ትኩሪቱም፡ ተምክር፡፡	
የዝን፡ ይስሐቄ፡ ነገር፡፡	

ብሐብል፡ በቃለ፡ ጐዝግም፡ ይንገር።
ሐፍሶ፡ አይፈጄ፡ አፈር።
መትሮ፡ አይፈጄ፡ ግራር።   L.60
እስኩ፡ ይንገር።
የአሳታዊ፡ ዳር።
ለበቀሎ፡ አልበቃው፡ መተከል።
ለፈረስ፡ አልበቃው፡ ጨንገር።
በሐብልም፡ በቃል፡ ጉማን፡ ይንገር።   L.65
ብዝቱን፡ የሚያቆጽር።
ሻንቅላ፡ ይንገር።
ፍየሉን፡ የሚያቄጽር።
ቢዛሞ፡ ይንገር።
ብዝት፡ የሚያቄጽር።   L.70
ሶቢ፡ ይንገር።
ብዝት፡ የሚያቄጽር።
በረድ፡ ይንገር።
ብዝት፡ የሚያቄጽር።
ቦጥ፡ ይንገር።   L.75
ገቸን፡ የሚያቄጽር።
ማለጉ፡ ይንገር።
ገቸን፡ የሚያቄጽር።
ሐረበዋሽ፡ ይንገር። መበሽ፡ ይንገር።
ገቸን፡ የሚያቄጽር።   L.80
አቢድራይ፡ ይንገር።
ገቸን፡ የሚያቄጽር።
ገምቦ፡ ይንገር።
ግብሩን፡ የሚገብር።
አብሸሎ፡ ተብቅል።   L.85
ግምጃ፡ ቤት፡ የሚጀጉል።
ሻት፡ ይንገር።
ገቸን፡ የሚገብር።
ድጋእት፡ ይንገር።
ዋማ፡ ይንገር።   L.90
ዜት፡ ይንገር።
ወርቁን፡ የሚገብር።
እናርያ፡ ይንገር።
ቦሽ፡ ይንገር።
ወርቁን፡ የሚገብር።   L.95
ዝንጀሮ፡ ይንገር።
ከምባት፡ ይንገር።
ፈረሱን፡ የሚያቄጽር።
እነሞር፡ ይንገር።
ቀረቀር፡ ይንገር።   L.100
ሐውዘኛ፡ ይንገር።
ፈረስ፡ የሚገብር።

ቀኔጨ፡ ይንገር።
ዝጎት፡ ይንገር።
የአንበሳ፡ መትከል፡ ብስ፡ ደንግያ፡ የኖር።   L.105
ኬራ፡ ይንግር።
ፈረሱን፡ የሚገብር።
ዛቶ፡ ይንገር።
ወላም፡ ይንገር።
ባሕር፡ ገሞ፡ ይንገር።   L.110
ሱፍ፡ ገሞ፡ ይንገር።
ፈረስ፡ የሚገብር።
ሐለባ፡ ይንገር።
ቅቤን፡ ይንገር።
ጎደብ፡ ይንገር።   L.115
ጉዴላ፡ ይንገር።
ባሊሶች፡ ይንገር።
ማና፡ ይንገር።
ዳሽላ፡ ይንገር።
ዝቡራ፡ ይንገር።   L.120
ጎን፡ ይስሐቁ፡ ትኩር።
አንደ፡ ኀበልሁስ፡ በቃል።
ሱማሌ፡ ይንገር።
ጽሙር፡ ይንገር።
ዘንክር፡ ይንገር።   L.125
አይደልይንገር።
ባሕር፡ ማጣባ፡ ይንገር።
በሰው፡ በላ፡ ሀገር።
አብርሃም፡ የሚሉ፡ ታቦት፡ ተከል።
ለቅዱሳን፡ ናኝ፡ ምድር።   L.130
በብረት፡ አስጀጉል።
በሪም፡ አስማገር።
ጎን፡ ይስሐቁ፡ ትኩር።
ትኩረቱም፡ ተምከር።
አንደ፡ ሐበልኹ፡ በቃል። ምጽዋ፡ ይንገር።   L.135
በምጽዋ፡ ምድር።
ጣረስምባው፡ የነበር።
እንጆራው፡ በምኩር።
ጸላው፡ በስፍር።
አብ፡ ተልጆ፡ ሲጨምር።   L.140
ጸፋዎች፡ ሲናሰር።
ጎን፡ ይስሐቁ፡ ከዘመት፡ ሀገር።
ተንቀሳቀስች፡ አድባር።
ጎማ፡ ኀዘኖች፡ በዱር።
ዓሣም፡ ኀዘነ፡ በባሕር።   L.145
ባሕሩም፡ ኀዘነ፡ በጅባር።
ጎን፡ ይስሐቁ፡ ሐወረር።

ግድ፡ የዝን፡ ሐርብይ፡ ወልድ፨
ዓለሙን፡ ገዝዋቾ፡ በግድ፨
አልገዘዋቾም፡ በውድ፨   L.150
ረጒም፡ ወርካ፡ ከተነሐድ፨
ባለ፡ ምሳር፡ ሐወረድ፨
ረጒም፡ ለዓምድ፨
ጕጭሩን፡ ለገደገድ፨
አስመስሎ፡ ገባሬ፡ ሐርድ፨   L.155
ዝን፡ ይስሐቁ፡ የግድ፨
መላሳይ፡ አለ፡ ኑንሒድ፨
ከዚሁ፡ ማን፡ ይጻመድ፨
ከእምሰማይ፡ ወረድ፨
ከመላእክታት፡ የተፈረድ፨   L.160
ሲይፈጀን፡ በሰላጢን፡ ሲሰጉድ፨
እንደ፡ ሣር፡ ስያሳጭድ፨
መለሳይ፡ አሉ፡ ንሒድ፨
ጒብ፡ የየሐዝ፡ ከበድ፨
ሐተን፡ ጠባጠብ፡ ብርንድ፨   L.165
አስመስሎ፡ ገባሬ፡ ሐርድ፨
ዝን፡ ይስሐቁ፡ የግድ፨
የዝን፡ ሐርቤይ፡ ወልድ፨

III.
ኢያማ፡ ዝን፡ ይስሐቁ፡ ኢያማ፨
አጉንም፡ ወዬትማ፨   L.170
ተመታእ፡ በገናኸማ፨
ወደል፡ ሐደሰማ፨
ጋቮ፡ ነፈሰማ፨
ምሥራቅ፡ ኾነች፡ ጨማ፨
ምዕራብ፡ ኾነች፡ ማማ፨   L.175
ተተከል፡ ቃራኸማ፨
መስቀል፡ ጸባማ፨
እንግዬህ፡ ወዬትማ፨
ዝን፡ ይስሐቁ፡ ኢያማ፨

3.1.3 Zär'a Ya'qob (1433-1467)

The poems that praise the deeds of emperor Zär'a Ya'qob presented in Tekle-Tsadik (1951 EC፡ 123) are similar with Bruce 88, presented below in I and II. The lyrics given in Amsalu (1976 EC፡ 156) is the one given below in III. For the reason mentioned above, we have given only from Bruce 88. Line numbers for lyric II continues from Lyric I. However, Lyric III starts with a new line number.

◈ THE ORIGIN OF AMHARIC

A Lyric for Zär'a Ya'qob (from Bruce 88)

I.

ገን፡ ቢድል፡ አማም።	L.1
አባት፡ የብእደ፡ ማርያም።	
አባት፡ የፀበለ፡ ማርያም።	
አመጹ፡ እለያ፡ ፀረ፡ ማርያም።	
ጸበበዎች፡ ዓለም።	L.5
ሲፍቀዋቾ፡ ኢጋም።	
ሲሉ፡ በእንተ፡ ማርያም።	
ሐረደዋቾ፡ እንደ፡ ላም።	

II.

ገን፡ ቢድል፡ ዘለቅ።	
አቤታቾ፡ የአዳል፡ መብረቅ።	L.10
ዝብ፡ እንደበላ፡ ጮምቅቅ።	
ባደል፡ ቢልባቾ፡ ብቅ።	
አማውታቾ፡ ዘቅ።	
አሞራ፡ የዳዊት፡ አሞራ።	
ተከተለኝ፡ በኋላ።	L.15
ሥጋ፡ አበላኸ፡ ሐበላ።	
የደም፡ አጠባኸ፡ ነተራ።	
ተከተለኝ፡ በኋላ።	
ወግዕቼ፡ ቢቃራ።	
ሰኸቼ፡ በጸመራ።	L.20
እኛስ፡ ብንበልዓኸ፡ መሓላ።	
ለጸር፡ ይስጠን፡ ለወርወራ።	
የክንፍ፡ በናደርግ፡ ጽላ።	
ለቀስት፡ ይስጠን፡ ለቀፈራ።	
ምን፡ ከበአሰን፡ ንበልእቹ፡ መሓላ።	L.25
ገላቾን፡ ከመሰል፡ የፈጠጋር፡ እምቢላ።	
አፈቾን፡ ከመሰል፡ በዓልቴቾ፡ የገባቾ፡ እንሶስላ።	
ፀዓታቾን፡ የመሰል፡ ቢደም፡ የዘራ፡ ጮራ።	
ስማቾን፡ ያገኑን፡ ተኮላ።	
አንበልዓም፡ መሓላ።	L.30

III.

ገን፡ ዘርአ፡ ያዕቆብ፡ ቢደል፡ ፀሓይ።	
ሐንገት፡ የዚከብራይ።	
ባለዋ፡ የባርዜላይ።	
በብራ፡ የበረቀ፡ ይመስል፡ ስማይ።	
ገን፡ ቢደበና፡ ቢታይ።	L.35
በዓልቴት፡ ያዘለቸው፡ ይመስል፡ ሥርናይ።	
ጋርን፡ ቢደበና፡ ቢታይ።	

238

አበባ፡ ይመስል፡ ገለገይ።
የመስከሮም፡ ይመስል፡ ጽገይ።
ሰይጣን፡ አውሬ፡ በድላይ።   L.40
የለመደው፡ በሐርጋይ።
ጋርን፡ ዘርአ፡ ያዕቆብ፡ ቢድል፡ ፀሐይ።
ቀለበው፡ እንደእምባይ።
አፈረጸው፡ እንደ፡ ሎሚይ።
ወጋ፡ አለዋቾ፡ ይታይ።   L.45
በትግሬ፡ በነገደ፡ ክርስቶስ፡ ገይ።
ግብፅ፡ የወጻ፡ ፈርሀነይ።
ይከምሩበት፡ ደንቴይ።
ሰማ፡ ዘርአ፡ ያዕቆብ፡ እንዳይቤይ።
በቅዳ፡ ሐሊይታይ።   L.50
ባለሸርጌ፡ በአንጐት፡ አለይታይ።
በለዊሳይ፡ ገይ፡ በአምሐራ፡ አለይታይ
በኢብቃለ፡ ጽዮን፡ ገይ። በጊዶም፡ አለይታይ።
በሐምበል፡ አቦከር፡ ገይ።
በኢይፋት፡ አለይታይ።   L.55
ምሽቱ፡ ዜነባ፡ እንድታይ።
ታንጐት፡ እንደ፡ መረወይ።
ትደቅነስ፡ እንደ፡ በርበረይ።
በፈጠጋር፡ አለይታይ። በሌዛርድ፡ ገይ።
ስሜ፡ ዘርአ፡ ያዕቆብ፡ እንደይበይ።   L.60
በደዋሮ፡ አለይታይ። በኔደራ፡ ገይ።
በባሊ፡ አለይታይ። በለአሊ፡ ገይ።
በሐድያ፡ አለይታይ። በለአመኖ፡ ገይ።
በገንዝ፡ አለይታይ። በለጠጣ፡ ገይ።
በወጅ፡ አለይታይ። በዜብዳር፡ ገይ።   L.65
በዳሞት፡ አለይታይ። በምተሎሟ፡ ገይ።
በጋፉት፡ አለይታይ። በአወላሞ፡ ገይ።
በጐዘርም፡ አለይታይ። በገንኸምር፡ ገይ።
ስም፡ የዘርአ፡ ያዕቆብ፡ ሐዳይበይ።
ይኸምሩበት፡ ደገይ።   L.70
ስም፡ በኍላ፡ ልጅ፡ ሕንዲቆይ።
እንተ፡ የጋንብ፡ ሐበይ።
ያልገደልኸ፡ ገደልኹ፡ ባይ።
ያላየኸ፡ ሆየኹ፡ ባይ።
ወሬኝ፡ እንደገጠን፡ ሀባይ።   L.75
ግዳይስ፡ ይኹነው፡ ለዳኛይ።
ወይሎሌ፡ ዳኛይ።
በሌሊት፡ ፀዕር፡ መቀደሸይ።
ይቀንዕ፡ በጐቶደደይ።
በግራ፡ እንደ፡ ጸመዳ፡ ብዕራይ።   L.80
ሲቀዳደም፡ በፈተይ።
ተአርዌ፡ በድላይ። ይግዳይ። በአተይ፡ ዳኛይ።

239

ও THE ORIGIN OF AMHARIC

ምሸት፡ ዊዘር፡ ባልኈነኝም፡ ለወይ፡፡
ሰፊሕ፡ ሀገር፡ ባልኈነኝም፡ ለወይ፡፡
አካል፡ ሓመር፡ ባልኈነኝም፡ ለወይ፡፡፡ L.85
ወርቅ፡ አምባር፡ ባልኈነኝም፡ ለወይ፡፡
ኪዳን፡ ይኍንኽ፡ በሰማይ፡፡
ጉልትኽን፡ አልስጥ፡ ለወይ፡፡
ይላል፡ ዝጐን፡ ዘርአ፡ ያዕቆብ፡ ቢድል፡ ፀሓይ፡፡ (Bruce 88)

3.1.4 Gälawdewos (1540-1559) (from Bruce 88)

ገመር፡ አጽናፍ፡ ስገድ፡ ገመር፡፡ L.1
ባለፈረስ፡ ብሉና፡ ባለጠብት፡ ባሕር፡፡
ለካ፡ ወጻኽልን፡ ወገር፡፡
ግራኝ፡ በኢትዮጵያ፡ ነግሦ፡ ነበር፡፡
ንዋየ፡ ቅድሳት፡ ሲመዘብር፡፡ L.5
በማመድ፡ ሲያዘምር፡፡
ፍቅረ፡ ማርያምን፡ ሲያስቄርር፡፡
ማተብ፡ ካንገት፡ ሲመትር፡፡
ታቦት፡ ኢያስብር፡፡
ቢያነግሥኽ፡ እግዚአብሔር፡፡ L.10
በዳዊት፡ መንበር፡፡
ቀኍጥዓ፡ እንደ፡ ጸጅ፡ ሰከር፡፡
ሰላጢን፡ እንደዘንግ፡ ወረወረ፡፡
ለግደይ፡ ተኰረ፡፡
ሐርብ፡ በኢስማን፡ ዝመር፡፡ L.15
አስከተል፡ በአመር፡ ወደ፡ ሸዋ፡ ቢዘር፡፡
በሸሜ፡ ስረም፡ ሀገር፡፡
እንደ፡ ጎሽ፡ ሺያናፍር፡፡ እንደ፡ አንበሳ፡ ሲጥነር፡፡
ቸኰል፡ አስኪርቅለት፡ ምድር፡፡
በወርኍ፡ ጥቅምት፡ ቆገት፡ ወረር፡፡ L.20
ነስረዲን፡ የማርያም፡ ጎሡር፡፡
መጻ፡ ሲፈከር፡፡
ጠልፎ፡ ጠሓለው፡ እንደ፡ ዓይነ፡ ምድር፡፡
ወደ፡ ደንቢያ፡ ቢሸገር፡፡
ዝመር፡ ከግራኝ፡ ሲወራወር፡፡ L.25
በተነው፡ እንደ፡ ሓሰር፡፡
በሰለባ፡ ተፈሡ፡ አቄት፡ ዝር፡፡
ግምጃ፡ እንዲያደርጉ፡ ቸገር፡፡
ድልወምበራ፡ ብትሸበር፡፡
ገቦቸ፡ መከተር፡፡ ሓባትዋ፡ ሀገር፡፡ L.30

240

Bruce 88 (Copy of the manuscript)

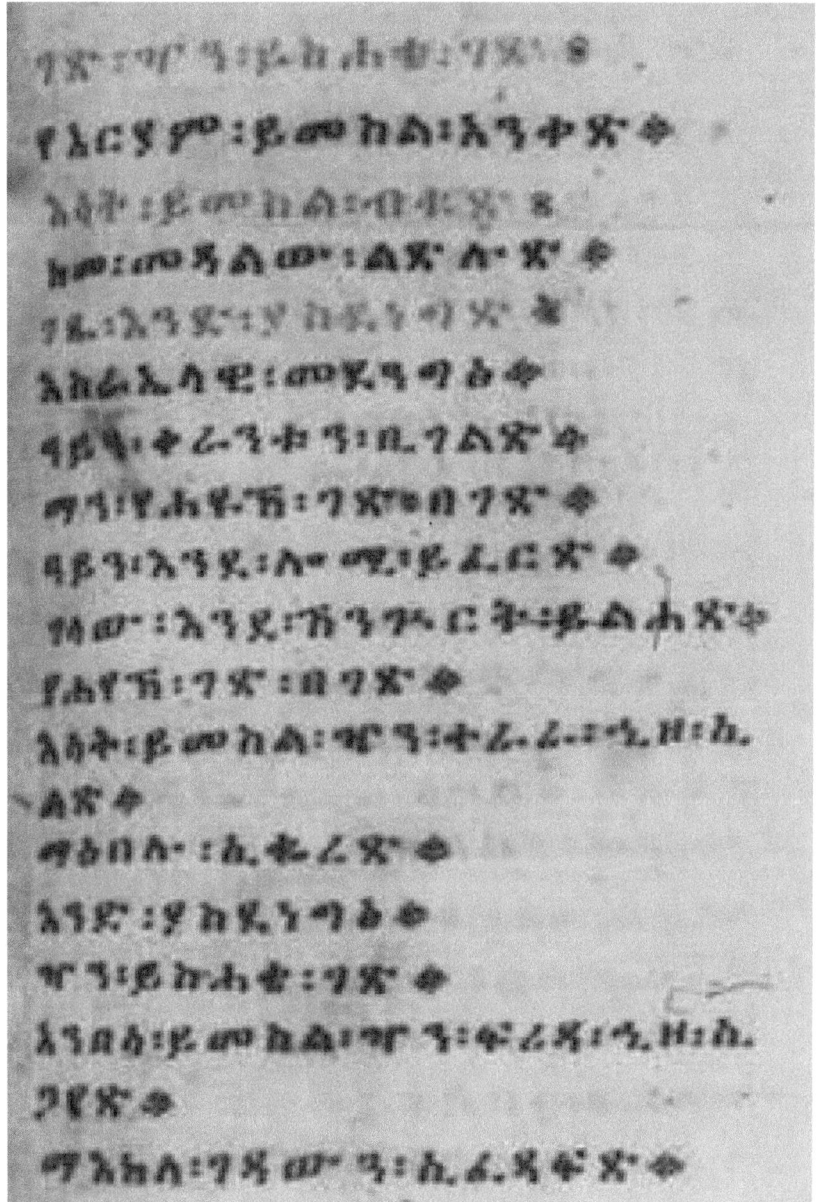

ጋማውን፡ሐገላጽቀ
እንድ፡ያክዲነግቦቀ
እንዲእት፡ታክተዲነግቦቀ
ነቤ፡ካሩላው፡ሒወጽቀ
ጹር፡በቀንዱ፡ሐጋልጽቀ
እክትንፉሑ፡ቢቀሬጽቀ
ደንግያ፡በእግሩ፡ሲፈልጽቀ
እንድ፡ያክዲነግቦቀ
እንዲእት፡ታክተዲነግቦቀ
ደንግኝ፡በቀልቀለት፡ሒርጽቀ
እርሑ፡በእርሑ፡ሲፉለጽቀ
እንድ፡ያክዲነግቦቀ
እንዲእት፡ታክተዲነግቦቀ
ኮክብ፡ትመክል፡ዝን፡በጽሩ፡ሰግ
ይ፡ሒርጽቀ
ወደ፡ምዕራብ፡ሒሠርቦቀ
ግጽኬ፡እንድ፡ያክዲነግቦቀ
ሒሩሠሬዊ፡ይመክል፡ዝንዱ
ሐምበል፡እልብስ፡ረመጽቀ
ጕጽን፡በሪም፡ሒፈጸጽቀ

ሐንገት፡በአይፉ፡ሊቄርጽ።
ገጽኩ፡እንድ፡ያከዲነግδ።
ዝን፡ይክሐቂ፡ገጽ።
ምልእት፡ይመክል፡ዝን።
ሀፉ፡ለአፉ፡ካንፈርዳጽ።
ወር፡ከከስሩ፡ነቅሎ፡ሊያርጽ።
እንድ፡ያከዲነግδ።
ገጽኩ፡የዞን፡ይክሐቂ፡እንዉ፡ያከ
ዲነግጽ።
ዝን፡ይክሐቂ፡ገጽ።
ፈረከሰር፡ሊ.ጋየጽ።
አለጢን፡ሳዘ፡የግብጽ።
ዘብያው፡ያይታ፡ወቅ፡bδ።
ማን፡ይሐይኼ፡ገጽ፡በገጽ።
ወምበይ፡ጠፉ፡ለዲምጽ።
ባይን፡በፉልሕ፡አታፈርጽ።
እጅ፡በብልሕ፡ላት፡ፊርጽ።
ጥበብሕ፡የግብጽ።
ሳይልኼ፡የሕዓδ።

THE ORIGIN OF AMHARIC

ዝኔዮክሐቁ፡ትክ-ርእ
ትክሬቁ፡ምተ፡ምክረ፦
የዝ-ኔዮክሐቁ፡ንገሬ
ብሐብል፡በቃል፡ጐዝም፡ይንገሬ፦
ሐፁ፦፡እየሬ ቼ፡እሬረ፦
መትሮ፡እየሬ ቼ፡ገሩረ፦
እክኑ፡ይንገሬ፦
የእከታዊ፡ዱ-ረ፦
ለበቁሎ፡እልበቃው፡መትክል፡
ለሬረክ፡እልበቃው፡ጨንገሬ፦
ይሐብልም፡በቃል፡ቱማን፡ይንገሬ፦
ብዝቁን፡የሚቄጽረ፦
ሸንቅለ፡ይንዓረ፦
ፉየሉን፡የሚያቄጽ ር፦
ቢዛም፡ይንገር ፦
ብዝት፡የሚያቄጽ ር፦
ስቢ፡ይንገሬ፦
ብዝት፡የሚያቄጽ ር፦
በሬጽ፡እንገሀ
ብዝት፡የሚያቄጽ ር፦
ወንጻዕል፡ቃቱ

በጥ፡ይንገር፨
ገቺን፡የሚያፊጽር፨
ማለጉ፡ይንገርተ፨
ገቺን፡የሚያፊጽር፨
ሐርበዋሽ፡ይንገር፨ሶወሽ፡ይንገር፨
ገቺን፡የሚያፊጽር፨
እበድራይ፡ይንገር፨
ገቺን፡የሚያፊጽር፨
ገምበ፡ይንገር፨
ጓብሩን፡የሚገብር፨
እብሽኦ፡ተብቅል፨
ጋምጃ፡ቤት፡የሚጄጉል፨
ሽት፡ይንገር፨
ገቺን፡የሚገብር፨
ድጋእት፡ይንገር፨
ዋማ፡ይንገር፨
ዜት፡ይንገር፨
ወርቁ፡የሚገብር፨
እናርያ፡ይንገር፨
በሻ፡ይንገር፨

245

THE ORIGIN OF AMHARIC

ወርቁን፡የሚገብር፡
ዝንጀሮ፡ይንግር፡-
ከምባት፡ይንግር፡
ፈረሑን፡የሚያቄጽር፡
እንሞር፡ይንግር፡
ቀረቅ፡ይንግር፡
ሐውዛኛ፡ይንግርዋ፡
ፈረከ፡የሚገብር፡
ቡጨ፡ይንግር፡
ዝርጎ፡ይንግር፡
የእንሳ፡መቶክልአብእኔንማየ፡
ዋር፡
ኳራ፡ይንግር፡
ፈረሑን፡የሚገብር፡
ዛቆ፡ይንግር፡
ወላሞ፡ይንግር፡
ዓሕር፡ገም፡ይንግር፡
ሑፉገም፡ይንግር፡
ፈረከ፡የሚገብር፡

ሐላባ፡ይንገር፠
ቄቤን፡ይንገር፠
ጎደብ፡ይንገር፠
ጉዴላ፡ይንገር፠
ዓሊሶች፡ይንገር፠
እንገሬ፡ይንገር፠
ማና፡ይንገር፠
ዳሺላ፡ይንገር፠
ዘዉሬ፡ይንገር፠
ጥን፡ይስሐቁ፡ትኩር፠
እንዶ፡ሳበሉሁክ፡በቃል፤
ሑማል፡ይንገር፠
ጅሙር፡ይንገር፠
ዝንከር፡ይንገር፠
እደል፡ይንገር፠
ባሐር፡ማተባ፡ይንገር፠
በሰው፡በላ፡ሀገር፠
እብርሃም፡የሚሉ፡ታቦት፡ተከል፤
ለቅዱሳን፡ናኛ፡ምድር፠
በብሬት፡እከጄ፡ጉልፀ

በሪም፡እማግርቈ
ሦንየክሐዊ፡ትኩርቈ
ትእሬቱም፡ተምከርቈ
እንደ፡ሐበልኸ፡በቃል፡ምጽዋ፡ያነ
ግርቈ

በምጽዋዕ፡ምድርፉ
ጣሬከም፡ባው፡የነበርቈ
እንጂራው፡በምኩርቈ
ጸላው፡በከፍርቈ

እብ፡ተልጄ፡ሊጨምርቈ
ጸፉዋች፡ይናስርቈ
ሦንየክሐዊ፡ከዘመቅ፡በገርቈ
ቶንቀላቀለጄ፡እድባርቈ
ዐማ፡ሳዘንች፡በዱርቈ
ባሣም፡ሳዘን፡በዐሕርቈ
ባሕሩም፡ሳዘን፡በጄባርቈ
ሦንየክሐዊ፡ሐወረርቈ
ባጽዋን፡ሕር፡ብያወልዷ
ሳለውክፐገየጽ፡በዓዞ።

እልገዛዋቾም፡ብሙድ፡
ረገርም፡ወርካ፡ከተገገድ፡
ባለ፡ምቅር፡ሐወረድ፡
ረገርም፡ለዓምድ፡
ሳጭሩን፡ለገደገድ፡
እከመክሎ፡ገበራ፡ሐርድ፡
ዝን፡ይከሐቁ፡የግድ፡
መለዕይ፡እለ፡ኑንሐዮ፡
ከዚኹ፡ማን፡ይጻመድ፡
ከእምሰማይ፡ወረድ፡
ከመለእከታት፡የተፈረድ፡
ሰይፈጀን፡በሕሳዉን፡ሒሕጉሩድ፡
እንዱ፡ሃር፡ከያዓጭድ፡
መለዕይ፡እሉ፡ንሂድ፡
ዝብ፡የየሐዝ፡ከበድ፡
ሐተን፡መባመብ፡ብርንድ፡
እከመክሎ፡ገበራ፡ሐርድ፡
ዝን፡ይከሐቁ፡የግድ፡
የዝን፡ሐርበይ፡ወልድ፡

ኢያማጒሥን፡ደክሐፉ፡ኢያማጒ
እኔን፡ሥ፡መዴ፡ትግ፡

ቀመታ፡እ፡በጋና፡ዥማ፡
ወደል፡ሐደ፡ስማቁ
ጋዝ፡ንፈስማቁ
ምሥራቅ፡ኹንች፡ጪማቁ
ምዕራብ፡ኹን፡ማማቁ
ተተእል፡ቃራኽ፡ማዕ
መከቀል፡ጸባማዕ
እንግዴህ፡ወዴትማዕ
ዞን፡ይእሐቁ፡ኢያማዕ

እንት፡ስብማግ፡ቀወብማግ
ሰምጋዝላኽ፡ያእኝን፡ፈትባ
ምኽት፡ስጥቱነኽ፡ዊዘር፡
እካል፡ስጥተነኽ፡ሐመር፡
አፈ፡ስጥተነኽ፡ሀገር፡
አምን፡ጸላኽ፡ው፡የኔኛን፡ፍቅር፡
ዳል፡ተመተር፡
ሐእበትኽ፡ሀገርዪ
ቢጸበ፡መከቀል፡

APPENDIX

ይከሐቁ፡ደረከ፡ከትልቀ
እንደ፡እግዓዘ፡ን፡ደምብረቀ
እንደ፡ቁር፡ብረርቀ
ሐልዮከን፡ቁደርቀ
ልጁ፡ምኽትኽን፡ዘርዝርቀ
ድሉ፡ተመተረ፡ሐእበትኹሀገር፡
ግን፡እንግደ፡የሉዋ፡ንገር፡
እንሉ፡ዓዋት፡ትኽሬ
ይበሉ፡እልጸፈጠው፡እኽሉ፡
ይጠጡ፡እሔጸፈሟው፡ቅምብር፡
ገነኩ፡ቢሁ፡ገበርቀ
በኽንዝ፡እሉ፡ስፈርቀ
ከንቱን፡እሔጽርቀ
የሐላበ፡ገበርቀ
የጠይዱ፡ገበርቀ
የለበሉ፡ገበርቀ
የገደብ፡ገበርቀ
ከንቱን፡እሔጽርቀ
የጉዴስ፡ገበርቀ
ኺፈከር፡ነበርቀ

251

ከን ኴስ እም ሐራ ንር ቀ
ለማይ ቢከን በልቀ
ኧናቆም ኢሉ ን በር በጸር ቀ
ኪፈ ከጹ ን በር ቀ
እጠፉዋ ቿ ለከር ቀ
ደር ሁ በ እን ዝ ለፈር ቀ
እጠፈዋ ቿ ለዝ ከር ቀ
ፈ ለ ቿ በ ኤ ለት ሐረር ቀ
እን በ ሁ ዳዊት ትኴር ቀ
እሉ ኼ ን ገ ብ ሯ
በ እ ብ ኼ የን በር ቀ
ፈረ ከ ኼ ን ና ቀ ብ ል ቀ
በ ት ሉ ኼ ን ና ቀ ብ ል ቀ
እን ጧ ፉ ለ ዘር ቀ
እን በ ሁ ዳዊ ት ተ ኤ ር ቀ
በ ደ በ ና ኼ መ ገን ቀ
በ ፈ ረ ከ ኼ መ ገን ቀ
በ ረ ም ኼ መ ገን ቀ
በ መ ሾ ት ኼ መ ገን ቀ
በ ሕ ቃ ና ት ኼ መ ገን ቀ

እማክስኺ፡ እትፍጀንቈ
ኤኛክ፡ፈቃዴሻንቈ
እንክም፡መንግሩሥ ትኸንቈ
ፈረክየተፈተንቈ
ወቅ፡የተመዘንቈ
ሕብቅ፡ቂራም፡ብለንቈ
ዓድርክ፡መንግሥ ትኸንቈ
እማክስኺ፡ እትፍጀንቈ
ዝንደሉኤለች
ደሐማሁትቱ
እንደተኩ፡ሐዋት፡በኤለት
እክሐረዋቹ፡ኤርሑም፡በኤለት
እንበሉ፡ዳዊት
ሐኡቸንጉረት
መለዙ፡ሔእንዲያንክ፡በለዓት
ደክ፡እወረደ፡በቿ፡የሔፍመዓት
ተጋየኡይ፡ጊለት
ትለለች፡እበቡት
ሐምልወፍፊዳዊት
የጋረቀኝ፡በልታት

በደብር፡ እላቿ ዷኢመላ ዞ ክትቄ
በኼተማ፡ ያላቿ ዷ፡ ሕዋናት ሦዋንተ
ወጋቿ ዷ፡ እቀ ችነ ጒሥ፡ በክረምት፡
ኺዘምትቄ
ወሪዷ፡ የሌእሲሉ፡ እለዷለትቄ
አለ ስኔነ ግን በትቄ
እንቲግቡ ፲ ወደስ ቡ ችተ እንበ ሉ፡ በድ፡
ልሉትቄ
እለመ ስከ፡ እለዋትቄ
ጀለ፡ ዝመትቄ
ማር ያምተ ዷን ሹ፡ እናትቄ
ሚካኤል ይ ዷን ኺ፡ እባትቄ
፲ ከተሉ ኺ፡ ሠፉዊ ተ መስ እክትቄ
ተነ ሣ፡ በተለ ችተ ፈጪማ ሀ ይሉ በቀ
ሉቀ ስትዑ
ሐርቡን ሰየሉ ኺተትዑ
በቀ ሉ ሀ ይሉ ለዓ ቀበ ትቄ
፲ ን ማን ሂ ወር ዴ፡ ቀሉ ቀሉ ሕ፡ ፲ ጒ
ኺ፡ተ ግነ፡ በሬትቄ

APPENDIX

ናኛዋጁ፡ ለእቱትም
አም፡ እከመ ክሉ፡የተጋሊለትም
የገድ፡መገሰሠርሃቸናትም
ጲርማን፡በተሰትም
ሐዋሽ፡መርማን፡በጽዋትም
ለዝያቹ፡ለመብፈ፡እገዊትም
ከታዝን፡የተውኖዋትም
ድለ፡ተመለከ፡ብከራትም
ከታዝን፡የተውኖዋትም
የሐዋሽንት፡ምለትም
እለከረገፈንም፡እበቁለትም
እለክፈታንም፡መገረትም
ድለ፡ተመለከ፡ብከራትም
እብለፊያ፡ብከረዋትም
ምንም፡እልሒኅም፡በለዋትም
ከታዝን፡የተውኖዋትም
የመቢ፡ምምለትም
እለከረገፈም፡እበቁለትም
እለክፈታንም፡መገረትም
ድለ፡ጊቹ፡ንገር፡መአጀትም

255

THE ORIGIN OF AMHARIC

ምንም፡እልዬንም፡በለዋትቀ
ለዚ፡ጀ፡ለወ፡ብሬ፡እግዊትቀ
ምን፡እል፡ዬንም፡በለዋትቀ
እንበሕዳዊትቀ
ጽርሐ፡ንጋሠ፡ትን፡ቃበትቀ
እንደተኬለዋት፡ቃበእለትቀ
እከረዋጀ፡እርሑም፡በእለትቀ
ደርኩ፡እወረጸበጀ፡ዮሌፍ፡መዓትቀ
ሐለ፡ተኸንጉርትቀ
መስዑ፡ሔ፡እንድያንክ፡በተለትቀ
እወረደበጀ፡ዮሌፍ፡መዓትቀ
እንበሕዳዊትቀ
ገግግ፡በጽልእማም።
እበት፡የብንደ፡ማሪያም።
እበት፡የፀበለ፡ማርያምቀ
እመዉ፡እለየ፡ፀረ፡ማርያምቀ
ጸበበዋጀ፡ዓለምቀ
ኪ፡ፎቀዋጀ፡አጋምቀ
ኢሁ፡በእንቱ፡ማርያምቀ

ሐረዴ ዎቺ፡ እንደ፡ ሳምዐ
ሩንበሂ፡ ሊዛለት፡
እስታጁ፡ የእዴሊ፡ መብረቅ፡
ገብ፡ እንደ፡ በሉ፡ ሳጅ፡ ትቅዐ
በደሉ፡ ቢለባቹ፡ ብቅዐ
እማዑታቹ፡ ዘቅዐ
እምራ፡ የዳዊት፡ እምሬዐ
ተከተለኝ፡ በሕሳዐ
ሥኑ፡ እስለኸ፡ ሐበሳዐ
የደም፡ እጠጠኸ፡ ንተራዐ
ተከተለኝ፡ በሕሳዐ
ወግዕቼ፡ በቃራዐ
ሌኸቼ፡ በደመራዐ
እኛከ፡ ብን በሐዓኸ፡ መሐላዐ
ለደዉ፡ ከጠን፡ ለወርወራዐ
የክንፉ፡ በናደርግ፡ ጽላዐ
እቀከ ትቼ ከጠን ለቀፈራዐ
ምን፡ ከበ እእን፡ ንበለ እኹ፡ መሐላዐ
ገላቹን፡ ከመልሑ፡ የፈጠጋር፡ እምብላዐ

THE ORIGIN OF AMHARIC

እፈቹን፡ከመአሕ፡በዓልቴት፡የገባቶ፡
እንአክሳቀ
ፀዳታቹን፡የመአሕ፡በዲም፡የዘራመሪዳ
ከማቾን፡የገዝን፡ተዙላቀ
እንበልዓም፡መሐላቀ
ሐሮብኛ፡ዓምዶ፡ፚ፡ዩን።
መላአፀ፡የወክን።
ወኽ፡እንደመከንቀ
መላሳፀየወእንቀ
ከወጅ፡ዜብዳርንቀ
ይሙረድ፡እድርገኸው፡ትጋፈውንቀ
ከወጅ፡ዜብዳርንቀ
ከገንገዝ፡ጠጣንቀ
ምን፡ቀረኽ፡በወእንቀ
እድይ፡እሜኖንቀ
ምን፡ቀረኽ፡በወእንቀ
ከበእ፡እሊንቀ
እዪዋዥ፡ዬዴራንቀ
ከፈጠጋር፡ዜላርድንቀ
ኤፈት፡እምበሐእበክርንቀ

258

እግዝምየዊአይንቀ
ከእናትችዝንእምሬንቀ
ከእገውእቤትእዝርንቀ
ከትግሬነገዴ፡ከርክቄከቄውሬድ፡
እደረግኸሙ፡ገንዙንቀ
እንዲከሬ፡ዳሙዝሙንቀ
ማን፡ቀረኸ፡በወአንቀ
እለጸፈኸሙሬቱንቀ
እለከማረኸሙ፡ልጅ፡ምኸቱንቀ
ከጎገሮም፡ዝንኸምርንቀ
ከጋፈት፡እወአምንቀ
በጸምት፡ምተአሚንቀ
ማን፡ቀረኸ፡በወአንቀ
ያለከጸፈኸሙሬቱንቀ
ያለማረኸሙ፡ልጅ፡ምኸቱንቀ
ሐርበኘ፡ዓምዲ፡ጽዮንቀ
መለኸ፡የወአንቀ
ዓምዲ፡ጽዮን፡ከም፡ይዘሬበ
በጠቁ፡እኬኩ፡በጥ፡አሞሬ

ቅፉይን፡ከኗንከ፡ቅፉሌንደ፡ጭፊቀ
በመንደጮ፡ገረገፊቀ
በሐድያ፡እክኩ፡ጒዴላቀ
በበሊ፡እክኩ፡ዔድፊቀ
በፀሐር፡እክኩ፡ኢርትፊቀ
ዳምደ፡ጵዮን፡ከም፡ይዛፊቀ
ዝን፡ዘር፡እያዕቆብ፡ደልፀ፡ሐየ
ሐንፕት፡የዚከብፊቀ
ባልዊ፡የባርዜላየቀ
ዝን፡በደበና፡ቢታየቀ
በብሊ፡የበረቁ፡ይመከሕ፡አማየ
ጋርን፡በደበና፡ቢታየቀ
በዓልቴት፡ያዘለቸው፡ይመከሕ፡ከር
ናየቀ
ጋርን፡በደባ፡ቢታኧ
እበባ፡ይመከሕ፡ገአገየቀ
የመከሮ፡ም፡ይመከሕ፡ጵገየቀ
አየጣን፡እውፊ፡በድላየቀ
የአመደው፡በሐር፡ጋየቀ
የአመደው፡በጋጄየቀ

ጋርን፡ዘርእ፡ያዕቆብ፡ብ፡በደሐፀሐይቀ
ቀለበሙ፡እንደሕምባየቀ
እፈረጸሙ፡እንደ፡ሉሚየቀ
ሙጋ፡እለዋቻ፡የታየቀ
በትግሪ፡በነገደ፡ክርክቆ፡ከገየቀ
ግብጽ፡የወጸ፡ፈር ዛንየቀ
ይኸ ምሩ በ ትዪደ ጌየቀ
ከማ፡ዘርእ፡ያዕቆብ፡ብ፡እንዳይቤየቀ
በቅዳ፡ሐሊይ ታየቀ
በለሸርጌየቀ በእንሳት፡እለይታየቀ
በለዊ ሊደ፡ገየቀ በእምሐራ፡እለይታየቀ
በእብቆሉ፡ጾ ንገዩቀ በግድምእለይታዩ፡
በሐምበሉ፡እበከር፡ገየቀ
በኢይፉት፡እለይታየቀ
ምኸ ቱ፡ዜነባ፡እንድታየቀ
ታንጉት፡እንደ፡መረወየቀ
ትደቁል፡እንደ፡በርበረየቀ
በፈጠ ጋር፡እለይታየቀ በሊዛርድ፡ገየቀ
ከሜ፡ዘርእ፡ያዕቆብ፡ብ፡እንደየበየቀ
በደዋሮ፡እለይታየቀ በሐደራ፡ገየቀ

በበሊ፡እለይታይቀበለእሊሊ፡ገይቀ
በሐድያ፡እለይታይቀበለእመጥ፡ገይቀ
በገንዝ፡እለይታይቀበለሐጠ፡ገይቀ
በመጅ፡እለይታይቀበዘብዳር፡ገይቀ
በዳምት፡እለይታይቀበምተሎሚ፡ገይቀ
በጋፋት፡እለይታይቀበእወላሞ፡ገይቀ
በጉንዝም፡እለይታይቀበገንኘምር፡ገይቀ
ከም፡ዋዛርእሃዖቹብሐዳይበይቀ
ዮኸምረበት፡ዴገይቀ
ከም፡ለዲሉሐጁ፡ሕንዲፉይቀ
እንተ፡ያገየን፡ብ፡ሐባይቀ
ያለገደልኸ፡ገዴለኜ፡በይቀ
ያለየኸ፡ሀየኜ፡በይቀ
ወፈኝ፡እደገጠን፡በባይቀ
ግደዮከ፡ዮኜነሙለዳኛይቀ
መደሉሔ፡ዳኛይቀ
በሌሊት፡ዓዕር፡መቀደሸይቀ
ዮቀን፡ዕበዳ፡ቶደዲይቀ
በግፉእንዴ፡ጸመዴ፡ብእፋይቀ

ኢቀዳደም፡ባፈተይቀ
ተእርዋ፡ብድስ ይንግዳይ፡በእተይዳ፺
ምሽት፡ዌዘር፡ባልሌናኝ ም፡ለዋይቀ
ኢፈሕ፡ህገር፡ባልሌናኝም፡ለዋይቀ
እካል፡ሐመር፡ባልሌንኝም፡ለዋይቀ
ወር፡ቀ፡እበር፡ባልሌንኝም፡ለዋይቀ
ኢዳንዶ፡ቱንኜ፡በ ሀማይቀ
ጉልትኜን፡እልብዋ፡ለዋይቀ
ይልሕ፡ዝን፡ዘር፡እ፡ያዕቆ፡ብድ፡ሕ፡ወሐ

ገመ፡ጸኘ፡ፉብ፡ለኖ፡ዋቁ
ባ፡ረ፡እሕ፡ባገር፡ዋ፡ባ፡ሦም፡እብ፡ተ፡በሕ
እክ፡ወዋኜል፡ን፡ወገርቁ
ብራኝ፡በ ኢትዮጵይ፡ንግም፡ንበርቁ
ንዋዋ፡ቅድስት፡ሂመዘብርቁ
በማመጽ፡ኢያዘም፡ርቁ
ፍቅረ፡ማርያም፡ን፡ሂያክ፡ፊ፡ርርቁ
ማተብ፡ካንግት፡ኤመቅርቁ
ታበት፡ኢያብርቁ
ቢያንግሥ፡ኜ፡ኚዋዚ፡እብ፡ሐርቁ
በጸዊት፡መንበርቁ

THE ORIGIN OF AMHARIC

ፉጥዓ፡እንዲ፡ጸጀ፡ሐከርቀ
አለጢኑ፡እንደዘን፡ጋወረመርቀ
ለግጀይ፡ተኩርቀ
ሐርብ፡በኢክማኑ፡ገሞርቀ
እክ፡ከተሉ፡በእመር፡ወደሽ፡ዋቢ፡ዛርቀ
በሽ፡ዌ፡ከረም፡ሀገርቀ
እንደ፡ጋሽ፡ሼያናፍርጫ፡ንደ፡ሐንበ፡ሑ
ቸ፡ኩ፡ሉ፡እክ፡ኢ፡ዴርቅ፡ለሕ፡ም፡ዴርቀ
በመርኡ፡ጥቅም፡ሑጀ፡ግት፡ወረርቀ
ነክረዲ፡ኑ፡የማርያ፡ም፡ላወርቀ
መጀ፡ሒ፡ረ፡ከርቀ

ጠል፡ፍ፡ጠ፡ሐ፡ለው፡ሼ፡ንደ፡ጋደ፡ነ፡ም፡ደርቀ
ወደደም፡ብ፡ጵ፡ቢ፡ሽ፡ገርቀ
ዝመር፡ከግፈ፡ኘ፡ሒ፡ወፈ፡ወርቀ
በተነው፡እንደ፡ሐከርቀ
በሰበ፡ተፈው፡እ፡ቁ፡ት፡ገርቀ
ግም፡ቸ፡እን፡ዲ፡ያደር፡ጉ፡ቸ፡ገርቀ
ድሐ፡ወም፡በፉ፡ብ፡ት፡ሽ፡በርቀ
ግ፡ባ፡ጬ፡መ፡ከ፡ተር፡ሐ፡በ፡ት፡ቀው፡ሀ፡ገርቀ

3.2 Timhirte Haymanot

Timhirte Haymanot "Teaching of the Faith' is undoubtedly one of the valuable materials for the study of Old Amharic. The text attached below is from Cowley (1974). Although this manuscript is not dated, Cowley (1974:602) suggests that it is most likely a 16th century work. The manuscript reproduced below also contains Ge'ez especially in Plate I. In this text all the basic Amharic letters are found. See, for instance, for ጩ /č'/, ቢጩምር (Plate II, column 2, line 5) and ጭብጥ (Plate V, column 2, line 4); for ሽ /š/, ይሻው (Plate I, column 2, line 20); for ች /č/, ማየች (Plate I, column 1, line 20); ኽ /x/, የሻኽ (Plate I, column 3, line 19) for ዥ /ž/, ዥመረ (Plate VI, column 3, line 6); for ኘ /ñ/, ሰኞ (Plate III, column 3, line 7-8) and for ጅ /ǧ/, አንጇ (Plate II, column 2, line 6).[220]

---

[220] See Cowley (1974) for the translation of the text and for some interesting analysis. See also Getatchew Haile (1980) for some remarks on Cowely.

PLATE 1

ሐተ፠ወዝንቱሰ፡ ይብስ፡ትስብእ ተሰምየ፡ዐ.ክር ቱስሕተ፡ወዘእን
ርስዓት፡ወ·እቱ፡ ትፂኢበጀሐ፡ኀነበ ስቶስ፠መንፈቀ በስ፡ትድምርት፡
ወንጋይ፡ሕዋግ፡ አካስ፡መለኮትፂ ነዊኃ፡ወመንፈ ·················
ሑ፡ስብእተወሰየም ሰዒ.ክርስቶስ፡ይ ቀ፡ሐዊረ፠እሳቂ ፠ ፠ ፠
ናትሒ፡ይትበሀሉ ስምይም፡መንፈ ቤሉ፡ክሰሀንቱ፡ ትምህርት·ነ·ዓሂ
በዝንቱ፡እስመ፡ ቀ፡ሐኢረ፠ወጐ መለኮት፡ኮኑት፡ ዋ·ት፡ዘደደሱ፡
ትርዓሚዓ፡ለቅብ ንረቀ፡ነዊ፡ጐቀ ስብእትወሀለ ሥህርዋሙ·ለእ
ዓተፃስተጋበ ዝንተቱ፡ከሀዴት ንታሁ፡ትእብኢ ሉስ፡ዞርስቲደ፡
ኀይስ፡ወክሂስ፡ ወጐተፃበእመ፡ ትኩኑ፡መለኮት ወየቀሀዋም፡
በከመ፡ይቤሉመ ይቤ፡ቀርስም·ስብ ዘንበስ፡ፍልጠ በዝንቱ፡እምቀ
ተርጐማጐ፡ወን ጀክፍልፀበወ ት፡ወዘእንበስ፡ጃ ድመ፡ጥምቀትፂ
ጌሉስሀለው፡እሱ ጽሐሪ፡እበዊነ፡እ ጠትፀወዘእንበስ ወቀርባነ፠መሰ

ትው፡ዓዲ፡እበው ትነው፡ከተወስ ጥይቅነው፡ከእ ·ብረክ፡እንፍት
መሃምርነ፡ደስብ ወሱስሕስኖፀመ ፕውምቀይቴ· ርርብዜከ፠ዓስም
ውዋም፡ስውስ ቀሎ፡በእንድ፡ሰ ደየው፡ከወደቀ በማ·መጻ·ዓስም·
ቶሙፀወለሰብኢ ብተመርምረነው ም፡ቢእዘው፡ዐ መንጋሰስተቀተ
ቤቶው፡ከመ·ኢ መርምሮም፡ከእ ጂ፡ይበለው፠ቀ ዐድሚ፡ከፈደም
ይኩኑ፡ትፉቃነ፡ መቀወቀ፠ግዝኢ ማዐ·ሐርነትፀመ ትር·ነ·ግዝ·እብ
በሃደማነቸ·ጻዜ ብሐርን፡ሻነው ውአተየሻክ·ስ ሐርቀስሱ·ሐ
ማነት፡ማየጂ፡ ሱ·ይሻወ·ብሐ ውቀክስዱዋግነ እደቀበቀቀማሆ
መተፃመፀወተቆ ሲናው፡ተግዛቶ ርነት፡ክንጠኢ አትንም፡ነነፊቱ·
እማዜእብሐር· ም·ካሻው፡በዓደ ትጻዝነተተካመ ከስል·ብቶጐዓ
መተፃመንም·እ ፉ·ባደሐየመ·ከበ ተመፃረት·ደዓ ምነንጐመነስር
ምነትመካማቸ በ·ቀንሂየ የገነው· ተሻፀበጀወ·ቀ·ዴ ከዶሱ·ቀርምቀ

266

PLATE II

PLATE III

PLATE IV

PLATE V

PLATE VI

PLATE VII

PLATE VIII

3.3 Fragmentum Piquesii

This manuscript shows more archaic features than TM appended above. We have adopted this manuscript from Cowley (1983), which he found in Jerusalem "housed in the library at the Ethiopian Archbishop's residence" (P. 2). Some words are not clearly visible in Cowley's attached copy. We have presented below the typed version first, then a copy of the manuscript.

በስመ፡ አብ፡ ወወልድ፡ ወመንፈስ፡ ቅዱስ፡ ፩አምላክ፡፡ ንጽሐፋለን፡ በጥቂቱ፡ ቸርነቱን፡ የእግዚአብሔርን፡ ለእኗ፡ ያደረገልን፡ ለበጄ፡ ባዩ፡ በንስሐ፡ ለተመለስ፡ የንለፊ፡ ንጢአቱን፡ ነዝኖ፡ አልቅሶ፡ ቢናዝዙ፡ የቀደመውን፡ ኁሉ፡ አይዘክርበትም፡፡ ርፉጎነው፡ ጌታቸነስ፡ እዬትና፡ ርፉጎነቱ፡ ያልኸኔ፡ እንደኖን፡ ኁለት፡ ቃል፡ ልንገርኽ፡፡ አልሰምጎኽምው፡ ቅዱስ፡ ጴጥሮስ፡ የክህደው፡ ጊዜ፡ ተሎ፡ አፍጥኖ፡ ቢያለቅስ፡ ሰግውና፡ በእንተ፡ ክህደቱ፡ መሐረው፡ ነገ፡ ሰልስትም፡ አላለውም፡፡ ገዮ፡ ርፉጎነቱን፡ ይኽን፡ ያደጋገር/ጌም፡ የማርያም፡ እንተ፡ ዕፍፈት፡ ወሬዋ፡ በተመሐሬበት፡ መጠን፡ ክርስቶስም፡ አፍጥኖ፡ እንደምሐረዋት፡ ጥቂቱ፡ ቆዩም፡ አላዋት፡፡ ነበረች፡ ሐንድ፡ ሴት፡ ዕኑዕ፡ መልክዓግ፡ ሐንድ፡ አይጋደሎት፡ ከጥርስ፡ ከዓይን፡ ከናፍር፡ ከአነጋጋር፡ ከእጅ፡ ጸት፡ ከእግር፡ ጸት፡ የጸጋዋ፡ ነገር፡ ብዙን፡ ያይጋደል፡

273

ወርቁ፡ ብሩ፡ ቁማሱ፡ ያን፡ ጉሉ፡ በዝሙት፡ የገዛቸ፡፡ ለዓለም፡ ትሽለም፡ ትኩሐል፡ ነበረች፡ ሐንደለት፡ ሳታሸለም፡ አትውዕልም፡ ለምን፡ ብትል፡ ታስሕትዝፖ፡ የንጢአቱዋንም፡ ብዝነቱን፡ ልንንረዋቾኑ፡ ትዕቢተኛ፡ ነበረች፡ ተፈጋዒ፡ ነበረች፡ ዘማዊ፡ ነበረች፡ ንፉግ፡ ነበረች፡ ቅናተኛ፡ ነበረች፡ ቁጣነኛ፡ ነበረች፡ ሀካይ፡ ነበረች፡ ከስብዐቱ፡ ንጢአት፡ ምንም፡ አይጋደለዋት፡ በከብት፡ የከበረች፡ የእኽል፡ በንጢአቱም፡ ክብር፡ ነበረች፡ ያም፡ ጸላኤ፡ ሰናያት፡ ሰይጣን፡ ያጣጥዕምላት፡ ነበር፡፡ ሐንድለት፡ እንደውትሮዋ፡ / ተሸልማ፡ በመስትሐዮት፡ ፊትዋንብትሐይ፡ የመልኩዓን፡ ነገር፡ ብትመለከት፡ ስታነክር፡ ሐንድ፡ ሰዓት፡ ቄየች፡ የዕለት፡ ምርጫቢ.ኖንላት፡ ሐጭር፡ ሐሳብ፡ ተመሰለላት፡፡ ስትል፡ ወዮ፡ ሞት፡ አል፡ ይኸ፡ ጉሉ፡ ይለወጣል፡ ይኸም፡ መልክዕ፡ ይደብሳል፡ ይኸም፡ ሽታ፡ ይገምአል፡ ይኸም፡ ነይል፡ ይደከማል፡ የጊሳ፡ ጊላም፡ የአሩዱአል፡ የሚወድም፡ ይጻልአል፡ እቀርብም፡ ያለ፡ ይርንቃል፡ ብዙነ፡ ነገር፡ አል፡ ምን፡ ይገናል፡ ኢየተቀመጡ፡ ግን፡ እዳ፡ በእዳ፡ ሲጨምሩ፡ ይኖሩዋል፡ ይልሀቅ፡ ኩኔ፡ ይፈደፍዳል፡ በሙሉ፡ ዓለም፡ ያለ፡ ክብት፡ ግን፡ በሰው፡ ከእርግናና፡ ከክፍአት፡ አያድንንም፡ ወፈርፋዱንም፡ ከሞት፡ አያመልጡም፡፡ ይኸስ፡ አይኾንም፡ አንቸ፡ ነፍሴ፡ ነይ፡ ምክራ፡ አለቸዋት፡ ምን፡ ታመኻን፡ ይኸን፡ ከዚያ፡ መኮንነ፡ ዓለም፡ የደረስኺ፡ ጊዜ፡ እርሱ፡ ግን፡ ይላል፡ እንዳገኘ፡ የሚናገር፡ ይኮናል፡ በደይን፡ ወይ / ነፍሴ፡ ማን፡ ይውሐስኺ ይኸን፡ ምን፡ ይውነጥሸ፡ ይኸን፡ ኄት፡ ትገቢው፡ ይኸን፡ ኄት፡ ትደርሽው፡ ይኸን፡ ትእዛዝ፡ የወጻ፡ ጊዜ፡ ከዚያ፡ ኡነኝ፡ ጌታ፡ ውሰዱዋት፡ ያለ፡ ጊዜ፡ ከዚያ፡ ጽልመት፡ ከዚያ፡ እሳት፡ የሰደደሽ፡ ጊዜ፡ እሳትም፡ ያይበርድ፡ እንጨቱም፡ አይነልቅ፡ ያነዱ፡ አይሻእ፡ በዜኽ፡ ብታ፡ ያመልጡዋል፡ አይምሰልሽ፡ ነፍሴ፡ አለ፡ አኹንም፡ ብርድ፡ አስሐትዮ፡ ንላ፡ የሚቁረጥም፡ ጥርስ፡ የሚያንቀጠቅጥ፡ ዕፍረት፡ የሌለው፡ ሞት፡ ቢሰምን፡ አይንኛ፡፡ ስሚዕ፡ አኹንም፡ ነፍሴ፡ ልምከርሽ፡ ማን፡ ይርዳሽ፡ ይመስልሻል፡ በዚያ፡ ዕለት፡ ማን፡ ይለምንልሽ፡ ይመስልሻል፡ ማላዱም፡ ኤል፡ ዋሀስም፡ አይነኛ፡ ዕለት፡ አይሉበት፡ ንስሐ፡ አይረሐበት፡ ገዓር፡ ጻዓር፡ አይቀረጽበት፡ የጥሐሉዋት፡ የመነኑዋት፡ ነፍስ፡ ይኸት፡ ቦታዋ፡ ስሚዕ፡ አኹንም፡ ነፍሴ፡ ልምከርሽ፡ አኛዋቶቸሸም፡ አይረብሐሽም፡ ዓለሙም፡ ንላፊነው፡ ወፈርፋዱንም፡ ወዳዮ፡ ቸሽ፡ ለንጢአት/ የሚያፈቅሩሽ፡ ዓይነዋን፡ ሐይታ፡ ስትል፡ ዓይኖቼ፡ ይኸ፡ ጉሉ፡ ኩሐል፡ ይረብሐዋቸሁን፡ ተስፋ፡ ይኾነዋቸሁን፡ ይኖን፡ ምት፡ የደፈነዋቾኑ፡ ጊዜ፡ ምን፡ ትሉ፡ ይኖን፡፡ ወይ፡ አፈ፡ ወዮ፡ ያን፡ የአኽል፡ ጽፕ፡ መብልዕ፡ ይረብሐሽና፡ ጽዋዕ፡ ሞት፡ ሳለ፡ መሪር፡፡ ወይ፡ አንደቤ፡ ስንቱን፡ የሸነገልሽው፡ ስንቱን፡ የሸፈጥሽው፡ ሞት፡ የዘጋሽ፡ ዕለት፡ ምን፡ ትናገር፡ ይኖን፡፡ / ለዚያለጉሉ፡ ጌታ፡፡ ወይ፡ እዶቼ፡ ትሸለሙ፡ የነበራቸሁ፡ በየቀልዑ፡ በወርቁ፡ አምባር፡ በብር፡ አምባር፡ በሰንኬች፡

APPENDIX

ጸዐቶቼ፡ በቀለበት፡ በፈርጽ፡ ብዙን፡ ዋጋው፡ እንዴት፡ ትንቀጠቀጡ፡ ይሆን፡ ምት፡ ቢደርስባቸሁ፡፡ ወይ፡ ጎንጤ፡ የተሸለምሸው፡ በወርቅ፡ በብር፡ በሰናፍጭ፡ በግባግብት፡ በእንጥልጥል፡ በሉል፡ በፈርጽ፡ እንዴት፡ ተቀጠፋው፡ ይኸን፡ በሞት፡፡ ወይ፡ ሥጋዩ፡ የተፈግዓገሸው፡ በቁማሽ፡ መልበሰ፡ በየነብሩ፡ እንዴት፡ ትኾነው፡ ይኸን፡ እራቁትሽን፡ ያቆሙሽ፡ ጊዜ፡ በእልፍ፡ አእላፋት፡ መላእክት፡ ፊት፡ በለዝያ፡ ማዕዝል፡ ክፋ፡ ምግባርሺን፡ ሲሰምልሽ፡ በዚያ፡ ዱለት፡ የሚያሳፍር፡፡ ወይ፡ ሥጋዩ፡ በላሽ፡ ጠጣሽ፡ አምሐርሽ፡ ሰሐሽ፡ ለመለምሽ፡ ለምስጥ፡ ሌላሰ፡ ሙአያኤለው፡፡ ወይ፡ እግሮቼ፡ እምትራወጹ፡ ለዝሙት፡ ጉላ፡ ጊዜ፡ እንበለ፡ እረፍት፡ እዩ፡ ሞት፡ የአስረዋቹጉ፡ ዕለት፡ እሸሽ፡ ቢሉ፡ አያምልጡ፡ በከብት፡ / አይማልድ፡ ቃልሐዜ፡ አያያል፡ እንድአዘዙ፡ የሚፈጅም፡ ዛታኽ፡ በቁጹ፡ ይበጀል፡፡ እስኩ፡ ክልባቸን፡ ንመራመረው፡ ይኸንን፡ ይኸን፡ ማዕሰርያቸን፡ በእግር፡ ብረትን፡ በሰንሰለትን፡ በገመድን፡ እንዴትን፡ ይኖን፡ ስትል፡ እንደምድራዊ፡ ንጉሥን፡ ገና፡ ያሰሩልናል፡ ይኸን፡ ወይም፡ ይዋዱልናለን፡ ይኖን፡ ከተአሰርም፡ ያመልጡዋል፡ ተሸሽነም፡ ይትነጡዋል፡ አይምሰልኽ፡ አይዶለም፡ እንዴኸስ፡ ግዱን፡ ሞት፡ አል፡፡ በዕድሜ፡ ብዝነት፡ ያመልጡዋል፡ ትል፡ እንደኖን፡ ከአዳም፡ ጀምሮ፡ እስከ፡ ዛሬ፡ ድረስ፡ የተፈጠሩ፡ ሌት፡ ደረሱ፡ ትላለኽ፡ አባታቸን፡ አዳም፡ ሙሉ፡ ፍጥረቱን፡ ያሰገደለት፡ በኑሉ፡ ላይ፡ ያነገሁው፡ ሌት፡ አል፡ ኖኅ፡ ጻድቅ፡ ዓለሙን፡ በማዮ፡ አይኑ፡ ሲያጠፋ፡ እርሱን፡ ያድነው፡ ሌት፡ አል፡ ሙሴ፡ ነቢይ፡ ተእግዚአብሔር፡ ቃል፡ ለቃል፡ የተነጋገረ፡ ሌት፡ አል፡ የቀሩም፡ ነቢያት፡ ሞቱ፡ እንኪያኽ፡ ጎይለኒ፡ ያመልጡው፡ ትል፡ እንደኖን፡ ናምሩድ፡ ጎያል፡ ሌት፡ አል፡ ሶም/ሶን፡ ሌት፡ አል፡ አግ፡ ጎያል፡ ሌት፡ አል፡ ጎልያድ፡ ጎያል፡ ሌት፡ አል፡ ባቀላ፡ የአኽል፡ ዳንገያ፡ የገደለው፡ የቀሩም፡ ብዙን፡ እንዴኽ፡ ያሉ፡ ሞቱ፡፡ የነገሁም፡ ያመልጥ፡ ትል፡ እንደኖን፡ ሌት፡ ደረሰ፡ ሳአል፡ ንጉሥ፡ ሌት፡ ደረሰ፡ ደዊት፡ ንጉሥ፡ የቀሩም፡ ነገሥታት፡ ጉሉም፡ ሞቱ፡፡ የተጠበበም፡ ያመልጥ፡ ትል፡ እንደኖን፡ ከሰሎሞን፡ ይልህቅ፡ ጠቢብ፡ አልተፈጠረም፡ እርሱም፡ ከሞት፡ አላመለጠም፡ መልክዓማ፡ ያመልጥ፡ ትል፡ እንደኖን፡ ስንቱት፡ ምልክዓሞቸ፡ የሞቱ፡ በዓለ፡ ጸጋ፡ ያመልጥ፡ ትል፡ እንደሆን፡ ሌት፡ አል፡ የሚሸለሙ፡ ኢያዕለቱ፡ ቁመሸ፡ ጉሉም፡ ሞ፡ ቱ፡ ከብቱም፡ የንልፋል፡ አይከተልም፡ ያለ፡ ቅሬና፡ አይወስድም፡ ያም፡ ለምስጥ፡፡ የገዙም፡ የንልፋል፡ አይከተልም፡ ያለ፡ ቅሬና፡ አይወስድም፡ ያም፡ ለምስጥ፡ የገዙም፡ የንልፋል፡ የበሉም፡ የጠጡም፡ የንልፋል፡ የስሐቁም፡ የተፈገዑም፡ የዘመውም፡ ሌላው፡ ጉሉ፡ እንዴኽ፡ ያለ፡ ነገር፡ የንልፋል፡ በዚኽ፡ ዓለም፡፡ እስኩ፡ ንማከር፡ ነፍጬ፡ ለጦንት፡ የሚሆንን፡ ነገር፡ እምይንልፋጉን፡ ቲተን፡ / እመንያልፋን፡ በማን፡ እንምነዎን፡ ይሆን፡ እምያስምህረን፡ ይኸን፡ ብላ፡ ስትናገር፡ ደረትዋን፡ ስትመታ፡ ለቃልዋም፡

ቢሐይ፡ እግዚአብሔር፡ ራርነለት፡ መንፈስ፡ ቅዱስ፡ ከሠተላት፡፡ ስትል፡ አላኮን፡ መድኔ፡ ዓለም፡ ከሰማይ፡ ወርዶ፡ ከድንግል፡ ተወልዶ፡ አለ፡ በእንተ፡ ፍቅረ፡ ሰብእ፡ ዕውር፡ ያበራህ፡ ሐንኪስ፡ ያረታዕ፡ ለምጽ፡ ያነጽሕ፡ መዛጉዕ፡ ያሸናረ፡ በ፴፬ቱ፡ ዓመቱ፡ ከተሐመመ፡ ሙት፡ ያነሣ፡ የርነበን፡ ያጸገብ፡ በጢቂት፡ ነገር፡ ንጢእን፡ እሚምህር፡ ሀለበት፡ ዚግ፡ ዕራር፡ ልሀድ፡ ደርሼ፡ ግዳጁን፡ ብነግረው፡ ይሰምዓኜ፡ እኸን፡፡ ድሮውነስ፡ ለማን፡ ብሎ፡ መጸ፡ ለንጢአተኝ፡ እንጄ፡ የተቀበለኜ፡ እንደኖን፡ ነገሩን፡ ምሉዕ፡ መሪነው፡ ርፉን፡ ዛሬስ፡ ቋይ፡ አለሰምዓሽም፡ ቢለጄም፡ አላጉረመርምም፡ አይሻልም፡ ንጢአትሸም፡ ብዙነነው፡ ቢለጄም፡ ለምና፡ በምድር፡ ስንኺ፡ አውቃለኑ፡ ጌታውን፡ ሰው፡ ቢበድል፡ መሐር፡ ብሎ፡ ቢሉ፡ ነገ፡ ይኹን፡ ጥቂት፡ ይብረድይ፡ ይላል፡ ስንኺ፡ ፈጣሪ፡ ሰማያት፡ ወምድር፡፡ ይሽነን፡ የአኸል፡ እዳ፡ ሳላብጄ፡ ለነገሩ፡ ቢኖን፡ ቀርበን፡ ሳል፡ ነይ፡ ዓይን፡ ደርቁ፡ ልኾዮ፡ በገዳ፡ በዓይን፡ ድርቀትዋ፡ አይዴሉ፡ ደም፡ ይውንዘዋት፡ የነበር፡ አሥራቱለት፡ ዓመት፡ የልብሱን፡ ዘርፍ፡ ብትይነገዝ፡ መሐረዋት፡፡ ተአማኒ፡ እንዲ፡ አይወድም፡ ብላ፡ አለቸና፡፡ ከዚያ፡ ተነሥታ፡ ከቤተ፡ መዘገብዋ፡ ገባቸ፡ ገብታ፡ ገረድዋን፡ ጸራቸና፡ እስኪ፡ ያን፡ ክብቴን፡ ጉሉን፡ አንጭ፡ አለቸዋት፡ ያለውን፡ ከብትዋን፡ በሙሉ፡ አውጻቸላት፡ አውዕታ፡ ብትሐይ፡ የግምቱውን፡ ብዘነት፡ የወርቁን፡ የብፉን፡ የነንነቱን፡ የጸዓቱን፡ የስብር፡ ስንጥርን፡ የቤት፡ አቀሐዋን፡ ቄጸሬታ፡ የሌለው፡ የአኸል፡ ብትሐይ፡ አንተ፡ ሸንጋጋይ፡ ከብት፡ ስንቱን፡ ያጠፋኽ፡ ከኔ፡ ቀድመኸ፡ ስንቱን፡ የሰንግልሽዋት፡ አለኑ፡ አለኑ፡ ስትል፡ ያትከተል፡ ወትሮ፡ ላ-- ያደልሐወን፡ ስትሸጄ፡ ያለውን፡ ስትቀበል፡ ወዳጁ፡ መስለኽ፡ ስታጠፋ፡ እስጦ፡ ኢያሱ፡ ይ--- ተኸል፡ ስትል፡፡ እንግዴኽስ፡ አወቁብኽ፡ ያልሽሽም፡ አያመልጥኽ፡ ይኸነን፡ አለቸና-- ዋን፡ ጸርታ፡ ሀጀ፡ ተሎ፡ አፍጦነኽ፡ ጽራልጄ፡ ያን፡ ነጋዬ፡ ዕፍረት፡ ያለውን፡ አለቻትት፡ / ገረድዋም፡ ተሎ፡ ሄደቸና፡ አመጸው፡ ስትለው፡ ያን፡ ጉሉ፡ መዘገብ፡ አሳየቸውና ---- ነን፡ ኽብቴን፡ ጉሉን፡ እስጥኽ፡ አያምልጥኽ፡ ከዕረተኽ፡ ስጠጄ፡ አለተው፡፡ ያ--- ያን፡ የአኸል፡ ከብት፡ ቢሐይ፡ ደነገጠ፡፡ ሲለዋት፡ ምንሸንሽ፡ እመቤቱ፡ መልክዓማን፡ ጉልማሳ፡ ሐይተሽ፡ በዜኽ፡ ሽታ፡ እሽንግለው፡ ብለሽ፡ ወይሽ፡ በዓለ፡ ብዘቱን፡ ከብትን፡ ብትሐይ፡ አስረገፈው፡ ብለሽ፡ ወይም፡ ወዳጀሽት፡ ሞቱ፡ ፈቱን፡ ትቀብዒው፡ መነው፡ ውስጡ፡ ይኽን፡ የአኸል፡ የእምያትገሀሽ፡ አለዋት፡፡ ስትለው፡ እርስዋም፡ ይኸ፡ ጉሉ፡ ያልኸን፡ ሁንኽ፡ መልክዕማን፡ ጉልማሳ፡ ሐይተሽ፡ በዜኽ፡ ሽታ፡ እሽንግለው፡ ብለሽ፡ ያልኹን፡ የተሽነገለይስ፡ እንደሆን፡ ለመልክው፡ ምሳሌ፡ የሌለው፡ በዓለ፡ ብዘቱ፡ ከብትን፡ ብትሐይ፡ አስረገፈው፡ ብለሽ፡ ያልኽጄ፡ አዋ፡ ከብቱም፡ ይኽን፡ የአኸል፡ ያይሉ፡ የተረፈው፡ የሚናጄ፡ ለኪስ፡ በጄስያለጄ፡ እንደኖን፡ አስረገፈው፡ ብዬ፡፡ ወዳጀሽት፡ ምቱ፡ ፈቱን፡ ትቀብዒው፡ ያልኽን፡ አዋ፡

276

እምወደው፡ እንደነፍሴ፡ እቅብዓው፡ ብዬ፡ ይኸነን፡ አለቻና፡ ያን፡ ጐሉ፡ መዘገብ፡ ሸጠቻው፡ ያን፡ ዕፍረት፡ ጨምራ፡ ስትኬድ፡ በእምነት፡ ልብ፡ ስትል፡ እግዚአብሔርስ፡ መሐሪ፡ ከነ፡ አባት፡ ልጁን፡ ቢቄጥዓው፡ አባቴሆይ፡ አቤቱ፡ ቢለው፡ ይራራን፡ ኤለን፡ እግዚአብሔርነም፡ አባቴሆይ፡ አቤቱ፡ ብለው፡ ይራነይ፡ እኮ፡ በአርአያው፡ በእምሳሉ፡ ፈጥሮኂ፡ ይጥገለኂን፡ ጠባዬ፡ ቢያርነቀን፡ እንጂ፡ አቱንም፡ ተመለስጉ፡ ብለው፡ አይሰደጂም፡ ጥንቱነኩ፡ መንግሥተ፡ ሰማያትን፡ ለማን፡ ሰርዓው፡ ለሰው፡ እንጂ፡ ምግባራቸን፡ አይደል፡ ቢከፋ፡ ሲኦል፡ ንወርዳለን፡ የተመለስነው፡ እንዲኸን፡ ለማን፡ ይሰጠው፡ ኖ፡ ለነፉ፡ ሐይታ፡ ሲደርሱ፡ ቢሰግሙ፡ ይሻል። ነገር፡ ዓዋቂ፡ ተሰው፡ የተጸላ፡ እንደኖ፡ ሐዳኒሳይደርስ፡ ቀድሞ፡ ቢታረቅ፡ እዳውም፡ የአንስለታል፡ ከዳኂነትም፡ ያመልጣል፡ ይኸን፡ ያልዓወቅ፡ እንደኖ፡ ግን፡ ብዙነ፡ እዳ፡ ይደርስበታል፡ ከብቱም፡ ይጠፋል፡ ተነጢአት፡ ይሞታል፡ ሲኦል፡ ይወርዳል፡ እንዴትን፡ ያልኸኂ፡ እንደኖን፡ ዳታን፡ ወአቤሮንን፡ ምድር፡ ወነጠቻዎቹ። ሰይም፡ ወገሞራነም፡ እንዴሁ፡ በእሳትና፡ በዋግራ፡ ኦነደዋቾ፡ እንደዚኸ፡ ያለ፡ ብዙነ፡ ኖነ፡ አንአውቅ፡ ላሉ፡ ሰው፡ ለአወቁ፡ ግን፡ ቢኖነ፡ ሰብአ፡ ነነዊን፡ መሐረዋቹ፡ ዮዲት፡ ሆሎፎርኒስን፡ ቸብቻውን፡ ቄረጸቻው፡ እግዚአብሔርነም፡ እንደዜኸ፡ የትእመነው፡ ሰው፡ አይጠፋም፡ የሰይጣነነም፡ ቸብቻውን፡ ደግሜ፡ አቄረጸው፡ አቱን፡ ጊዜውት፡ ብላ፡ ሄደቻ። ኢየሱስ፡ ክርስቶስም፡ ጌታቻን፡ በቤተ፡ ስምዓን፡ ተቀምጦ፡ ሳለ፡ ደረስቸበት፡ በዓይን፡ ድርቀተዋ፡ ገባቻና፡ እግሩን፡ የታሸቸው፡ በእንብዓዋ፡ ሐጸበቻው፡ በራስ፡ ጭገርዋ፡ መዘመዘቻው፡ ያን፡ ዕፍረት፡ ስትቀብዓው፡ ስትል፡ አቤተ፡ ነጢአቴን፡ መሐረኂ፡ ድሮውነም፡ ለምሕረት፡ ወረድኸ፡ ለምና፡ ንጥአንን፡ እምህር፡ ብለኸ፡ አንተ፡ አልኸ፡ ባይለወጥ፡ ታልኸ፡ ኢመጻዕኩ፡ ዕጸውዕ፡ ጻድቃነ፡ አላ፡ ንጥአነ፡ ለንስሐ፡ ከኔ፡ የበአሰ፡ ንጥዕ፡ ማን፡ አለ፡ አቤቱ፡ ለጻድቃንስ፡ ምነም፡ አይኂደስኮን።

THE ORIGIN OF AMHARIC

APPENDIX

ጸሐፊ የኅርያም እንዳይፋቅረት ወረዲበተሎ
ሐረጽበቲ መጠንንክርስቶስም እፍጥም
እንደም ለየዋት ጥቄ ተሎ አሳለየ
ት፡ኅባሪቾ ሐንደ ሔተ ፅፀቆ መልክዓ
ሐንጽ እደግ ደሰ ወጥ ክፕርሑ ከ ነደሕ
ከ ነፍር ክ እ ነ ጋጋር፡ ክ እጭ ጸ ተ ክ እ ግር
ቻት የጸግዋነ ገር፡ብዞሩ ደደኤኧ ልወር
ተ ብረ ተ ግማ ሉ ፡ ፀ ፀ ሒሊ ጠ ወ ት የ ገዚ
ጮ፡ ሊ ዓል ዓ ዋ ተ ሾ ም ተ ኸ ሔ ል ነ በ ረ ጽ
ሐን ደ ስ ቲ ስ ቅ ኛ ላ መ እ ተ ወ ዕ ልማ ስ ዎ
ኝ ባ ተ ል ተ ኡ እ ጥ ነ ግ ። ፡ የ ዳ ጠ እ ተ ወ ን
ዖ ጠ ዛ ቄ ዔ ል ን ገ ረ ዋ ቁ ሑ ። ተ ዐ በ ተ
ፀ ነ በ ረ ቾ ተ ለ ገ ዔ ነ በ ረ ት ዛ መ ዌ ነ ገ ለ ገ
ቸ ነ ል ገ ነ ስ ተ ቀ ኛ ተ ፌ ነ በ ረ ቁ ወ
፡ ነ በ ተ ወ ነ ሒ ተ ፀ ሔ ተ ቾ ፡ ልስ ብ ዓ ፁ ነ
ጨ እ ተ ም ጠ ሑ እ ደ ገ ጸ ስ ዋ ቱ ለ ነ

ተጸልሚ በእትሐ የጎ ፊትዋንዝኅሐይ።
የመልኩዓን ነገር ብትመስካተስኃ
ክር ሐንዱ ሰዓት ቴ የቻ የዐስቲምር
ጊቡኖ ንዐት ሐጽር ሐላተመሰበላጊ።
ከትልመዶምቲ አል ይከ ሥሉ ይሰወ
ግል ይከሞ መለ ክል ይደ በሰል ይዞም
ከኢይግምል ይከም ነይሉ ይደከግል
የግሉ ዷነዩ የአረዱ ዋል የግወደሮ
ሾልሐ አቀራበዊ የሉ ዮርቀል ብዙ
ዓጋር ከል ማን ይነፋሉ ኢየተቀሙጓን
አይ በአደ ሐመዋር ይናርዋል ያሉህተሽ
ኬይደ ጻናርል በመሐዋሴየሰክንብትግ
ዞብ ሰው ክአር ግፍና ቱ ህፉ አትኢ የደሳንፀ
ወደፋደከየወሐ አያመለውዓ የከ
ለአድክንየ አገደነዕሐ ከክምዒ አለጥ
ቲዎጓተወናቀ ይኛነሐደ ደወሳደንዥዓ
መያደረከን ጊኩ እርሐ ግጻፉሰዐኳን
ዷንኜ የግናየዒ ይዕሥናርለዋጕተመ

ናፉሑ ማን፡ ይወሊስኜ፡ ይኸነ፡ ምነ፡ ይወ
ኃኛኸ፡ ይኸነ፡ ሬትቀነቢ ወ፡ ይኸነ፡ ሬ
ቲት ደርኸወ፡ ይኸነ፡ ትእዛዝ፡ የወዳ ጊዚ
ካዚይ፡ ኤነኗ፡ ጀታ ወል ደዋት ያሉ፡ ዚ ከ
ዘይ፡ ዉለመሉ ከ ዚይ እስኝ፡ ይስ ደዱኸ
ዚሁ፡ እስተወያይ ደበርኽ፡ እንወተም እይኗ
ል ቱ ይነደ፡ ኤደኸ እ፡ በዜኸ ብቱ ይመስወ
ፖል አይመስልኸ ናፉ ሑ፡ እለ፡ እኛr ነም ብር
ይ እሕቀይ ገስ፡ ይዉ ቱረ ነዓ ኖርኽ የዓይ
ነወቀ ዓረ ቱየ ለወ ሙት ቢለምቱ እይነ
ኂ ስወሉ ኡነም ናፉለ ልይ ከርቤ ማነደረ
ኗ፡ ይወልስተል፡ በዘይ ዕለ ቱወነ የላም ንሉኸ
ምለ ስተልጋ ኡ ይ ኤሑ ወሁም እይንኔ ዕ
ለት እይለ ብቁ የስሑ እይረብ ለ ብቁ ነገር ይኖር
እይረጊቀወየነ ሑ ወቲ የወነዱቀ ነፉለ ያ
በኸ ነት፡ ወ ወልእኝ ወም ናፉለ ልም ከርኸ
እ ኛም ም ተ ስአ ለ ደ ኒ በዙ ም

የማይረርሽ፡ ዓይንዋን፡ ያይታስተል ዳይሩሯ፡

ይኸኔሉ ዞኔለ ይረብኧ ዋቴሁን ተካፉ፡
ይኸነጥጣኖኒ፡ ይኖን፡ መት የደረናዋቃ
ኡ፡ ዚዜ፡ም? ትሉይ ኞን፡፡ ወይ እረዋዩ፡
ን? የእኸለ ሸፈቀ፡ መብለ፡ ይረብእኺና
ቅየ ዎትለሰ መረር ፡፡ ወይ፡ እንደበቲስ
ነቀን፡ ያሽነ ለኽወ፡ አንቂን የሸረዋክወ፡
መት የዞገኘ፡ ስለቱ ምን ትናገር፡ ይነን፡፡

ሰዚደሰ'ኑሉ ጌታ። ወደ እዶቼ ትሸሰው።
የናብራችሏ። በየትልው በወርቅ እምባር
በብር እምባር ቢሰነኪት ጸዓቶቼ በቀሰ
በጕቦረቁ ብዙኋ ዋገው እንዴጕት
ነቀጠቀቡ ይሆን ምትቢጸርጓገችሏ። ወ
ይሏንጌ የተሸሰምእውበወርቅ በብር በለ
ናፍጭ በጋባግብኹ በእንጥልጥሉ በሱል
በፈርጽ እንዴቲ ትተወፈው ይኗን በምጭ።
ወይ ሥጋ ዩ የተፈግዓሸው በቁጣሸ መልበ
ስ በየሩብራ እንዴት ትኹነው ዶኑኔ እሬቲ
ትሽነ የ ቆሙኺ ጊዚ በእልፍ እአባፉ ሕመ
ሳእክትፈኅትበሰዝያማዕሬ ክፈ ምግባ
ርሺነሄ ሰውልሼ በዚዩዱ ላት የጊ የሰፍር።
ወይ ሥጋ በሳኽ ጠጋኽ እምሕርኽ ሰብፈ
ጹ ሰመሰምኽ ሰ ምስጥ ሲሳኑሉ ደእሳ
ው። ወይ እባርቺ እምትራወደ ላዛውኽኗ
ሰጊዚ እንበለ እረፈት እይሞቱ የእሰረዋ
ችሏ ዕል እሽኽ ቢሏ እየመልበው በ ክብት።

283

THE ORIGIN OF AMHARIC

ይመስለያልሐዊ. አህዶስ ከጉዴዘዉ።
ኗሚሉኑ. ዛሬታኜባተ ጁ. ደጠፅል ። እእ
ሙከስባቶን ኃጠ ፈመረው ደጎንን ደ
ኗሧ ግዕለርሃቹን ብእግሩ ብረቶን በእን
ስስተኗ በገመደን እንደተኜደኗሁ ኩተ
ፈእንደሥዐረዊንተሥን ገኛያለፈልኗስ
ዎዎተ ደም ደየረስናለኑ ይኗን ካተል
ጎቹራመዋል።
ለም ዎመልጡዋል ተሸገኗ እይማልኜ።
ለሰም ከንደኜስ ግሩንጥከል።በይ
ስተኗስ ዎመልጥል ተል እንደኗንኾኄደ
ሥርኃል።በሩ መሩብ የተፈመሩ ጉተ
ሥርጎስ ከተኘን ከደዎመእሯዊ
ሥርስተኗተ ዘኗሱ ለደዖንገሠው ካህ
ሥርር ጀዉከ ዐለሙን በዎደከይፈሊጣ
ከንደሥኑ ሃከለለ መኮፈልየ
ከንደዎስኜስኗ ኗንገተፈ ከአለሥ
ከንደኗነስአለ። ዘኗ ለስ ዎመ
ከንደመስፈደ ተከአ ዕሳ።

ሰን ሄት፡ እል፡ እንዳናሩትእል ገልያሮ፡ ፡
የል፡ሂት፡ እል፡ግቲል፡ የእኸልያ፡ ገነዋ፡ የነያለ
መየረማብሩ፡ እንደኛቶመቱ ፡ የነገw
ዮንመልኝ ትል፡ እንደኛ ሂተይ፡ ስ፡ እልገኑ
ሂትደረሁ፡ ደየትገም፡ የቀረም፡ ነገ ሥተቱ፡
ሉመ ም ቱ ፡፡ የቱመጠበ ም፡ የመልት ትል፡ እ
ን ፳ና ን፡ ከእሉመን፡ ይልህቀ መቢብ፡ እልተረመ
ረማ እር ሑመ ዃመቱ፡ እሳመሰመም፡ መልኝ
ግቱ፡ የመልኝ፡ ትል፡ እን ደሩ ን፡ እንቱት፡መ
ከራመቱ፡ የመተበዓሉ፡ ደነ፡ የመልኝ፡ ትል፡ እንደ
ቡንደተተሥየመቋ ሽለመ፡ እየ ደ ቱ ቀመነሽ፡
ሂሉመመቱ፡ ከብተም፡ የኻል ፈል፡ እ ደክተ
ልም፡ የለ፡ የዃ እ የመበ ቱም፡ የመ ሉመ ቱኝ
የገሑ፡ የኻቀረቱ፡ የበሱም፡ የጠየ፡ የኻል
ፌልከተ መደ የሩደንተ ወ የዘመጡ ለ
ለመኞ፡ እየደን የለ ው፡ተከመሕለብ
ደየ ፡ ልስ መ፡ እስ ከመተ ከ መ ለ ተ ን
ቱመተመ ም መ ሉ ደ

THE ORIGIN OF AMHARIC

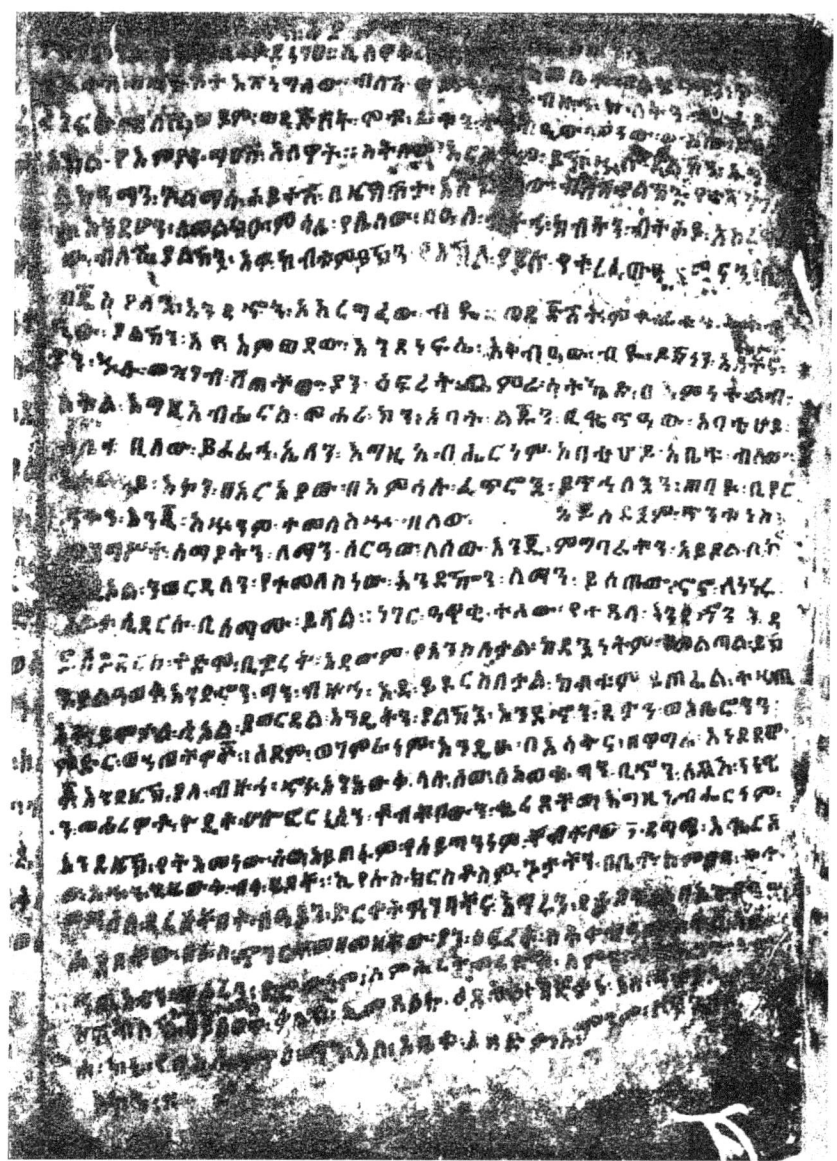

3.3 Texts from the 19th century

3.3.1 *Däbtära* Zeneb's Mäshafä č'äwata Sïgawi Wämänfäsawi

Although further research is needed, it seems that this work of *Däbtära* Zeneb, which contains amusing secular and spiritual stories, is one of the greatest works of its time. It is still worth to read this work for its literal quality. The book is a short one and divided into two parts. The first part is called *Mäshafä č'äwata Sïgawi* 'Book of Amusing Worldly (Stories)', and the second *Mäshafä č'äwata Mänfäsawi* 'Book of Amusing Spiritual (Stories)'.

መጽሐፈ ፡ ጨዋታ ፡ ሥጋዊ ።
ክፍል ፡ ፩ ።

እግዚአብሐር ፡ አስቲሻር ፡ ሚካኤል ፡ አስቲዎት፡ ምን ው ፡ በኖርሁኝ ። ገብርኤል ፡ ሲያንቀላፉ ፡ ሩፋኤል ፡ ሲደ ክም ፡ ሐስተኛው ፡ ዲያብሎስ ፡ ንስሐ ፡ ይገባል ።

ክረምት ፡ ሲመጣ ፡ ሰማይ ፡ እንዲክብድ ፡ የጠሉትም ፡ ሰው ፡ ሲመጣ ፡ እንደዚያ ፡ ይከብዳል ። ዘወትር ፡ ከሚያጋ ድል ፡ አህያ ፡ ተሸክሞ ፡ መሄድ ፡ ይሻላል ። ከማያስተክክል ፡ መላክተኛ ፡ የማለዳ ፡ ወፍ ፡ ትሻላች ፡ ምነው ፡ ቢሉ ፡ ንግቱን ፡ ትንግራለችና ።

ደንጋይና ፡ ጭቃ ፡ ቢቀጣጠሉ ፡ ታላቅ ፡ ቤት ፡ ረጅም ፡ ቅጥር ፡ ይሆናሉ፡እንንተም፡መረታውያን፡ሰዎች ፡ እንደዚህ ፡ ብትረዳዱ ፡ ጥበባችሁና ፡ ኃያላችሁ ፡ ከሰማይ ፡ በደረሰ ።

ክሰኖ ፡ ክረምት ፡ ፊት ፡ ይመራል ፡ ኂላ ፡ ግን ፡ ደስ ፡ ያሰኛል ። ድሪ ፡ ምንድር ፡ ነው ፤ ገንዘብን ፡ ለመቆራኘት ፡ የተሁራ ፡ ሰንሰለት ፡ ነው ። እሬት ፡ መብላት ፡ ቢለመድ ፡ ባ ልተለቀቀም ፡ ነበር ፤ ዝሙትም ፡ ላለመደው ፡ ሰው ፡ እንደ ዚህ ፡ ነው ።

ጣዝማ ፡ እጅግ ፡ ብልህ ፡ ናት ፡ መሬት ፡ ቀዳ ፡ ገብታ ፡ እንደዚያ ፡ ያለ ፡ መድኃኒት ፡ የሚሆን ፡ ማር ፡ ትሠራለች ። ምነው ፡ እናንት ፡ ሰዎች ፡ ወይ ፡ ከፈጋሪ ፡ ወይም ፡ ከሰው ፡ ብልሀትን ፡ አትፈልጉምን ።

የምሥራች ፡ ክራቅ ፡ አገር ፡ በመጣ፡ጊዜ፡የሰው ፡ ልብ በደስታ ፡ በሕር ፡ ይሰጥማል ። እርንን ፡ ከፍቶ ፡ ቢተውት ዝንብና ፡ ድመት ፡ ይጫወትብታል ። አገርንም ፡ አቅኖ ፡ ሰው ፡ ካላስቀመጡበት ፡ ተመልሶ ፡ ዳር ፡ ይሆናል ።

287

መጽሐፈ ፡ ጨዋታ ፡ ሥጋዊ ፡

ባባቱ ፡ የሚከራ ፡ ሰው ፡ ጆሳ ፡ ነው ። የሰው ፡ እባቱ ፡ እንድ ፡ እዳም ፡ አይደለምን ። ሔትን ፡ ወንድ ፡ እንድ ፡ ጊዜም ፡ ይደርስባታል ፡ መንታ ፡ ትወልዳለች ፡ እህልም ፡ እንዲት ፡ ፍሬ ፡ ተዘርታ ፡ ብዙ ፡ ታፈራለች ፡ ይህ ፡ ነገር ፡ ከቶ ፡ እንዴት ፡ ነው ፡ እንጃ ፡ ማን ፡ ያውቀዋል ፡ ያ ፡ የጠቢቦች ፡ ጠቢብ ፡ ያውቀው ፡ እንደሆነ ፡ ነው ፡ እንጂ ።

ፈረስ ፡ በብረት ፡ ልጓም ፡ ይገታል ፡ የሕዝብም ፡ ልጓሙ ፡ ንጉሥ ፡ ነው ፡ መቃብር ፡ መልካም ፡ ጉታ ፡ ነው ፡ ብስሉንና ፡ ጥሬውን ፡ ይከታልና ። ወዳጅ ፡ ቢወዳት ፡ ይወዳል ፡ መሬትም ፡ ቢበሉት ፡ ይበላል ።

በርበሬ ፡ ላይን ፡ ቀይ ፡ ሆና ፡ ይታያል ፡ ምነው ፡ ቢሉ ፡ በብልሐት ፡ ገብቶ ፡ ሊለብብ ። ክፉ ፡ ሰውም ፡ ቀስ ፡ ብሎ ፡ ገብቶ ፡ ኋላ ፡ ንግሩን ፡ ያመጣል ።

ቸር ፡ ሰው ፡ ለወዳጁ ፡ ጠቃ ፡ ነው ፡ ፍቅሩ ፡ ያስከራልና ። ዝናም ፡ ከዘነመ ፡ በጓላ ፡ ቡቃያ ፡ ያበቅላል ፡ ንጉሥም ፡ ከወደደ ፡ በጓላ ፡ ይሾማል ።

ሽክላ ፡ እጅግ ፡ ክፉ ፡ ነው ፡ ወይ ፡ ኦርስ ፡ አሠርቶት ፡ መከታ ፡ እየሆነ ፡ እሳትን ፡ ያስወጋዋል ። ክፉም ፡ ሰው ፡ እንደዚያ ፡ ነው ። ወንፊት ፡ ዱቄትን ፡ እንዲነፉ ፡ ዘርዝራም ፡ ሾጋ ፡ ጠጁን ፡ እንዲያወርድ ፡ ባለቤቱም ፡ ያልቻሉን ፡ ምሥጢር ፡ ሴለው ፡ ሰው ፡ አይችልም ።

ቅቤ ፡ ከይብና ፡ ከንት ፡ እንዲላይ ፡ በላይም ፡ እንዲሆን ፡ ዳድቅም ፡ ሰው ፡ እንደዚያ ፡ ነው ።

ክፍል ፡ ፮ ።

ደመና ፡ ሰማይን ፡ እንዲሸፍነው ፡ ንጉሥም ፡ በሠራዊቱ ፡ እንደዚያ ፡ ነው ። ሳግና ፡ አጸሊት ፡ ለምለም ፡ መ

መጽሐፈ ፡ ጨዋታ ፡ ሥጋዊ ።

ስለው ፡ እንዳለበልቡ ፡ መናፍቃንም ፡ ሲቀርቧቸው ፡ እንደዚያ ፡ ናቸው ።

በቀስታና ፡ በዝግታ ፡ የተበጀ ፡ መዘውር ፡ ኋላ ፡ ጉልበት ፡ ይሆናል ። ወረቀት ፡ መልካም ፡ እርሻ ፡ ነው ፡ ብዙ ፡ ነገር ፡ ይዘራልና ፡ ጉታም ፡ አይሻ ፡ እርሱ ፡ ክቶት ፡ ይና ራልና ።

ማር ፡ ሁለት ፡ ጊዜ ፡ ያገለግላል ፡ አንድ ፡ ጊዜ ፡ መጠጥ ፡ እንድ ፡ ጊዜ ፡ መብራት ፡ ሆኖ ። ምነው ፡ ቢሉ ፡ የብልሕ ፡ ሥራ ፡ ነውና ፡ አሰርም ፡ የለው ።

ሕዝብና ፡ ሕዝብ ፡ ደጋና ፡ ቆላ ፡ ናቸው ። ንጉሡ ፡ ግን ፡ ገበያ ፡ ነው ፡ ሁሉን ፡ ያገናኛልና ። ሸክላ ፡ ከተሰበረ ፡ በጓላ ፡ ገል ፡ ነው ። መኳንንትም ፡ ከተሻሩ ፡ በጓላ ፡ ሕዝብ ፡ ናቸው ።

ክፉ ፡ ሰው ፡ ሽንቱን ፡ በሽን ፡ ጊዜ ፡ ኋላ ፡ ጉንፋን ፡ ይሆናል ፡ ምነው ፡ ቢሉ ፡ ግብሩ ፡ ተጉድፎ ፡ የተወሐደ ፡ ነውና ፡ ማርና ፡ እሬትን ፡ ቢመዝኑ ፡ ማን ፡ ይደፋል ፡ እሬ ት ፡ ምነው ፡ ቢሉ ፡ ክፉ ፡ መራራ ፡ ነውና ።

ክብዙ ፡ ቀን ፡ ደስታ ፡ ያንድ ፡ ቀን ፡ መከራ ፡ ይበል ጣል ። ንጉሥ ፡ ምሰሶ ፡ ነው ፡ ሠራዊት ፡ ግድግዳ ፡ ናቸ ው ። መኳንንት ፡ ግን ፡ ማገር ፡ ናቸው ፡ ለጎጥ ፡ ልጡ ፡ እንዲማልግ ፡ እንጨቱም ፡ ቀሊል ፡ እንደሆነ ፡ ወስላታም ፡ ወዳጅ ፡ እንደዚያ ፡ ነው ።

ጨዉ ፡ በዓለም ፡ ሁሉ ፡ ይዘራል ፡ ምናልባት ፡ ሰል ችተው ፡ ይተውኛል ፡ ብሎ ፡ ነውን ፤ ክሬት ፡ ጋራ ፡ ይጋባ ፡ እንደሆነ ፡ ነው ፡ እንጂ ፡ የሚለቀው ፡ የለም ።

አንድ ፡ ዓይንና ፡ አንድ ፡ ጎን ፡ ያላቸው ፡ ተጋብተው ፡ ሁለት ፡ ዓይን ፡ ያለው ፡ ልጅ ፡ ወለዱ ፡ ይህ ፡ ነገር ፡ ም ንድር ፡ ነው ፡ እንዱ ፡ ካባቱ ፡ አንዱ ፡ ከናቱ ፡ ነዋ ። የዚህ ፡

መጽሐፈ ፡ ፘፈዋታ ፡ መንፈሳዊ ።
ክፍል ፡ ፮ ።

ቅቤ ፡ ለመጽሐፍ ፡ ዘመዱ ፡ አይደለም ፡ መጽሐፍ ፡ ግን ፡ ለሰው ፡ ቅቤ ፡ ነው ፡ እታክልት ፡ ሆና ፡ ካላፈራ ፡ ሰው ፡ ሆና ፡ እግዚአብሔርን ፡ ካልፈራ ፡ መቀረጥ ፡ አይቀርስትም ፡ ከትኒችና ፡ አራሚ ፡ የሌለው ፡ እትክልት ፡ አይረባም ። ን ጉሥና ፡ መምህር ፡ የሌላትም ፡ አገር ፡ እንደዚህ ፡ ናት ፡ ጋቢ ፡ እት ፡ ስትሠራ ፡ ደስ ፡ ይላታል ፡ ጓላ ፡ ግን ፡ ፍሬ ፡ ስታፈ ራ ፡ ፍሬዋ ፡ እሬት ፡ ይሆናል ።

ከረጊት ፡ መሰፋቱ ፡ የወርቅ ፡ መያዣ ፡ ነው ፡ የሰው ፡ ልብም ፡ መፈጠፉ ፡ ክፉን ፡ በት ፡ ለማወቅ ፡ ነው ። የጆሮት ፡ ልቢ ፡ እሾህ ፡ ነው ፡ የዲያብሎስም ፡ ልብሱ ፡ ክፋት ፡ ነው።

ሸንኩርትና ፡ ድንች ፡ ፍሬያቸው ፡ በሥራቸው ፡ እንደ ሆን ፡ ጻድቃንም ፡ በሥራቸው ፡ ለማፍራት ፡ የአምላካቸው ን ፡ ነገር ፡ በልባቸው ፡ ይተክላሉ ።

በገና ፡ ሆዱ ፡ አንድ ፡ ሆና ፡ ለወፍራሙም ፡ ለቀጭኑ ም ፡ እንደ ፡ ጠባያቸው ፡ እንደሚርቁህ ፡ እግዚአብሔርም ፡ አንድ ፡ ሲሆን ፡ ለፋጥረቱ ፡ ሁሉ ፡ እንደጠባይ ፡ እንደ ጠባዩ ፡ ይሰጠዋል ።

የተምር ፡ ፍሬ ፡ እንዳጋፍጥ ፡ የጻድቃንም ፡ ሥራ ፡ እንደዘያ ፡ ነው ፡ ቅል ፡ በዝናም ፡ ይበቅላል ፡ ሸክላም ፡ በውህ ፡ ይሠራል ፡ ጓላ ፡ ግን ፡ ሁለቱም ፡ ለመህ ፡ ማደሪ ያ ፡ ይሆናሉ ።

ሰውንም ፡ እግዚአብሔር ፡ ከፈጠረው ፡ በጓላ ፡መል ካም ፡ ሰው ፡ የሆነ ፡ እንደሆነ ፡ ማደሪያዳ ፡ ይደርገዋል ። መሰል ፡ መልካም ፡ ነው ፡ ብርትን ፡ ይስለዋና ፡ መጽሐ ፍም ፡ መልካም ፡ ነው ፡ ልብን ፡ ያበራዋና ።

መጽሐፈ ፡ ጨዋታ ፡ መንፈሳዊ ፡፡

ክፍል ፡ ፮ ፡፡

እግዚአብሔር ፡ ፈሪ ፡ ነው ፡ እኛ ፡ ብንበድለው ፡ ል
ጁን ፡ ልክ ፡ ቀስ ፡ ብለህ ፡ ተዛምደህ ፡ ና ፡ ብሎ ፡ በልጁ
ታረቀን ፡ አሁን ፡ ምን ፡ ያደርገኝ ፡ መስሎት ፡ ነው ፡ ለ
ክ ፡ በየቤቱ ፡ ፍሬት ፡ አይታጣም ፡ እኛ ፡ ስለበደልነው ፡
የምንክሰውን ፡ እርሱ ፡ ካሰነ ፡፡

እንግዴህ ፡ ወዲህ ፡ ሥጋችን ፡ ክሆነ ፡ በስብ ፡ ባስ
ባብ ፡ ብለን ፡ እርስቱን ፡ እንክፈላዋለን ፡ ጥቀት ፡ ሥጋ ፡
እንዴ ፡ መርፌ ፡ ትወጋ ፡ እንደሚሱት ፡ እንኳን ፡ ልጁን ፡
ልክ ፡ ተዛመደን ፡፡

የክርስቶስ ፡ ነገር ፡ እዮግ ፡ አስቸገረ ፡ ልጅ ፡ ስለሆነ ፡
ይሆን ፡ እንድ ፡ ጊዜ ፡ ተርቤ ፡ አላብላችሁኝም ፡ ይላል ፡ እ
ንድ ፡ ጊዜ ፡ እምስት ፡ እንጀራ ፡ ለእምስት ፡ ሽህ ፡ ሰው ፡
አብቶ ፡ አትርፎ ፡ ያስናሳል ፡፡

ለበሬ ፡ ቀንድ ፡ አለው ፡ ለነገሥም ፡ ዘውድ ፡ አለው ፡
እረ ፡ ለእግዚአብሔር ፡ የምንሰጠው ፡ ክብር ፡ ምንድር ፡
ነው ፡ እንለይለትምን ፡ አምልክ ፡ ስግደት ፡ ምስጋና ፡ ለ
ርሱ ፡ ነው ፡ በጋም ፡ እንዛው ፡ እንለጋመጠውም ፡፡
እንታጠቅለትም ፡፡ ታላቅ ፡ ጌታ ፡ ሰዬ ፡ ነሽ ፡ ነውና ፡፡

እዴኛም ፡ ገዳይም ፡ እርሱ ፡ ነውና ፡፡ በሰግይና ፡ በ
ምድርም ፡ ክርሱ ፡ በቀር ፡ ሌላ ፡ የለም ፡፡ ሁሉም ፡ ክርሱ
ነው ፡ የተገኘው ፡ ሁሉም ፡ የሆነው ፡ በርሱ ፡ ነው ፡፡ አለ
ርሱ ፡ ምንም ፡ የሆነ ፡ የለም ፡ ምስጋና ፡ ይገባዋል ፡ ለዘለ
ዓለም ፡ አሜን ፡፡

እግዚአብሔር ፡ ዕሩቅ ፡ ነው ፡ ጥበቡ ፡ አይታይምና ፡፡
እግዚአብሔር ፡ ቅርብ ፡ ነው ፡ ቶሎ ፡ ይሰግልና ፡፡ እግዚአ
ብሔር ፡ መኰንን ፡ ነው ፡ ቶሎ ፡ ይፈርዳልና ፡፡ እግዚአብ

መጽሐፈ ፡ ፊፌዋታ ፡ መንፈሳዊ ።

ሔር ፡ እንግዳ ፡ ነው ፡ ቶሎ ፡ ወሬ ፡ ይሰማልና ። እግዚአብ
ሔር ፡ ትሑት ፡ ነው ፡ ሰውን ፡ አይንቅምና ። እግዚአብ
ሔር ፡ መሐሪ ፡ ነው ፡ ቶሎ ፡ ይቅር ፡ ይላልና ፡ ራኅሩኅ ፡ ነው ።

እግዚአብሔር ፡ ሐኪም ፡ ነው ፡ ሁሉን ፡ በጥበብ ፡ አ
ድርጓልና ። እግዚአብሔር ፡ ምስጉን ፡ ነው ፡ ፀሐይን ፡ ጨ
ረቃን ፡ ፈጥሮአልና ። እግዚአብሔር ፡ ክቡር ፡ ነው ፡ ሰ
ማይና ፡ ምድር ፡ የርሱ ፡ ናቸውና ።

እግዚአብሔር ፡ ባለጸጋ ፡ ነው ፡ ለሁሉ ፡ ይመግባልና ። እ
ግዚአብሔር ፡ ረቂቅ ፡ ነው ፡ አይጨበጥምና ። እግዚአብ
ሔር ፡ ግዙፍ ፡ ነው ፡ በዓለም ፡ ሁሉ ፡ ሞልቷልና ። እግ
ዚአብሔር ፡ ብሩህ ፡ ነው ፡ ጨለማ ፡ የለበትምና ። እግዚአ
ብሔር ፡ ኃያል ፡ ነው ፡ የሚቋቋመው ፡ የለምና ።

እግዚአብሔር ፡ እሳት ፡ ነው ፡ እዬግ ፡ ያስፈራልና ።
እግዚአብሔር ፡ መካር ፡ ነው ፡ መጻሕፍትን ፡ ሰጥቶናልና ።
እግዚአብሔር ፡ አባት ፡ ነው ፡ አሳድጐናልና ። እግዚአብሔ
ር ፡ ወንድም ፡ ነው ፡ ሰው ፡ ሆኖዋልና ። እግዚአብሔር ፡
ወዳጅ ፡ ነው ፡ የሁዳን ፡ ነግሮናልና ።

እግዚአብሔር ፡ አገር ፡ ነው ፡ እንዓርበታለንና ። እግዚ
አብሔር ፡ ማርና ፡ ሱካር ፡ ነው ፡ ይጣፍጣልና ። እግዚአብ
ሔር ፡ ገናን ፡ ነው ፡ የሚያሀለው ፡ የለምና ። እግዚአብሔ
ር ፡ ትልቅ ፡ ነው ፡ ስፍሬ ፡ አይበቃውምና ። እግዚአብሔ
ር ፡ ጥልቅ ፡ ነው ፡ በዋና ፡ አይገኝምና ። እግዚአብሔር ፡ ፋ
ሲካ ፡ ነው ፡ ለሁሉ ፡ ታርዷልና ። እግዚአብሔር ፡ ዓመት ፡ በዓል ፡
ነው ። ለሁሉ ፡ ደስታ ፡ ነውና ። እግዚአብሔር ፡ ጨው ፡ ነው ፡
ሁሉን ፡ ያጣፍጣልና ። እግዚአብሔር ፡ ክረምት ፡ ነው ፡ ሁሉን ፡
ያበቅላልና ። እግዚአብሔር ፡ አይጠረጠርም ፡ ሁሉን ፡ ያውቃ
ልና ። እግዚአብሔር ፡ አይዘነጋም ፡ በሁሉ ፡ ዝክም ፡ የለበት
ምና ። እግዚአብሔር ፡ አይሰጋም ፡ የሚሸረው ፡ የለምና ።

3.3.2 Letters

Letter 1

Aleqa Engida to Alfred Ilg
April 23, "1890" (Bairu Tafla 2000:82)

ይድረስ፡ከጌታዬ፡ሙሴ፡ኢልግ፡ሞድንጌ
ቫለም፡ጤና፡ይስጥልኝ፡ብዬ፡እጆ፡እነሳለ
ሁ፡፡   ፡፡ለተክስ፡አረጋይና፡ላብተወ
ልድ፡ሻየብር፡ሰጁ ስሁ ና፡ክራ ይም፡ቀ
ረጥም፡እንደ ያሠነኩ ብኝ ፡፡ ብሞ ትም
፡ ሰደጄ፡እንደ አሠጡልኝ፡፡፡፡ የሳል፡
አሶቷ ፡እንዳደ፡

በማዝየ፡በ፲፰ቀን፡ተጣፈ፡በእንጦጦ፡

THE ORIGIN OF AMHARIC

Letter 2

Abba Jifar to Alfred Ilg
June 26, 1890 (Source Bairu Tafla 2000: 86)

Letter 3

Menilek II to Alfred Ilg
November 4, 1890 (Source: Bairu Tafla 2000:90)

ሞዓ፡እግበሰ፡ዘእምነገደ፡ዲሁዳ፡ዳግማዊ፡ምኒልክ፡ሥዩ
መ፡እግዚአብሔር፡ንጉሠ፡ነገሥት፡ዘኢትዩጵያ
ይዕ ለ፡ከመ፡ሴ፡አ ልግ፡እንዲት፡ሰነበታኩ፡እኔ፡እግዚ
አብሔር፡ይመስገን፡ዳኅና፡ነኝ፡ወእንግሊ ዝ ግ
ግሥት፡ የሚሃዱወን፡ ይብደቤ፡ ጽሌህ፡ የሰደዱ
ህሌኝ፡እንደላን፡ብለን፡ከምበሰየ፡እውጥ ፈን፡
ከነየ ወ፡እየፋ፡ነከው ፡ተባለሸ፡እግይ፡ንሁ፡
እነደጸፉ፡መልክተኞቹ ፡ ሮ ምሬ፡ዳብደቤው
ነ፡ሰይ ሏ፡ልሃለሁ፡ ጽ ፈህ፡ሰጥሃከ ው፡እዛሽ፡
ወልዉ፡ንው ቱ፡ሻጃቼ ቾው፡በዚ ው፡በኩል፡እነ
ዴሄ ዴ፡ዶሁ ን፡ ደብደ ቤው ን ም፡እፈስ፡መኮ ን
ን፡እዴታ ት፡ነውን፡ የሚሠደ የው፡እ ም ሰ ሎኝ፡
እንዲደገ ው ም፡ ዲሁ ን ፡ በጥቅምት፡በ፳፬ቀ
ን፡ባይ ሰ፡አ ባ ከ ቱ ባ፡ተጻፈ፡
በ፲፬ ፻ ፰፫ ዓመት፡ ም ህረ ት፡

3.4 Sample Amharic Texts of the Early 20ᵗʰ Century

This appendix contains three additional sample texts - one a proclamation and two descriptive essays - of Amharic from the beginning of the 20ᵗʰ century. As pointed out in chapter seven, although Amharic was reduced to writing around the 14ᵗʰ century (or even earlier), until recently it was not developed as a standard written language. As can be seen also in the following sample texts, the language is more of a spoken language and the usage of punctuation marks is not standardized.[221] Moreover, it seems that only three punctuation marks, namely *hulet net'ib* (፡), *dirib serez* (፤) and *arat net'ib* (።), were functioning at that time.

---

[221] All the texts below are taken from Eadie (1924); "An Amharic Reader". See also Eadie (ibid) for additional Amharic short texts of various genres of the beginning of the 20ᵗʰ century and for explanation on the usage of some terms and phrases of the texts adopted here.

Text one: Proclamation

አዋጅ። ሲነገር።

ስማ፡ ስማ፡ መስማሚያ፡ ይንሳቸው፡ የማርያምን፡ ጠላት።

ስማ፡ ስማ፡ መስማሚያ፡ ይንሳቸው፡ የጌታችንን፡ ጠላት።

ሰው፡ በተጣላ፡ ጊዜ፡ ከባላጋራው፡ ተቋም፡ እልፍ፡ ጅራፍ፡ እሰጥ፡ ሺ፡ ጅራፍ፡ እሰጥ፡ እያለ፡ ውርርድ፡ የሚተክለው፡ ሁሉ፡ ይቅር፡ ብያለሁ፡ ውርርድም፡ ማር፡ ይሁን።

እጅግም፡ ቢበዛ፡ ፈረስ፡ እሰጥ፡ በቅሎ፡ እሰጥ፡ ይባል፡ እንጂ፡ ከዚህ፡ በላይ፡ ኤትከል። ደኛም፡ ከዚህ፡ በላይ፡ ውርርድ፡ አስተክሎ፡ አያሚግት፡ የውርርዱም፡ ዕዳ፡ በበቅሎ፡ የተረታ፡ ጁ፡ ብር። በፈረስ፡ የተረታጡ፡ ብር፡ በማር፡ የተረታ፡ ፬፡ ሩብይከፈል። ዳኝነትም፡ ጁ፡ ሩብ፡ ይሁን፡ በወንጀልም፡ እየተያዘ፡ መሬቱ፡ የሚነቀል፡ ሰው፡ ሁሉ፡ ወንጀልም፡ ቢገኝበት፡ በሰውነቱ፡ ይቀጣ፡ እንጂ፡ መሬቱ፡ አይነቀል፡ ብያለሁ። ነገርግን፡ ነፍስ፡ ገድሎ፡ በመንግስት፡ ክፉ፡ ነገር፡ የሰራ፡ ይነቀላል።

ርስትም፡ ማለት፡ ያበት፡ የናት፡ መሬት፡ ደግሞ፡ በዐርቁ፡ የገዘው፡ መሬት፡ ነው፡ እንጂ፡ የመንግሥት፡ መትከያ፡ አይደለም። ደግሞ፡ የመትኪያም፡ መሬት፡ ቢሆን፡ መንግሥት፡ ርስት፡ ያደረገለት፡ ይረጋል።

መካንም፡ የሞተ፡ እንደሆነ፡ እናት፡ አባቱ፡ ገንዘቡንም፡ ርስቱንም፡ ይውሰዱ፡ እንጂ፡ ሹም፡ አይውረስ። እናት፡ አባት፡ የሌለው፡ እንደሆነ፡ ወንድሙ፡ እሁቱ፡ ይውረሱ፡ እናት፡ አባት፡ ወንድም፡ እህት፡ የሌለው፡ እንደሆነ፡ ግን፡ ለዕርብ፡ ዘመዱ፡ ይሁን፡ ደግሞም፡ ከዘመዶቹ፡ ለይቶ፡ ለገሌ፡ ይሁን፡ ብሎ፡ የተናዘዘ፡ የተናዘዘለት፡ ይውሰድ። ካራት፡ ትውልድ፡ ወዲያ፡ የሆነ፡ እንደሆነ፡ ግን፡ ሹም፡ ይውረሰው፡ ብያለሁ።

መስከረም። ፲፻፡ ቀን፡ ፲፰፻፶፡

When the proclamation is made:-

Listen, listen, may the enemies of the Church lack unity.

Listen, listen, may the enemies of Mary lack unity (or agreement).

Listen, listen, may the enemies of our master lack agreement.

I have ordered that, when a man quarrels with another and confronting his opponent, the bet that he makes, saying, "I give ten thousand – one thousand – lashes," shall cease. Let the wager be honey.

At the most let it be said "I will give a horse or a mule," more that this let him not wager. The judge also, having allowed him to wager more than this, let him not allow him to plead. He who loses, the debt of his wager being a mule, let him pay $20, who loses by the wager of a horse, $10, by honey, 4 quarters (of a dollar). Everyone

297

who being arrested for fraud and whose land is confiscated, I have ordered that if he be guilty of fraud he is to be personally punished, but his land is not to be confiscated. A murderer however or a man who has done evil to the government (his land) will be confiscated.

"Rist" is the land of father and mother also that brought by money; it is not that given by the government. Again, if this "matkaya" land be that which the government has made as "rist" to him, it is not confiscable (lit. it is settled).

If a person dies without children let his father and mother take his property and "rist" (i.e. his personal and real property) and let not the chief inherit it. If he has no father and mother, let his brother and sister inherit. If he has no father, mother, brothers, or sisters however let (the property) go (lit. be) to his nearest kinsman up to four generations. Also having excluded (the inheritance) from his relatives, if he makes a will in favour of so and so, let the person in whose name the will is made inherit. But if (the heir) be after four generations I have ordered that the Chief inherits.

16 Maskaram 1901.

Text Two: Descriptive Essay

የጦር አቀድ።

ዘመቻ፡ ሲፈለግ፡ አዋጅ፡ ይነገራል፡ ከንደዚህ፡ ያለ፡ ስፍራ፡ በገሌ፡ ቀን፡ በገሌ፡ ወር፡ ከተት፡ ተብሎ፡ ይነገራል፡፡ ዘመቻው፡ ንጉሥ፡ ለንጉሥ፡ እንደሆነ፡ ሕዝቡ፡ ሁሉ፡ ነው፡ የሚታዘዝ፡ ቁላ፡ ባለሽ፡ ተብሎ፡ ነው፡፡ ከታዘዘበት፡ ስፍራ፡ ድረስ፡ ይከታል፡፡ ከዚያ፡ ስፍራ፡ የጦሩን፡ አቀድ፡ ወይ፡ ፈታቸው፡ የሚደረገውን፡ ሁሉ፡ ይመክራሉ፡ ማለት፡ እገሌ፡ በንደዚህ፡ ስፍራ፤ እገሌ፡ በንደዚህ፡ ያለ፡ ስፍራ፡ ይዋል፡ እገሌ፡ ባስፈለገው፡ ነገር፡ ምልክቱ፡ እንደዚህ፡ እንደዚህ፡ ያለ፡ ይሁን፡ ተብሎ፡ ይታቀዳል፡፡ ተዚህ፡ ወዲህ፡ ሁለት፡ ሶስት፡ ቀን፡ ርቀት፡ የሚቀድሙት፡ ፈታውራሪዎች፡ አንዱ፡ ፈታውራሪ፡ አበጋዝ፡ ይሾማል፡ ለሎርነት፡ ጊዜ፡ ነው፡ እንጂ፡ ይህ፡ ሹመት፡ አይረጋም፡ ማለት፡ እገሌ፡ ፈታውራሪ፡ ከነገሌ፡ ፈታውራሪዎች፡ የጦርነት፡ አቀድ፡ ያውቃል፡ ተብሎ፡ ይመረጣል፡ የተቆጠሩለት፡ ፈታውራሪዎች፡ በርሱ፡ እግር፡ ይጓዛሉ፡፡ ቀጥሎ፡ ፈረሰኛ፡ ባንድ፡ ሹምእግር፡ ሁለትና፡ ሶስት፡ ቀን፡ ርቀት፡ ይጓዛል፡ እነ፡ ቀኝ፡ አዝማች፡ ግራ፡ አዝማች፡ ናቸው፡ ለነዚሁም፡ ፈታውራሪ፡ አላቸው፡፡ ከዚህ፡ ቀጥሎ፡ ገዳም፡ ጦር፡ ይለጥቃል፡ ቀጥሎ፡ ንጉሥ፡ እንዳስ፡ ንጉሥ፡ እንበለዚያ፡ ዋና፡ አበጋዝ፡ የጦር፡ ጠቅላይ፡ ይለጥቃል፡ ቀጥሎ፡ ኢታ፡ ቤት፡ ይከተላል፡ ቀጥሎ፡ ደጀን፡ ይለጥቃል፡ የደጀን፡ ስራው፡ የሞተ፡ ለመቅበር፡ የደከመውን፡ ለማንሣት፡ የተነሳውን፡ ለመደገፍ፡ ነው፡ በቀኛም፡ በግራም፡ ቀኝ፡ አዝማችና፡ ግራዝማች፡ አለበት፡ ቡፉ፡ ደጋም፡ ግራና፡ ቀኝ፡ ታዘም፡ ቢሆን፡ ባይታዘዝ፡ ፋኖ፡ የሚባል፡ ጦር፡ ፈረሰኛና፡ እግረኛ፡ ያገኘውን፡ አውዳሚ፡ እንደ፡ አንበጣ፡ ርቄ፡ ይወርል፡ እዝም፡ አይሰማ፡ ሴራ፡ አይል፡ ዲና፡ አይል፡ አገር፡ አጥፊ፡ ነው፡፡ የዚህ፡ ሁሉ፡ ከፍል፡ ጦር፡ በግሩ፡ ያለትን፡ ሹማም(ን)ት፡ አበጋዝ፡ አለው፡ ደጋሞም፡ መልክት፡ ከንቱሥ፡ ወይም፡ ከፍናው፡ ጦር፡ ጠቅላይ፡ እዝ፡ እየመጠበት፡ ነው፡ ወራሪም፡ ወደ፡ ፊቱና፡ ወደ፡ ኋላው፡ ነው፡ አወራራሁ፡ ይህ፡ ሁሉ፡ ከፍል፡ ጦር፡ በተሰማርበት፡ ባዝኖ፡ እንደይቀር፡ በፊት፡ የቀደመው፡ አበጋዝ፡ ፈ(ሬ)ታውራሪ፡ የቤተ፡ መንግሥትን፡ ድንኳን፡ አስቀድሞ፡ ያስተካከላል፡ ሠራዊት፡ ድንኳኑን፡ አያየ፡ ይሰፍራል፡ ደሞ፡ የነጋትና፡ የመለክት፡ ድምጥ፡ እየሰማ፡ ይከተላል፡ ድምጡ፡ በፉቅ፡ ይሰማልና፡ ነጋሪት፡ የሚያስጭኑ፡ መለከትና፡ እምቢልቲ(ታ)፡ የሚያስፉ፡ ራስና፡ ደጃዘማች፡ የሆነ፡ ብቻ፡ ነው፡ እንጂ፡ ሌላ፡ ሹም፡ ሁሉ፡ አይገባውም፡ በዚህ፡ አግር፡ ይለጥቃል፡ እንጂ፡ አንዱ፡ ራስ፡ ወይም፡ አንዱ፡ አበጋዝ፡ ከጦርነት፡ የተነሣ፡ የላላ፡ እንደሆነ፡ ከገዳም፡ ጦር፡ ወይም፡ እዝ፡ ጠባቂ፡ ጦር፡ ወይም፡ እገሌ፡ ጦር፡ እገሌን፡ ገስግሰህ፡ እርዳ፡ ተብሎ፡ ይታዘዝለታል፡፡ ተፈጸመ።

The Rules of War

When a military expedition is desired, proclamation is made, it being said, "collect in such and such a place, on such and such a day, in such and such a month". If the expedition be one of King against King, the whole populace is ordered, "all males" being said. They collect in the place they were ordered. There they consult on the entire plan of the campaign which will be performed in the future, that is to say it is arranged that so and so shall stay in such and such a place, and for the thing that so and so needs the signal will be such and such (lit. like this). After this, one of the advanced guard leaders who go in front at a distance of two or three days is appointed "Abagaz." This appointment is for the period of the war however, it is not permanent. That is to say it being said that a certain Fitaurari out of certain Fitauraris knows tactics (lit. the plan of war) he is selected (for Abagaz), and Fitauraris who are appointed to him are under his orders. Again the cavalry marches under the command of a leader at a distance of 2 or 3 days. They (i.e. the cavalry) have right- wing and left-wing commanders and these also have Fitauraris. The right- wing commanders and skirmishes on the right, and the left-wing commanders and skirmishes on the left, after this follows the main body. Next, if the king is there, the king follows, otherwise the chief Abagaz, the Commander-in-Chief. Next the transport (lit. store-house) follows and then the rear-guard. The work of the rear-guard is to bury the dead, to pick up the weary and to support those unable (to carry on). It has on the right a right-wing, and on the left a left-wing, commander. Far away also on the right and left, whether they are ordered or not, the army called Fano consisting of cavalry and foot, plunders afar, destroying all they find like locusts. They do not obey orders; they devastate the country, no matter whether it be loyal or rebel. Of all these parts of the army there are Commanders-in-Chief for the subordinate officers. Also it (i.e. the army) takes a signal from the king of from the Commanders-in-Chief. The skirmishers skirmish to the front and rear. So that all these parts of the army may not lose their way in the country, who goes on ahead, causes to be pitched first the king's tent. The army seeing the tent, camp themselves. Again they collect on hearing the sound of the drums and bugles, for their noise is heard far away. But it is only Rases and Dajazmaches who have drums beaten (lit. Loaded, i.e. taken with their troops) and bugles and fifes blown; all the other chiefs have not the right, but follow the orders of these others. If a Ras or Abagaz gets weak from the fight (i.e. suffers heavy losses), (some one) from the main body, reserve, or any army crops is ordered to make a forced march and reinforce him. Finis.

Text Three: Descriptive Essay

የጋብቻ ሕግጋት።

የቁርባን፡ በቤተ፡ ክርስትያን፡ ጋብቻ፡ መጽሐፈ.(ፍ)፡ ቅዱስ፡ እንዳዘዘው፡ ነው።፡ ቆርባን፡ አልባ፡ በቤተ፡ ክርስትያን፡ ሳይሆን፡ ጋብቻ፡ አግቢ፡ አማላጅ፡ ወደ፡ ሴት፡ አባትና፡ እናት፡ ይልካል፡ ልጃችሁን፡ ስጡኝሲል፡ እሺ፡ ባለ፡ ጊዜ፡ ለፍጥሙ፡ ቀን፡ ይታቀድለታል። ቀኑ፡ በደረሰ፡ ጊዜ፡ ዳኛ፡ አማኝ፡ ይቀመጣል፡ የሴት፡ አባት፡ የተላኩትን፡ ምንትፈልጋችሁ፡ ብሎ፡ ይጠይቃል፡ አግቢውየነገር፡ አቱኙና፡ ባልንጀሮቹን፡ ነው፡ ይዞ፡ የሚመጣው፡ የነገር፡ አባት፡ ልጅ፡ ልታረጉኝ፡ ብለን፡ ነው፡ የመጣነው፡ ብሎ፡ ይመልስለታል፡ የሴት፡ አባት፡ እንዲ፡ ምን፡ እጃችሁ፡ ተምን፡ ብሎ፡ ደሞ፡ ይጠይቃል፡ ጌጥ፡ ልብስ፡ ካባ፡ በቀሎ፡ ምድር፡ የተቻለውን፡ ያህል፡ ይቆጥራል፡ ግል፡ የፈለገው፡ እንዴህን፡ ይህ፡ ምድር፡ እንደዚህ፡ እንደዚህ፡ ያለ፡ ነገር፡ ግሌ፡ ነው፡ ብሎ፡ ለዳኛ፡ ለማኝ፡ ያስታውቃል፡ ይቼነን፡ ሁሉ፡ ንግግር፡ ደብዳቤ፡ ጸሐፊ፡ ይዶፋል፡ ተዚህ፡ በኋላ፡ እግሊት፡ ማለት፡ ስሚን፡ ጠርቶ፡ ምኔልክ፡ ይሙት፡ ምስቴ፡ ነች፡ ብሎ፡ ይፈጠማል፡ ባሌ፡ ነው፡ ብይ፡ ብለው፡ ዘመዶች፡ የዘዋታል፡ ስለምን፡ ታቶራለች፡ ቃል፡ ትሰባለች፡ የነገር፡ አባቷ፡ ምኔልክ፡ ይሙት፡ ባሌ፡ ነው፡ አለች፡ ይላል፡ የምትቀመጥበትም፡ ከሴቶች፡ ጋራ፡ ነው፡ እንጂ፡ ዳኛና፡ ምስከር፡ ካለበት፡ ስፍራ፡ አትደርስም፡ ይህ፡ ሁሉ፡ የሚገባውን፡ ነገር፡ ተተፈጸመ፡ በኋላ፡ አግቢውን፡ ጥንድ፡ ዋስ፡ ለዓይነዋ፡ ለራሲ፡ ለጥሪሲ፡ ጥራልን፡ ይሉታል፡ ጀዋስ፡ ይጠራል፡ ማለት፡ ድንገት፡ ባልና፡ ምስት፡ የተጣሉ፡ እንደሆነ፡ ይመታትና፡ አካላ፡ ጎደሎ፡ እንዳያረጋት፡ ነው፡ ዋስ፡ መጥራቱ፡ ይህ፡ ሁሉ፡ ደምብ፡ ተተፈጸመ፡ በኋላ፡ ግቡ፡ ይባላል፡ ትሽ፡ ድግስ፡ ተደግሷል፡ ከዚያ፡ ያሉትን፡ ሁሉ፡ አብልተው፡ ይሰድዋዋል፡ ተዝይ፡ ዋና፡ የሥርግ፡ ድግስ፡ አግቢው፡ ይድግሳል፡ የሴት፡ አባት፡ ደሞ፡ ይደግሳል፡ የሴት፡ አባት፡ ድግስ፡ ሲደርስ፡ አማችን፡ ይቼነን፡ ሁነሁ፡ ና፡ ብለው፡ ይልኩበታል፡ ሲመጣ፡ ጌጡን፡ የተረከበውን፡ ሁሉ፡ ይዞ፡ ይመጣል፡ ያመጣው፡ ሁሉ፡ በደብዳቤ፡ ይጻፋል፡ ተዚህ፡ በኋላ፡ ክቤተ፡ ገብተው፡ ይበላሉ፡ ይጫወታሉ፡ ድንግት፡ ባልና፡ ምስት፡ ጠብ፡ አነስተው፡ ከመፋታት፡ የደረሱ፡ እንደህን፡ የሚፋቱት፡ በነገር፡ አባታቸው፡ ነው፡ የተቂጠሩትን፡ ገንዘብ፡ እኩል፡ ይፈልሉ፡ ተግል፡ ገንዘብ፡ በቀር፡ ምኔልክ፡ ይሙት፡ ፈታሁ፡ ይላል፡ እርሲም፡ ይቼነኑን፡ ትላለች፡ ምናልባት፡ ባማላጅ፡ ደሞ፡ ይታረቃሉ፡ የጁ፡ ጋብቻ፡ ሕግጋት፡ ይህ፡ ነው።

የጭን፡ ገረድ፡ (ገሬድ)

የጭን፡ ገረድ፡ ስለ፡ ምስት፡ ያህል፡ ናት፡ ሰማንያ፡ ብቻ፡ ነው፡ የሚነል፡ በስተቀረ፡ ልክ፡ እንደ፡ ስማንያ፡ ምስት፡ ናት፡ ብድር፡ በቀሎ፡ ጌጥ፡ ሁሉ፡ ይሰጣታል፡ ምንአልባት፡ የተጣሉ፡ እንደህን፡ ሁሉኑም፡ ይዛ፡ ትሄዳለች።

አንደኛዋ፡ ዓይነት፡ ገረድ፡ ደሞ፡ ከጄ፡ ይዞ፡ እስከ፡ ፰፡ ብር፡ ድረስ፡ ነው፡ ደሞዝዋ፡ አስቀድም፡ ጥሎሽ፡ ጥሎ፡ በሰው፡ ፈጅቶ፡ ነው፡ ሰማንያ፡ የላትም።

ተራ፡ ገረድ፡ ደሞ፡ ተጄ፡ ብር፡ ይዞ፡ እስከ፡ ፪፡ ብር፡ ድረስ፡ ነው።

The Rules of Matrimony

The marriage of (i.e. with) the sacrament in Church is in accordance with what the Bible lays down. The man who wishes to get married without the sacrament, and not in Church, sends go-betweens to the parents of the girl saying "Give me your daughter."

When they accept, they fix a day for the solemn declaration. When the day arrives, the judge and witness sit down. The girls father asks those who are sent what they want. The bridegroom comes with his legal advisor and comrades. The lawyer answers him saying, "We have come that you may make us your sons." The girl's father asks those who are sent what they want. The bridegroom comes with his legal adviser and comrades. The lawyer answers him saying, "We have come that you may make us your sons." The girl's father also asks "How! What have you in your hands?" He (the lawyer) enumerates to the extent of his power ornaments, cloths, silk mantles, mules, land. If he wishes for "gil" he informs the judge and witnesses that such and such things will not be divided up him in case of divorce. The scribe writes down all this conversation. After this (the bridegroom) makes a solemn declaration saying, "Such and such a woman, i.e. naming her, by the death of Menelik she is my wife." Her relations order her saying, "Say you that he is my husband." Because she is shy, she gives her word and her lawyer says, "She has said by the death of Menelik he is my husband." Where she sits however is with the women, she does not approach the place where the judge and witness are. When all these necessary things are finished, they (i.e. the girl's father and lawyer) say to the bridegroom, "Call for us two guarantees for her eyes, head, an teeth." He calls these two guarantees. That is to say if by chance the husband and wife quarrel and hit each other, the security is given that he may not damage her body. When all these formalities are completed they say "enter," and a small feast is given, and having entertained all the people who are there, they send them away. After that the bridegroom gives the main marriage feast. The girl's father also makes a feast. When the time of the girl's father banquet arrives he sends to him (i.e. the bridegroom) saying "Come so many of you (my) son-in-law!" When he comes he brings all the ornaments that he can. All that he brought will be written down in a paper. Afterwards they go inside and eat and chat. By chance the husband and wife having started a quarrel, if it comes to divorcing they carry it out through their lawyers. With the exception of the "gil" property, they divide equally the property that they had each enumerated. He says, "By the death of Menelik I have divorced you," and she says the same. And perhaps also by the help of conciliators they may make it up.

This is the manner of marriage by oath.

Concubines.

A concubine is equivalent to a wife; 'tis only the oath (lit. "80" i.e. 80 dollar oath) which is lacking; for the rest she is exactly like the wife married by oath. Land, mules, ornaments, etc., are given her, if perchance they quarrel she takes all away.

Another kind of concubine again has a salary of from 5 to 30 dollars (a month). Beforehand, the having paid the "Tilosh" settles the matter before witness. She is not married by oath.

Ordinary (i.e. common) concubines also are of from 2 to 4 dollars.

3.5 Remarks

As mentioned in the introductory chapter and as the title of this book indicates, this work is not a history of Amharic. Its main aim is to investigate the much-misunderstood origin of Amharic and its less-known early spread. Due to this, we have limited ourselves in discussing the development of Amharic as a written language. Integrating all the texts appended here in the body will take us out of the scope of this work. However, the inclusion of this appendix is based on two assumptions. First, these appended texts, which are carefully selected, are intended to provide additional information of what has been discussed in the main body, especially that of chapter seven and eight. Second, as the attached texts are from different periods, they may show not only the development of Amharic as a written language but also the changes that it made through time. In order to provide a complete picture of Amharic history among other issues, we need to understand at least the lexical changes that it made through the course of time as well as its diachronic grammar and development as a written language more in detail than what has been presented in chapters seven and eight. Although it is difficult to address the diachronic grammar of Amharic and its development as a written language based on only the appended texts, these (especially the oldest ones) are definitely some of the major texts to consult for such investigation.

Index

Abbadie, 170, 174, 181, 192, 215
Abebe, 33, 34, 36, 38, 39, 40, 43, 131, 134, 135, 215
Abraham, 56, 89, 90, 215, 229
Afar, 16, 35, 57, 130, 139
Afework, 152, 171, 215
Afroasiatic, 1, 23, 57, 66, 67, 68, 77, 86, 93, 94, 95, 96, 97, 98, 100, 117, 118, 119, 120, 126, 202, 217, 224
Agew, 2, 10, 11, 12, 14, 27, 32, 43, 45, 46, 65, 102, 117, 141, 143, 216
Ahmed, 33, 36, 131, 135, 215, 224
Akkadian, 42, 65, 84, 85, 86, 87, 92, 100
Al 'Umari, 33, 36, 39, 132, 141
Alamirew, 2
Aliyu Amba, 188, 190, 193, 195
Amdä Seyon, 5, 6, 13, 16, 33, 133, 143, 145, 146, 163, 177, 179, 184, 227, 232
Amhara province, 20, 130, 138, 214

Amsalu, 4, 13, 15, 22, 127, 145, 150, 215
Appleyard, 4, 13, 14, 15, 22, 39, 45, 46, 52, 75, 79, 80, 88, 89, 91, 93, 127, 130, 215, 216
Argobba, xviii, 15, 25, 33, 34, 35, 36, 38, 39, 40, 41, 42, 43, 44, 46, 81, 129, 130, 131, 132, 133, 134, 137, 138, 142, 143, 214, 215, 222, 223
Armbruster, xiv, 171, 173, 181, 216
Axum, 14, 37, 43, 103
Axumite, 2, 3, 12, 14, 15, 32, 36, 58, 89, 101, 103, 104, 105, 114, 116, 125, 134, 137, 214
Ayalew, 2, 12, 14, 43, 53, 138, 216
Ayele Bekeri, 108, 216
Bach, 48, 216
Bairu, 171, 216, 293, 294, 295
Balashova, 146, 216
Bale, 35, 130, 134, 214
Banti, 131, 216
Bashilo, 10, 14, 16, 32, 34, 44,

129, 130, 213, 214
Bashilo River, 10, 130
Baye, 2, 9, 11, 12, 14, 22, 31, 32, 50, 52, 213, 216, 222
Beja, 1, 43, 68, 93, 117
Belay, 3, 54, 216
Bender, xvii, 2, 9, 10, 11, 12, 13, 14, 20, 21, 22, 24, 26, 27, 28, 31, 32, 34, 39, 40, 41, 42, 43, 44, 45, 46, 47, 48, 49, 50, 52, 53, 61, 62, 64, 67, 74, 77, 78, 86, 89, 93, 99, 100, 117, 130, 213, 216, 217, 219, 220, 221, 225
Bender and Fulass, 2, 9, 12, 14, 31, 32, 34, 41, 46, 64, 213
Bent, 104, 217
Berber, 1, 68, 77, 86, 93, 117, 126
Bernal, 57, 59, 67, 68, 92, 94, 95, 96, 101, 102, 120, 217
Biraile, 23, 139
Blench, 70, 77, 93, 95, 100, 118, 217
broken plural, 24, 77, 87
Bruce, xiv, 108, 110, 113, 147, 163, 166, 167, 177, 180, 181, 217, 227, 229, 232, 233, 237, 238, 240, 241
Budge, 59, 217
Central Semitic, 63, 65, 72, 75, 79, 81, 87, 226
Central South Ethio-Semitic, 138
Chadic, 1, 67, 68, 86, 93, 117, 126
Chaha, 25, 81, 123
Chernetsov, 16, 20, 21, 142, 217
Cohen, 12, 13, 61, 217
complementizer, 48, 201

Cooper, 13, 21, 139, 217, 219
Cosmas, 104, 133, 224
Cowley, xiv, 6, 61, 151, 170, 173, 174, 178, 180, 181, 182, 184, 185, 187, 188, 190, 192, 194, 196, 197, 198, 199, 200, 202, 203, 204, 205, 207, 208, 209, 210, 211, 216, 217, 219, 265, 273
Crass, 208, 210, 218, 220
Crummey, 39, 218
Cushitic, xvii, 1, 2, 5, 10, 14, 20, 22, 27, 28, 41, 43, 45, 46, 47, 48, 49, 50, 52, 55, 56, 57, 58, 64, 65, 68, 70, 77, 78, 86, 90, 91, 92, 93, 94, 95, 99, 100, 117, 125, 126, 141, 214
Cushomotic, 11, 49, 50
Da'amat, 103, 107
Damte, 216
Daniels, 105, 106, 110, 113, 218
Dawit, 6, 145, 147, 148, 163, 166, 179, 195, 227
Desta Tekle-Wold, 218
Dillmann, 15, 181, 218
Drewes, 41, 58, 62, 63, 70, 105, 106, 113, 218
Eadie, 18, 153, 218
Ehret, 47, 118, 218
Endegeñ, 25, 123
Epigraphic South Arabian, 63, 73, 81, 107
Eritrea, 1, 10, 35, 57, 58, 88, 89, 120, 121, 130, 134, 136, 137, 175, 214
ES, 1, 4, 15, 26, 28, 41, 42, 55, 58, 59, 60, 61, 63, 64, 65, 66, 67, 70, 71, 73, 74, 75, 76, 77, 78, 79, 80, 81, 82, 83, 86, 87, 88, 89, 90, 91, 92, 93, 99,

116, 117, 120, 121, 123, 125, 126, 127, 131
Ethiopian Semitic, 1, 25, 42, 44, 45, 58, 60, 64, 66, 71, 75, 76, 79, 81, 84, 92, 93, 94, 102, 114, 116, 126, 221, 222, 225, 228
Ethiopic, xviii, 50, 58, 60, 62, 63, 75, 76, 89, 90, 91, 92, 99, 105, 106, 110, 114, 120, 216, 218, 219, 220, 221, 223
Ethiopic script, 105, 110, 114
Ethio-Semitic, xviii, xix, 1, 3, 4, 5, 15, 23, 24, 25, 27, 28, 33, 34, 38, 40, 41, 42, 43, 44, 47, 49, 50, 51, 52, 53, 54, 55, 56, 58, 61, 64, 65, 66, 69, 74, 75, 76, 77, 78, 79, 82, 87, 89, 91, 92, 95, 99, 100, 115, 119, 120, 121, 126, 127, 131, 135, 137, 142, 202, 210, 212, 213, 216, 220, 221, 225, 226, 227, 228
Ezana, 105, 106, 107
Ezha, 25, 123
Faber, 24, 65, 66, 71, 72, 73, 74, 75, 76, 81, 82, 83, 86, 88, 218
Fauvelle-Aymar and Hirsch, 36, 131, 135, 218
Ferguson, 49, 50, 64, 74, 219
Fleming, 61, 64, 76, 219
Fragmentum Piquesii, 180, 217, 227, 232, 273
Gafat, 21, 25, 40, 70, 81, 123, 124, 210, 223
Gälawdewos, 6, 38, 145, 179, 227, 232, 240
Gamst, 2, 21, 101, 102, 219
Gaspari, 57, 60
Ge'ez, xi, 2, 3, 4, 6, 10, 12, 15, 22, 24, 25, 27, 28, 31, 41, 42, 45, 48, 49, 50, 51, 60, 61, 62, 63, 64, 70, 72, 77, 79, 81, 84, 85, 86, 90, 91, 92, 106, 107, 108, 110, 111, 112, 113, 116, 123, 125, 142, 145, 147, 149, 150, 151, 152, 159, 161, 162, 163, 166, 167, 168, 176, 177, 178, 180, 181, 193, 202, 208, 219, 220, 222, 265
Gedem, 131
Getatchew, xix, 6, 51, 151, 152, 168, 169, 170, 173, 180, 181, 184, 185, 186, 187, 199, 200, 201, 210, 219, 222, 265
Gezahegn, 150, 166, 219, 232
Girma, xv, xix, 23, 25, 28, 44, 48, 62, 64, 77, 87, 93, 159, 218, 219, 220
Girum, 3
Gogot, 25, 62, 123
Gojjam, 17, 20, 21, 124, 133, 136, 141, 143, 175
Goldenberg, 80, 147, 210, 220
Gondar, 108, 143, 148
Gonder, 20, 136, 141
Gragg, 63, 90, 220
Greenberg, 93, 220
Greenfield, 60, 220
Gregory, 70, 150, 167, 178
Guidi, 148, 171, 180, 182, 183, 184, 185, 186, 187, 192, 193, 194, 195, 196, 197, 198, 199, 201, 220, 232
Gurage, 18, 36, 38, 40, 43, 44, 52, 74, 77, 91, 93, 99, 117, 121, 122, 123, 124, 130, 193, 196, 200, 206, 210, 211, 220, 221, 223
Haile-Gabreil, 175, 220
Hailu, xiv, xix, 4, 70, 99, 116,

307

148, 179, 216, 218, 220
Harar, 33, 35, 36, 44, 130, 131, 134, 139, 143, 155, 176, 214
Harari, 6, 25, 40, 43, 44, 81, 86, 93, 130, 131, 188, 193, 196, 210, 223, 226
Heran, 142, 221
Hetzron, 2, 24, 25, 27, 28, 33, 34, 39, 40, 41, 42, 43, 44, 49, 53, 56, 58, 61, 62, 64, 65, 71, 72, 73, 74, 75, 76, 77, 78, 79, 80, 81, 83, 84, 88, 89, 91, 92, 95, 99, 121, 122, 125, 126, 132, 195, 201, 218, 220, 221, 226
Houghton, 61, 221
Hudson, xiv, xix, 24, 40, 44, 47, 66, 67, 88, 92, 93, 120, 121, 125, 201, 212, 221, 222
Huntingford, xiv, 16, 33, 37, 39, 141, 149, 166, 223
Hussein, 35
Hussien, 26, 33, 34, 36, 222
imperative, 26, 187, 227
imperfective, 24, 26, 84, 86, 185, 196, 197, 198, 199, 200, 201, 228
Indo-European, 67
Irvine, 125, 222
Isenberg, xiv, 152, 173, 175, 181, 183, 222
Jewhar, 35, 224
Kane, 145, 146, 150, 152, 222
Lalibela, 12, 43, 53, 133, 138, 142, 214
Lapiso, 13, 14, 16, 222
Last, xv, 60, 222
Leslau, xiv, 21, 24, 26, 33, 34, 50, 58, 60, 75, 84, 181, 219, 221, 223, 224, 225
Levine, 14, 16, 21, 32, 114,

130, 140, 223
lisane niguss, 12, 13, 15
Little, 181, 203, 223
Littmann, 106, 150, 171, 223
Ludolf, xiv, 13, 16, 51, 70, 150, 151, 167, 168, 169, 171, 172, 174, 176, 178, 180, 181, 196, 217, 223
Ludolphus, 16
Makzumite, 36, 39, 135
Mänz, 21, 51, 131, 133, 140, 225
Maqrizi, 16, 33, 37, 39, 141, 149, 166, 167, 168, 174, 223
Marcus, 70, 101, 102, 103, 105, 113, 224
Mäsqan, 25, 81, 123
McCall, 67, 93, 224
McCrindle, 104, 224
Menilik II, 13, 16, 21, 214
Mersie Hazen, xiv, 224
Messay, 114, 115, 224
Meyer, xiv, xix, 2, 13, 14, 15, 21, 22, 127, 130, 139, 140, 141, 179, 193, 210, 218, 220, 224
Muhamed, 35, 224
Muher, 25, 62, 123
Munro-Hay, 102, 105, 107, 115, 224
Murtonen, 23, 42, 44, 74, 75, 76, 87, 88, 89, 92, 93, 94, 98, 99, 212, 224
NES, 3, 24, 41, 55, 70, 76, 77, 78, 80, 81, 82, 83, 86, 87, 121, 122
Nilo-Saharan, xvii, 10, 14, 41, 57
Noldeke, 70, 116
North Ethio-Semitic, 24, 41, 42, 44, 61, 89, 121

North Gurage, 25, 123
Nosnitisn, 148, 151, 176, 222
Nosnitsin, 216, 224
O'leary, 224
O'Leary, 56, 57
Old Amharic, 38, 46
Old Egyptian, 1, 93, 126
Old South Arabian, 63, 66, 73, 74, 75, 88
Omotic, xvii, 1, 10, 14, 22, 27, 41, 48, 49, 50, 51, 64, 68, 86, 93, 94, 95, 96, 100, 117, 118, 126, 141, 214
Oromo, 20, 21, 22, 44, 45, 46, 48, 57, 59, 95, 130, 134, 143
OSA, 63, 74, 75, 76, 79, 80, 82
Outer South Ethiopic, 24, 25
Palmer, 64, 225
Pankhurst, 33, 39, 60, 133, 222, 225
perfective, 11, 24, 26, 79, 80, 82, 83, 84, 86, 87, 182, 187, 188, 189, 192, 193, 195, 196, 200, 201, 228
Praetorius, xiv, 150, 181, 201, 225
Punt, 102, 110
Reminick, 131, 133, 225
Richter, 2, 21, 139, 148, 150, 224, 225
Rodgers, 73, 74, 76, 225
Rose, 51, 225
Sabaean, 60, 62, 63, 64, 66, 70, 80, 82, 90, 91, 103, 105, 106, 107, 108, 113, 114, 115, 116, 218
Salt, 116, 225
Schlözer, 56, 71
Semitic, xvii, xviii, 1, 2, 3, 4, 5, 10, 11, 12, 15, 20, 22, 23, 24, 26, 27, 28, 29, 31, 33, 38, 39, 40, 41, 43, 44, 45, 46, 47, 48, 49, 50, 51, 52, 53, 54, 55, 56, 57, 58, 59, 60, 61, 63, 64, 65, 66, 67, 68, 69, 70, 71, 72, 73, 74, 75, 76, 77, 78, 79, 80, 81, 82, 83, 84, 85, 86, 87, 88, 89, 90, 91, 92, 93, 94, 95, 96, 98, 99, 100, 101, 103, 105, 110, 113, 114, 115, 116, 117, 119, 120, 121, 125, 126, 127, 130, 131, 132, 140, 179, 182, 183, 190, 193, 195, 196, 199, 202, 203, 206, 211, 212, 213, 217, 218, 220, 221, 222, 223, 224, 225, 226
Sergew, 14, 15, 43, 53, 57, 59, 60, 90, 97, 103, 115, 116, 138, 142, 143, 169, 177, 225
SES, 3, 24, 41, 48, 55, 71, 76, 77, 80, 81, 82, 83, 84, 85, 86, 87, 122, 123, 124, 131
Shoa, 17, 33, 34, 36, 38, 134, 135, 143
Shoa Robit, 188, 190, 192, 193, 195
Shonke-Tollaha, 183, 188, 190, 192, 193, 195, 211
Sidama, 46, 50, 57, 210
Silte, 6, 25, 40, 130
Soddo, 25, 62, 81, 123, 210
Sokolinskara, 131, 133, 225
Solomon, 159, 167, 177, 225
Solomonic, 12, 16, 20, 33, 36, 142, 143, 151, 168, 177
Solomonic dynasty, 16, 36, 142
Somali, 43, 48, 57, 139
Soqotri, 65, 73, 76, 79, 89, 99
South Arabia, 44, 55, 58, 64, 76, 78, 90, 99, 101, 103, 114, 115, 121
South Arabian, xi, 5

58, 62, 63, 64, 65, 66, 69, 71, 73, 74, 75, 76, 78, 79, 81, 82, 83, 87, 88, 89, 90, 99, 102, 103, 104, 105, 106, 107, 110, 112, 113, 114, 115, 116, 117, 120, 125, 222, 228
South Arabian script, 105, 107, 114
South Ethio-Semitic, 24, 38, 40, 42, 44, 47, 53, 56, 61, 76, 87, 89, 210
South Semitic, 23, 63, 64, 65, 66, 72, 73, 74, 75, 76, 77, 78, 79, 80, 81, 82, 83, 84, 85, 86, 87, 88, 90, 224, 225
SOV, 6, 22, 28, 48, 202, 203, 211, 216, 228
substratum, xvii, 2, 10, 41, 43, 90
Sumner, 60, 225
superstratum, xvii, 2, 10, 41, 44, 92
Taddese, xix, 14, 20, 32, 36, 134, 142, 218, 225
Taye, 3, 15, 21, 54, 177, 225
Tegegne, 20, 225
Tekle-Tsadik, 148, 226, 232, 233, 237
Theodore II, 12, 145, 152
Tigre, 24, 25, 41, 61, 62, 77, 81, 84, 86, 93, 99, 120, 220
Tigrinya, 3, 4, 22, 24, 25, 41, 47, 48, 49, 51, 61, 62, 70, 77, 81, 92, 93
Timhirte Haymanot, 151, 228, 232, 265
Transversal South Ethiopic, 25, 44

Tsehaye, 15, 226
Ullendorff, 2, 28, 51, 58, 59, 60, 64, 125, 226
Voigt, 24, 58, 60, 61, 63, 75, 78, 79, 116, 226
VSO, 6, 48, 202, 203, 204, 205, 206, 208, 211, 213, 228
Vycihl, 94, 95, 96, 226
Wagner, 44, 226
Wällo, 16, 21, 33, 36, 130, 134, 140, 143
Western Gurage, 25, 62, 123
Western South Semitic, 73, 74, 75, 76
Wetter, 33, 34, 38, 183, 220, 226
Wolane, 25, 40, 81, 130
Wollayta, 52
Yayneshet, 90
Yeha, 90, 105, 107
Yifat, 21, 33, 36, 37, 38, 39, 42, 130, 131, 132, 140, 141, 149, 167, 168
Yikuno Amlak, 3, 20, 133, 138, 214
Yishaq, 6, 145, 147, 148, 179, 228, 233
Yohannis VI, 138
Zague, 2, 12, 14, 43, 53, 134, 138, 143, 214, 216
Zär'a Ya'qob, 6, 38, 179, 228
Zär'a Ya'qob, 13, 16, 37, 39, 42, 143, 145, 147, 237, 238
Zay, 6, 25, 40, 81, 130, 131, 210, 224
Zelealem, 21, 226
Zeneb, x, 152, 171, 226, 232, 286